Exploitation, Ethics and Law

Focusing on a matter of continuing contemporary significance, this book is the first work to offer an in-depth exploration of exploitation in the doctor-patient relationship. It provides a theoretical analysis of the concept of exploitation, setting out exploitation's essential elements within the authors' account of wrongful exploitation. It then presents a contextual analysis of exploitation in the doctor-patient relationship, considering the dynamics of this fiduciary relationship, the significance of vulnerability, and the reasons why exploitation in this relationship is particularly wrongful. Two case studies – sexual exploitation and assisted dying – are employed to assess what the appropriate legal, ethical and regulatory responses to exploitation should be, to identify common themes regarding the doctor's behaviour (such as the use of undue influence as a conduit through which to take advantage of and misuse patients), and to illustrate the effects of exploitation on patients. A recurring question addressed is how exploitation in the doctor-patient relationship *is* and *should be* dealt with by ethics, regulators and the law, and whether exploitation in this relationship is a special case.

The book provides a critical, interdisciplinary evaluation of exploitation in the doctor-patient relationship that will be of interest to health care lawyers, bioethicists, legal academics and practitioners, health care professionals and policymakers.

Suzanne Ost is Professor of Law at Lancaster University. Her publications on health care law and bioethics, and child sexual exploitation, include *Medicine and Bioethics in the Theatre of the Criminal Process* (with Margaret Brazier), and *Child Pornography and Sexual Grooming: Legal and Societal Responses*.

Hazel Biggs is Emeritus Professor of Healthcare Law and Bioethics at the University of Southampton, having retired in September 2020. Throughout her career, she published widely on the legal and ethical aspects of numerous areas of health care law and bioethics, including end of life care, medical research and human reproduction.

Biomedical Law and Ethics Library

Scientific and clinical advances, social and political developments and the impact of healthcare on our lives raise profound ethical and legal questions. Medical law and ethics have become central to our understanding of these problems, and are important tools for the analysis and resolution of problems – real or imagined.

In this series, scholars at the forefront of biomedical law and ethics contribute to the debates in this area, with accessible, thought-provoking, and sometimes controversial, ideas. Each book in the series develops an independent hypothesis and argues cogently for a particular position. One of the major contributions of this series is the extent to which both law and ethics are utilised in the content of the books, and the shape of the series itself.

The books in this series are analytical, with a key target audience of lawyers, doctors, nurses, and the intelligent lay public.

Series Editor: Sheila A. M. McLean

Professor Sheila A.M. McLean is Professor Emerita of Law and Ethics in Medicine, School of Law, University of Glasgow, UK.

Available titles:

Restrictive Practices in Health Care and Disability Settings
Legal, Policy and Practical Responses
Edited by Bernadette McSherry and Yvette Maker

Assisted Suicide and the European Convention on Human Rights
Stevie Martin

Exploitation, Ethics and Law
Violating the Ethos of the Doctor-Patient Relationship
Suzanne Ost with Hazel Biggs

For more information about this series, please visit:
www.routledge.com/Biomedical-Law-and-Ethics-Library/book-series/CAV5

Exploitation, Ethics and Law
Violating the Ethos of the
Doctor-Patient Relationship

Suzanne Ost with Hazel Biggs

LONDON AND NEW YORK

First published 2022
by Routledge
2 Park Square, Milton Park, Abingdon, Oxon OX14 4RN

and by Routledge
605 Third Avenue, New York, NY 10158

Routledge is an imprint of the Taylor & Francis Group, an informa business

© 2022 Suzanne Ost and Hazel Biggs

The right of Suzanne Ost and Hazel Biggs to be identified as authors of this work has been asserted by them in accordance with sections 77 and 78 of the Copyright, Designs and Patents Act 1988.

All rights reserved. No part of this book may be reprinted or reproduced or utilised in any form or by any electronic, mechanical, or other means, now known or hereafter invented, including photocopying and recording, or in any information storage or retrieval system, without permission in writing from the publishers.

Trademark notice: Product or corporate names may be trademarks or registered trademarks, and are used only for identification and explanation without intent to infringe.

British Library Cataloguing-in-Publication Data
A catalogue record for this book is available from the British Library

Library of Congress Cataloging-in-Publication Data

Names: Ost, Suzanne, author. | Biggs, Hazel, author.
Title: Exploitation, ethics and law : violating the ethos of the doctor-patient relationship / Suzanne Ost with Hazel Biggs.
Description: Abingdon, Oxon ; New York, NY : Routledge, 2021. | Series: Biomedical law and ethics library | Includes bibliographical references and index.
Identifiers: LCCN 2021006836 (print) | LCCN 2021006837 (ebook) | ISBN 9781138238756 (hardback) | ISBN 9781032041131 (paperback) | ISBN 9781315296890 (ebook)
Subjects: LCSH: Medical laws and legislation. | Medical ethics. | Physician and patient.
Classification: LCC K3601 .O88 2021 (print) | LCC K3601 (ebook) | DDC 174.2–dc23
LC record available at https://lccn.loc.gov/2021006836
LC ebook record available at https://lccn.loc.gov/2021006837

ISBN: 978-1-138-23875-6 (hbk)
ISBN: 978-1-032-04113-1 (pbk)
ISBN: 978-1-315-29689-0 (ebk)

Typeset in Galliard
by KnowledgeWorks Global Ltd.

Contents

Table of statutes vi
Table of cases viii
Acknowledgements xi

1 Introduction 1

2 What is exploitation? Philosophical foundations 10

3 Wrongful exploitation in the doctor-patient relationship 47

4 Patient vulnerability and exploitation 91

5 Sexual exploitation in the doctor-patient relationship 114
  Part 1: Sexual boundary breaches and sexual exploitation 114
  Part 2: The appropriate legal response to sexual exploitation 142

6 Assisted dying and exploitation 167

7 Reflecting on exploitation in the doctor-patient relationship 199

References 228
Index 247

Table of statutes

Canada

Criminal Code
s.273.1(1)(2)(c), s.265(3)(d)

Protection of Patients Act 2017
Schedule 2 s.51(5)

England and Wales

Consumer Protection from Unfair Trading Regulations 2008
Regulation 7

Corporate Manslaughter and Homicide Act 2007
s.1, s.25

Human Fertilisation and Embryology Act 1990
s.41, sch 3

Human Tissue Act 2004
s.5, s.32

Local Authority Social Services Act 1970
s.7

Medical Act 1983
s.35

Mental Capacity Act 2005
ss.2(1), s.3(1), s.4(5), s.4(6)

Modern Slavery Act 2015
s.2, s.3

Offences Against the Person Act 1861
s.18, s.20, s.47.

Protection from Harassment Act 1997
s.7(3)(a)

Sexual Offences Act 2003
ss.1–4, Ss.16–24, s. 21(4), ss.34–37, ss.38–41, s.42(3), ss.48–50, s.51(2), s.53(A), s.67, s.74, ss.75, s.76, s.78

Theft Act 1968
s.21

Germany

German Criminal Code
s.217

Netherlands

Termination of Life on Request and Assisted Suicide (Review Procedures) Act
s.2

United States of America

California Civil Code
§ 1575 (1872)

California Probate Code
§ 86

California Welfare and Institutions Code
§15610.30, § 15610.70

Texas Penal Code
§ 22.011(b)(9)

Table of cases

Australia

Breen v. Williams (1994) 35 NSWLR 522; (1996) 186 CLR 71
Health Care Complaints Commission v. Dr Baez [2014] NSWCATOD 3

Canada

Geffen v. Goodman Estate [1991] 2 SCR 353
McInerney v. MacDonald [1992] 2 SCR 138
Norberg v. Wynrib [1988] 6 WWR 305; [1992] 2 SCR 226
Ontario (College of Physicians and Surgeons of Ontario) v. Ghabbour, 2017 ONCPSD 38
Ontario (College of Physicians and Surgeons of Ontario) v. Sundaralingam, 2019 ONCPSD 11
R v. Hogg (2000), 148 C.C.C. (3d) 86 (Ont. C.A.)
R v. Kilian 2018 ABQB 273
R v. Snelgrove 2019 SCC 16
R v. TD 2019 ONSC 3761
Re ATU, Local 113 and Toronto Transit Commission 2018 CarswellOnt 12619

England and Wales

A Local Authority v. Mrs A and Mr A [2010] EWHC 1549 (Fam)
A Local Authority v. DL, RL and ML [2010] EWHC 2675 (Fam)
Airedale NHS Trust v. Bland 1 All ER 821
Allcard v. Skinner (1887) 36 ChD 145
AMP v. Persons Unknown [2011] EWHC 3454 (TCC)
An NHS Trust v. Mr Y (by his litigation Friend, the Official Solicitor) and another [2018] UKSC 46
Appleton v. Garrett [1996] PIQR P1
Attorney General's Reference No 3 of 2003 [2004] EWCA Crim 868
B v. An NHS Hospital Trust [2002] EWHC 429 (Fam)
Bank of Credit and Commerce International SA v. Aboody [1990] 1 QB 923
Boardman v. Phipps [1967] 2 AC 46
Bolam v. Friern Hospital Management Committee [1957] 1 WLR 583
Bristol and West Building Society v. Mothew [1996] 4 All ER 698
Campbell v. MGN [2004] UKHL 22

Chester v. Afshar [2004] UKHL 41
Daniel v. Drew [2005] EWCA Civ 507
De Gregory v. GMC [1961] AC 957
Dent v. Bennett (1839) 4 Myl & Cr 269
Dowson v. Chief Constable of Northumbria Police [2010] EWHC 2621 (QB)
Earl of Chesterfield v. Janssen (1750) 28 Eng. Rep. 82
Evans v. Llewellin (1787) 1 Cox CC 333
Freeman v. Home Office [1984] QB 524
GMC v. Spackman [1943] AC 627
Goldsworthy v. Brickell [1987] 2 WLR 133
Hall v. Hall (1868) LR 1 P&D 481
Hammond v. Osborn [2002] EWCA Civ 885
Hart v. O'Conor [1985] AC 1000
Huguenin v. Baseley (1807) 14 Ves 273
Lau v. DPP [2000] 1 FLR 799
Montgomery v. Lanarkshire Health Board [2015] UKSC 11
Norton v. Relly (1764) 2 Eden 286
Pearce v. United Bristol Healthcare NHS Trust [1999] PIQR 53
Pretty v. DPP [2001] UKHL 61
R (Nicklinson) v. Ministry of Justice [2014] UKSC 38
R (on the application of Conway) v. The Secretary of State for Justice v. Humanists UK, Not Dead Yet (UK), CNK Alliance Ltd [2018] EWCA Civ 1431
R (on the application of Purdy) v. DPP [2009] UKHL 45
R (on the application of) Quincy Bell and A v. Tavistock and Portman NHS Trust and others [2020] EWHC 3274 (Admin)
R v. Adomako [1994] UKHL 6
R v. Attorney General for England and Wales [2003] UKPC 22
R v. Brown [1994] AC 212
R v. Cosford [2013] EWCA Crim 466
R v. Cox (1992) 12 BMLR 38
R v. Department of Health, ex p Source Informatics (1999) 49 BMLR 41
R v. Hinks [2001] 2 AC 241
R v. Hughes (2014) 1 Cr App R 6
R v. Human Fertilisation and Embryology Authority, ex parte Blood [1999] Fam 151
R v. Jheeta [2007] EWCA Crim 1699
R v. McNally [2013] EWCA Crim 1051
R v. Olugboja [1981] 1 All ER 443
R v. SK [2011] EWCA Crim 1691
R v. Tabassum [2000] 2 Cr App R 328
R v. Whitaker (1914) KB 1283
Re L (No 2) [2012] EWCA Civ 253
Re SA (Vulnerable Adult with capacity: Marriage) [2005] EWHC 2942
Re T (Adult: Refusal of Treatment) [1993] Fam 95 (CA)
Re Z (Local Authority: Duty) [2004] EWHC 2817 (Fam)
Rhodes v. OPO [2015] UKSC 32
Royal Bank of Scotland v. Etridge [2001] UKHL 44
Sidaway v. Board of Governors of the Bethlem Royal Hospital and the Maudsley Hospital [1985] AC 871
Tchenguiz v. Imerman [2010] EWCA Civ 908

Thomas v. *News Group Newspapers Limited and another* [2001] EWCA 1233
Three Rivers D.C. Bank of England (No. 3) [2003] 2 AC 1 (HL)
Thompson v. *Foy* [2009] EWHC 1076 (Ch)
U v. *Centre for Reproductive Medicine* [2002] EWCA Civ 565
Universe Tankships Inc of Monrovia v. *International Transport Workers Federation (The Universe Sentinel)* [1983] 1 AC 366
W v. *Egdell* [1990] Ch. 359 CA
W v. *M* [2011] EWHC 2443 (Fam)
X v. *Y* [1988] RPC 379

New Zealand

Smith v. *Auckland Hospital Board* [1965] NZLR 191

United States of America

Barber v. *Superior Court*, 147 Cal. App. 3d 1006 (1983)
Lintz v. *Lintz* (2014) 222 Cal.App.4th 1346
Lockett v. *Goodill* 430 P.2d 589 (Wash 1967)
Moore v. *Regents of the University of California* 793 P. 2d 479 (1990)
Neade v. *Portes* 739 N.E.2d 496 (Ill.2000)
Pegram v. *Herdrich* 530 US 211 (2000)
Re Piatt 191 Ariz. 24, 951 P.2d 889 (Ariz.1997)

Acknowledgements

We are grateful to our good friends and colleagues, Sara Fovargue, for her painstaking review of numerous draft chapters and Alexandra Mullock, for kindly reviewing chapter 6. The blame for the existence of this book lies with John Coggon, as it was his suggestion some years ago that we should turn an article that we had asked him to comment on into a monograph. We are grateful to him for making us realise that the only way that we could do justice to the subject was to devote the level of analysis to it that a monograph allows. We also owe a debt to John Murphy who offered very helpful advice on finer details regarding the torts of battery and misfeasance and the legal concept of undue influence. Our sincere thanks to Alison Kirk, Emily Summers and Richard Kemp at Routledge for their patience and support throughout the project. Thanks to Carolyn Dodds, our fantastic copyeditor, who corrected grammatical and typographical errors, whilst also ensuring consistency in style and presentation.

Suzanne would like to acknowledge the support of Lancaster University and the Faculty of Arts and Social Sciences in enabling me to take a sabbatical, without which at least three of the chapters in this book would not have been completed. I thank my long-suffering husband, Alisdair Gillespie, for his willingness to engage in countless late-night discussions on the criminal law and on the proposed offences in chapters 5 and 6 and for his unwavering support. Thanks also to my colleague, Steven Wheatley, for organising a coercion roundtable event for the Centre for Law and Society at Lancaster University in December 2018. I was lucky enough to hear Grant Lamond's presentation on coercion at this event, and I am grateful to Grant for providing valuable comments on the presentation I gave, which included parts of the analysis of coercive offers in chapter 5. Finally, and as ever, I am immensely grateful to Margaret Brazier. Without Margot, I doubt that this book would have appeared, since the ideas that lay at its core were conceived during *The Impact of the Criminal Process on Health Care Ethics and Practice* AHRC-funded project, which she led, and I had the pleasure of working with her on. But more than this, she continues to offer her support and share her wisdom (although I know that she would never acknowledge the latter to be such), and she is one of an extremely small number of people who have achieved the amazing feat of cooking food that all of my children (aka fussy eaters) enjoy!

Hazel acknowledges the support of Southampton University Law School, and, in particular, colleagues David Gurnham and Claire Lougarre who generously gave time and encouragement during the production of this book. Huge thanks also go to my husband Jeremy Garlick who, as a non-academic, has been on a steep learning curve about the mysteries of the process of research and writing. My three sons, their partners and children provided endless support, pleasure and distraction. Going forward, having recently retired, I can't wait to spend more time in their company. I would also like to thank a wide community of like-minded and supportive colleagues, too numerous to mention individually, for the insights and influences provided throughout my career in the legal academy. You know who you are, and I wouldn't have wanted to do it without you!

This book is dedicated to our families: Alisdair, Lily, Matthew and Elin, and Jeremy, Michael, Jonathan and Tim, together with Vicky, Julia, Ruby, Teddy and Florence.

1 Introduction

'Exploitation' has increasingly become a high-frequency word in health care ethics and law, often featuring in debates regarding surrogacy, organ donation and transplantation and clinical research, for instance. But it is rarely given centre stage. In fact, it is often the case that when the term exploitation is used, the very spectre of exploitation is powerful enough for it to be deemed unnecessary to provide further explanation. In this work, we shed light on this concept, bringing to the fore what is often left to operate in the background as a significant factor that underpins ethical opposition to certain practices.

Take, for instance, the British case of Diane Blood.[1] Hers is commonly conceived of as a case in which a wife succeeded in circumventing the strict legal regulations in England and Wales surrounding the use of gametes in assisted reproduction after death.[2] She was able to take her deceased husband's sperm abroad to use in her fertility treatment even though he had not consented to its extraction, and her case was thus presented as a victory for autonomy and assisted reproduction 'rights'.[3] However, whilst Mrs Blood attested that she and husband had been trying to conceive for some months prior to him catching meningitis, the fact remains that sperm was extracted from a dying patient without his consent, when he was incapable of consenting. True, much of the commentary surrounding the case considered whether this was ethical. But there is also the matter of a battery being committed on a comatose patient[4] for his wife's benefit, for ends that Mr Blood *may* have desired (and certainly this is what Mrs Blood contended[5]). If, therefore, the case had been explored through the lens of exploitation, we suggest that it may have been viewed very differently. In another example, which came to court

---

1   R v. *Human Fertilisation and Embryology Authority, ex parte Blood* [1999] Fam 151.
2   Under which written prior consent is required before gametes can be used after a person's death (sch.3 of the Human Fertilisation and Embryology Act 1990).
3   For examples in the literature, see Morgan and Lee 1997; Price 1997; Bennett 1999; Clare Dyer, 'Diane Blood law victory gives her sons their legal father' *The Guardian* (London, 19 September 2013).
4   Whilst Mrs Blood consented to the extraction of her husband's sperm, she was not *entitled*, at law, to consent: Biggs 1997.
5   R v. *Human Fertilisation and Embryology Authority, ex parte Blood*, 159.

in Canada almost a decade earlier, a doctor agreed to provide his patient with a drug that he knew she was addicted to in exchange for sexual favours. The subsequent legal case brought against him was presented as a case involving a variety of wrongful acts: sexual assault, negligence, breach of fiduciary duty and breach of contract.[6] Yet, in our view, the nub of the doctor's wrong was most aptly summed up by one of the Supreme Court Justices, McLachlin J, in her comment that the patient had a 'striking personal interest in obtaining professional medical care *free of exploitation for the physician's private purposes*'.[7] As we seek to demonstrate throughout this work, focusing on exploitation can draw attention to the crux of the issue, and may result in us arriving at a different legal and ethical place.

This work explores the nature of exploitation in the specific context of the doctor-patient relationship, and considers what the ethical and legal responses to such wrongful behaviour are, and should be. In some instances where patients suffer physical or psychological injury at the hands of their doctors, this is the result of them being taken advantage of and misused, for their doctors' own ends.[8] This exploitation is facilitated by the nature of the doctor-patient relationship and, often, the harm that the patient suffers is exacerbated because of the abuse of trust that has enabled the doctor to take advantage of the patient. Traditional notions of harm do not convey the deep-seated nature of the effects of exploitation by their doctors that patients experience. In short, the harm suffered is intensified by the exploitation of the victim.

Given the contexts in which a patient's encounters with her doctor take place, the possibility of exploitation occurring in the health care setting is not remote, as alluded to by Colt et al:

> the risks for patient exploitation exist in virtually every aspect of the medical system ... the sexualisation of the doctor-patient relationship; the involuntary incarceration of those labelled mentally disturbed; ... the advancements in technology that prolong death rather than life; the (very human) prejudices and biases of physicians; ... the use of pharmaceutical choices based on drug company incentives ... direct financial incentives for recruitment of patients from a physician's practice, so-called 'finder's fees,' for participation in research protocols ...[9]

Contemporary examples demonstrate a wide range of exploitative behaviour, with instances in the UK including surgeon Simon Bramhall, who branded his initials on the organs of two patients during transplant surgery;[10] Ian Paterson, who provided unnecessary and inappropriate surgery to patients for cancer

---

6 *Norberg* v. *Wynrib* [1988] 6 WWR 305; [1992] 2 SCR 226.
7 *Norberg* v. *Wynrib* [1992] 2 SCR 226, [74] (emphasis added).
8 We are not concerned with cases with no element of exploitation, e.g. where the harm caused to patients is due to their doctors' negligence, or medical error which falls short of negligence.
9 Colt and others 2011: 299.
10 See chapter 3, n.232; Ost 2019; Ost 2020.

treatment in a private hospital;[11] and a doctor's alleged profiting from the sale of private tests for COVID-19 in 2020.[12] Whilst our primary jurisdictional focus is the UK, in the Netherlands, there is the example of a fertility doctor using his own sperm in assisted reproduction treatment that he offered his patients,[13] and in the United States, gynaecologist Dr Nikita Levy took covert, explicit photographs of his patients during pelvic examinations over a 25-year period.[14]

Although most of the cases that we examine in this work involve *doctors* perpetrating exploitation, this is not always the case. It is the patient's wife in the afore-mentioned *Blood* case who might be perceived as the exploiter; one of our case studies on assisted dying also focuses on the patient's relatives as potential exploiters, and we recognise too the patient can, on occasion, be the exploiter.[15] This raises the question of why we have chosen to focus, primarily, on exploitation occurring in the doctor-patient relationship. This is a more selective approach than, for instance, Pattinson's analysis of undue influence in the context of medical treatment decisions, which extends to both doctors and nurses as potential perpetrators of undue influence, viewing both as 'medical advisors' who could look 'to press [their] own ethical views upon the patient'.[16] Similarly, whilst we recognise that other health care professionals can be the ones who are exploited rather than, or as well as, patients,[17] this is not our chosen focus. We have chosen to be more discriminating chiefly because we wish to explore the particular dimension of power within, and the intimate nature of, the doctor-patient relationship, and subject exploitation within this relationship to a more intense scrutiny than would have been possible had we extended our focus to include nurses and other health care professionals.

1) Our key themes

i) What makes exploitation wrongful?

Although not all exploitation is considered to be morally wrong, it is a term commonly used to condemn a certain practice or behaviour. Yet whilst the

---

11 See chapter 3, text accompanying nn.93–94.
12 Rupert Neate, 'GMC concerned about doctors exploiting coronavirus fears' *The Guardian* (London, 22 March 2020).
13 Anon, 'Dutch fertility doctor used own sperm to father 49 children, DNA tests show' BBC News (12 April 2019), at https://www.bbc.co.uk/news/world-europe-47907847 accessed 9 April 2020; chapter 3, text accompanying n.97.
14 See chapter 3, text accompanying nn.34–35.
15 See chapter 7 and chapter 5, section 4.
16 Pattinson 2002: 311. Although Pattinson's analysis is not directed towards exploitation it still bears relevance since, as we will discuss in subsequent chapters, some instances of exploitation can occur through the vehicle of undue influence.
17 On junior doctors and exploitation, see Parker 2019. For an anecdotal account of exploitation of junior doctors by consultants, see Kay 2018. On sexual exploitation of doctors by their colleagues, see Launer 2018; Minkina 2019.

concept has a powerful moral impact, ambiguity remains as to what exactly it is that makes exploitation normatively wrong.[18] Thus, one of our core objectives is to provide a theoretical account of exploitation. As should become apparent, the conceptualisation of wrongful exploitation that we provide is distinctive in revolving around *mis*use of another rather than taking unfair advantage of, or degradation, with taking advantage of another's vulnerability for one's own ends being a common example of misuse. The matters of both wronging and harming are also central to our account. This account grounds our subsequent analysis of exploitation in the doctor-patient relationship, thereby enabling us to evaluate when a doctor's behaviour is exploitative, and what the appropriate ethical and legal responses to instances of exploitation should be.

ii) The connection between exploitation and vulnerability

In exploring the nature of exploitation in the context of the doctor-patient relationship, we say much on vulnerability and its connection to exploitation. The general relevance of this theme becomes apparent through our consideration of the nature of wrongful exploitation and how instances of wrongful exploitation can involve taking advantage of a person's vulnerability. We also focus more specifically on the particular vulnerabilities that patients may possess within the doctor-patient relationship which can be taken advantage of.

In light of the popularity of universal vulnerability theories, the analytical position that we take may be controversial, since we reject the notion of the universal vulnerable subject as our starting point. As we see it, this goes too far in assuming the omnipresence of vulnerability. However, we accept that vulnerability can readily arise in relationships where there is an unequal balance of power, and we see the concept of *shared* vulnerability in universal vulnerability debates as providing a valuable means of approaching the questions of whether a patient is vulnerable to exploitation and, if so, what the implications of this should be. For us, the starting point should be one of *potential* vulnerability.[19] All of us are potentially vulnerable, and there are situations such as poverty, illness, addiction or certain relational statuses which make anyone *more likely* to be vulnerable to exploitative tactics. These are situations and contexts where our shared vulnerability is apparent. What we seek to avoid in our analysis of the relational connection between vulnerability and exploitation is making assumptions, without evidence, that an individual is vulnerable *per se* because they are part of a group perceived to be vulnerable

---

18 In Mayer's words, 'for most wrongs – like murder, theft, or lying – it is easy to understand why the conduct is bad. But exploitation is different. We know it is wrong to be an exploiter but it is not clear *why* it is wrong': Mayer 2007: 137 (emphasis added).
19 Although an obvious exception for a certain group indicative of a more universal shared vulnerability would be very young children.

in and by society.[20] Such assumptions pose the real risk that members of such groups are given the blanket label of vulnerability in a paternalistic, and what may be an offensive, way.[21]

iii) The nature and effects of exploitation in the doctor-patient relationship: a special case?

In the doctor-patient relationship, exploitation perpetrated by a doctor on their patient occurs in the setting of a power imbalance between the parties, where the patient – who may be suffering ill-health – has vested their trust in a professional whose knowledge and expertise they are relying on. In these circumstances, as the cases that we explore demonstrate, the doctor's professional role can be used as a tool of perceived legitimacy to gain a patient's acquiescence to what are, in fact, exploitative acts, thereby enabling exploitation, and can potentially offer numerous opportunities to perpetrate exploitation on one, or perhaps more, patients. Furthermore, when doctors exploit their patients, the dynamics of the doctor-patient relationship mean that this exploitation involves a serious breach of trust, and is especially likely to both wrong patients by way of violating their rights, and to cause harm by way of a setback to their interests. And the effects can have long-term ramifications where the patient's awareness of the doctor's exploitation causes them to suffer a loss of trust in the medical profession more broadly.[22] It is the combination of these factors that causes us to present exploitation in the doctor-patient relationship as a special case, although we also recognise certain commonalities with exploitation in other intimate and confidential professional relationships.[23]

iv) Undue influence and the doctor as fiduciary

The significance of undue influence (that is, pressurising or persuading the patient so that their free will is invaded) as the conduit through which doctors can take advantage of and misuse their patients is demonstrated in various cases that we discuss throughout this work. Consequently, we examine the relevance of the legal concept of undue influence and whether it might provide a suitable framework for dealing with some instances of exploitation.

Important factors that give rise to a finding of *undue* influence pertain to the nature of the doctor-patient relationship, and the deferential trust that the patient places in the doctor. We argue that this deferential trust imposes a

---

20 Such groups can include the elderly, disabled and chronically ill, for instance, and perhaps anyone labelled as patient. See further chapter 2, section 3.i.b; chapter 4, section 2; chapter 7, section 2.
21 As alluded to by Ries and Thomson 2020: 298.
22 See, e.g. the examples we discuss in chapter 3, section 2.
23 See chapter 3, section 1; chapter 5, part 2, section 1, text accompanying nn.51–55; chapter 7, text accompanying n.142.

fundamental *fiduciary* obligation on the doctor. We focus on the relevance of the fiduciary framework to illustrate what lies at the core of the doctor's duties in the doctor-patient relationship – to act in the interests of the patient and not out of self-interest – and to demonstrate how exploitation of patients violates this fundamental element of the relationship. As will become apparent, this shapes the conceptual basis of the ethical (professional medical education and regulatory) response to exploitation that we propose.

2) Overview of the book

Our analysis proceeds as follows. In chapter 2, we explore the intricacies of the concept of exploitation. Whilst existing conceptions of exploitation have much to offer, we explain why we take issue with approaches that focus on the *outcome* of the interaction between the parties and why, notwithstanding our support for alternative approaches which concentrate on the *process* of the interaction between the parties, particular aspects of such accounts still leave us unsatisfied. Having identified what we see as key commonalities in the existing accounts, we then provide our own account of exploitation which is orientated towards Kantian liberalism. We identify and scrutinise its primary elements and the way in which it connects with, but also differs from, certain other conceptions of exploitation that highlight the wrongful treatment of others.

Chapter 3 turns to our contextual focus of exploitation in the doctor-patient relationship. In demonstrating how exploitation in the doctor-patient relationship is particularly wrongful, we present this relationship as an *intimate and confidential professional relationship*, with trust and an imbalance of power at its core. We also explain why it is a fiduciary relationship, and how exploitation violates the ethos of this relationship. When considering instances of doctors exploiting their patients, we examine cases involving stark exploitation and 'greyer' areas where the presence of exploitation is more contestable. Given that the doctor-patient relationship can be situated in both public and private health care systems in the UK, we explore how the nature of the relationship, and the opportunities for exploitation, might be affected by each system. We reflect on how philosophical medical ethics and professional medical ethics construe exploitation, before turning, briefly, to consider how the law categorises exploitation in the doctor-patient relationship. It is here that we introduce the relevance of undue influence as a legal doctrine, and as a means through which exploitation can be perpetrated.

Chapter 4 offers our primary analysis of vulnerability. We examine the question of what it means to be vulnerable, engaging with Fineman's work on universal vulnerability and shared vulnerability in particular.[24] Whilst we reject a starting point of universal vulnerability, we advocate *potential* vulnerability as the place from which to begin a relational analysis of vulnerability, with illness

---

24 Fineman 2008; Fineman 2010; Fineman 2013; Fineman 2019.

or feared ill-health being situations which can make anyone more vulnerable to exploitation. We set out our position that it is essential to enhance and restore autonomy, alongside recognising vulnerability, if we seek to address susceptibility to exploitation. Having provided a theoretical analysis, we then explore how autonomy *and* vulnerability can be recognised in practice in medical research. The matter of exploitation in medical research has already been the subject of analysis in the existing literature,[25] and thus we have chosen to contribute to this literature by centring our consideration of medical research on the connection between vulnerability and exploitation. Alongside medical research, and in the context of private health care, cosmetic surgery also offers a valuable lens through which to test our account of vulnerability.

The case studies that we have chosen in the two subsequent chapters enable us to explore what the appropriate legal, ethical and regulatory response to types of exploitation should be, and to explore the commonalities (in terms of the doctor's behaviour and the effects of exploitation on patients) between them. Chapter 5 brings us to our first case study. Since the 1990s, the occurrence of sexual misconduct by (some) doctors against their patients has been highlighted as a result of numerous government investigations, task force reports, media coverage of cases of misconduct involving sexual misconduct brought before professional medical bodies, and the creation of specific professional ethical guidance.[26] Yet exploitation has not yet been used as a core conceptual analytical framework through which to explore and address this sexual misconduct. Now, in the wake of the #MeToo movement and increased societal awareness and disclosure of sexual harassment and assault, this is an especially apt time to subject this form of doctor misconduct to the lens of exploitation. Notably, this chapter provides the most substantial of our two case studies because of the complexities of sexual exploitation and sexual boundary breaches in the doctor-patient relationship, and the multiple issues that warrant consideration. Consequently, the reader will find that this chapter is split into two parts. In the first part, we focus on when sexual boundary breaches perpetrated by doctors are exploitative, tackling in particular the contentious issue of consent and exploitation through offering inducements, and evaluating whether the professional zero-tolerance approach to sexual boundary breaches between doctors and patients is appropriate. In the second part, we explore the legal response to this form of exploitation, assessing when a doctor's sexual exploitation is criminalised and identifying a gap in the criminal law. We propose to fill this gap with a new abuse of trust offence: intentionally causing a relevant sexual act to occur through exploiting another by exercising undue influence. We also evaluate the potential of existing civil law remedies and the appropriateness of fiduciary law as a means to address doctors' sexual exploitation of their patients. Finally, we consider whether the reverse situation – in which patients initiate sexual activity with their doctors – can be exploitative of doctors.

25 Perhaps most notably Wertheimer 2011: chapter 5.
26 The footnote references in chapter 5 offer a sample of these various sources.

Our second case study, in chapter 6, applies our account of exploitation to groups commonly perceived to be vulnerable in the context of assisted dying, including: older adults; the terminally ill; and patients with disabilities. One of our main focuses is the way in which a patient's perception that they are a burden, and their desire to die, could be exploited. We assess how both patients and doctors could be the parties who are exploited. Notably, this chapter involves a shift in the (primary) identity of the exploiter: in contrast to the rest of this work, it is not the matter of the doctor, but the matter of relatives and society doing the exploiting that we address here. Lastly, we consider how the law might respond to the risks of exploitation that we identify and, once again, we recognise the relevance of undue influence, both as a means of facilitating some cases of exploitation and as a conceptual legal framework for tackling this exploitation.

Chapter 7 brings together the strands of analysis and the insight that our case studies provide to convey the common characteristics that exploitation in the doctor-patient relationship possesses, and reflects on the connection between exploitation and vulnerability. We then turn, finally, to our assessment of the responses to exploitation in professional ethics and law. We call for an explicit focus on exploitation in medical ethics education and continuing professional development, within a fiduciary ethical framework. The fiduciary obligation not to act out of self-interest is also our concern when we then consider the General Medical Council's (GMC) responsibility to enforce ethical guidance through regulation. We advocate the mandatory disclosure of doctors' conflicts of interest in a centrally held, publicly accessible register, and careful enforcement of this duty by the GMC. Looking to the legal response, we draw attention to the piecemeal protection from exploitation that the current law offers patients. However, our analysis of the variety of behaviours that are exploitative causes us to recognise the unworkability of a more tailored response by way of a new tort or criminal offence of exploitation. Rather, following the school of thought that draws a connection between undue influence and fiduciary obligations, we propose a modification to existing legal frameworks in order to offer what we argue is a more appropriate legal response to exploitation in the doctor-patient relationship.

3) Caveats and a point on our choice of gender pronouns

In drawing this introductory chapter to a close, we wish to express two caveats in an effort to avoid misconceptions about what we have set out to do and what this book is about. First, we do not intend to make sweeping assumptions that all doctors do, or will at some point, exploit their patients. Nor are we suggesting that exploitation in the doctor-patient relationship is rife and that doctors are prone to using their powerful position in the relationship to their advantage. We cannot put an actual figure on how many doctors abuse their patients' trust through exploitation since there are no available statistics evidencing prevalence. However, high-profile, publicised cases such as those we discuss in the chapters in this book demonstrate that exploitation by medical professionals can, and does, occur.

Secondly, it may surprise some readers that we have not included surrogacy or organ donation and transplantation in the case studies which feature in this book. Whilst we recognise that these are areas in which exploitation can and does occur, they have already been the contextual subject of important existing literature in the field.[27] Further, the exploitation that is commonly discussed in these areas – the exploitation of the economically and socially disadvantaged – is not necessarily generated in, or by, the doctor-patient relationship.[28] Because we have striven to balance our theoretical and contextual analysis, we have, necessarily, needed to be selective in our case studies. We have chosen those areas which are most pertinent and timely, and where we are of the view that we can make the greatest contribution to the literature.

We should also explain the approach to gender pronouns that we have chosen to adopt. We use 'he' and 'she' interchangeably when referring to the person who exploits and the person being exploited, in order to avoid making generalisations and to dispel beliefs and stereotypical assumptions regarding gender, such as that it tends to be men who exploit and women who are exploited. Perhaps the most obvious example here is that which we explore in chapter 5 regarding sexual exploitation: the existing research suggests that sexual boundary breaches tend to involve male doctors and female patients. This indicates that female patients *might* be more vulnerable to sexual exploitation, but we subject this assumption to analysis: are all sexual boundary breaches exploitative and is gender (always) a critical factor?

As we discovered when embarking on this project some years ago, exploitation is a vast and rich topic for study. The scope which this monograph offers has enabled us to provide the first intensive, theoretical and contextual account of what we conceive to be the key issues and concerns when exploitation occurs in the doctor-patient relationship. Our aim in so doing has been to offer the groundwork for further analysis that we hope will follow in the future.

---

27 See, e.g. Wilkinson 2003; Wilkinson 2016; Hill 1994.
28 Whilst we also acknowledge that the identity of the potential exploiter is not the doctor in our assisted dying case study in chapter 6, the doctor's involvement is crucial in order for a lawful assisted death to occur, and the doctor-patient relationship is an important part of the framework we suggest for tackling the exploitation that we discuss (see chapter 6, section 4).

2 What is exploitation? Philosophical foundations

Our first substantive chapter involves a philosophical exploration of the concept of exploitation. In an effort to tease out what exploitation is, and our moral perceptions of it, we examine existing conceptions and accounts of exploitation and highlight commonalities that they share. We present what we see as the essential elements of exploitation and consider whether consensual exploitation is wrongful. Finally, we explore how exploitation can both wrong and harm the exploited person, drawing upon Feinberg's analysis of wronging a person and setting back their interests.

Readers who wish to see an analysis of the way in which exploitation occurs in the doctor-patient relationship might feel impatient that this is preceded by a detailed philosophical and conceptual account of what exploitation is within this chapter. They may consider such an account to be unnecessary and, indeed, it has been contended that moralised philosophical accounts are unhelpful, contributing conceptual confusion to the question of what we mean by the term exploitation.[1] But exploring what exploitation is and what we conceive to be wrongful about it is a necessary first step to achieve conceptual clarity – at least for the purposes of this book – before we undertake our substantive tasks of assessing how exploitation occurs in the doctor-patient relationship and whether exploitation in the context of this relationship is a special case. In setting out our own account of exploitation, we do not seek to provide a philosophical account that will convince all. Such a task would be nigh on impossible to accomplish given the ambiguities surrounding both the concept and the matter of what makes exploitation wrongful.[2] Rather, we aim to provide a defensible conceptual foundation to sustain our subsequent analysis of exploitation in the doctor-patient relationship.

1) The concept of exploitation: preliminary matters

Exploitation is a commonly used term to refer to conduct occurring in numerous contexts where one party (or parties) in some way takes advantage of another

---

1 Wood 1995: 141.
2 See also Logar 2010: 332.

person (or other persons) for their own ends. It is a frequently used descriptor for certain behaviours perceived to exemplify this practice, such as trafficking in persons[3] and unfair practices in the workplace.[4] In particular, it is inexorably connected to the use of children for sexual purposes, with 'child sexual exploitation' being the overarching term used to encompass a wide range of behaviour including sexual abuse, involving a child in abusive images and involving a child in prostitution.[5] Yet the concept of exploitation is frequently applied without any real investigation of its meaning. Indeed, it often seems to be taken for granted that there is a generally accepted understanding of its meaning.[6]

The *Oxford English Dictionary* (OED) provides three definitions of exploitation, the latter two of which are most relevant for our purposes here:

> the action or fact of deriving benefit from something by making full or good use of it
> the action or fact of taking advantage of something or someone in an unfair or unethical manner; utilization of something for one's own ends.[7]

At the crux of these two definitions is the idea of *A* using *B*, or taking advantage of *B*. In Goodin's words, 'the nub of the matter is always "taking advantage" in one way or another'.[8] It is hard, if not impossible, to envisage how *B* could be exploited if *A*'s use of him does not involve taking advantage of him or something that is inherently connected to him.[9] To conceive of exploitation in such circumstances would surely be to miss the element that is essential to what it means to exploit.

Wertheimer[10] and others have contended that exploitation is a moralised concept and that, consequently, it 'is, at least, *pro tanto* morally wrong'.[11] However, we would challenge any account that exploitation is *always* a moralised concept, for the term can be used to describe behaviour involving utilising something

---

3   United Nations Office on Drugs and Crime 2015: 8.
4   Askola 2007; Monzini 2005; Zia Mansoor 2006.
5   See Gillespie 2008a: 1–2.
6   See also Wertheimer 1996: 5.
7   OED Online at https://www.oed.com/view/Entry/66651?redirectedFrom=exploitation#eid accessed 5 January 2021. There is nothing about these lay person's definitions to suggest that only people can be exploited. Indeed, it is far from unusual in common parlance to refer to objects and natural resources as being exploited too. (See also Goodin 1987: 167. And see the other definition provided by the OED: 'the action of deriving value from a natural resource by harvesting'.) However, we say very little else about the exploitation of anything other than persons, since such exploitation falls outside our remit.
8   Goodin 1987: 168.
9   Hereafter, other than in particular example scenarios, we refer to the exploiter as *A* and the exploited person as *B*. As discussed in the introductory chapter, we use 'he' and 'she' interchangeably when referring to *A* and *B*.
10 Wertheimer 1996: 6; Jansen and Wall 2013: 385.
11 Jansen and Wall 2013: 385.

which we are morally neutral towards.[12] Returning to the OED definitions above, the first definition is morally neutral; there is nothing within it to suggest that 'making full or good use of' something (or someone) is somehow wrongful. For example, a harpist exploits her musical talents by playing at weddings and receiving payment for her services. It would difficult to conceive of how this could be considered to be morally wrong. And there are some situations in which exploitation may well be perceived to be admirable. Consider the example Wood provides of a chess player who wins the game by taking advantage of her opponent's lapse of attention.[13] In this context, two opponents are engaged in a competition that both seek to win. Both are undoubtedly seeking opportunities to outmanoeuvre each other and surely have the expectation that the other will take any such opportunity. Would the audience not be impressed by one player's skilful exploitation of the other's loss of concentration?

It is thus more appropriate to conceive of exploitation as a concept that *can be* (and often is) moralised, rather than a concept that is always moralised. The second OED definition above offers such a moralised notion of exploitation through inclusion of the words 'unfair' and 'unethical'. It demonstrates that exploitation is commonly used to describe behaviour that we view pejoratively. Here the term may be employed to describe *mis*use rather than use, suggesting acting in a way that is morally wrong. It is this idea of exploitation as wrongful behaviour that we are concerned with, and which concerns the authors whose accounts we analyse below. We also limit our focus to behaviour towards others. The harpist example above is an instance of self-exploitation but, given this book's concentration on one person's behaviour towards another occurring in the context of a (special) relationship, we leave the question of whether it is possible to wrongfully exploit oneself for others to address.[14] We turn next to exploring existing conceptions of exploitation.

2) Existing conceptions

> The ambiguous and ill-defined concept of exploitation has been widely applied, taking on an open-textured and almost all-encompassing meaning ... no clearly defined necessary and sufficient conditions govern the application of the concept of exploitation. Nor is there an adequate theoretical basis for understanding exploitation ...[15]

---

12 See Wilkinson 2003: 11; Wertheimer 2007: 248.
13 Wood 1995: 138.
14 We also note that exploitation can occur at micro and macro levels. It can be perpetrated by more than one person, by organisations and by societies (see Goodin 1987: 193, n.11 for an example of societal exploitation). Whilst our primary focus is on exploitation perpetrated by one person upon another, we do concern ourselves with organisational exploitation when, e.g. we consider whether private health care providers might exploit their consumers (chapter 3, section 5.ii), and whether a society that offers assisted dying exploits those who wish to avail themselves of an assisted death (chapter 6).
15 Hill 1994: 631–632 and 635.

i) Process- and outcome-based conceptions of exploitation

Explaining what makes behaviour exploitative is a far from easy task. The afore-mentioned dictionary definition and common usage of the term clearly revolve around using and taking advantage of another. But this provides a hazy picture; *how* does the way in which one person uses and takes advantage of another make the interaction between the two parties exploitative? The answer to this question is elusive, as Hill's statement above suggests. Because of the ambiguity surrounding 'use' and 'taking advantage of', it should come as no surprise that various academic explanations of exploitation have been offered and that, whilst commonalities are often present, each author tends to provide an account which is in some way unique.

To assist in understanding what exactly it might be that makes behaviour exploitative, we suggest that it is helpful to organise existing conceptions according to predominant approaches in the philosophical literature which orient towards alternative points to explain what makes behaviour exploitative. Two typologies offer a useful means of categorising conceptions of exploitation in this way: the first centres on the process of the interaction between the parties and the second focuses on the outcome(s) of the interaction. Jansen and Wall see process-based accounts as those which conceive exploitative interactions as occurring where 'one party plays on a weakness or vulnerability of the other in order to advance his ends'.[16] The focus is thus on what occurs *during* the interaction between the parties. In contrast, outcome-based accounts explore the interaction's result, requiring that 'at least one party benefits unfairly from the [interaction]'[17] in order for it to be described as exploitative. Jansen and Wall observe that some accounts can be most accurately described as a combination of these two approaches, so that '[an interaction] is exploitative if, and only if, one party plays on a weakness or vulnerability or another to advance his or her ends *and* benefits unfairly from the [interaction]'.[18]

We leave aside our view as to which approach centres on the correct focal point until we have examined some of the conceptions of exploitation that have been put on the table by previous authors. Whist we do not seek to provide a comprehensive assessment of each account of exploitation, we identify particular issues regarding the authors' conceptions of exploitation which we perceive to be problematic, consider which typology each of these conceptions falls within, and highlight their commonalities.

ii) Feinberg on exploitation

> The exploiter [must] be a gainer. Exploitation in the usual pejorative sense is the wrongful turning to some advantage by one party (*A*) of some trait or circumstances of another party (*B*).[19]

---

16 Jansen and Wall 2013: 383.
17 Ibid.
18 Ibid (emphasis in original).
19 Feinberg 1988: 192.

Feinberg appears to adopt an analysis which is both process- and outcome-based. The first part of the quotation above clearly evidences a view that where A does not gain from his interaction with B, there is no exploitation. Hence the question of whether or not exploitation has occurred involves an assessment of the outcome for A.[20] The outcome for B would seem to be less important, however. Having stated that 'we would not normally speak of exploitation ... (at least in any blameable sense) when B himself gains from the use to which A puts him', Feinberg goes on to say that 'B's not gaining, however, may ... be too strong a requirement. B could gain from his own exploitation, I suppose, but be badly used because A gained disproportionately.'[21] The crux of the matter regarding outcome, then, is (disproportionate) gain for A.

Yet beside this emphasis on outcome, Feinberg also centres on the process of the interaction; he refers to A's wrongful taking advantage of B. In terms of what it is about B that A exploits, Feinberg considers not only traits that we perceive to be weaknesses, but also traits which we appreciate as strengths (such as B's good will or loyalty) to be potential candidates for A's exploitation.[22] In such cases, 'part of what seems outrageous ... is that A, who is morally defective, should gain relative to B ... precisely because B ... [is] morally superior to him'.[23] And he notes that circumstances as well as characteristics can be exploited. Great moral repugnance may be felt towards A's exploitation of B's misfortune, for example, especially if A has been involved in some way in creating this misfortune.[24] Thus, any trait or circumstance can potentially be exploited, 'provided only that they are causally relevant to the exploiter's purposes'.[25] Feinberg's approach is effective in conveying the multitude of factors that can make B vulnerable to exploitation and challenges more limited conceptions of characteristics or circumstances that make a person susceptible to exploitation.[26] He presents us with the disconcerting truth that we are all potentially vulnerable to being exploited. This position could be seen to be sympathetic to universal vulnerability theories. But it could also connect with our preferred approach to vulnerability which, as will become apparent, is that we are all more likely to vulnerable in certain situational contexts and it is in such contexts that we possess a shared vulnerability.[27]

In explaining the pejorative nature of the process of the exploitative interaction, Feinberg uses the word 'wrongful'. This leaves what it is that is morally wrong about A's treatment of B open to interpretation. Albeit noting that 'it is ... difficult to characterize the nature of ... wrongfulness', Feinberg's

---

20 'all interpersonal exploitation involves ... (A) profiting from his relation to ... (B)': ibid: 178.
21 Ibid: 193.
22 Ibid: 179 and 183.
23 Ibid: 202.
24 Ibid: 184-185.
25 Ibid: 181.
26 See, e.g. the text accompanying n.49.
27 On universal vulnerabilities and our approach to vulnerability, see chapter 4.

approach is to use unfairness (regarding the treatment of *B* or the outcome for *B*) and injustice as measures of wrongfulness.[28] This then leads to his consideration of types of exploitation that he believes we would conceive to be the 'most unfair', such as that involving deception and coercion and exploiting *B*'s trust and virtues and those instances where the outcome is a significant loss for *B* or a substantial gain for *A*.[29] Again, his concern with both process and outcome is evident here.

The implications of Feinberg's requirement that *A* must gain are significant; even if the process of the interaction is wrongful because, for example, *A*'s exploitation of *B*'s virtue is an instance of what Feinberg suggests we would perceive as the 'most unfair' (exacted through deception or coercion for instance), we cannot say that exploitation has occurred where the outcome of gain for *A* is absent. Since the reasons for any lack of intended gain for *A* are not explored, this would presumably be the case regardless of the reason for *A*'s lack of gain. For example, Feinberg does not consider whether there is a difference between a situation where, after the interaction between *A* and *B*, someone else's intervention prevents *A* from receiving the expected benefit, and a situation where *A* changes her mind before she acquires the benefit and therefore chooses not to avail herself of it. Yet our moral response to these two situations could differ, and we might have good reason to perceive one or both as involving exploitation.

iii) Wertheimer on exploitation

Wertheimer's understanding of exploitation echoes Feinberg's when it comes to casting unfairness as the measure of wrongfulness. He explores the claim that 'A exploits B when A takes unfair advantage of B'.[30] In terms of what exactly is meant by 'taking unfair advantage', he states that this:

> first ... may refer to some dimension of the *outcome* of the exploitative act or relation, and this, it seems, has two elements: (1) the benefit to A, and (2) the effect on B ... Second, to say that A takes unfair advantage of B may imply that A has been able to turn some characteristic of B or some feature of B's situation to his or her advantage. We imply that there is some sort of defect in the *process* by which the unfair outcome has come about or the formation of the agreement between A and B.[31]

It thus appears that both outcome and process are also important to Wertheimer's account. However, whilst he goes on to say that 'it seems plausible to argue that A does not exploit B simply because there is unfairness in the distribution of

---

28 Feinberg 1988: 199.
29 Ibid: 204.
30 Wertheimer 1996: 16.
31 Ibid: 16 (emphasis in original).

rewards, that exploitation also depends on the way in which that distribution came about',[32] it can be inferred that his account is, in fact, predominantly outcome based. For, in explicating the significance of a beneficial outcome for *A*, he emphasises that 'it seems that A *cannot* take unfair advantage of B *unless* A gets some advantage from B'.[33] This suggests that what Wertheimer presented as the first way in which an interaction can be understood to be exploitative, in his earlier statement above, is actually a prerequisite in order for exploitation to occur.[34] This is supported by his contention that cases where *A* attempts to gain an advantage in his interaction with *B* but fails to do so are not cases where *A* actually exploits *B* but merely '"acts exploitatively" toward B'.[35] We suggest that it confuses the issue to differentiate between exploitation and acting exploitatively towards *B*; for they are surely two sides of the same coin if we take the view that the outcome is irrelevant to the existence of exploitation. It would thus seem most appropriate to describe Wertheimer's approach as primarily outcome based, with some consideration of process. The end result would appear to be that in a situation where A's treatment of B is seriously wrongful, with *A* taking advantage of *B* to achieve his own ends, there is no exploitation *unless* *A* gains a benefit.

iv) Goodin on exploitation

> Exploiting a person is ... essentially a matter of "taking unfair advantage" of that person.[36]

Upon initial examination, Goodin would appear to offer a similar conception of exploitation to Feinberg and Wertheimer since he argues that the unfairness associated with exploitation demonstrates its inherent wrongness: 'Built into the concept of exploiting a person is a notion of "unfairness" (of "taking

---

32   Ibid: 25.
33   Ibid: 17 (emphasis added). A similar approach (focused on outcome and the extraction of an (excessive) benefit by *A*) is taken by Valdman 2009. See also Mayer 2007: 139.
34   We note Wertheimer's comment at the outset of his monograph that he is not aiming to 'advanc[e] a set of necessary and sufficient conditions for the proper use of the word "exploitation"', but rather to reveal the 'morally relevant features' of interactions that are claimed to be exploitative (Wertheimer 1996: ix). However, the implication of the quoted statement from Wertheimer above (text accompanying n.33) is that exploitation does not occur absent a beneficial outcome for *A*.
35   Wertheimer 1996: 17 (n.57). Note too that he later states that 'a mutually advantageous transaction is (wrongly) exploitative only if the *outcome* is (in some way) unfair to B': Ibid: 22 (emphasis added). See also Jansen and Wall 2013: 406, n.3, who cite Wertheimer 2011: 202 to suggest that there is at least one occasion in his works where he appears to see outcome as the only consideration. Cf. Wertheimer 2007: 250: 'A transaction is (wrongly) exploitative only if the outcome is (in some way) unfair to B *or* A wrongfully uses B' (emphasis added).
36   Goodin 1987: 171.

unfair advantage")'.[37] But Goodin's account is primarily process-based; he sees *A*'s treatment of *B* in an unfair manner as the essential conduit through which exploitation flows.

Yet, before we explore this further, there is some outcome-based thinking apparent in Goodin's account. Whilst he sees one particular outcome of the interaction (*B* suffering a loss or losses) to be unnecessary in order to define it as exploitative,[38] he also says that 'interpersonal exploitation must *necessarily* entail some benefit for the exploited [*B*]'[39] and that, if *A* receives no benefit, 'it was not a *successful* act of exploitation or else it was not an act of *exploitation* at all'.[40] Both of these statements suggest that Goodin places at least some significance on certain outcomes (that both *A* and *B* receive some benefit from the interaction), thereby indicating that he also adopts an approach which incorporates a degree of outcome-based thinking. His specific focus in terms of outcome is interesting and somewhat unusual, given that a beneficial outcome for the exploited person is rarely presented as a necessity in outcome-based accounts. Indeed, it is more common to see outcome-based accounts which construe *B*'s suffering a loss as a consequence of *A*'s action to be a necessary condition of exploitation.[41]

Notwithstanding this consideration of outcome, Goodin's paramount concern lies with process:

> the concept of 'exploitation' must necessarily refer to a *process*, rather than just to some end-state … It is not a matter of how things *end up* at all. It is instead a matter of how you got there. The essence of exploitation must be sought in some characteristic of the process, rather than in some characteristic of the end results.[42]

We suggest that an interpretation of Goodin's account as predominantly process-based is supported by exploring the tensions that would follow if we see outcome as central to his account. For if it is a necessary condition that *B* must receive a benefit from the interaction with *A*, this would presumably exclude instances where *A* takes unfair advantage of *B* but *B* has no knowledge of this and is thus unable to avail himself of any opportunity to receive a benefit, or where *A*'s treatment of *B* does not offer any beneficial opportunity for *B*.[43] But if the principal focal point is 'taking unfair advantage of' *B*, why should such instances fall outwith the conception of exploitation? There appears to be a

---

37 Ibid: 167 (emphasis in original), 173–174. See also Archard 1994: 96: 'the core understanding of exploitation [is] one side taking unfair advantage of another'.
38 Goodin 1987: 173.
39 Ibid: 173 (emphasis added).
40 Ibid: 172 (emphasis in original).
41 Ibid: 172.
42 Ibid: 181 (emphasis in original) and see 195, n24.
43 For an example of the latter, see our *Dr X* and *Mr Y* scenario, discussed later in section 3.iii.

tension here between the process and outcome(s) of the interaction; can the process take precedence over the outcome notwithstanding the emphasis that Goodin places on the need for a beneficial outcome or outcomes? His reference to the essence of exploitation as 'taking unfair advantage' of B suggests that it should, and the consequence of this is that B gaining in some way from the interaction would not be a *necessary* element of exploitation, albeit that we might wish to see this as a *commonly occurring* element.[44]

For Goodin, the characteristic of the interaction's process which reveals the essence of exploitation resides in the 'wrongful uses of people and their circumstances'.[45] Having framed this as A taking unfair advantage of B, he later explains that this occurs when A takes advantage of someone who is vulnerable to her. For, in so doing, she breaches a moral duty to protect the vulnerable:

> Occasions for exploitation arise when one party is in an especially strong position vis-à-vis another. Those same circumstances impose upon the stronger party a heavy moral responsibility to protect the weaker ... the analysis of exploitation [is] parasitic upon an analysis of this duty to protect the vulnerable.[46]

Goodin provides a catalogue of situations in which A would interact with a vulnerable person, including, for instance, where B is outmatched in his interaction with A because of 'vastly disproportionate bargaining power', or because B is the victim of a grave misfortune.[47] He chooses not to provide a specific list of vulnerabilities.[48] This can be contrasted with the approach taken by Hill, who specifies a particular type of vulnerability in his concept of exploitation: 'For an offer to be exploitative, it must serve to create or to take advantage of some recognized psychological vulnerability which, in turn, disturbs the offeree's ability to reason effectively.'[49] As we see it, this specified type of vulnerability is too restrictive, as is the contextual setting which requires that an offer is made. It would exclude numerous instances of exploitation such as those involving exploitative requests as opposed to offers and those where the exploited person is not offered any opportunity to give consent to the exploitation.[50]

---

44 We suggest that this could be the case if we were to adopt a broad interpretation of 'some benefit'. For instance, a sex worker may receive some (financial) benefit from her employment whilst at the same time being exploited by her employer who chooses to keep for himself a large proportion of the money that her clients pay.
45 Goodin 1987: 182.
46 Ibid: 167.
47 Ibid: 185–186.
48 See the John and Sandra and *Dr X* and *Mr Y* scenarios discussed in section 3.i.b, 3.iii and 3.iv.
49 Hill 1994: 637.
50 See chapter 4 for our detailed exploration of vulnerability.

Goodin's broader approach towards ascribing vulnerability does seem apposite in cases where exploitation occurs in the context of relationships of trust involving 'vastly disproportionate power' and A's abuse of her more powerful position over B. But surely there will be other cases where Goodin's requirement of a duty to protect the vulnerable is not as obviously met, in which it is still possible for exploitation to occur.[51] In response to this potential objection, we might note that Goodin perceives this moral duty to be incumbent on everyone; we must all protect the interests of anyone else whose interests are 'strongly affected by … our own actions and choices, regardless of the particular source of their vulnerability'.[52] Presented in this way, however, it is an extremely broad, unwieldy duty that Goodin would hold us all to, especially since he expands it to require us to prevent '*anyone* (ourselves or others)'[53] from taking unfair advantage of the person whose interests are strongly affected by our own actions. From where would such a far-reaching duty derive?

We do not, therefore, support such a framing of the concept of exploitation around a duty to protect the vulnerable. Yet whilst we object to the imposition of such a duty, Goodin's focus on vulnerability does raise significant questions regarding the role that the relationship between A and B plays in exploitation and, more specifically for our ends, what it means to be vulnerable in the context of the doctor-patient relationship. Are all patients vulnerable because of their status (in terms of their (ill-)health and less powerful position), or is it paternalistic to perceive them in this way? We will explore these matters further in subsequent chapters.[54]

v) Sample on exploitation

> Exploitation involves interacting with another being for the sake of advantage in a way that degrades or fails to respect the inherent value in that being.[55]

Sample's presentation of 'exploitation as degradation' is sympathetic to violations of Kantian norms on how to treat others in a way that respects them as persons.[56] Her account is undoubtedly process-based, centring on the way in which A interacts with B. It is an approach that allows for a finding that exploitation has occurred regardless of the outcome of the interaction for A or B in a way that Feinberg's and Wertheimer's do not. She is sympathetic to Goodin's concern

---

51 Such as Feinberg's lonely hero scenario: Feinberg 1988: 218. And see the text accompanying n.142 in section 3.iii. See also Logar 2010: 339.
52 Goodin 1987: 187. See also 196, n.33.
53 Ibid: 187 (emphasis in original). See also Sample's critique: Sample 2003: 49.
54 See chapters 4 (in particular) to 7.
55 Sample 2003: 57.
56 Ibid: 56–62.

regarding the wrongful use of others and also draws a connection to his focus on vulnerability.[57] In her view:

> exploitation as Degradation is connected to vulnerability because vulnerability is typically (if not always) at the root of exploitation. When we exploit others, we make use of their genuine need for the sake of advantage in ways that fail to respect them.[58]

In its reference to a person's 'genuine need', this extract from her account also evidences a significant point of divergence from Goodin's conception of exploitation; rather than linking vulnerability to interactions in which B's interests are strongly affected by A's behaviour in the way that Goodin does, Sample hones in on certain, fundamental needs: 'when what brings a person to interact with us in the first place is a need to meet his basic needs, then that person is vulnerable to us'.[59] She goes on to explain that 'needs include not only those objects necessary for physical survival, but also conditions of purposeful employment, the prerequisites of psychological well-being, and constraints on interaction that are necessary for self-respect'.[60]

It is, therefore, the taking advantage of an individual's *basic needs* which lies at the heart of Sample's conception of exploitation. Drawing on Nussbaum's work on capabilities,[61] Sample sees a basic need as being something 'that is a prerequisite of or constitutive of human flourishing'.[62] This concentration on basic needs is an integral part of the uniqueness of her approach, but it means that her understanding of the kind of interactions in which exploitation can occur is more restrictive than, say Feinberg's, given that Feinberg offers a broader construction of what characteristics can make us vulnerable to exploitation. For, as Logar observes:

> Sample is adamant that taking advantage of basic needs is a *necessary* condition of exploitation; therefore, if we take advantage of someone's mere desire, that is, of their wish for something that is not objectively essential to their flourishing, we cannot be said to be exploiting them, no matter how degrading our manner of taking advantage is.[63]

Logar proffers the example of a rich man who exploits a relatively poor woman's desire for a graduate school education by offering to pay for this provided she becomes his mistress.[64] The woman's desire to undertake a graduate programme

---

57 Ibid: 70.
58 Ibid: 75.
59 Ibid: 70.
60 Ibid: 74.
61 Ibid: 76–84.
62 Ibid: 84.
63 Logar 2010: 340 (emphasis in original).
64 Ibid: 342.

is hardly a basic need and yet we would surely still conceive of this as exploitative. Moreover, 'examples that involve exploiting another person's generosity, sense of moral duty, or even one's greediness, all seem to invalidate the assertion that we can only exploit others' basic needs, since the exploitees' basic needs can be easily assumed to be adequately satisfied in such examples'.[65] Logar's critique thereby neatly demonstrates that requiring that *A* takes advantage of *B*'s basic needs is too specific. Whilst we agree with Logar on this, Sample's account is important in its encapsulation of the essence of exploitation as *A*'s failure to treat *B* as a person in pursuit of *A*'s ends.

vi) *Jansen and Wall on exploitation*

> An interaction between two parties is exploitative if one party, A, interacts with the other, B, under unfavorable framing conditions, in order to advance A's ends *and* it is true that B, under favorable framing conditions, would not rationally consent to the interaction with A (or consent to the interaction with A on the same terms).[66]

It is clear from this extract that Jansen and Wall's account is process-based, centring on the conditions under which the parties interact. Before analysing their conception further, explanation is needed as to what they mean by framing conditions. They describe such conditions as those which 'affect the quality or nature of the interaction that takes place'.[67] In Jansen's and Wall's account, an unfavourable framing condition would be the presence of a weakness or vulnerability possessed by *B* and favourable framing conditions would be present if this was absent.[68] This element of unfavourable framing conditions requires an objective assessment related to the unfairness of *A*'s treatment of *B*: 'when one person exploits another, she [treats] the other unfairly'.[69]

In addition, there is a subjective aspect to the assessment of whether exploitation occurs since, notably, Jansen and Wall's conception of exploitation requires consideration of both *A*'s and *B*'s states of mind. *A* must be aware of and take advantage of whatever vulnerability *B* possesses and be motivated to advance her ends, and *B* provides a consent that is not rational because *A* is playing upon whatever vulnerability he possesses. The attention that this conception requires to be paid to *B*'s state of mind and the matter of consent is noteworthy and, we argue, problematic for the following reasons. First, giving priority to consent can give the impression that consent is the crux of the issue when it comes to exploitation. But, as we will discuss later, it is possible to have consensual exploitation and

---

65 Ibid: 340.
66 Jansen and Wall 2013: 390 (emphasis in original).
67 Ibid: 389.
68 Ibid.
69 Ibid: 387.

exploitation where 'the issue of consent does not seem to arise at all'[70] (when, for example, B remains unaware that A has exploited him). Where there is an absence of consent, or invalid or compromised consent, then whilst this is likely to be part of the wrong, it is not a necessary element of exploitation that must always be present. In other words, the question of whether B has given real consent to the interaction with A *might* be relevant depending on the particular interaction, but consent can otherwise be a distraction, drawing attention away from other matters which could (and should) be essential elements of what we conceive exploitation to be.

Secondly, rather than concentrating on what the exploiter does, Jansen and Wall's approach turns our attention to what the exploited person would or would not have done under favourable framing conditions. This can surely only be speculative. Whilst one response to this might be that their inclusion of the element of rationality enables an objective assessment of whether B would have consented under such conditions, the introduction of this element raises further difficulties because of the ambiguity surrounding rationality.[71] For instance, according to Jansen and Wall, 'a person rationally consents when she is aware of sufficient relevant information and is not impaired by various incapacities and distorting influences'.[72] But conceptions of what constitutes a distorting influence or an incapacity can differ from person to person.[73] Moreover, focusing on B's state of mind could also encourage the perception that B has acted irrationally in consenting to the exploitative interaction with A, rather than assessing A's behaviour, with the potential result of blame-shifting. For these reasons, we suggest that Jansen and Wall's process-based conception is focused on an element which is not at the core of the matter. Whilst B's state of mind can sometimes be relevant, it should not be a defining element of exploitation.

vii) *Commonalities in existing conceptions*

We have shown how some authors incorporate both process- and outcome-based approaches within their accounts of exploitation, and that there can be connections between approaches that are predominantly or exclusively based on process or outcome. For example, unfairness is the chosen measure of the wrong of exploitation for both Goodin and Wertheimer and it also appears in Jansen and Wall's account. Feinberg presents unfairness as the measure of the wrong in some cases, but not all, and considers whether the more generally applicable measure is injustice, with

---

70 Wertheimer 1996: 25.
71 We are critical of Hill's concentration on rationality for the same reason and note that, despite his focus, he recognises that 'there are a number of philosophical problems with the concept of rationality': Hill 1994: 674 and 699.
72 Jansen and Wall 2013: 389.
73 This is implicitly acknowledged later in the paper, where the authors discuss a case involving someone who has 'unusual' views which would lead to him not consenting under favourable framing conditions. See ibid: 408, n.20. See also Hill 1994: 688.

unfairness being one form of this.[74] In contrast, an application of the standard of unfairness is absent from Sample's account, with her prioritisation instead of A's treatment as degradation and a failure to respect B as a person. We will consider whether unfairness best encapsulates the wrong of exploitation in our account below.

The common element of taking advantage of a weakness or vulnerability possessed by B is perhaps most evident in Goodin's account, with his focus on A taking advantage of someone who is vulnerable to her. Sample too centres on taking advantage of vulnerable individuals, specifically those who share the characteristic of being dependent on their exploiters for their basic needs. As we saw, Feinberg adopts what appears to be a broader conception of the traits possessed by B that can be taken advantage of, referring to strengths and virtues alongside vulnerabilities and weaknesses. This is surely correct because one's strengths and virtues can become vulnerabilities in the context of an interaction with a person looking to exploit, as we discuss later.[75] Moreover, both Feinberg and Wertheimer recognise the potential vulnerabilities to exploitation that B's characteristics *and* situation may present, as do Jansen and Wall in their reference to 'personal' and 'extrapersonal' circumstances when explaining what an unfavourable framing condition could be.[76] We will explore whether this common element most appropriately conveys what A is doing to B in the pejorative sense, or whether A's taking advantage of B's weakness or vulnerability is actually a *category* of behaviour within a broader taxonomy of treating B in a way that makes us conceive of his exploitation as wrongful.[77]

A further common element is apparent in the extract provided at the start of the previous subsection, in which Jansen and Wall expressly state that exploitation occurs for the advancement of A's ends. Sample's account is also premised on exploitation involving 'using another person ... to advance one's ends'.[78] She does recognise that unintentional exploitation can occur in cases where exploiters are mistaken in their beliefs as to what constitutes the respectful treatment of others. However, she is clear (and succinct) in her view 'that a person cannot be accused legitimately of exploitation if she is not trying to gain from an interaction'.[79]

Feinberg is hazier on this matter. He makes it clear that A must gain on his account, but it is not apparent from this in itself that A's *intention* has to be to gain. However, he does say later that we should understand gain both 'in the strict sense and [as the] fulfilment of one's aims, purposes or desires'.[80] The implication here is that he construes A's purpose as being to gain. Thus, there is no explicit emphasis placed on A's intention in Feinberg's account; instead, he appears to take it as a given that A acts with the intention of bringing about the advantageous outcome

74 Feinberg 1988: 199–200.
75 See n.111.
76 Jansen and Wall 2013: 389.
77 See section 3.i.b.
78 Sample 2003: 15.
79 Ibid: 58.
80 Feinberg 1988: 193.

for himself. That said, Feinberg adopts the position that unplanned, unpremeditated exploitation can occur, where A's exploitation tends to be passive rather than brought about through circumstances he has actively sought to bring about.[81]

As with Feinberg, Goodin's consideration of A's intention lies at the periphery of his account. He does make implicit reference to this when he states that 'an act of exploitation ordinarily redounds to the benefit (advantage) of the person who performs it. Otherwise, such acts would not be performed at all.'[82] He also provides a more explicit acknowledgement of the purpose of advancing one's ends when he refers to exploiters' attempts to manipulate those they exploit 'in ways conducive to their larger goals' and playing for advantage and for their own gain.[83] However, this is not accompanied by any discussion or analysis of such purposes. Likewise, Wertheimer pays some attention to this issue, considering that an interaction with B is exploitative when 'A expects to gain something of value from [it].'[84] He goes on to say that 'we might say that the motivation of the exploiter is crucial, that A exploits B ... if A *expects* to gain from the [interaction] and if that expectation is an important motivating consideration'.[85] However, this is not followed by any analysis of this motivation. It is thus apparent that A's intention to achieve self-gain is a commonly occurring element of exploitation that exacerbates its wrongfulness, but this element is present implicitly rather than explicitly in some authors' accounts. There is also the question of what the advancement of A's ends encompasses and what we mean by gain.

There are, therefore, some clearly discernible commonalities within the various accounts of exploitation. However, the (often significant) differences in the approaches and the focus for each author are also clearly apparent. They face the same challenge: to provide a convincing philosophical and ethical explanation for the intuitive feeling that exploitation is wrong so that 'exploitation claims ... are not merely a rhetorical placeholder for expressing disapproval'.[86] As Hill has noted:

> exploitation has long been a greatly overused and misused concept, serving to fill the vague intellectual gap between the pre-analytic intuition that there is something wrong with this [interaction] and the post-analytic determination as to what this something wrong is, exactly.[87]

It is no surprise, then, that the fundamental differences in the accounts of exploitation discussed here reside in the authors' explanation of what it is that makes exploitation wrongful.

---

81 He refers to such cases as 'passive unjust enrichment': Feinberg 1988: 198–199 and 209–210.
82 Goodin 1987: 168.
83 Ibid: 168 and 185.
84 Wertheimer 1996: 167.
85 Ibid: 168 (emphasis in original).
86 Ibid: 5.
87 Hill 1994: 699.

3) Our account of exploitation

Building on some of the common elements of the explanations discussed above and our critique of these explanations, we now explicate what we understand exploitation to be; presenting, unpacking and rationalising our account of exploitation. In this book we are only concerned with exploitation that is wrongful and this is reflected in our account here. In adopting this approach, we note Wood's observation that those who draw a distinction between moralised and non-moralised understandings of exploitation tend, by and large, to focus upon what it is that makes exploitation wrongful and thus 'provide ... a "moralized" account of exploitation. That is, they suppose that the term "exploitation" (in the "pejorative" sense) already has wrongfulness or moral badness built into its very meaning.'[88] As our discussion in the first section should make clear, we do not make the assumption that exploitation is always wrongful, and, indeed, one significant element which we identify below is not built into instances of exploitation that we react to in a morally neutral way. But, for reasons of brevity, unless stated otherwise, when we refer to exploitation hereafter in this book we mean exploitation that is wrongful in the way that we will proceed to explain.

i) The essential elements of exploitation

We see exploitation as *the taking advantage of and misuse of another person for one's own ends*. It can be observed from this that our approach is process-centred. The essential factors which cause an interaction to be exploitative relate to the way in which the exploiter *treats* the other individual and the objective behind her behaviour. We do not consider it necessary to evaluate the outcome of the interaction and measure any benefit received by the exploiter in order to describe their interaction with another as exploitative. Provided that *A* has taken advantage of and misused *B* with a view to achieving *A*'s ends, then *A* has exploited *B*. It is true that if *A* gains an excessive benefit then this may exacerbate our moral reaction to his behaviour, but this is not an essential element which makes his behaviour exploitative. Similarly, the absence of any benefit for *A* does not mean that his behaviour was not exploitative,[89] albeit that it may well mean that the act of exploitation was unsuccessful for *A* because the intended outcome did not materialise.[90] Rather than the actual outcome, what is central to the occurrence of exploitation is *A*'s treatment of *B* and *A*'s purpose of acting to achieve his own ends. And whether or not *B* receives a benefit or loss is equally irrelevant, in our view. As Wood notes, the fact that the exploited party often stands to gain in some way from the outcome of their exploitation explains why exploitation frequently

---

88 Wood 1995: 137.
89 See also Jansen and Wall 2013: 395; Collins 2015: 142. Cf. Valdman 2009: 2
90 See also Goodin 1987: 172.

can be voluntary and consensual.[91] But the existence of any benefit for *B* does not mean that no exploitation has occurred. This is evident if we consider a scenario where, for instance, *A* is aware that *B* is facing serious financial hardship and thus makes her an offer of £1,000 for one of her kidneys, knowing that she will find this offer very hard to resist. The outcome of receiving the money may benefit *B* but, regardless of this, she is still exploited because she has been misused by *A*, as should become clear through our subsequent analysis in this subsection.

Conversely, *B* can be exploited albeit that she may not suffer any loss.[92] Moreover, not only is the existence of a beneficial outcome to *A* and/or loss to *B* a non-essential element of exploitation, an unfair distributive outcome can occur in situations which involve no exploitation, as Jansen and Wall persuasively explain:

> bad luck and coordination difficulties can explain how unfair distributive outcomes come about in a variety of settings. They might explain, for example, an unfair distributive outcome that results from participation in international biomedical research. Some parties might benefit unfairly from the participation of other parties in the research; but the unfairness might have nothing to do with exploitation or a desire on the part of anyone to take unfair advantage of anyone else.[93]

We note also that outcome-based approaches would seem to be more common in the context of economic exploitation involving transactions and the unfair distribution of goods. Thus, they do not offer as neat a fit with the context in which the exploitation that we explore in this book occurs: the relationship between a doctor and patient.[94]

In order to convey the factors that make behaviour exploitative in our view, it is necessary to unpick and tease out three elements from the above conception: taking advantage of; misuse; and for one's own ends.

a) *Taking advantage of*

We have already noted that taking advantage of *B* in the sense of using *B* is the essential element of exploitation: *A* utilises something that is inherently connected to *B*. This is what we hereafter allude to as *taking advantage of*

---

91 Wood 1995: 148. See also Sample 2003: 10–11 and 57. We discuss consensual exploitation in section 3.ii.
92 See Goodin 1987: 173 and our later scenario involving *Dr X* and *Mr Y*, discussed in section 3.iii.
93 Jansen and Wall 2013: 384.
94 See also the allusion to 'a transaction' and 'unfair distribution outcomes' with reference to outcome-based accounts in Jansen and Wall 2013: 384 and their statement that 'exploitation refers, in the main, to transaction-specific interactions' at 385. We note, however, that we do consider the doctor-patient relationship in the context of private health care in chapter 3, section 5.ii, where there may be a greater degree of similarity with economic interactions involving transactions.

(using) – that is, the concept of taking advantage of in its primary utilisation sense. It may be *B* himself who is used, or something about *B*, such as his labour or his standing in the community, for instance. As Wood has observed, in some cases, this distinction may not be clear-cut.[95] It might be *B*'s artistic skills that are exploited by *A*, for example. However, *B* may feel sufficiently demeaned by the use of his skills (say *A* demands that he paint a picture which violates his sense of artistic integrity), or feel that these skills are so personally connected to himself, that he considers it to be he himself who has been exploited.[96] For the purposes of explaining our conception of exploitation, either or both of these applications of taking advantage of (using) could apply.

b) Misuse

It is misuse which separates exploitation that is wrongful from exploitation which we feel morally neutral towards. Our position is that exploitation is wrongful when *A*'s taking advantage of (using) *B* involves *misusing B* by treating him in a way which fails to respect him as a person and does not 'take seriously the requirements of living a *human* life'.[97] We conceive of misuse as a taxonomy of behaviour which occurs when *A* treats *B* in such a manner and infringes his right to demand respect equal to that paid to other human beings. In short, *A* fails to recognise the value of *B*'s life and the essence of his individuality. Albeit acknowledging that we may not all agree on what respect for persons entails precisely, we concur with Sample that 'we have a general idea of what respect demands of us'.[98] Thus, a failure to respect *B* as a person might involve a failure to respect his dignity or treating him in a demeaning way. As we see it, therefore, exploitation is linked to Kantian ideas regarding the treatment of others and the ethical responsibility to treat individuals as ends in themselves.[99] This can be differentiated from a situation where *A* takes advantage of (uses) *B*, but there is no such wrongful treatment. Consider, for instance, that a pupil uses a driving instructor's knowledge of the road and driving skills in order to learn how to drive a car, with the end which he is seeking to achieve being to pass his driving test. Whilst this would meet the morally neutral OED definition of exploitation discussed in the first section,

---

95 Wood 1995: 146.
96 We acknowledge that whether something about *B* is integral to his sense of self will be culturally variant. See Benn 1984: 232.
97 Sample 2003: 69 (emphasis added). And see Schwartz: 1995: 177: 'to exploit others ... is to take from them their humanity'.
98 Sample 2003: 73.
99 Kant 1999: 37. 'Exploiting people is using them for one's own purposes, without regard for their own purposes, and in a way that prevents them from setting and acting on their own purposes': Schwartz 1995: 176–177. See also Buchanan 1985: 87; Sample 2003: 70; Collins 2015: 128. See text accompanying n.114 for an explanation of how we adopt a broadly Kantian approach when it comes to misuse, rather than a strict understanding of his second categorical imperative.

provided that the pupil respects his instructor as a person in his interactions with her, taking account of her purposes and the value of her life, there is no misuse.[100]

We can also see the difference between use and misuse by way of a 'free-rider' or 'harmless parasitism'[101] scenario such as the following: during a work meeting in a very hot room, John sits behind Sandra who is fanning herself and he receives the benefit of the breeze she makes, whilst not affecting her receipt of this same breeze. Whilst John is taking advantage of (using) something inherently connected to Sandra – the breeze that she has created through her labour – it is unlikely that we would perceive this as exploitation which is wrongful. John is not failing to recognise the value of Sandra's life or infringing her right to equal respect. No misuse occurs and thus there is no wrongful act. Whilst John has utilised Sandra's labour, she possesses no weakness or vulnerability that he has taken advantage of here, for instance; the opportunity to benefit from the breeze is enabled simply by virtue of him sitting behind Sandra and she is not being deprived of anything. Our perception of the situation changes, however, if we amend the scenario in the following way. John is Sandra's boss. He is aware that Sandra is seeking a promotion and that she does not wish to do anything that would make him less likely to support her promotion. He passes her a note asking her to continue fanning herself in a way that ensures that the breeze she creates reaches him. Sandra obliges, even though she was going to stop fanning herself. Here John's treatment of Sandra is indicative of misuse. He has taken advantage of her, acting in the knowledge that she is unlikely to refuse his request for fear of making his response to her promotion application less favourable. In making this request, he has failed to respect Sandra as a person by misusing her to achieve his own purposes, and it may well be that Sandra feels demeaned by his use of her labour.

Further consideration is required of how A could treat B in a way which fails to respect B as a person. One common way in which misuse occurs is when A does not treat B as being equal to herself because she takes advantage of a vulnerability, weakness or other characteristic he possesses which thereby enables her to misuse him. This is exemplified in both the revised John and Sandra scenario above and the scenario discussed earlier involving A's taking advantage of a vulnerability possessed by B – her serious financial circumstances – in order to gain her consent to the purchase of her kidney for a low sum. As expressed by Wood:

> proper respect for others is violated when we treat their vulnerabilities as opportunities to advance our own interests ... It is degrading to have your weaknesses taken advantage of, and dishonorable to use the weaknesses of others for your ends.[102]

---

100 See also Wilkinson 2003: 38; Mappes 1985: 204. As we go on to explain, however, much depends on context. See the discussion in the paragraph of text accompanying n.150.
101 As coined by Feinberg 1988: 14.
102 Wood 1995: 150–151.

This is what we refer to as taking advantage of in its secondary sense, when the exploiter *takes advantage of the exploited person's vulnerability*[103] and it is a characteristic of exploitation which is almost always present.[104] Indeed, Wood conceives of this as the factor which *enables* exploitation to occur.[105] The vulnerability may be internal (*B*'s personal characteristic or trait) or external (the circumstances that *B* finds herself in). Whatever the origin of the vulnerability, its essential characteristic is that it makes *B* more susceptible to *A*'s exploitation and *A* knowingly takes advantage of this. Unconsciousness is an obvious example of a vulnerability that patients undergoing medical procedures will often possess, and an example of this vulnerability being taking advantage of occurred when a surgeon branded his initials on the organs of patients whom he was operating on during transplantation surgery.[106] Such an act is a blatant example of misuse, of treating these patients as objects rather than persons.

Simply because one individual has taken advantage of a vulnerability possessed by another for their own ends, this does not mean that misuse has definitely occurred, however. For, in ascertaining whether *mis*use as opposed to use occurs, much is dependent upon the normative context.[107] If we return to Wood's chess scenario, the successor takes advantage of a temporary vulnerability possessed by her opponent (his lapse in concentration) and uses this lapse for her own ends, to win. But there is no misuse because of the context in which this exploitation occurs. The interaction between the parties is one where they

---

103 The way in which we have explained the two senses of 'taking advantage of' shares similarities with Wood's division of exploitation into benefit-exploitation ('we exploit some attribute of the person from which we derive... use to achieve our end'), and advantage-exploitation ('we exploit someone's weakness or vulnerability, which gives us hold or advantage over the person'), which he sees as 'a complementary pair'. Wood 1995: 142. Despite this similarity, we choose not to adopt Wood's explanation because we seek to make the essence of *A*'s wrongful behaviour explicit in our conceptualisation of exploitation.

104 See also Wolff 1999: 111. Note also Mayer's view that exploitation 'is an abuse of vulnerability': Mayer 2007: 143.

105 Wood 1995: 142–143. He also appears to imply that, absent 'advantage-exploitation' (see n.103), the scenario is one of 'simple use' rather than exploitation (at 142). However, he then seemingly contradicts this by his subsequent statement that 'exploitation *usually* involves some element of vulnerability on the part of what is exploited, and also some use of the attribute benefitting some project of the exploiter' (at 145, emphasis added). This suggests that there can be instances of exploitation without taking advantage of a vulnerability and we agree. Neither of our cases involving the harpist or John/Sandra (the original version) involve a vulnerability being taken advantage of, but we argue that they are still situations involving exploitation. It is notable that these two cases are examples of innocent exploitation, exploitation that we feel morally neutral towards, thus supporting the point made above that taking advantage of a vulnerability is almost always present in instances of wrongful exploitation.

106 See chapter 3, n.232; Ost 2019; Ost 2020.

107 See also Wilkinson 2003: 42 and 43. On the importance of normative context, albeit outside the setting of exploitation, see Uniacke's analysis of the ethics of retaliation. Uniacke 2004: 177–181. And see Ganuli Mitra and Biller-Andorono 2013.

are on an equal playing field,[108] both have an expectation that each will take any legitimate opportunity to win. There is no evidence to suggest that the victor is failing to respect the other player as a person or demeaning him. Thus, misuse relates to the way in which *A* has treated *B* in the context of the interaction between them. This bears relevance to the focus of this book, the doctor-patient relationship; a patient's ill-health is an obvious potential vulnerability that could be taken advantage of by a doctor who might be acting for unscrupulous reasons, or out of paternalism, to achieve her own ends.

On the matter of taking advantage of a vulnerability, 'weakness' and 'vulnerability' are typically used in the existing literature to refer to a characteristic that makes *B* susceptible to *A*'s exploitative behaviour.[109] If we take Wolff's explanation of being vulnerable to exploitation, we can see how these terms could be interchangeable: 'you are vulnerable if (other things being equal) you are poorer, more ignorant, less intelligent, less cunning, or less ruthless than another, or have some other bargaining weakness with respect to them'.[110] Each example that Wolff refers to here might be perceived as a weakness which makes *B* more vulnerable to being exploited.[111] In our account of exploitation, we have chosen to refer to taking advantage of a vulnerability possessed by *B* because of the significant (albeit not essential) connection between exploitation and vulnerability that we explore further in chapter 4. However, we steer away from Goodin's contention that exploitation involves breaching a moral duty to protect the vulnerable. This is an argument that we critiqued earlier because of the unwieldly nature of such a duty.[112] What is more, we would not wish to specify that only certain vulnerabilities possessed by *B* can be taken advantage of by *A* in order to avoid being too restrictive in the way that, for instance, Sample's account of exploitation is.[113]

Whilst, above, we draw a connection with Kantian approaches and our understanding of misuse, it is important to note that we are not saying that misuse *only*

---

108 Wood certainly states nothing to suggest otherwise. Wood 1995: 138 and 152. On the matter of context, see also Goodin 1987: 183.
109 We note that a growing body of literature on vulnerability theory challenges the negative association of vulnerability with weakness. See Fineman 2008; Fineman 2019: 342; chapter 4, section 1.
110 Wolff 1999: 111.
111 Notwithstanding what we have suggested here regarding the interchangeability of the two terms in the literature, we argue that it may be more apt to refer to the characteristic possessed by *B* which *A* exploits as something that makes *B* vulnerable to *A*'s exploitation, rather than a weakness. This is especially so where the characteristic in question is generally considered to be a strength or virtue rather than a weakness, such as loyalty. However, in the context of the interaction with *A*, such characteristics might become weaknesses if *A* can utilise them to her advantage: see our sister and brother scenario in the text accompanying n.135. See also Sample 2003: 90. We are also sympathetic to criticism of the association between vulnerability and weakness in the vulnerability literature: see n.109.
112 See section 2.iv.
113 See section 2.v.

occurs where A treats B *solely* as a means to an end.[114] We can envisage situations in which misuse occurs where *A* does, in some respect, treat *B* as an end as well as a means. Take a surgeon who carries out a risky, invasive procedure on the basis that it might be good for his career prospects if the slim chance that it will cure the patient's rare medical condition materialises. He does want to cure her and knows she desires to be cured. He also knows that the patient will only agree to having the procedure if he presents it as the best treatment option, which he duly does. He is not treating the patient *merely* as a means to an end because there is a chance that the procedure will work, thereby achieving the patient's own purposes and desires. However, this does not alter the fact that he is misusing her by exposing her to a relatively high risk of physical harm for his own ends.

It is because we see exploitation as closely connected to misuse and Kantian ideas regarding the treatment of others that we have chosen not to use *unfairness* as the measure of the wrong of exploitation.[115] To explicate the nuances between misuse and unfairness as measures of the wrong, we can consider the following scenario presented by Jansen and Wall:

> Joan, who is poor and out of work, is presented with the option of participating in a two-month experimental trial designed to test the safety and efficacy of a new drug, one known to have potentially serious side effects. Participation in the trial will not benefit Joan medically, and it will subject her to significant risks of discomfort and serious harm. The trial has the potential to advance scientific understanding that could benefit future people, but Joan is not motivated to participate out of altruistic concern. Those conducting the trial persuade her to participate by offering to pay her $100.[116]

Jansen and Wall proceed to say: 'those conducting the trial take *unfair* advantage of Joan's poor economic circumstances to get her to agree to participate at the very low rate of compensation they are offering … She is in no position to press for a higher level of compensation'.[117] They clearly view the wrong in question as relating to unfairness, which they connect to the way in which the researchers take advantage of Joan.

In our view this encapsulates some of the wrong, but not all of it, and not the crux of it. Assuming that other participants are offered the same amount or more than Joan, the researchers are offering a greater enticement for Joan to

---

114 That is, there does not have to be a violation of Kant's second categorical imperative in order for misuse to occur. However, in section 3.iii, the consequence of our utilisation of this imperative to frame a moral right that can be violated by exploitation is that this particular moral right can *only* be infringed when A treats B *merely* as a means to an end.
115 See also Sample 2003: 7.
116 Jansen and Wall 2013: 382.
117 Ibid: 382 (emphasis added). Cf. Wertheimer 2007: 250, who considers that where 'B's background conditions are unjust, it does not automatically follow that A's proposal is unfair to B [if] A bears no responsibility for B's unjust background condition'.

32 *What is exploitation?*

participate by taking advantage of her vulnerability due to her financial situation. They realise that it will be difficult for Joan to say no because of her circumstances and that it will be much harder for her to say no than other participants who are not facing this financial hardship. They are infringing Joan's right to demand respect equal to that paid to other human beings in making an offer which they know she will find hard to resist. Yes, this is unfair. But it is also demeaning and reflects a failure to respect Joan as a person in a way that takes into account her difficult circumstances.[118] The wrong to Joan is thus more fully encapsulated by *misuse* rather than unfairness.

c) For one's own ends

A crucial part of the reason why we understand behaviour to be exploitative is because the exploiter is acting to fulfil her ends and, usually (but not always), this means that she behaves as she does for her own benefit.[119] Whilst this motivation is significant, 'own ends' can and should be broadly understood and it should not be assumed that these ends will always (or only) be selfish: 'it is true that those who [misuse] others for their own ends typically do so for selfish ends, but there is nothing requiring that the ends be selfish'.[120] This is starkly conveyed by Jonathan Swift's satire of society's indifference to the poor and England's oppression of Ireland, in which he proposes that the children of the poor be exploited in the most horrific manner for the 'publick good' of the country.[121] We might also conceive of a situation where the exploiter has mixed motives, such as where the exploiter's ends include the achievement of a higher good, as could occur where *A* extracts tissue from *B* without *B*'s knowledge or consent in order to establish a cell line because she is searching for a cure for a particular medical condition for the good of humankind. But, alongside this altruistic motivation, the exploiter is also acting to achieve her own ends; whilst finding a cure and thereby benefitting humankind is the exploiter's goal, her desired end, she will also gain from the achievement of it, whether through achieving altruism or desired fame, wealth, etc. She thus has a self-interest in achieving it. Similarly, it may be that the exploiter acts with the aim of benefitting another person (her own son who suffers from the particular condition, for example). Again, however, she is also acting in order to

---

118 We might ask whether the alternative of excluding Joan from the trial because of her financial status is not ethically problematic in itself. Although not our focus here, we note that some instances of exploitation *may* be defensible. See further chapter 3, n.30.
119 See Wilkinson 2003: 21.
120 Wood 1995: 153, n.29. We have substituted the word 'misuse' in this quotation for Wood's own wording 'use the weakness of'. The difference here lies in the fact that Wood sees the wrong of exploitation more narrowly – as taking advantage of a weakness – whereas, for reasons discussed above, we see taking advantage of a vulnerability as an example of the broader wrong of misuse, depending on the context of the interaction. See also Feinberg 1988: 193.
121 Swift 1729.

fulfil her own ends of benefiting her son and will gain from this even if the gain is purely psychological, such as knowing that she has helped her son.

It might even be the case that the exploiter's ends are to benefit the person she is exploiting. Returning to the *Blood* case that we referred to in the previous chapter (regarding which we raised the question of whether Mrs Blood acted exploitatively), Diane Blood may have considered that extracting her husband's sperm would have benefited him in the sense that it is what he would have wanted – the possibility of having children. She might have been of this view notwithstanding that he was incapable of consenting to what occurred and would have remained unaware of the occurrence of the procedure in the brief time before he died. By way of a further example, it is also possible to conceive of a situation where A considers that the most effective means of benefitting B involves taking advantage of (using) B and misusing him. Consider a scenario in which B is a tissue match for his ill sibling, C, and no other suitable donor can be found. Doctor A takes advantage of B's bone marrow to save C by misusing B, extracting bone marrow against B's wishes in the face of B's strong objection (let's say that B fears that he will die if his bone marrow is removed). A acts as she does because she considers that saving C will benefit B. Because of B's fear, A does not see any other realistic means of fulfilling her ends of benefiting B. A's motivation may be benevolent (albeit misguided and paternalistic), but she still exploits B, acting to achieve her own ends.

In sum, then, our process-based account of exploitation centres on the way in which A treats B (the taking advantage of and misuse of B) and A's purpose in so doing (the achievement of their own ends). Having set out and explained what we see as the fundamental elements of exploitation, we turn to consider next the matter of whether B can be consensually (and wrongfully) exploited.

ii) Can acquiescent exploitation be wrongful?

The first point that we note here is that, in cases where the exploitation occurs *without* any consent on the part of the exploited individual, the exploiter's failure to obtain B's acquiescence seems to exacerbate the wrongful nature of the exploitation. On this issue, we should note our disagreement with Wilkinson that there can only be exploitation '*where there is (at least) "minimal consent" from the exploitee*'.[122] He adopts this position because it seems intuitively odd to label the main evil of wrongs that intrinsically involve a lack of consent – such as rape – as exploitation. In his view, it is not possible for a crucial element of exploitation – taking advantage of a weakness for gain – to occur when B's 'will, or conscious choice' is completely bypassed.[123] Yet, when women are forced into prostitution because of social circumstances (and thus it can be said that they are forced into sex, giving a minimal form of consent), there seems to be no

---

122 Wilkinson 2003: 74 (emphasis in original).
123 Ibid: 74.

similar awkwardness in applying the exploitation label.[124] This leads Wilkinson to argue, therefore, that some degree of consent from B is a necessary element involved in the categorisation of an act as exploitative.

A (partly) legal analysis helps to illustrate the difficulties that we have with this argument and the role that it assigns to consent in delineating exploitation. Whenever a doctor touches an unconscious patient, under the tort of battery, she commits a tort that involves the absence of consent (albeit that the doctor is provided with the defence of necessity in emergency cases). Thus, since the treatment of the unconscious patient is a wrong which revolves around no consent, seemingly, on Wilkinson's analysis, this wrong could not involve any exploitation. But there are any number of exploitative acts that a doctor could carry out where the patient is unconscious, taking advantage of this vulnerability for his own purposes, such as the example of the surgeon branding his initials on the organs of patients that we discussed above.[125] As a further example, consider the practice of medical students being encouraged to do intimate pelvic examinations on unconscious patients undergoing gynaecological surgery without their knowledge or consent, a practice which research has revealed to be 'alive and well' in teaching hospitals in the UK and US.[126]

For Wilkinson, the nub of issue seems to be that, for exploitation to occur, A must take advantage of B's vulnerability in order to obtain her 'minimal consent' to whatever A desires to occur. True, it might often be the case that A is able to exploit B by obtaining her minimal consent, but we see no reason why B's vulnerability cannot be taken advantage of *without* B's (minimal) consent or, indeed, awareness. As we have shown directly above, unconsciousness itself can be a vulnerability that can be taken advantage of for A's purposes. In short, the patient's lack of consent does not address the key question of whether exploitation occurs.[127] Whilst cases involving no consent and no awareness might be less common,[128] they can and do exist.

---

124 Ibid: 72–73.
125 See text accompanying n.106.
126 Friesen 2018. Remember that, on our account, the ends behind exploitation can be beneficial to others rather than selfish, such as educating medical students: the doctor who permits students to do this is still acting in order to fulfil her own ends of educating her students.
127 We are grateful to John Murphy for helping to shape our thinking on this. Our preferred explanation for the conundrum that Wilkinson presents is one that he himself finds unsatisfying (Wilkinson 2003: 73): moral occlusion clouds our intuitions (that is, rape does amount to exploitation, but we instinctively feel that this is a relatively 'lesser' evil of rape when compared to its violation of autonomy and the body). At the same time, we should also be sensitive to Buchhandler-Raphael's caution that 'conceptualising rape as non-consensual sex not only fails to provide an accurate account of the harms inflicted, but also to capture the wrongdoing embodied in rape ... rape [should] be defined as an act of abuse of power and as an exploitation of dominance and control': Buchhandler-Raphael 2011: 154.
128 See also Collins 2015: 213, n.64. On her analysis, the complexity of the consent issue is such that 'exploitation's relationship to consent may vary depending on the type of interpersonal exploitation in question (be it financial, sexual, bodily, labour exploitation) and ... there may be no sound reason to underplay the complexity of the relationship between consent and exploitation in doctrinal terms': Collins 2017: 185–186.

Alongside cases of exploitation involving no consent, there are cases in which B does consent but A behaves in a way which causes us to question the validity of B's consent because, for example, B has been coerced or presented with a seductive offer, or A fails to inform B of a significant matter.[129] Whilst some would conceive of cases involving such compromised consent as non-consensual exploitation,[130] we prefer to see these as cases where consent is given but we have reason to query the validity of B's consent. This is because, albeit on a superficial level, consent is present.[131]

A lack of consent or questionable consent on B's part is not a constant element of exploitation, however. We explained earlier that consent is a sometimes significant but not essential element of exploitation, and presenting it as essential can draw attention away from the possibility that consensual exploitation can be wrongful.[132] Indeed, it is possible that a person might be willing and even content to consent to their own exploitation in certain circumstances.[133] Despite risks to her health, Joan may still willingly give consent to her exploitation in Jansen and Wall's clinical trial scenario, for instance.[134] As another example, consider a woman who has made numerous attempts to have her novel published, without success. Her brother has also laboured for some time over a novel, which he has now completed, and which she knows is better than her own. She asks him if she can send it to the publisher, stating her name as the author. Her brother agrees because he is distressed to see her so downhearted and the book is accepted for publication. Here, although the brother is complicit in his own consensual exploitation, he has still been exploited. His sister has taken advantage of a vulnerability that her brother possesses (his love for her, his desire for her to do well) for her own ends.[135] She is misusing him, treating him disrespectfully by misappropriating his work and passing it off as her own, thereby failing to recognise his ownership of the work and his right to demand respect equal to that she pays to herself; she is using him solely as a means to her end. Although she is taking into account his desire for her to do well, this is not because she is

---

129 We have chosen not to include the matter of whether B's consent is rational here, having expressed our reservations about invoking the concept of rationality earlier in this chapter (section 2.vi).
130 Wertheimer 2007: 249.
131 See also Wilkinson 2003: 75.
132 On the way in which an act validly consented to can still be wrongful, see Gardner 2018: 60–61.
133 See also Wolff 1999: 113; Wertheimer 2003: 250.
134 We note the argument here that the researchers' offer of $100 could constitute a seductive offer to Joan because of her serious financial hardship. This might lead us to consider that her consent is questionable, albeit that this is contestable. We explore such matters further in the context of the doctor-patient relationship in chapter 4, sections 3 and 4 and chapter 5, part 1, sections 3.i and 3.ii.
135 'in personal relationships we can exploit others' generosity, gullibility, fear, affections, and so on, in order to get them to do things that promote out interests, aims, and goals': Logar 2010: 330. See also Formosa 2013: 105–106.

respecting his values and aims and thereby respecting him as a person. Rather, she is taking account of this desire in order to acquire his consent to accomplish what she seeks to achieve. It is therefore possible for acquiescent exploitation to be wrongful on our account and, consequently, we do not exclude cases where B consents.

iii) How exploitation can wrong the exploited person through violating their moral right(s)

The account of exploitation we have offered thus far in this section sets out the elements that make certain instances of exploitation wrongful and hence objectionable in a moral sense. However, exploitation is also morally objectionable because of its effects; it can frequently have a negative impact upon the exploited person by wronging and/or harming them, as we will now explain through utilising an aspect of Feinberg's analysis of wrongful behaviour and wronging.[136]

Feinberg draws a distinction between wrongful behaviour (which he regards exploitation as an example of), and a wrong to a person that constitutes moral harm (which exploitative behaviour can sometimes involve): 'exploitation is normally a way of using someone for one's own ends, which is somehow wrongful or blameworthy, whether it wrongs the other person or not'.[137] For Feinberg, an individual is wronged when the other person's conduct violates his right(s).[138] In terms of what amount to rights in this context, Feinberg states that it is a person's *moral rights* that are at issue.[139] A moral right 'is a claim backed by valid reasons and addressed to the conscience of the claimee or to public opinion' and 'welfare interests ... are the grounds for valid claims against others (moral rights) *par excellence*'.[140] Utilising Feinberg's analysis, it should therefore follow that if exploitation violates a moral right which is important for the individual's welfare, it wrongs that individual.

Whether or not the exploitee's moral right has been violated can depend upon the circumstances surrounding the situation in which the exploitative behaviour occurs.[141] To provide an illustration of a situation where no moral right is infringed, Feinberg presents a scenario that involves a talented author who makes vast profits from writing a book about a lonely hero's inspirational life. She does

---

136 Feinberg 1988; Feinberg 1984:105–125. We note that Feinberg's analysis is framed within his exploration of the moral limits of the criminal law, and this different context means that we do not adhere to all aspects of his account of harm. See further the text accompanying nn.198–201.
137 Feinberg 1988: 177. Cf. Goodin 1987: 173, who considers that 'an act of exploiting a person always constitutes a wrong'.
138 Feinberg 1984: 34. See also Holtug 2002: 379.
139 Feinberg, ibid: 111. Feinberg's explanation of wronging does not convince everyone. For instance, Stewart has pointed to ambiguities regarding the relationship between rights and wronging in Feinberg's account: Stewart 2001.
140 Feinberg 1984: 110 and 112 (emphasis in original).
141 Uniacke 2004: 180.

not share any of her profit with the hero, who is still alive. Feinberg concludes that: 'no wrong has been done the man, no promises broken, no harm inflicted. He has been left exactly as he was, no better, no worse'.[142] The fact that the hero has not consented to the author writing a book about him is not enough to cause Feinberg to conclude that he has been wronged. He would presumably argue[143] that there is no moral right to give consent in these circumstances; no such moral duty is owed by the author to the hero in this context. Whilst this might be true, we would dispute the conclusion that the hero is not wronged. The wrong committed against the lonely hero lies in the author's particular misuse of him, her unjust treatment.[144] She is using him solely for her own end, failing to respect him as a person, and simply seeing him as a means to make a profit. Although it could be contended that she is recognising the value of his life by recognising that it is worth writing about, his life is of value to her *purely* because she can profit from it.

In cases where the exploiter misuses the exploited individual to the extent that she treats him *merely* as an object to achieve these ends, she infringes Kant's second categorical imperative and we would argue that this constitutes a wrong to that person. It is not conducive to the lonely hero's welfare to be used to promote the welfare of the author; it demeans his worth as a person. Support for the existence of a moral right not to be treated solely as a means to an end can be derived from Uniacke's claim that the only right individuals possess unconditionally 'is a right not to be treated merely as a means of promoting the welfare of others. Substantive rights implied by this more general right would include the right not to be … treated merely as an object'.[145] Accordingly, an exploiter's failure to respect the other individual as an end in herself violates this right, and represents one possible (and common) way in which *A* wrongs *B*.[146] Notably, this is a moral right which is not context specific. Whilst, for instance, whether or not there is a moral right to consent depends upon the circumstances in which the exploitative behaviour occurs, the moral right not to be treated merely as an object is possessed by all persons, regardless of the context in which *B* interacts with *A*.

This wrong is not always present in an exploitative scenario, however, since an exploiter might not treat the exploitee *only* as a means to an end. As Archard notes, 'the Kantian principle does not proscribe treating another as a means; it rules out treating the other merely as a means. It is permissible to treat another as a means provided that one also treats them as an end.'[147] He goes on to explain that:

---

142 Feinberg 1988: 218.
143 We say *presumably* because Feinberg does not offer any explicit consideration of why a failure to obtain the lonely hero's consent would not amount to wronging him.
144 In legal terms, it might also constitute an infringement of his intellectual property rights.
145 Uniacke 2004: 180. See also Wolff 1999: 112–114. The concurrent duty to act in accordance with this right 'can be more onerous when dealing with the highly vulnerable': Formosa 2013: 107. On vulnerability, see chapter 4.
146 See also Bogg and Stanton-Ife 2003: 415–416 and Wolff 1999: 111.
147 Archard 1998: 41.

to treat the other as a means is to have regard for the other insofar as she serves one's own ends. To treat the other as an end is to have regard for her own purposes and desires, taking these into account in the formulation of one's own actions towards her.[148]

As such, a moral right derived from Kant's second categorical imperative can only be infringed when B is treated *merely* as a means to A's ends. '"Merely using" is to be understood as refusing to acknowledge the value of [B] by refusing to take her genuine interests seriously.'[149] Returning to Feinberg's lonely hero scenario, let us say, for example, that the author spends time with the lonely hero in order to get to know him. Whilst, in part, this might be with a view to being able to provide a more personal account of his character and thereby enhance the book, if it is also with a view to making him feel less lonely, then the author would be giving the lonely hero at least some respect as a person and recognising the value of his life and his genuine interests. She would thus not be treating him *solely* as means to an end. We might still conceive of her treatment of him as misuse – for example, the lonely hero could rightfully feel that she has played on his loneliness to achieve her ends – but there would be no violation of a moral right not to be treated solely as an object. There would, therefore, be no wrong unless another moral right has been violated.[150]

To offer a further example of an exploiter who does not violate the patient's moral right not to be used *merely* as a means to an end, we can make a modification to a scenario we considered in our earlier discussion. Returning to our surgeon who carries out a risky, invasive procedure in order to serve his career prospects as he knows that there is a small chance it could cure his patient's rare medical condition,[151] let's say that he is prepared to run the risk with this patient because she is a woman. That is, he is prepared to take more of a risk with a female patient because he is a misogynist. But he does not violate his patient's moral right not to be used merely as a means to an end because he wishes, in part, to cure her and knows that she desires to be cured. However, a moral right that exists within the doctor-patient context has still been violated. The doctor's female patient has a right to moral equality – to be treated as equal to his other patients, to be given equal concern and respect. This has been infringed by the doctor choosing her as the 'guinea pig' for the new drug, because he is prepared to take the risk with her rather than his male patients.[152] Whilst this can be premised upon a broader right to equality that it has been claimed all in society possess,[153] it is given particular strength in the doctor-patient context through

---

148 Ibid.
149 Sample 2003: 70.
150 Note that just because there is no wrong, this does not mean that no harm is caused. See our later discussion of this manipulated scenario in section 3.iv.
151 See text following n.114.
152 See also Wellman 2005: chapter 9, on the moral right to equitable treatment.
153 Dworkin 1977: 370.

putting into practice Beauchamp and Childress's principle of justice,[154] and is recognised by the NHS Constitution in the UK.[155] This misuse poses a clear threat to the patient's welfare, thereby making it more likely that the patient has a moral right to equality on a Feinbergian analysis. Furthermore, if the doctor fails to inform her that this is a risky procedure, he has violated her moral right to be provided with information necessary to enable her to make an informed choice.[156] This is a right generally considered to be grounded in the interest of autonomy (on which we say more shortly) and is again recognised by the NHS Constitution.[157] The doctor disrespects her as a 'chooser',[158] and the failure to inform would also cause us to question the validity of her consent.[159]

Another doctor-patient scenario offers further examples of moral rights that are specifically protected in the context of this relationship and could be violated by an exploitative interaction. Let us imagine that *Mr Y* is a patient in *Dr X*'s clinic. *Dr X* asks *Mr Y* to get undressed for an examination and then secretly takes a photograph of him in the nude. The examination is actually unnecessary and *Dr X* keeps and uses the photograph for her own sexual gratification. *Dr X* has violated her patient's right to privacy, a right that protects him 'from unauthorized intrusions'[160] into his private sphere. For in agreeing to undress, *Mr Y* has acted under the reasonable expectation that he has undressed in the privacy of the examination room strictly and only for the purposes of a medical examination. Whilst we recognise that whether there is a general moral right

---

154 Beauchamp and Childress 2013: chapter 7.
155 The first principle of the *NHS Constitution for England* states that 'The [NHS] service … has a duty to each and every individual that it serves and must respect their human rights. At the same time, it has a wider social duty to promote equality through the services it provides': Department of Health and Social Care 2015: 3.
156 For a real-life example of such exploitation, see the account given by a patient of surgeon Ian Paterson in Paterson Inquiry 2020: 94 and see 115. We discuss Paterson in chapter 3, section 4.
157 Consider, for instance, Beauchamp and Childress's explanation of autonomy as 'self-rule that is free from both controlling interference by others and limitations that prevent meaningful choice, such as inadequate understanding': Beauchamp and Childress 2013: 101. For analysis of the right to know, see Chadwick and others 2014. According to the *NHS Constitution for England*: 'You have the right to be given information about the test and treatment options available to you, what they involve and their risks and benefits': Department of Health and Social Care 2015: 8. We recognise that there would also be a violation of the patient's legal right to give informed consent (*Montgomery* v. *Lanarkshire Health Board* [2015] UKSC 11), but legal rights are not our concern here.
158 A term we have borrowed from Benn 1984: 230. Note that a *complete* failure to respect his patient's autonomy could be perceived to amount to treating her *only* as a means without regard to her purposes and desires, thereby violating Kant's second categorical imperative (see the text accompanying n.174). However, the fact that the doctor takes into account her autonomy regarding her wish to be cured means that there is no violation of this right here.
159 Wertheimer 1996: 257.
160 Corlett 2002: 331.

to privacy is contested,[161] we argue that since privacy is necessary for a person's well-being and dignity, it should be recognised as a fundamental value in health care.[162] This is especially the case in the context of the doctor-patient relationship;[163] were a moral right to privacy not to exist, the relationship between doctor and patient would be at threat. This relationship is structured 'according to an understanding of what [it is] and what accordingly is due to [the two parties] and from them'.[164] Both parties understand that the doctor is under a duty to respect her patient's privacy.[165] Following on from this, the repercussions for their health and well-being would be grave if patients did not have an assurance of privacy in their interactions with their doctors and thus chose not to seek medical advice when ill.[166]

The scenario involving *Dr X* and *Mr Y* is a particularly apt one to demonstrate how a moral right to privacy can be traced back to Kantian ideas of respect for persons. In taking advantage of *Mr Y*'s agreement to be examined for a medical purpose, *Dr X*'s scrutiny for her own purposes, her failure to respect *Mr Y*'s privacy, amounts to a failure to respect him as a person; she is treating him solely as an object. She gives no consideration to the effect that her behaviour could have on his perception of himself and the nature of what he is doing.[167] As noted by Benn, if a doctor 'has occasion to make someone an object of scrutiny ... the patient will have grounds for resentment if [the doctor] appears insensible to the fact that it is a person [s]he is examining'.[168]

Moreover, in failing to obtain *Mr Y*'s consent to the taking of the photograph, *Dr X* has violated his right to autonomy. Whilst recognising the existence of varying and sometimes competing versions of autonomy,[169] we have in mind here *Mr Y*'s right to self-govern himself, to make decisions on matters regarding himself 'freely and independently and without ... let or hindrance',[170] whilst also recognising the impact of interpersonal interaction and relationships on

---

161 Ibid.
162 '[A] certain level of privacy, and a right to it being respected, is necessary for one to even attempt to become an authentic (project pursuing) self in society ... the right to privacy is needed to protect a citizen's interest in becoming or maintaining a *self to respect*': ibid: 333 and 336 (emphasis in original). See also Scanlon 2009: 74.
163 See DeCew 2000 (albeit DeCew focuses on medical information specifically).
164 Benn 1984: 235.
165 According to the *NHS Constitution for England*: 'you have the right to privacy and confidentiality and to expect the NHS to keep your confidential information safe and secure': Department of Health and Social Care 2015: 8.
166 This is not to say that there can never be exceptional circumstances where a right to privacy can be justifiably violated to protect others, e.g. as in W v. *Egdell* [1990] Ch. 359 CA, but discussion of such circumstances is beyond our focus.
167 Benn 1984: 230.
168 Ibid: 228.
169 Brazier and Ost 2013: 238–239. We are not applying Kantian principled autonomy here, for instance: see O'Neill 2002.
170 Gillon 1986: 60.

autonomy.¹⁷¹ Autonomy can certainly be claimed as 'one of the elements of well-being', a moral right grounded in the individual's welfare interests.¹⁷² What is more, the existence of this moral right within the doctor-patient relationship is supported by, for example, Beauchamp and Childress's bioethical principle of autonomy.¹⁷³ *Dr X*'s complete failure to respect *Mr Y*'s autonomy can be perceived to amount to treating him *only* as a means without regard to his purposes and desires, thereby violating Kant's second categorical imperative.¹⁷⁴

To conclude, exploitation often wrongs the person who is exploited. Even in cases where the exploiter does not treat the exploited person *merely* as a means to an end, another moral right could well have been violated. As we discuss in the next chapter, this is especially likely in the context of particular professional relationships in which exploitation frequently involves violating not only moral rights, but also the very ethos of the professional relationship.

iv) How exploitation can harm the exploited person through setting back their interest(s)

Besides wronging the exploited individual, exploitation can also cause them harm. We begin our analysis here by noting that we do not take the view that exploitation is *always* harmful to the exploited individual. As Wood notes, 'exploitation ... is not necessarily harmful to the interests of the exploited'.¹⁷⁵ According to Feinberg, if harm is not caused, the exploitation in question is an instance of harmless wrongdoing.¹⁷⁶ Thus, whilst we would still morally object to such exploitation, this is on the basis of the principle that it is wrong to take advantage of and misuse another for one's own ends rather than because *A*'s behaviour in such instances causes *B* harm. Whilst we agree that *A*'s wrongful behaviour towards *B* does not wrong and/or harm *B per se*, we suggest that it is difficult to conceive of cases involving wrongful exploitation where no wrong is done *or* harm is caused to *B* at all, because misusing a person so often involves the violation of at least one of their moral rights and/or causes harm.

---

171 As will become apparent, we are sympathetic to definitions of autonomy that reflect a more relational conceptualisation. See chapter 4, section 2.
172 Mill 1996: 123.
173 Beauchamp and Childress 2013: chapter 4.
174 'to treat someone as an end... is to respect his right to use his own reason to determine whether and how he will contribute to what happens': Korsgaard 1993: 46. See also Wilkinson 2003: 30. The doctor's unnecessary examination itself could also constitute misuse involving using *Mr Y* merely as a means to an end if it is done for no other purpose than facilitating the taking of photograph. It would constitute a violation of *Mr Y*'s right to bodily autonomy too. Again, whilst we have noted that we are not concerned with legal rights in this chapter, the tort of battery may well have been committed, since there is deceit as to the purpose of examination (*R v. Tabassum* [2000] 2 Cr App R 328).
175 Wood 1995: 149.
176 See Feinberg 1988: 211–220.

Following Feinberg's account, an individual is harmed if his interests, defined as 'things in which one has a stake', things that are vital to an individual's well-being,[177] are set back or, left 'in a worse condition than [they] would otherwise have been in had the invasion not occurred at all'.[178] Feinberg utilises the term 'welfare interests' to refer to those interests that provide the means for an individual to achieve his or her ultimate goals.[179] There is what may appear to be an overlap here with Feinberg's conception of moral rights and his view that welfare interests can be the best exemplar for grounding moral rights. However, the distinction lies in the difference between rights and interests. Rights commonly reflect fundamental values and demand a prima facie ground for respect.[180] In contrast, although interests can be conceptualised as 'the anchor of rights',[181] whether an individual's particular interest should be protected depends upon consequential considerations and the balancing of this interest against any competing interests.[182] This raises an interesting issue since an instance of exploitation could promote one of B's interests, whilst at the same time setting back another of her interests, thereby being both beneficial and harmful.[183] For our purposes in this chapter, we do not need to explore this further as we are merely concerned with how exploitation can cause a setback to B's interests.

Our interest in health is an obvious example of a welfare interest since without good health it may be difficult, if not impossible, to achieve many of our ultimate goals. Examples of harms that exploitation can cause which are connected to this welfare interest include psychiatric injury (particularly if the exploitation is of a sexual nature),[184] and mental and physical suffering. An unscrupulous employer's demand that a financially crippled employee works long hours in a physically demanding and/or stressful job at lower than the minimum wage, can represent an example of exploitation which leads to such harms. Alternatively, the exploitation could cause harm in the sense of financial loss (say where a carer exploits an older person's memory loss to receive double her usual payment),[185] or loss of reputation (such as when an innocuous photograph of a woman is manipulated to create a morphed pseudo-image of pornography and people she knows are presented with the image and have their perceptions of her altered by it). Such examples could clearly have a 'substantial effect on one's behaviour

---

177 Ibid. See also Uniacke 2004: 174: 'We can harm someone in this sense by inflicting physical, psychological, financial or other forms of damage on him, with or without his consent.'
178 Feinberg 1984: 34.
179 Ibid: 37.
180 Dworkin 1984: 153–167; Peerenboom 1995: 361; Waldron 1984: 14.
181 Scanlon 2009: 76.
182 Ibid: 78; Peerenboom 1995: 361.
183 We explore this matter further in chapter 3, section 2, text accompanying nn.23–32. See also Sample 2003: 85.
184 See the discussion in Chapter 5, part 1, text accompanying n.50, and chapter 5 part 2, text accompanying n.21.
185 Consider also the case of *R v. Hinks* [2001] 2 AC 241. See Bogg and Stanton-Ife 2003 for analysis of the carer's exploitation in this case.

or life',[186] which would be inherently harmful. Furthermore, when exploitation occurs in the context of a professional relationship involving the exploited person's reliance on the exploiter, the harm caused to welfare interests is likely to be greater for reasons we identify in the next chapter.

Not all cases of exploitation will cause B to suffer a setback to his interests, however.[187] We can return here to Feinberg's lonely hero scenario prior to our manipulation of it. We challenged Feinberg's view that the author commits no wrong to the lonely hero, but agree with him that there is no setback to his interests because these interests are left in no worse a position than they would have been in had the author not written the book. But the situation is not always clear-cut. In some hard cases, whether there is a setback to interests needs careful analysis. Consider, for example, a situation considered by numerous authors where an exploiter takes advantage of the fact that another person is unconscious or intoxicated with drugs or alcohol to rape her, and the victim remains unaware that she has been raped.[188] Whilst she has clearly been wronged, she perceives no immediate consequences of the rape and there are no overt consequences or harmful effects. It thus might be concluded that she has only been wronged.[189] But the exploiter-rapist has invaded the victim's interest in liberty, 'an interest in [herself] tying down the future in a certain respect and determining through [her] own choice what is to happen'.[190] The conditions necessary for the victim's interest in liberty to be fulfilled are absent (consciousness and capacity) and in acting as he does, the rapist thereby thwarts this interest. This suggests that we may be able to establish the existence of harmful exploitation which sets back her interests. It might be contended, however, that in a case where the victim remains completely unaware of the rape, there can be no setback to her interest in liberty because the lack of knowledge of the invasion means her well-being will not be negatively affected; the victim's prospects are not 'diminished or indeed affected at all, by the rape'.[191] Yet Archard's analysis pinpoints the interest that is set back *regardless* of the victim's knowledge: '[a] woman's interest in her sexual integrity is set back when she undergoes sex to which she does not consent, even if she does not know that at the time or even subsequently'.[192] A further, less discussed example is one involving a person's interest in dignity.

---

186 A phrase used by Wolff to describe the effects of severe cases of exploitation. Wolff 1999: 115.
187 Feinberg 1988: 176.
188 Discussed by Archard 2007. See also Gardner and Shute 2007 and Madden Dempsey and Herring 2007.
189 Gardner and Shute 2007: 5.
190 Feinberg 1984: 35.
191 Gardner and Shute 2007: 6.
192 Archard 2007: 379. See also Bogart 1995: 166–167; Schulhofer 1998: chapter 6 on sexual autonomy; and see further our discussion in chapter 5, part 2, section 1, n.62. Any exposure to the risk of becoming infected with a sexually transmittable disease would also set back a further interest, the victim's welfare interest in health. See Madden Dempsey and Herring 2007: 476–478; Bogart 1995: 172.

44   What is exploitation?

Here we draw on, but also reimagine, a scenario offered by Foster.[193] Imagine that an unconscious man is on a stretcher in hospital in a ward. A person passing by pulls the blanket off the man, leaving his body exposed for all to see. Notably, in both these examples, even though the victims suffers no physical or psychological hurt, they still suffer a setback to their interests. It should, therefore, be clear that harm in the sense of a setback to interests is a broader notion of harm than harm by way of personal injury (physical or mental).

Turning back to our *Mr Y* and *Dr X* scenario, the setting suggests that *Dr X* has invaded the strong interest in privacy that *Mr Y* has as a patient attending the clinic for the purpose of medical diagnosis and treatment. It is easy to envisage that the breach of trust resulting in *Dr X*'s secret photographing of *Mr Y* would, if it subsequently became known to *Mr Y*, cause feelings of hurt and betrayal that might also lead to mental distress and suffering. Or if he discovers later that *Dr X* has committed this wrong against other patients, this knowledge could cause *Mr Y* to question whether it has happened to him also, thus setting back his interest. If either of these possibilities do occur, then the wrong caused by treating *Mr Y* merely as a means to an end without his consent or knowledge is intensified by the resultant anguish. But suppose that *Mr Y* remains unaware that he has – or others have – been photographed,[194] and thus *Dr X*'s taking of and any subsequent use of the photograph has no impact on his well-being. Although we have argued that his moral right to privacy is violated, can we say he has suffered a setback to his interests? We contend that we can. As a patient attending the clinic for the purpose of medical diagnosis and treatment, *Mr Y*'s interest in privacy has been intruded on by *Dr X*'s actions; this interest is set back because it is left in a worse condition than it was prior to the invasion.[195]

Sometimes, as in the above scenario, wronging a person and harming them by way of a setback to interest can amalgamate.[196] We have argued that in his situation, *Mr Y* has both a moral right to privacy and an interest in privacy that can be set back. Essentially, *Dr X* has a moral duty to protect *Mr Y*'s privacy interest, a duty that is imposed by *Mr Y*'s right to privacy and a duty that she has failed to adhere to, and this leads to *Mr Y*'s interest being set back.[197] Take as a different example *Dr C*, who refuses to provide IVF treatment to

---

193 See his scenario involving a teenage girl with profound learning disabilities in Foster 2011: 2.
194 What Wertheimer refers to as 'nonvolitional exploitation': Wertheimer 1996: 26.
195 Feinberg refers to an interest in privacy as a welfare interest: 1984: 61–62. Note too that Feinberg recognises that we can suffer harm through a setback to our interests of which we have no knowledge. He states that his interest in a good reputation 'can be seriously harmed without my ever learning of it': Feinberg 1984: 87.
196 More generally, see Duff 2003: 43 and 48; Scanlon 2009: 75.
197 'If one has a right to privacy, and one's right to privacy is violated, then one has been harmed in the requisite sense of having one's interest in one's privacy being set back': Corlett 2002: 340.

Patient D on the National Health Service (NHS) unless she agrees to donate some of her eggs. If the eggs are healthy, *Dr C* intends to use them when treating other patients to improve her IVF success rate. *D* is actually under no obligation to donate her eggs, but *C*'s more powerful, authoritative position enables her to exploit *D*'s lack of knowledge and understanding regarding the criteria for IVF treatment on the NHS. As is the case with our misogynist doctor who fails to advise his female patient that the procedure is risky, *C* has violated *D*'s right to give informed consent. We could also argue that, through this wrong, *D* has suffered an invasion of her interest in liberty. In other words, the violation of her right to give a free and informed consent also involves an invasion of her interest in liberty. This intrusion could constitute a setback to her interest in liberty if she would not have chosen to donate her eggs anyway, ergo her interest in liberty is then in a worse condition than if the intrusion had not occurred.

Just as it is possible to wrong a person but not to cause them harm, it is also possible to set back their interests without wronging them. Take our manipulated version of Feinberg's lonely hero scenario. We argued that no wrong is caused where the author does not treat the lonely hero merely as a means to her end, by spending time with him (in part) to make him feel less lonely. However, the lonely hero's welfare could still be affected, constituting harm by way of a setback to his interest in health. He may now distrust anyone who tries to engage in conversation with him because of the fear that they will use him in the same way, causing his loneliness and consequent mental suffering to be exacerbated further.

Interestingly, according to Feinberg's construction of harm, exploitation is only harmful if it both wrongs an individual *and* sets back her interests.[198] Whilst we find Feinberg's assessment of the way in which exploitative behaviour can negatively affect others to be useful in our task of illustrating how exploitation can both wrong the exploited person and set back their interests, we have chosen to separate wronging and harming rather than to view them both as variants of harm.[199] This is because, for our purposes, referring to two varieties of harm (normative harm by way of wronging and harm as setbacks to interest, as Feinberg sees it) unnecessarily complicates the issue.[200] Moreover, requiring that both a wrong and a setback to interests occur in order for exploitation to be rightly perceived as harmful would lead to untenable conclusions. Take, for instance, our *Dr X* and *Mr Y* scenario. Even if our arguments that *Mr Y* has moral rights to privacy and autonomy fail to convince, he has still suffered harm by virtue of the setback to his interest in privacy. However, in the absence of a

---

198 Feinberg 1984: 36. For a critique of Feinberg's account of harm, see Duff 2001.
199 We thus reject the contention that, for instance, breaching the Kantian categorical imperative not to treat a person solely as a means 'is to harm her'. See Wertheimer 1996: 23–24.
200 See also Wilkinson 2003: 69. We note, however, that construing harm in such a way was arguably necessary for Feinberg's very different purpose of formulating a harm principle that could be applied to place appropriate constraints upon the criminal law.

wrong, no matter that *Mr Y* suffers mental distress from discovering what *Dr X* has done, *Dr X*'s behaviour could not be construed as harmful exploitation on Feinberg's account. This surely cannot be right.[201]

We have shown that exploitation can have the effects of both wronging and harming *B*, but that there are also cases in which it *only wrongs B* or *only harms B*. We recognise that, in taking into consideration both wronging a person and setting back their interests, our account of the way in which exploitation can negatively affect the exploited person is broad. It encompasses more than a standard Feinbergian approach to wronging by invoking a Kantian perspective in recognising a (universal) moral right not to be treated solely as object. But we adopt this broader Kantian liberal account because it is better suited to explicating the wrongful nature of exploitation as we see it – the misuse of another person for one's own ends – and the way in which this can have a wide-reaching impact on the exploitee. That said, to return to a point we made earlier, it is difficult to conceive of cases where there is no wrong *or* harm.[202]

In sum, whilst the account of exploitation that we offer in this chapter sits comfortably alongside other process-based accounts which are concerned with the wrongful treatment of others provided by Goodin and Sample, the originality and significance of our explication of exploitation lies in its prioritisation of misuse as opposed to taking unfair advantage of, or degradation and taking advantage of basic needs. Drawing on Feinberg's work, this account provides a unique analysis of how exploitation can wrong and/or harm the exploitee through invoking a Kantian liberal approach. Our conceptualisation of exploitation provides a framework for the analysis of exploitation in the doctor-patient relationship in the remainder of this work. The next task is to map this context, exploring the characteristics of exploitation in the doctor-patient relationship.

---

201 We do not concern ourselves here with the question of legal redress for the repercussions to *B* of *A*'s exploitative behaviour, but note in passing that unless a moral right is recognised and protected by law, it is generally harms connected to set back to interests that the law recognises as actionable. See further chapter 7, section 4.ii.

202 One example could be our manipulation of lonely hero scenario where there is no moral right violated, but only where there is no harm to the interest in health as we suggested might occur. See the first paragraph on p. 28 and the second paragraph on p. 45.

3 Wrongful exploitation in the doctor-patient relationship

In this chapter, we begin our exploration of whether exploitation in the doctor-patient relationship can constitute a special case of wrongful exploitation (that is, taking advantage of and misusing another person for one's own ends), by setting out certain common characteristics of exploitation in professional relationships involving unequal power. We then scrutinise the particular dynamics of the doctor-patient relationship, exploring the crucial elements of trust, reliance, the doctor as a fiduciary, and the inequality of power between the parties. We consider the fact that the relationship presents unscrupulous doctors with the opportunity to exploit patients – potentially many patients – and the significance of the patient's state of ill-health in facilitating a doctor's exploitation. Next, we address what influence, perceived or real, the context of a publicly funded National Health Service (NHS) in the UK has on the nature of the relationship between doctor and patient, and the opportunities this may present for patient exploitation, comparing this to the doctor-patient relationship in private health care. Finally, we explore how exploitation can be situated within philosophical medical ethics and professional medical ethics, before turning, briefly, to consider how the law categorises exploitation in the doctor-patient relationship.

As we noted at the start of this book, we are not claiming that all doctors do, or will at some point, exploit their patients. We are mindful that those who enter the profession generally do so because of desire to do good and to help others.[1] But we should not assume that doctors' personal ethics and integrity, their practice of the contemporary biopsychosocial model of medicine,[2] and training that they receive

---

1 As portrayed so effectively in Adam Kay's account of his time as a junior doctor: Kay 2018.
2 This model 'includes the patient as well as the illness … [The doctor] must weight the relative contributions of social and psychological as well as biological factors implicated in the patient's dysphoria and dysfunction as well as in his decision to accept or not to accept patienthood and with it the responsibility to cooperate in his own health care': Engel 1977: 133. See also Coulter 2002; Bauman and others 2003. Note the requirement in the GMC's *Good Medical Practice* guidance to doctors that in assessing the patient's conditions, they must take 'account of their history (including the symptoms and psychological, spiritual, social and cultural factors), their views and values': General Medical Council 2013b: 7[15(a)].

as part of current medical education on making their practice patient-orientated,[3] for instance, guarantee that they are all immune to the temptation of abusing the doctor-patient relationship for reasons of self-interest. Membership of the medical profession does not make doctors any different from the rest of us in that sense. Hesketh has argued that 'a more realistic approach is needed: rather than polarizing doctors either as the benevolent ideal or as "another Shipman" (and therefore evil almost beyond compare), it would be better if doctors were viewed as ordinary people conferred with special privileges that they may or may not abuse in the course of their work'.[4] This is the position that we adopt here.

1) Exploitation in intimate and confidential professional relationships

> The relationship between professional and client is characterized by a fundamental inequality in a variety of respects: dependency, power, status, and expertise. She is dependent on his help; he is not on hers. He has power significantly to affect her future, whereas she does not have the power to affect his future.[5]

In many respects in everyday life, we are involved in professional relationships of unequal power, either as the client or sometimes as the professional: when we seek legal advice from a solicitor; when we approach our line-manager at work; when we consult an architect about an extension to our house; and when we assess our students' work at university, for instance. Looking to Archard's statement above, it is not always true to say that, in such relationships, the client has *no* power to affect the professional's future. A colleague's allegation of sexual misconduct against her line manager could have significant implications for this manager's career, for example, even if the allegation is subsequently proven to be false. However, Archard's general point about the fundamental power imbalance in these relationships is surely correct; this imbalance is inevitable since the client enters into such relationships because he seeks the professional's expertise upon a matter regarding which he is inexperienced and unqualified.[6] Of course, the level of dependency differs depending on the nature of the professional relationship. Turning again to Archard's analysis, he identifies three characteristics shared by certain professional relationships of unequal power:

> The first is an ethos of intimacy, closeness, trust, openness, and confidence. The second is the relative dependence and vulnerability of the client. The third is the esteem, respect, and admiration which the client has for the professional.[7]

---

3   See Gerteis and others 1993.
4   Hesketh 2011: 73.
5   Archard 1994: 96.
6   For further discussion of the inequality of power between doctor and patient, see section 4.
7   Archard 1994: 98.

Arguably the most obvious example of such a professional relationship – which we refer to as an *intimate and confidential professional relationship* – is that which we are focused upon: the relationship between doctor and patient. But there are other examples we can consider first. Take, for instance, the relationships between lawyers and their clients, and between priests (or other religious leaders in a similar role) and their parishioners.[8] All of these relationships involve a level of intimacy and trust: the client confides in her solicitor, providing highly confidential information, as does the parishioner who seeks absolution for his sins from his priest. Both clients are dependent on the professional (the first to represent her in legal proceedings, the second to offer him religious advice and guidance), and both could be emotionally vulnerable, depending on the reason why they need the professional's help. It is also probable that the elements of respect and esteem will be present.

When exploitation occurs in such intimate and confidential professional relationships, when the professional takes advantage of her client in pursuit of her own ends, this violation is likely to breach the very foundations upon which the relationship is set: trust, reliance and reasonable expectation. For such relationships cannot operate without trust and are based upon the client's reasonable expectation, arising from their reliance, that the professional will always act in the client's interests. This is the ethos of these relationships, crucial to the shared understanding that both parties have about the scope of the relationship and the professional's duties; the client 'knows what to expect from the professional and … the professional understands the scope of the relationship he enjoys with his client'.[9] Indeed, the nature and scope of the relationship is enshrined in professional regulation.

Breaching this relationship ethos through exploitation is also likely to violate the moral rights[10] of, and cause a setback to the interests of, the exploited person. This is because the existence of such a relationship of reliance makes it easier to violate the client's (*B*'s) moral rights, since *B* is vulnerable to *A*'s exploitation because of his dependency on *A* for a matter that is vital to him, such as his health. This is a shared vulnerability that clients in these relationships are likely to possess because of the very nature of such professional relationships. And through the very existence of the relationship, *A* is provided with an opportunity to fail to act in the client's interests in pursuit of her own and to treat *B* solely as a means to an end, for instance. Moreover, *A*'s exploitation of *B* is highly likely to harm *B*

---

8   Archard provides the following as examples of such relationships: 'doctors, teacher, therapists, counsellors, and even priests in a pastoral role': Archard 1994: 92. Whilst recognising these relationships as falling into the broad category of intimate and confidential professional relationships, we distinguish the doctor-patient relationship (and we subsume therapists/psychiatrists within this) from other such relationships in the final section of this chapter.
9   Archard 1994: 96.
10 In the previous chapter, we utilised Feinberg's analysis to explain that moral rights are claims supported by valid reasons against others, and we highlighted the importance of moral rights pertaining to an individual's welfare interests, such as the moral right to autonomy. An individual is wronged if their moral right is violated (see chapter 2, section 3.iii). We will say more upon the issue of moral rights shortly, when we turn specifically to exploitation in the doctor-patient relationship (see the subsequent sections 2, 6 and 9).

by way of mental distress and suffering, because such behaviour is so damaging when it occurs in intimate and confidential relationships of trust.[11] This is what makes exploitation in such relationships especially wrongful.[12] Given this, we go further than Archard does when he states that '[(sexual) exploitation] ... which benefits the professional exceeds the scope of the professional relationship',[13] and we conceive of exploitation in such intimate and confidential relationships as being *exploitation that violates the very ethos of the professional relationship*.[14] It is now necessary for us to explore the particular characteristics of the doctor-patient relationship in order to illustrate how exploitation that violates the ethos of the doctor-patient relationship is especially wrongful.

2) The doctor-patient relationship: a relationship based on trust and reliance

> All prospective patients – everyone, that is – want doctors to be trustworthy. And, so, all doctors must accept *seek trust and deserve it* as their moral law, as their creed. In deciding what to do and how to do it they must pay attention to promoting trust and not eroding it.[15]

Whilst the current legal, ethical and professional regulatory model of the doctor-patient relationship is dominated by patient autonomy rather than medical paternalism,[16] this does not mean that patients' reliance upon their doctors has necessarily diminished. Nor does it mean that the knowledge that the doctor is legally obliged to respect their autonomy extinguishes the need for the patient's trust, as we argue below. First, in order to gain a better understanding of the characteristics of the doctor-patient relationship, it is essential to consider the circumstances that the patient finds herself or himself in. The patient's ill-health or feared ill-health is a key feature of these circumstances. Crucially, this means that

---

11 See the cases discussed in the next section, in the text accompanying nn.33–40.
12 As Archard notes, 'exploitation of a professional relationship is both wrong and destructive': Archard 1994: 98.
13 Archard 1994: 98.
14 As a side issue, we note that exploitation can violate the ethos of personal relationships too. Consider a family member, *A*, who has assumed the role of carer for their older relative, *B*. The personal relationship between *A* and *B* is highly likely to possess the first characteristic of a relationship of intimacy and trust. Furthermore, *B* is dependent on *A* for a vital matter to *B* – her welfare – and, consequently, is vulnerable to *A*'s manipulation. Thus, Archard's second characteristic is also likely to be present. Whilst the third characteristic of *B* holding *A* in high esteem might not be present, this characteristic could be replaced in personal relationships (albeit not all personal relationships) with love and an emotional bond between *B* and *A*. See chapter 6 for our exploration of the potential exploitation of those who desire an assisted death by their relatives.
15 Rhodes 2001: 496 (emphasis in original).
16 See, e.g. *Chester* v. *Afshar* [2004] UKHL 41; *Montgomery* v. *Lanarkshire Health Board* [2015] UKSC 11; O'Neil 2002: 168; Coggon 2007; General Medical Council 2013b.

whilst the patient's consent gives the doctor the authority to act, the patient is surrendering her agency, albeit temporarily, as Gardner neatly explains:

> Armed with your consent, so long as various other conditions hold, your doctor can legitimately manipulate and intrude into your body, ply you with substances, extract and replace parts of you, and even subdue you with anaesthetics in order to do such things. Your doctor does such things *to* you. That is the sense in which you are her patient. By consenting here, it is true, you exercise your autonomy, and *a fortiori* your agency. But you do so in such a way as to confine or qualify, or even surrender, your own agency in respect of what your doctor and her team will then proceed to do. The doctor will not be conducting the surgical procedure with you but *on* you … You will not be exercising any autonomy, joining in with anything or playing any active role, because for the time being you will not be an agent. For the duration of the procedure, you will be exclusively a patient …[17]

With health being the central cause for concern, the patient is required to place faith in the doctor's knowledge and expertise,[18] and to grant the doctor unparalleled access to her body and mind, in comparison to other intimate and confidential professional relationships. Trust is integral to patients laying themselves bare (sometimes literally),[19] for 'in what other circumstances would you find yourself nearly naked discussing the intimate details of your life with a person you met scant minutes before'?[20] Moreover, 'when patients and their loved ones are pre-occupied with illness … they want doctors they can trust', indeed, ill-health *forces* trust.[21] Tauber outlines the experience of being a patient in modern-day health care as follows:

> the fear of the unknown, the dissolution of identity accompanying pain in its multifarious forms, the dehumanization of being subjected to the administrative processes of health care, and the psychological dependence resulting from each of these challenges combine to make patients emotionally dependent on health-care providers.[22]

---

17 Gardner 2018: 57 (emphasis in original).
18 On this type of 'deferential trust', see n.72. As Pellegrino and Thomasma note, patients trust doctors whilst carrying 'a burden of anxiety, pain, or suffering', possibly all three of these. Pellegrino and Thomasma 1993: 68.
19 Archard 1998: 61. See also Pellegrino and Thomasma 1993: 68.
20 Colt and others 2011: 298. See also Rhodes 2001: 495.
21 Irvine 2005: 1265; Pellegrino and Thomasma 1993: 65.
22 Tauber 2005: 47. In this extract, Tauber also refers to the 'loss of autonomy' but we have omitted this here, since autonomy is only lost when the patient no longer possesses the capacity for autonomy. Moreover, when capacity to make a decision about one's care or treatment has been lost, the patient's autonomy (values and wishes) should still be respected through the best interests test under the Mental Capacity Act 2005, s.4(6). On the patient's experience, note also the Supreme Court's highlighting of 'the social and psychological realities of the relationship between a patient and her doctor, whether in the time-pressured setting of a GP's surgery, or in the setting of a hospital. Few patients do not feel intimidated or inhibited to some degree.' *Montgomery* v. *Lanarkshire Health Board*, see n.16, [58] (Lords Kerr and Reed).

The aspects to which Tauber alludes are frequently present in the practical realities of health care, as is further apparent if we consider the following exploitative scenario from Jansen and Wall which effectively conveys the significance of the patient's reliance and trust:

> David is physically weak and ill. He visits his physician, who recommends a particular procedure that is in David's best medical interests. Despite being fully informed about the procedure and the consequences of forgoing it, David refuses the procedure. However, his physician is able to pressure David into agreeing to the procedure in part by taking advantage of the trust David places in him and in part by taking advantage of David's weak condition and his consequent lack of motivation to resist pressure.[23]

There is an interesting question here that we address initially: does this scenario actually involve exploitation according to the account of exploitation's essential elements that we provided in the previous chapter?[24] There is *misuse* by way of taking advantage of a vulnerability, since the doctor takes advantage of the trust that David places in him and David's weak condition, and this occurs for the doctor's *own ends* (to ensure that David has the procedure that the doctor considers to be in his best medical interests). But is the doctor *taking advantage of (using)* David or something inherently connected to him? We consider that this element is also present since the doctor takes advantage of (uses) David's capacity as a decision maker. As Wertheimer puts it, 'A [can] exploit B's capacity as a decision-maker in order to (paternalistically) benefit B'.[25]

The elements of trust and reliance play a significant role in facilitating the exploitation and in regard to its impact upon David. Dealing first with what enables the exploitation, David ultimately gives his consent because of the situation that he is in and the doctor takes advantage of this situation. His doctor exerts undue influence, knowing that David is more susceptible to pressure because of his weakened state and, particularly, to pressure from him because David trusts, and is reliant upon him. Indeed, this position of trust is part of the reason why David is vulnerable to exploitation.[26] In Baier's words, 'not all the things that thrive when there is trust between people, and which matter, are things that should be encouraged to thrive … Exploitation … thrive[s] better in an atmosphere of trust.'[27] And even though David may trust others, we can ask ourselves whether he would have been as likely to succumb to pressure from anyone else he trusts in the same way as he does

---

23 Jansen and Wall 2013: 400.
24 See chapter 2, section 3.i.
25 Wertheimer 1996: 254.
26 See Baier 1986: 235: 'Trust … is accepted vulnerability to another's possible but not expected ill will (or lack of good will) toward one.' See also Barnard 2016: 294; Collins 2015: 154.
27 Baier 1986: 232.

when it comes from his doctor. Whilst a close family member might have been able to exert significant influence by virtue of their personal relationship and David's trust in them, this would be because of other elements likely to be present in a close familial relationship, such as a desire to act in accordance with a loved one's wishes.[28] But the different dynamics of their relationship with David could have had an alternative effect, with David being better able to resist the pressure because of his loved one's subjectivity, and lack of medical knowledge and involvement in his medical care. In short, it is the particular dynamics of the professional relationship between David and his doctor that overcome David's autonomous wishes.

Turning next to the outcome of the doctor's behaviour and its impact upon David, what occurs in this scenario may not actually be construed as exploitation following outcome-based approaches to conceptualising exploitation *provided* that the end result is that David benefits from the treatment. However, reflecting on what occurred might make David suspicious of the medical profession in the future, causing him not to seek medical advice when this is required. It is the doctor's violation of David's trust that could well lead to this consequence, and thus the breach of trust exacerbates the wrong. And it is the context of the special relationship regarding a crucial aspect of David's life – his health – that gives rise to any negative outcome that could arise from David's subsequent avoidance of health care.

Process-based accounts of exploitation such as ours emphasise that, regardless of whether the outcome is beneficial for David or not, the doctor is failing to respect David as a person. He has misused David by taking advantage of a vulnerability that he possesses and wrongs him through violating his moral right to autonomy by pressurising him to consent. The doctor has breached his professional ethics and has gone beyond the boundaries of the contemporary patient autonomy model of the doctor-patient relationship[29] in effectively making the decision for David rather than advising him. The scenario also provides a good illustration of the way in which the motives underlying a doctor's exploitation of his patient may not be selfish, but he could still be considered to be acting to achieve his own ends (getting David to consent to treatment that he considers being in his best medical interests). Despite the doctor's ends and David's medical best interests being aligned, and the fact that the doctor is acting in what he perceives David's best interests to be, this does not alter the wrong done.

In addition, this scenario raises the interesting issue of the exploited person having competing interests. David's interests in autonomy and his future health might be set back through his doctor's exploitation, but his interest in his health in the immediate and short term is promoted. Consider too our misogynist doctor scenario: the doctor's exploitation may promote his female patient's interest in health in the unlikely event that the procedure does actually cure her,

---

28 See further chapter 6 on potential exploitation in family relationships.
29 On which see the next section.

but his exploitation causes a setback to her interests in equality and liberty.[30] Such conflicts between *B*'s interest in health and other interests can occur in the doctor-patient relationship in scenarios such as that involving David when the doctor puts the patient's best medical interests before the patient's autonomy.[31] Whilst serving at least one of *B*'s interests does not mean that there is no exploitation on our account, it could have a bearing on the shape of the impact that the doctor's exploitation has upon *B*: Sample has contended that 'it may be the case that an action [is exploitative], but that the other benefits of the action outweigh the [exploitation], making the action nonharmful overall'.[32] Thus, in the particular case, the end result might be that, overall, being exploited by the doctor has more positive than negative repercussions for the patient. However, this is not to say that this rights the wrong done.

Whether the doctor's exploitation of the patient is well meaning but undoubtedly paternalistic, as it appears to be in Jansen and Wall's scenario, or whether the doctor exploits her patient with her own self-interest as her focal concern, we contend that exploitation in the doctor-patient relationship is especially likely to have a negative impact upon patients' interests and cause them harm because of the significant breach of trust. The most powerful illustration of the effects of exploitation, as exacerbated by the patient's reliance and trust, come from real-life examples. According to the official Kerr/Haslam Inquiry into two consultant psychiatrists' sexual exploitation of their patients in the UK, which we return to in chapter 5, 'in most if not all cases, the effect upon the women of the breach of trust that occurred has been devastating'.[33] We can also look to the impact on patients exploited by Dr Nikita Levy, a gynaecologist based at Johns Hopkins Hospital in Baltimore. Utilising a spy camera that looked like a pen, Levy was able to take covert, explicit photographs of his patients during pelvic examinations over a period of 25 years. Lawyers for his victims commented that 'when learning of Dr. Levy's behavior, our clients were extremely distraught … They felt a great breach of faith and trust. They felt betrayed'.[34] One of Levy's patients experienced such a betrayal of trust that she

---

30 For this scenario, see the text accompanying nn.151–159 in the previous chapter. We could also think again about Jansen and Wall's scenario involving Joan and researchers conducting an experimental drug trial: her interest in health could be affected if she suffers side effects from taking drug, but her interest in improving her financial situation is served by her receiving $100 payment (see chapter 2, text accompanying nn.116–118). This also raises the issue of whether some consensual instances of exploitation might sometimes be acceptable or, at least, a more tolerable option where the alternative is worse. See further Sample 2003: 5 and 87; Wertheimer 2011: 148.
31 Consider, e.g. the approach taken by the health care team caring for the patient in *B v. An NHS Trust* [2002] EWHC 429 (Fam).
32 Sample 2003: 85.
33 Department of Health 2005: 4. See also chapter 5, part 2, n.47 and the text accompanying n.47 in part 1 of the same chapter.
34 See Matt Pearce, 'Johns Hopkins gynecologist with camera: Victims to get $190 million' *LA Times* (Los Angeles, 21 July 2014). See also Paterson Inquiry 2020: 28.

had been unable to see another gynaecologist since Levy's exploitation came to light: 'I can't bring myself to go back ... You're lying there, exposed. It's violating and it's horrible, and my trust is gone.'[35] Thus, experiences such as this can have far-reaching effects on the patient's future health and her future trust in the medical profession;[36] the trust relationship and '*network* of trust' with the profession has become 'morally rotten'.[37] For patients such as the one quoted here who have experienced exploitation at the hands of their doctors and the related severe breach of trust, the awareness of the impact of this, and the possibility of the same occurring, means that they may run the risk of the significant disadvantages that not seeking future medical treatment poses to their health.

As a further example, a doctor based in Detroit, Farid Fata, prescribed and administered unnecessary drugs and dangerous treatments to 553 patients for profit by submitting fraudulent claims to Medicare[38] and private medical insurance companies. In some cases, he made false diagnoses of cancer. His exploitation had serious implications for his patients' health; indeed, some may have died because of his interventions.[39] In one of the many victim impact statements, a patient of Fata commented that:

> I don't trust any doctor or medical professional, I doubt everything they say. When I start thinking about it I can't function, I become so anxious that I can't even go to work, and if I have a doctor's appointment for myself or my son I cancel it. I thought it would get better with time, but it hasn't. How am I supposed to go thru [sic] the rest of my life not trusting the medical profession?[40]

---

35 Ibid. See also Moriah Balingit, 'A gynecologist secretly photographed patients. What's their pain worth?' *Washington Post* (Washington DC, 14 January 2017).
36 Doctors such as Levy thus violate their 'fundamental *prima facie* moral imperative': Rhodes 2001: 495. 'As beneficiaries of their predecessors' trustworthiness and as those who create the reputation which the next generation of physicians will inherit, doctors also have the responsibility of acting to ensure that the profession of medicine will have its necessary trust.': Rhodes 2001: 495–496.
37 To use Baier's terminology: Baier 1986: 255 (emphasis in original). The commonality of this impact on patients' long-term trust in the medical profession is starkly demonstrated by the volume of statements from Ian Paterson's patients to this effect. See Paterson Inquiry 2020: 15, 19, 21, 23, 26, 28, 29, 31, 33, 34, 36, 37, 41, 42, 43, 45, 52, 60, 64, 76, 78, 81, 82, 84, 87, 94 and 96. On Paterson, see section 4.
38 The national social insurance programme in the United States, administered by the federal government.
39 US Department of Justice Press Release, 'Detroit-Area Doctor Sentenced to 45 Years in Prison for Providing Medically Unnecessary Chemotherapy to Patients' 10 July 2015, at https://www.justice.gov/opa/pr/detroit-area-doctor-sentenced-45-years-prison-providing-medically-unnecessary-chemotherapy accessed 22 July 2020. Dr Ian Paterson's provision of unnecessary and inappropriate surgery that he told patients was needed for cancer treatment and which may well have also led to some patient deaths, offers a somewhat similar UK-based example. See the text accompanying n.93; Paterson Inquiry 2020: 2; Dyer 2017a;
40 Justice Department 2015: 22.

Although some breaches of trust such as that perpetrated by Fata are stark, in other cases, the doctor and patient may have differing views as to what behaviour constitutes exploitation, and the related breach of trust, in the doctor-patient relationship. Doctors may use their patients but not *mis*use them, and might not themselves consider that they have breached the patient's trust by their actions. Yet the patient could feel differently.[41] Take the following question, posed by therapists Twemlow and Gabbard: 'are therapists justified in making use of their patients for their own education, for case studies published in scientific papers, and for clinical material to be used in didactic seminars'?[42] In pondering this, they refer to two patients who discovered that their cases featured in a scientific paper written by their therapist:

> Although neither reacted negatively at the time of the discovery, in reanalysis each expressed the feeling that he had been 'raped'... Whilst we are not suggesting that using a patient for a case report or for one's own education is tantamount to exploitation, we are noting that a subtle continuum exists in the area of deriving personal gratification from one's patients ... This continuum reminds us that the potential for exploitation of patients exists in all of us. It exists in activities that are generally considered professionally and ethically acceptable, and none of us can assume that he or she is immune to the temptation for exploitation.[43]

Did the therapist exploit the patients here? We address this question by considering whether, applying our account, exploitation has occurred. The therapist has taken advantage of (used) the patients by utilising their cases in the paper they wrote for their own research-related ends. But in order to wrongfully exploit the patients, the therapist must also have misused them. To reiterate, we argue that misuse occurs when the exploiter's treatment fails to respect the other party as a person; it could involve treating them in a demeaning way or not recognising the value of their life and the essence of their individuality. Let us assume that the therapist ensures that they have not breached the patients' confidentiality when presenting their cases. And unlike Feinberg's talented author who, we argued, uses the lonely hero purely as a means to her ends, there is nothing to suggest that the therapist has failed to respect the patients as persons, nor that they have not respected their autonomy, values and rights whilst treating them. However, the therapist has taken advantage of a vulnerability that the patients possess by taking advantage of their mental suffering. Even if, until the point of discovering that their cases feature in the publication, they have been successfully treated

---

41 For instance, in the particular context of sexual boundary breaches perpetrated by doctors, the Council for Healthcare Regulatory Excellence (CHRE) notes 'that individual patients may construe even activities identified as less serious as wholly abusive': Council for Healthcare Regulatory Excellence 2008b: 14.
42 Twemlow and Gabbard 1989: 72.
43 Ibid: 72.

by the therapist to the extent that they no longer require any mental health treatment, their previous vulnerability – their past suffering – has been taken advantage of.

There is also the question whether the patients had a reasonable expectation that their therapist would not feature their anonymised cases in a research publication without their consent. In other words, did they have a moral right to give consent to this, which the therapist has violated? One answer to this would be that the existence of moral right to consent in this context would depend upon whether the possible inclusion of the patient's case in future research publications is something that is normally flagged up by responsible therapists.[44] However, attempting to resolve the matter in such a way would appear to be at odds with the contemporary doctor-patient model that emphasises patient autonomy and the law on informed consent.[45] An alternative answer would be that the existence of a moral right to consent would depend upon whether the reasonable patient receiving mental health therapy would expect to be asked to consent to the inclusion of their anonymised case in a research publication.[46]

What is clear is that we cannot reach a conclusion here on the basis of philosophical analysis alone. For, as Wertheimer acknowledges, whether or not an interaction is exploitative 'is an *empirical* question' that 'will not be solved by philosophical discussion'.[47] However, a particular point that we seek to make is that the empirical question may be hard to answer too, because of the existence of differing perceptions of the therapist's behaviour.[48] We argue that the resolution to this question resides in the matter of trust. Because it is the patients who have reasonably placed their trust in their therapist with the equally reasonable expectation that this trust will not be breached, *they*, rather than the therapist, should have the discretion to decide 'what should count as failing to meet [their] trust'.[49] The fact remains that whether or not the doctor recognises his behaviour as exploitative, where patients perceive that there has been a breach of trust and betrayal by their doctor, this example of the therapist and the other real-life cases discussed in this section evidence the enormity of this for patients. In short, the impact that exploitation has upon damaging trust in the doctor-patient relationship cannot be underestimated.

---

44 Ethically, a 'responsible' therapist would meet the standards set in professional guidance such as the GMC's *Good Medical Practice* (General Medical Council 2013b). In the legal context, the parallel here would be the *Bolam* standard (*Bolam v. Friern Hospital Management Committee* [1957] 1 WLR 583).
45 *Montgomery v. Lanarkshire Health Board*.
46 As reflected more broadly in, e.g. the Court of Appeal judgment in *Pearce v. United Bristol Healthcare NHS Trust* [1999] PIQR 53.
47 Wertheimer 2007: 253 (emphasis in original).
48 To quote the novelist Margaret Atwood, 'There may not be one Truth — there may be several truths — but saying that is not to say that reality doesn't exist.': Marilyn Berlin Snell, 'Margaret Atwood' *Mother Jones* (July/August 1997), at https://www.motherjones.com/media/1997/07/margaret-atwood/ accessed 22 July 2020.
49 See generally Baier 1986: 238.

3) The doctor as a fiduciary

The connection between exploitation, the violation of the ethos of the doctor-patient relationship and breach of trust can be further illustrated by exploring the notion of the doctor as fiduciary. A popular dictionary definition of fiduciary is 'held or given in trust' and 'dependent on public trust'.[50] Because the doctor occupies 'a role to which specific social meanings and expectations attach', the doctor-patient relationship is one in which a 'thicker form of trust' arises.[51] As a legal concept, the term fiduciary is applied to relationships in which one party (the fiduciary) is entrusted with a power regarding the beneficiary's legal or practical interests. Where the law of equity recognises a relationship as a fiduciary one, this gives rise to fiducial obligations, limiting the fiduciary's power to act on the beneficiary's behalf 'exclusively for the other-regarding purposes for which it is held'.[52] We return to fiduciary law in chapter 5 in the specific context of doctors who sexually exploit their patients, and in our concluding chapter when we consider the appropriate way to deal with exploitation in the doctor-patient relationship at law. Here, however, we focus on the broader, non-legal construction of the doctor-patient relationship as fiduciary because of the doctor's professional responsibilities neither to breach the patient's trust, nor to act out of self-interest.

Some have argued that the conceptualisation of the doctor-patient relationship as fiduciary is a relic of the past, more paternalistic model of health care.[53] However, the paternalistic interpretation of what it means to be a fiduciary can be modified to better fit the contemporary model of health care without altering the fundamental prohibition that a fiduciary obligation contains: not to act out of self-interest.[54] The doctor personifies one of society's paradigm professionals. She acts for the good of her patients[55] (and under the contemporary model of health care this involves respecting their autonomy and values), and is trusted by both society and her patients to be dedicated to her role and to perform that role professionally,[56] notwithstanding her monetary reward gain. Unlike in the context of personal relationships, patients are generally lacking in any knowledge of doctors' characters and thus rely on doctors' membership of the profession in order to have the necessary faith to place their trust in them:

---

50   Elliott 1997.
51   Harding 2013: 84.
52   Fox-Decent and Criddle 2009: 312.
53   See, e.g. Wang 2016: 7–8.
54   Flannigan 2004: 52.
55   See also Rhodes 2001: 495.
56   Moline 1986. Gill and others 2012: 2

> As a patient is typically not familiar with her doctor's personal moral values, trust in her doctor's goodwill requires trust that the doctor possesses 'moral competence' and is motivated to adopt the ethical standards of the medical profession ...[57]

There is both a societal and individual expectation that patients receive 'professional medical care free of exploitation for the physician's private purposes'.[58] This is why public reaction is so strong when scandals involving medical professionals who fail to act in accordance with this expectation emerge.[59]

Whilst there has been a change in emphasis in professional practice from acting paternalistically in the patient's best interests to respecting her rights, autonomy and values,[60] in our view, trust and the obligation not to act out of self-interest remain integral to the doctor-patient relationship. We dispute Wang's contention that the contemporary move towards a more contractual model of health care has caused trust to be abandoned due to decision-making responsibility being removed from the doctor to the patient. He claims that:

> the underlying message of the contract is that the doctor cannot be trusted, and that the patient must trust himself only. At the same time, the doctor is discouraged from going the extra mile for his patient. Each party in this model is more keen to fulfil his end of the contract rather than building a relationship of trust. Hence, trust and good-faith are no longer required in the doctor–patient relationship.[61]

In contrast, we argue that trust remains vital in order for patient and doctor to engage in the exchange of ideas necessary to ensure the patient's role as the autonomous decision maker within today's shared decision-making model of

---

57   Rogers and Ballantyne 2008: 57. Interestingly, a UK-based study involving members of the general public suggests that participants did not wish to know about their doctors' personal lives: 'it was felt to assist in maintaining trust in doctors for patients to know nothing about their personal life and for professional boundaries to be maintained. That is to say, participants did not feel patients would like to know if a doctor is experiencing challenges or difficulties as this may undermine how confident they felt about their medical judgement.' Gill and others 2012: 14.
58   *Norberg* v. *Wynrib* [1992] 2 SCR 226 [74] (McLachlin J).
59   It was the public reaction to the Shipman case that led to the decision to make the intended privately held inquiry a public one. See Hutter and Lloyd-Bostock 2017: 125. Hall has drawn attention to the way in which the public reaction to breaches of trust by doctors can be 'overly punitive' because an emotional connection is experienced; the public feels 'a strong empathetic sense of betrayal': Hall 2005: 160.
60   See, e.g. O'Neil 2002: 17
61   Wang 2016: 8. Note also O'Neill's view that 'the older personal, trust-based model of doctor-patient relationships seems increasingly obsolete' because the patient's relationship is with 'complex organisations staffed by many professionals' and the professional relationship is 'constrained, formalised and regulated in many ways': O'Neill 2002: 39.

the doctor-patient relationship.[62] The information that the doctor shares with the patient is technical and medical, whereas the patient's information concerns her preferences, values, life situation and plans.[63] Indeed, Dyer and Bloch have argued that, as applied to doctors and their patients, the fiduciary principle is one of partnership[64]: 'in medicine the doctor decides with the patient, a process dependent on the development of the latter's trust. Although the fiduciary principle in medicine is a two-way street, requiring mutual trust, it particularly calls on the doctor to be trustworthy.'[65] Trustworthiness is a virtue that we expect the medical professional and profession to possess; it is essential to upholding the profession's reputation.[66] And, as we explored in the previous section, trust continues to be the essential premise on which the patient's relationship with her doctor operates. When she approaches the doctor for medical advice/treatment, she trusts that the doctor will put her autonomy values and interests first. Just as was the case under the previous paternalistic model, the patient enters into the relationship on the basis that the doctor will not act out of self-interest, and this leaves her exposed: 'trusting involves granting discretionary powers and makes the [patient] vulnerable to the [doctor]'.[67] Placing trust in their doctor's duty of loyalty can thus give rise to a vulnerability shared in common with other patients. As we see it, exploitation in the doctor-patient relationship occurs where the doctor ignores the societal and ethical requirements of her fiducial role, allowing a conflict between her duty of loyalty to the patient and her own self-interest to occur. In other words, this breach of the fiduciary relationship is part and parcel of the doctor's wrongful exploitation.[68]

4) The inequality of power between doctor and patient and the opportunity to exploit numerous patients

Although something of a truism, we return here to Goodin's point, as noted in the previous chapter, that 'occasions for exploitation arise when one party

---

62 See also Ost 2016: 231 and Gill and others 2012: 2. On the shared decision-making model, see Smith and Newton 1984 and Kon 2010. See O'Neil 2002 for an engaging account of the way in which versions of more individualised approaches to autonomy can undermine trust. On the high level of trust that the public continues to have in GPs, see Lacobucci 2018b.
63 Charles and others 1999.
64 See also General Medical Council 2013b: 16[49]: 'you must work in partnership with patients, sharing with them the information they will need to make decisions about their care'.
65 Dyer and Bloch 1987: 15.
66 Beauchamp and Childress 2013: 39–40. And beyond the micro-level doctor-patient relationship, the public's trust in the medical profession also requires faith in the General Medical Council's regulation of the profession. The findings of the fifth report of the Shipman Inquiry strongly suggested that this faith was misplaced at that time. See Smith 2004; Irvine 2005.
67 Rogers and Ballantyne 2008: 48.
68 See also Tan 1997: 252.

is in an especially strong position vis-à-vis another'.[69] In the doctor-patient relationship, the doctor's authority,[70] her power, emanates from two different sources. First, this power is Aesculapian[71] and impersonal, stemming from her as an individual medical professional because of the knowledge and expertise she possesses.[72] Indeed, this is why the patient is involved in his relationship with his doctor: 'the patient has to believe in the physician ... Intrinsic to such a belief is the patient's conviction that his physician not only can be trusted but also has some special knowledge that that patient does not possess. He needs... a physician whom he invests with authoritative experience and competence.'[73] This Aesculapian power has been diffused somewhat by the patient-centred and autonomy-led contemporary model of the doctor-patient relationship, in which the patient is the ultimate decision maker. That is, the patient (with capacity) is the more powerful one in the relationship when it comes to decision-making concerning whether to take the available treatment or have the surgery that the doctor suggests.[74] But it is still the doctor who possesses the special medical knowledge and expertise and advises the patient. The doctor generally influences the patient's understanding of the condition and available treatments and their success rates,[75] notwithstanding the access to medical information, diagnoses and medical treatment products now available to the patient online (which we discuss further below).

---

69 Goodin 1987: 167.
70 For an account of the nature of authority in professional relationships such as the doctor-patient relationship, see Schneebaum 2015: 367–374. On her account, 'the categorization of doctor-patient relations as authority relations makes sense to anyone who has been party to such relations and has experienced their hierarchical nature': Schneebaum 2015: 376.
71 A term that we borrow from Brody 1992.
72 And this connects to the type of trust that the patient vests in the doctor: deferential trust. See Flannigan 1989: 286: 'this kind of trust may be created over time or may arise immediately because of the knowledge, expertise or office occupied by the trusted person. It is a "deferential" kind of trust in the sense that the trusting person will defer to the judgement of the trusted person.'
73 Ingelfinger 1980: 1509. See also Goodyear-Smith and Buetow 2001: 452: 'doctors need specialist knowledge and power to be their patients' advocates. Patients are unlikely to choose a doctor whom they perceive or know to be powerless'.
74 And see Goodyear-Smith and Buetow 2001: 451.
75 Rates which can, of course, be presented in misleading way. Whilst a critique aimed at some private sector clinics rather than doctors at such clinics specifically, in 2019, the Chairwoman of the Human Fertilisation and Embryology Authority stated that 'some of the private sector clinics use very selective success rates in their sales tactics' in order to persuade women in their forties to undergo fertility treatment. See Laura Donnelly, 'Older women being exploited by IVF clinics – when just two a year will achieve success rate after the age of 44' *The Telegraph* (London, 21 April 2019).

Secondly, the doctor's power is also institutionalised, stemming from his or her membership of a particularly influential profession.[76] Since the mid-nineteenth century, the medical profession has been one of the most eminent professions.[77] Whilst the *dominance* of the medical profession has diminished over recent decades, it remains true that 'there is, as yet, little evidence of a marked decline in the power of medical authority'.[78] Indeed, the profession's influence has arguably increased further since the latter part of the last century because of the phenomenon of increased medicalisation (the 'process by which nonmedical problems become defined and treated as medical problems'[79]) in public policy and popular thinking.[80] As Hesketh puts it:

> patients acknowledge (albeit sometimes subconsciously) the underpinning structural assumption that doctors, as a profession, have a certain monopoly on, for example, the categorisation of illness, its diagnosis and often (but not always) the treatment of illness, prescription of drugs, etc. In other words, although the patient might decide ... to decline the doctor's advice or to refuse treatment, the patient (and doctor) must accept that the doctor's power is institutionalised. This amounts to a situation where the doctor as an individual might share power with the patient as an individual, but as a member of a profession that is a key player in a healthcare system ... the doctor's role has power.[81]

This dual basis for the doctor's power – Aesculapian and institutionalised – separates the relationship between doctor and patient from other intimate and confidential professional relationships such as that between lawyer and client, and priest and parishioner. We contend that neither of these professions possesses the level of power that the medical profession does. The legal institution may wield power in the courtroom, but not to the monopolistic degree that the medical profession does over our everyday lives regarding our health and health care. Although, for example, a client accused of a criminal offence is likely to be highly dependent on his lawyer, not all clients experience and are affected by

---

76 What Brody refers to as 'social power': Brody 1992: 17. We use the construct of institutionalised power rather than Brody's construct of social power, which he sees as stemming from the doctor's high status in society (Brody 1992 and see also Schneebaum 2015: 368), since this high status can be held by other professionals, such as university Vice Chancellors, for instance. Our preferred construct of institutionalised power draws attention to the particular influential professional institution that a doctor is part of, on which we say more shortly. In addition, Brody also refers to charismatic power which emerges from the doctor's personal characteristics, such as firmness and kindness. We have chosen not to include this element of power here since, as with all individuals, this will vary from doctor to doctor depending upon their individual characters.
77 Kelleher and others 2006: xiv.
78 Wiles and Higgins 1996: 342.
79 Conrad 2007: 4. See also Ost 2010: 499–500.
80 Lowenberg and Davis 1994: 582.
81 Hesketh 2011: 56.

the legal process, and not all legal advice is as crucial as advice regarding health and heath care. And, notwithstanding the presence of high clergypersons in the House of Lords, the Church's institutional ecclesiastical power within society continues to wane.

The inequality in power between doctor and patient remains, even though more and more patients may be taking advantage of care offered through 'collaborative health' rather than relying solely on health care provided by the more traditional conceptual framework involving the doctor-patient relationship.[82] The availability of collaborative health care means that patients are now able to receive health care advice and treatment, monitor their own health, share their experiences of symptoms with others, join self-help groups,[83] and take part in research projects via online health care services and platforms such as Babylon, PatientsLikeMe and 23andMe.[84] Millenson sees this as having an impact on the medical profession's power and control:

> Collaborative health describes a shifting constellation of collaborations for sickness care and for maintaining wellbeing that is shaped by people based on their life circumstances. The result is ... a transfer of power in which the traditional system loses some of its control. That system will often be a part of wellbeing and care relationships ... but other times (and not by choice) it will be excluded.[85]

Yet, whilst advances in technology and the emergence of alternative organisations and services related to health have meant that patients can gain a certain level of knowledge regarding their medical conditions and health, this knowledge may not always be accurate, well understood or interpreted, or emanate from a reliable online source. And although patients might not always need to be dependent upon their doctors for their health care now, and the organisation of the NHS has given rise to a 'reconfiguration of professional power',[86] it is still by and large the medical profession that the patient relies upon when ill. It is through their doctor that they are provided with access (*free* NHS access in the UK) to health care and treatment, such as required surgery.[87] Moreover, their doctor is the gatekeeper who possesses the procedural and policy knowledge in relation to the particular local Clinical Commissioning Group's (CCG) NHS treatment rationing decisions, for instance.[88]

---

82 Millenson 2017.
83 See Kelleher 2006.
84 https://www.babylonhealth.com; https://www.patientslikeme.com; https://www.23andme.com/en-gb; all accessed 9 April 2020;
85 Millenson 2017: 358.
86 Kelleher and others 2006: xxix.
87 See also Lazarus 1988: 45.
88 Hesketh 2011: 60. On rationing in the NHS, see Butler 1999; Robertson and others 2017; Witting 2001.

The existence of this dually based power can be exploited by a doctor who fails to act in accordance with her fiduciary duties. And the existence of this imbalance of power in each relationship that a doctor has with her patients, coupled with the elements of trust and reliance, means that patients can be misused on multiple occasions. For instance, Levy's access to patients' bodies as a gynaecologist enabled him to exploit enough patients to create more than 1,200 explicit video clips and images.[89] And whilst convicted for the murder of 15 patients, reports estimate that the actual number of patients whom Harold Shipman exploited and murdered was between 215 and 260.[90] In the words of Dame Janet Smith, Chair of the Shipman Inquiry, 'Shipman was trusted implicitly by his patients and their families. He betrayed their trust in a way and to an extent that I believe is unparalleled in history.'[91] He was able to perpetrate exploitation at this level, in large part, because he selected vulnerable, older patients and was trusted by these patients to the extent that he visited them alone in their homes, with the result that his exploitation and criminal responsibility for their deaths was harder to discover.[92] Similarly, Ian Paterson employed exploitation on a grand scale when he provided approximately 500 NHS and private patients with unnecessary surgery which he advised them was needed as part of their treatment for cancer. His professional position meant that his exploitative actions could be masked as reasonable and appropriate medical treatment.[93] One of his victims commented that '[Paterson] used the respectability and cloak of professionalism that came with being a consultant breast cancer surgeon to commit grotesque violent acts against me and the other victims'.[94] Albeit on a smaller scale, another doctor, Robert Trossel, offered stem cell therapy treatment to nine patients with multiple sclerosis, treatments which were held to be

---

89 See n.34. It is apparently impossible to know exactly how many patients Levy exploited because the images he recorded frequently focused solely on patients' genitals, but more than 8,000 women have been identified as potential victims.
90 Smith 2002: 179.
91 Ibid: 201.
92 See further ibid: 182, 189; Rogers and Ballantyne 2008: 54–56. He was also able to perpetrate murder on such a mass scale because of 'systems failures' and weaknesses in the (then) professional regulations: Smith 2002: 200–201; Smith 2004.
93 Paterson Inquiry 2020. And see generally Baier 1986: 239.
94 Dyer 2017a. Another instance of a doctor providing experimental treatments without informed consent is that of consultant maxillofacial surgeon, Roger Bainton: see Dyer 2017b. For an earlier case involving a dentist who provided unnecessary, painful treatments to patients, see *Appleton* v. *Garrett* [1996] PIQR P1. A further example is GP Manish Shah's conviction for the sexual assaults upon more than 20 patients between 2009 and 2013. He was able to commit these acts by advising that patients had regular breast and vaginal examinations when these were not clinically needed (see Metropolitan Police, 'Disgraced former family doctor jailed for multiple sexual assaults', 7 February 2020, at http://news.met.police.uk/news/disgraced-former-family-doctor-jailed-for-multiple-sexual-assaults-393870 accessed 9 April 2020).

'unjustifiable' on the basis of medical evidence and inappropriate by the GMC's Fitness to Practise Panel.[95] Although the stem cells were not designed for human use and Trossel exaggerated the benefits of the treatment, it seems that he genuinely believed that the treatment would be in their medical interests. He was found to have failed to fully inform patients and to have abused his position as a doctor by the panel. As a final example, there have been increasing reports that infertility doctors in various countries have used their own sperm in their patients' artificial insemination treatment following the use of consumer DNA tests.[96] One prominent case in the Netherlands involved the now deceased Dr Jan Karbatt who owned a fertility clinic in Rotterdam. DNA results have established that, whilst his patients were advised their artificial insemination involved the use of sperm from donors, Karbatt fathered at least 49 children.[97]

The opportunity to engage in numerous instances of exploitation is undoubtedly augmented because patients are disempowered by the circumstances within which they find themselves. Whilst vulnerability is an issue which we focus on in the next chapter, it is important here to highlight the way in which their ill-health can constitute a common situational vulnerability to exploitation that makes patients easier to exploit and reinforces the imbalance of power.[98] Unconsciousness, feeling too weak to resist (physically and/or mentally), being in a confused state or state of anxiety, perceiving a benefit or possible benefit if they do as their doctor requests because it might improve their health, are all factors that can play a role in exacerbating patients' vulnerability to exploitation by the more powerful party in the relationship. And certain conditions can give rise to particular fears and concerns that can be taken advantage of. For instance, in sentencing Ian Paterson for seventeen counts of wounding with intent to cause grievous bodily harm and three counts of unlawful wounding, Baker J emphasised that he had 'deliberately preyed on their worst fears, either by inventing or

---

95 Press Association, 'Doctor may be struck off for exploiting "desperate" MS patients' *The Guardian* (London, 10 September 2010); Dyer 2010. The GMC is the principal medical regulator in the UK, a statutory body recognised under the Medical Act 1983. Since 2012, disciplinary proceedings against doctors have been heard by, and sanctioning powers bestowed upon, the Medical Practitioners Tribunal Service (MPTS). The MPTS exists independently within the GMC.
96 See Jacqueline Mroz, 'Their Mothers Chose Donor Sperm. Their Doctors Used their Own' *New York Times* (New York, 21 August 2019), at https://www.nytimes.com/2019/08/21/health/sperm-donors-fraud-doctors.html accessed 20 November 2019.
97 Agence France-Presse in The Hague, 'Dutch fertility doctor "secretly fathered at least 49 children"' *The Guardian* (London, 12 April 2019).
98 Ill-health or feared ill-health causes the power imbalance to be maintained even where there appears to be, on the face of it, a more equally balanced power relationship between doctor and patient: 'Even if we [as patients] are physicians … ourselves, our capacity for objectivity is compromised when we are ill … We have to choose between our own judgment and that of someone we trust to have knowledge and a commitment to our well-being.' Pellegrino and Thomasma 1993: 69.

66 *Exploitation, doctors and patients*

deliberately exaggerating the risk that they would develop cancer'.[99] In sum, all the cases of exploitation that we have discussed in this chapter, real and fictional, illustrate how the inequality in the doctor-patient relationship can be utilised by the doctor to take advantage of any susceptibility that the patient's possesses and achieve his own ends.

5) The nature of the doctor-patient relationship in a publicly funded health care system and in private health care[100]

The clinical setting is not merely a backdrop for interactions but is an integral part of the doctor-patient relationship, helping to determine how people act and how much power the physician sustains.[101]

i) The relationship in publicly funded health care

Being in a publicly funded health care system such as the UK's NHS has the major benefit of access to 'free'[102] health care.[103] Moreover, the move to a more consumerist NHS model in more recent years[104] has led to the bestowal of patient rights via the NHS Constitution,[105] and wider patient choice as to treatment providers and care services[106] (at least in theory).[107] This could lead us to contemplate whether, in the UK at least, public and private health care models increasingly bear more similarities, so that the relationship with his doctor that the patient experiences is little affected by the system that it exists within.

---

99 Dyer 2017a.
100 Our particular focus in this section is the UK's NHS.
101 Lazarus 1988: 49.
102 'Free' because in a system such as the NHS, a proportion of the tax and National Insurance contributions that citizens pay to the government funds the health care system.
103 One of the three core founding principles of the NHS is that access to services should be based on clinical need, not an individual's ability to pay. See Principle 2 in the NHS Constitution for England: Department of Health and Social Care 2015.
104 In *Montgomery* v. *Lanarkshire Health Board*, Lords Kerr and Reid noted that patients are now 'widely treated as consumers exercising choices' ([75]). See also Veitch 2019; Guy 2019.
105 Department of Health and Social Care 2015.
106 See http://www.nhs.uk/conditions/social-care-and-support-guide/Pages/choosing-care-services.aspx accessed 20 November 2019. Interestingly, for Veitch, this also means that NHS patients have an *obligation* to act as consumers: Veitch 2019: 14.
107 According to a survey conducted for NHS England in 2014, less than 40 per cent of patients said that they were given a choice of hospital by their GP on being referred for an outpatient appointment: NHS England, 'Survey reveals more needs to be done on choice for patients' 7 August 2014, at https://www.england.nhs.uk/2014/08/choice-for-patients/ accessed 20 November 2019. And, of course, much will depend on the patient's location regarding the availability of alternative treatment providers.

However, notable differences between patient experiences of health care in each system remain.

Focusing first upon the NHS, numerous tensions and strains are placed on the doctor-patient relationship by limited resources, funding cuts,[108] the service's organisation and the way in which the health care it funds is delivered (with an increasing move towards privatisation and marketisation).[109] There is an inevitable negative impact on patients' perceptions when cost-cutting is a key concern in the delivery of health care: 'the level of trust between the two parties is corrupted when physicians are required to incorporate economic factors into their medical advice.'[110]

Whether or not patients actually receive particular treatments can be dependent upon both the budgeting priorities and rationing decisions of their CCG[111] and National Institute for Health and Care Excellence (NICE) recommendations as to what treatment should be available on the NHS.[112] This has been evidenced by NICE's decision not to recommend an immunotherapy drug that has been shown to extend the lives of patients with advanced head and neck cancer (who have a survival expectancy of around six months) by an extra three months, because the drug is considered too expensive.[113] Doctors, general practitioners (GPs) in particular, are thus the gatekeepers. Whilst they can recommend treatments, advise patients and refer them to treatment providers, decisions regarding the availability of treatment are largely out of their hands. The managerial[114] and clinical governance constraints that such factors place on doctors' ability to perform their role effectively in their relationships with patients are likely to be a cause of frustration for both patients and doctors alike.[115]

---

108 Robertson and others 2017; Youseff El-Gingihy, 'How the "humanitarian" crisis in the NHS is paving the way for private healthcare' *The Independent* (London, 12 January 2017). The COVID-19 pandemic's impact on resources is also significant.
109 See Veitch 2019 and chapter 7, n.11. Privatisation ('the expansion of private sector delivery of NHS services from the early 2000s onwards': Guy 2019: 480) has increased since the early 2000s and the Health and Social Care Act 2012 is framed around a market regulation-based approach. See Guy 2019. See House of Lords Select Committee on the Long-Term Sustainability of the NHS 2017: 28–29, for criticism of the market regulation approach in the 2012 Act.
110 Garzino 1997: 563.
111 Or, indeed, whether they receive *any* treatment: see Iacobucci 2019.
112 All CCGs are legally obliged to fund medicines and treatments recommended through NICE's technology appraisals.
113 Sarah Boseley, '"Gamechanging" cancer drug rejected for use on NHS' *The Guardian* (London, 11 April 2017). As a further example, after NICE rejected a drug for treating cystic fibrosis in 2016 because it was not cost effective, it was finally made available for NHS patients at the end of 2019 following three years of negotiation to reach an agreement with the manufacturer to provide the drug at an affordable price to NHS England. See Lizzie Roberts, 'Cystic fibrosis "wonder drug" to be provided on the NHS after 3 year fight' *The Telegraph* (London, 24 October 2019).
114 On which, see Hunter 2006.
115 See, e.g. the depiction in Kay 2018.

68   *Exploitation, doctors and patients*

Limited resources and staffing shortages mean that NHS patients often face waiting times and delays in receiving treatment.[116] Whilst there has been a target of 92 per cent of patients receiving treatment within 18 weeks of referral since 2008,[117] for hip or knee replacements and other non-urgent operations, the number of cases where this target was not met rose by 100,000 between 2016 and 2017.[118] In 2017, it was announced that the NHS was 'significantly relaxing' this required target.[119] In the wake of increasing cuts to NHS budgets, a report has revealed that there has been a 15 to 25 per cent annual rise in uninsured patients paying for private treatment and 'there's no doubt that NHS waiting lists are at the heart of this growth in self-pay'.[120] Another report revealed that 61 per cent of the private patients in one study cited the avoidance of NHS waiting lists as an important factor in their decision to turn to the private sector.[121] Moreover, working in a publicly funded communitarian health care system experiencing financial and staffing strains, such as the NHS, creates what may be an inevitable tension between the doctor's duty to the individual patient and her duty to the system. The length of time that a doctor can spend with each patient is necessarily limited and patients' experiences of their relationships with their doctors can be negatively affected because of concerns about other patients' needs, which prevent some patients from asking too many questions and taking up too much of their doctors' time.[122]

The need to account for resources can also place strains on doctors' relationships with their patients. As noted by Dorr Goold and Lipkin 'the use of the primary care clinician to coordinate ... access to other services involves the primary care clinician in accountability for resource use as well as for care of individual patients'.[123] The potential conflict this may cause is well illustrated by a prescribing incentive scheme rolled out by Oxfordshire CCG in 2017. GP practices were offered half of the savings achieved if GPs reduced the amount of drugs being prescribed to patients in care homes 'as encouragement and reward to improve the quality, safety and cost effectiveness of prescribing', according

---

116 Although beyond the scope of this book, we note that due to the staff shortages we refer to here, NHS Improvement (a body that oversees NHS foundation trusts, NHS trusts and independent care providers providing NHS funded-care) has alleged that locum medical professionals are exploiting the NHS. See Anon, 'Locum doctors make up to £43,000 a month from NHS "bidding war"' *The Week* (London, 22 March 2017), at http://www.theweek.co.uk/82827/locum-doctors-make-up-to-43000-a-month-from-nhs-bidding-war accessed 20 November 2019.
117 Department of Health 2004b: 6.
118 Denis Campbell, 'NHS "waving white flag" as it axes 18-week waiting time operation target' *The Guardian* (London, 31 March 2017).
119 Ibid.
120 Denis Campbell, 'NHS waiting times "driving people to turn to private treatment"' *The Guardian* (London, 11 September 2017).
121 Wiles and Higgins 1996: 345.
122 Ibid: 346.
123 Dorr Goold and Lipkin 1999: S27. See also Chisholm and others 2006: 68–70.

to the CCG.¹²⁴ GPs were asked to consider whether they could improve the effectiveness of prescribing without compromising the quality of patient care. If GPs within those practices that signed up to the scheme frame their assessments around prescribing to ensure appropriate patient care, then this should not prevent the needs of the particular patient being served. But if the starting point is to achieve cost savings, this places the financial benefits to the NHS CCG (along with the extra funds that practices would receive) above the needs of individual patients, thereby interfering with doctors' fiduciary duty to act for the good of their patients.

Because of the way in which NHS-funded treatment and care is delivered (the NHS's internal market),¹²⁵ the doctor's ability to recommend where the patient should go for NHS-funded treatment and incentives that doctors may be offered for selecting a particular provider could also affect the dynamics of the doctor-patient relationship. It is concerning that, in 2015, evidence was given to the Parliamentary Health Committee that doctors were receiving fees from private health care providers for sending patients to private hospitals for NHS-funded treatment.¹²⁶ The allegations followed an investigation into the private health care market by the Competition and Markets Authority (CMA). The CMA reported in 2014 that there were 'certain benefits and incentive schemes provided by private hospital operators which reward (directly or indirectly) referring clinicians for treating patients at, or commissioning tests from, their private healthcare facilities'.¹²⁷ This caused there to be a 'distortion of referral decisions to their private healthcare facilities and distort[ed] patient choice of diagnosis and treatment options'.¹²⁸

As we see it, taking such fees can encourage patient exploitation because doctors are incentivised to refer patients on the basis of self-gain rather than putting their patients' interests, autonomy and values first. Misuse (a necessary requirement on our account of exploitation) could consequently occur, with the doctor taking advantage of the patient's potential vulnerability, their ill-health, and thereby failing to respect the patient as a person. Moreover, we contend that patients would be wronged if doctors breach their moral right to autonomy by failing to inform them when recommending a private health care provider that they will receive a fee upon referral.¹²⁹

---

124 Sally Nash, 'GPs to keep savings under £1.4m scheme to slash care home prescribing' *Pulse* (London, 31 May 2017), at http://www.pulsetoday.co.uk/clinical/prescribing/gps-to-keep-savings-under-14m-scheme-to-slash-care-home-prescribing/20034434. article accessed 20 November 2019.
125 For critical analysis of this, see El-Gingihy 2015; Veitch 2019.
126 Andy Lines, 'NHS doctors taking bribes from private healthcare firms and hospitals, leading medic reveals' *Mirror* (London, 10 February 2015).
127 Competition and Markets Authority 2014: 2[8].
128 Ibid: 2[8].
129 The issue of doctors profiting from the doctor-patient relationship is addressed by GMC guidance: General Medical Council 2013a: 24[78]. Arguably, however, not enough is being done to uphold this guidance, as we discuss in chapter 7, section 3.

After the CMA investigation's findings were published, the CMA made an Order which, since 2019, has placed a duty upon consultants to provide fee information to the Private Healthcare Information Network (PHIN) and requires PHIN to publish fees information on its website.[130] The Order requires consultants to provide letters to patients prior to consultations setting out, inter alia, potential conflicts of interest,[131] but this duty is only stated in respect of *private* patients. No reference is made to doctors' referral of NHS patients to private hospitals.[132] Broader ethical concerns regarding doctors receiving payment for treating patients might exist no matter how the doctor is paid. According to Dorr Goold and Lipkin, payment can 'represent a conflict of interests for physicians and violate the fiduciary nature of the relationship. All mechanisms for paying physicians, including fee-for-service reimbursement, create financial incentives to practice medicine in certain ways.'[133] Thus, on the issue of payments, concerns regarding the effects on the doctor-patient relationship are not necessarily limited to the private health care context, although the commercial nature of this relationship in that context may raise particular issues that we consider in the following subsection.

Earlier, we presented trust as an integral part of the doctor-patient relationship. Our exploration of this would be incomplete if we considered trust in the doctor-patient relationship in isolation from the health care system that the relationship is operating within. The broader setting of health care has implications for the patient's trust, which could exist at both the micro (interpersonal) and macro (institutional and system) levels: a patient might 'trust a doctor but distrust the underlying system. Moreover, patients can mistrust a doctor working in a trustworthy system.'[134] Conversely, in contemporary models of publicly funded health care, within which patients are less likely to see their named GP when making an appointment, patients who are familiar with and trust in the values underpinning the NHS may make assumptions that they can place their trust in an unknown, perhaps locum, GP.[135] Indeed, a patient who does not have the financial means to receive anything other than publicly funded health care may feel that their only option is to place their trust in both doctor and system, even if they are aware of actual or potential failings within that system. Individuals constrained by the wider social structure still need

---

130 Competition and Markets Authority 2017: 2(10).
131 From 31 December 2017.
132 For reference to the duty upon NHS organisations to hold a register which includes declarations of doctors' private practice, see chapter 7, section 3.
133 Dorr Goold and Lipkin 1999: S27. At a more macro level, consider the fees received by doctors who are involved in assessing whether drugs should be offered on the NHS: Edward Malnick, 'Individual NHS doctors receiving £100,000 per year from drugs firms' *The Telegraph* (London, 13 June 2016).
134 Ward and others 2015: 299.
135 See also ibid: 300, 302; Hall 2005: 162.

and wish to receive medical care.[136] Researchers in a study conducted in South Australia found that the participants who received publicly funded health care 'articulated a kind of "forced or resigned trust" in the doctors ... and were willing to accept and sometime[s] excuse or justify the "problems" of the system in order to maintain their trust'.[137]

Trust is also challenged by recent and ongoing reforms in the management of the NHS, one of the most notable being the government's push for more integrated provision across service sectors in England, with the plan having been to achieve integrated health and social care by 2020.[138] Such integrated delivery places further responsibilities on doctors, such as information sharing: 'with integration come[s] new responsibilities for doctors and other health care practitioners for communication, teamwork, and a more longitudinal approach to patient care'.[139] As a consequence of this, the patient's trust needs to be placed not only in medical professionals and the NHS, but in other professionals and systems too. Moreover, this shift in the provision of care increases the risk that continuity of care takes second place to efficiency in delivery. Continuity of care has obvious advantages for the doctor-patient relationship in that it 'encourages trust, provides an opportunity for patients and providers to know each other as persons and provides a foundation for making decisions with a particular individual'.[140] In explaining his experience of health care, Hoff has lamented that:

> I am never able to see my 'regular' primary care doctor, and every access point into the system is barricaded by a maze of phone systems, complex directions for how to seek out care, and poorly paid and motivated staff. The 'convenience' I get is often a superficial and incomplete service or product that is only good for the most basic of my health care needs. In the meantime, I am told repeatedly how much the quality of my 'experience' matters to insurance plans, medical offices, and hospitals, even as that experience involves bonding with or even seeing a given doctor less and less.[141]

---

136 A point highlighted by Lazarus 1988: 47.
137 Ward and others 2015: 297.
138 The ambitions behind this plan included improving joint working and reducing costs by, e.g. reducing acute hospital activity. A National Audit Office report released in 2017 found that, at that point, the Better Care Fund (the principal integration initiative) had not achieved the expected savings, better outcomes for patients or reduction in hospital activity, and the achieved target time of 2020 was at 'significant risk': National Audit Office 2017. However, the final 13 integrated care systems in England were rolled out in April 2021: see Anon, 'NHS achieves key Long Term Plan commitment to roll out integrated care systems across England' (19 March 2020), at https://www.england.nhs.uk/2021/03/nhs-achieves-key-long-term-plan-commitment-to-roll-out-integrated-care-systems-across-england/ accessed 2 April 2021.
139 Dorr Goold and Lipkin 1999: S28.
140 Ibid: S29. See also Nicola Davis, 'Keeping the same doctor reduces death risk, study finds' *The Guardian* (London, 29 June 2018).
141 Hoff 2017.

The end result of such reforms to the management and organisation of publicly funded health care can be that the 'medical record, not the doctor'[142] becomes the main link between the patient and health care. In this milieu, very little space is available for the doctor-patient relationship to develop and be nurtured. On the one hand, this may make it harder for NHS doctors to exploit their patients because the element of trust generated by a long-term relationship that can be effectively taken advantage of is absent.[143] On the other hand, more joined-up care could make it harder for doctors to conceal any exploitative behaviour. Yet the patient continues to be reliant upon the doctor and in a state of ill-health; the inequality of power between them, and the need for trust, remains. Even in the current shape that publicly funded health care in the UK is in, 'given the intensity of the need for trust and a patient's helpless dependency on a physician's skill and judgment when suffering from a serious illness',[144] the doctor-patient relationship is pivotal to the patient's experience of health care and treatment. There may thus be some reassurance to be had from Veitch's conclusion that, notwithstanding the shift from its original vision to more neoliberal policies, the NHS:

> continues to assert the principle of access to healthcare free at the point of need and to implement this in practice, insofar as it is possible to do so; and its professionals continue to characterise themselves as public servants devoted to their patients.[145]

ii) *The relationship in private health care*

It seems a logical assumption that having the financial means to select one's health care provider on the basis of reputation and quality of care places the private patient in a more secure position than the recipient of publicly funded health care.[146] And if something goes wrong due to a breach of duty or the doctor unduly influences her, for instance, she will be able to seek redress through remedies under the law of contract that would be unavailable to the patient receiving publicly funded health care.[147]

Rightly or wrongly, the expectation is that private patients will receive a higher quality of service and a better doctor-patient relationship experience. The aforementioned case of Ian Paterson reveals that such an expectation is not always well placed, for his exploitation was perpetrated against patients

---

142 Lazarus 1988: 48.
143 Although we are not suggesting here that any absence of, or reduction in the level of, patient trust as a result of 'managed' health care is a good thing in itself. See generally Hall 2005.
144 Hall 2005: 165.
145 Veitch 2019: 294.
146 See also Wiles and Higgins 1996: 343.
147 We discuss how the law of contract can deal with exploitation in section 8.

in both publicly funded and private health care.[148] This case has also highlighted failings in both the monitoring by, and governance of, independent care providers.[149] However, the majority of private patients in a UK-based study reported experiencing an enhanced relationship of mutuality with their doctors.[150] According to research from Australia, private patients treated in public hospitals were indeed treated differently than public patients treated in the same hospitals, experiencing a third less waiting days and being admitted for treatment with higher urgency. They were also provided with more medical and diagnostic procedures during hospitalisation.[151] In the UK-based study, Wiles and Higgins found that one of the factors motivating patients to opt for private health care was greater access to medical professionals. This also played a role in patient satisfaction levels following private treatment, with some patients who had been under the care of the same doctor in both NHS and private health care noting that the doctor had more time for them in the private sector.[152] What is more, research has evidenced a perception amongst private patients that competition in the private sector leads to better quality of care. Since the doctor's reputation influences private patients' choices about who to be treated by,[153] and thus doctors who maintain a strong reputation are more likely to receive private patients, the self-interests of doctors working in the private sector were perceived to be better aligned with quality care than those of doctors in the public sector.[154]

These findings suggest a more positive perceived experience for the private patient, but does the commercial nature of the relationship between doctor and patient in the private sector – the fact that the doctor profits from his interaction with the patient - have a negative effect on the doctor-patient relationship? According to Feinberg:

> In the most general nonpejorative sense, physicians 'exploit' sick persons by turning to their own profit the unhappy circumstances of their patients. But they achieve this gain by helping the other party, and unless the fee charged is extortionate, the patient cannot claim that he was exploited since he too profited from the process ... even in the rare case of the ambulance-chasing physician motivated entirely by greed, his patient cannot complain of exploitation if the fees were standard and the treatment beneficial. At the most, we can say that the physician's motives or intentions in that case were 'exploitative' – all he cared for was what was in it for him. But even then it

---

148 Paterson Inquiry 2020: 2. And the inquiry report highlights how difficult it was for private patients in particular to obtain compensation: Paterson Inquiry 2020: 163–164.
149 See Care Quality Commission 2018: 4; Paterson Inquiry 2020: 124–126.
150 Wiles and Higgins 1996: 347.
151 Shmueli and Savage 2014.
152 Wiles and Higgins 1996: 345–346.
153 Ward and others 2015: 305.
154 Ibid: 306.

cannot be true that his conduct exploited his patient in any blamable sense that provides the patient with a moral basis for complaint.[155]

Feinberg appears to suggest that whilst obtaining a standard financial benefit is not morally blameworthy on the doctor's part, since the patient also benefits from the arrangement, obtaining an *excessive* financial benefit would be; presumably this could make the doctor's treatment of the patient unjust on his account of exploitation.[156] We can deal with the issue of whether *B* (the patient) receives a benefit fairly briefly, since we have already noted that, on our process-based account of exploitation, the issue of *B* (the patient) benefitting from the interaction is not decisive in terms of whether the interaction between doctor and patient can be described as exploitation. In the previous chapter, we explored how an exploitative interaction that benefits *B* can still be morally blameworthy through *A*'s misuse of *B*.[157] That the patient gains from the interaction may be of relevance to the question of whether the doctor's exploitative behaviour should be subject to professional and legal sanction, but we do not address this matter here.[158]

The question that we do address at this point is whether the mere fact that the doctor in private health care receives a direct benefit (profit) from the patient means that the doctor exploits the private patient, regardless of the patient gaining a benefit. Our response to this is directed again by our process-based account. We identified above how exploitation might occur in the context of *public* health care above, when the fee incentive of referring a patient to a particular service provider could cause the doctor to put her own interests before her patient's, leading to misuse by taking advantage of the patient's ill-health for financial gain. Similarly, where a doctor in the private sector puts her *own* interests (her direct financial benefit) before the patient's, exploitation could occur. Financial incentives for consultants to refer patients to private hospitals have been cause for concern in the UK, with it being noted that more than 637 consultants either own shares or equipment in private hospitals where they work, refer patients and receive a fee for so doing.[159] And on the matter of *excessive* benefit which is Feinberg's cause for concern, following our account, exploitation might also happen where the doctor receives an excessive financial benefit from the private patient by charging the patient more for the same treatment than she is charging her other private patients for the same treatment in the same circumstances; she would be infringing the patient's right to demand respect equal to that paid to

---

155 Feinberg 1988: 193–194.
156 For a theory of wrongful exploitation that centres on excessive benefit, see Valdman 2009.
157 See chapter 2, section 3.i.
158 Although in chapter 7, sections 3 and 4, we engage in a broader consideration of the most appropriate professional and legal response to exploitation in the doctor-patient relationship.
159 Rowland 2019: 7 (with 546 of these being NHS consultants). The report cites the Ian Paterson as 'one of the largest ever recorded instances of "over-treatment" of patients in a private hospital … Both the private hospital and the surgeon will have made significant amounts of money from this unnecessary treatment': Rowland 2019: 5.

other human beings.¹⁶⁰ Exploitation could also occur through inflating prices for treatment or tests where a doctor takes advantage of patients' anxieties, as illustrated by reports in 2020 that a doctor in the UK was profiting from selling private tests for COVID-19 at a high price.¹⁶¹ But we agree with Feinberg that it is not exploitative *per se* for the doctor to receive a direct financial benefit.¹⁶² Otherwise, we would have to say that wherever *A* receives payment for services rendered to *B* who is in need (perhaps *dire* need) of these services, *A* exploits *B*. So *A*, a plumber, would exploit *B* by providing *B* with a 24-hour call-out boiler repair service for an annual or monthly payment.¹⁶³

Whilst private patients report positive experiences of their health care and relationship with their doctors in the studies that we have referred to, it has been suggested that doctors who are involved in private health care alongside their work for the NHS are negatively affecting the doctor-patient relationship in public health care.¹⁶⁴ In the view of one NHS consultant cardiologist who has taken the ethical decision to no longer work in the private sector, 'time spent in the private sector deprives the NHS of a valuable resource' and 'private practice creates a perverse incentive to increase your NHS waiting times – after all, the longer they are, the more private practice will accrue'.¹⁶⁵ The latter of these claims, if accurate, could reveal the exploitation of NHS patients; doctors would be taking advantage of and misusing patients for their own ends. They would take advantage of the weakness possessed by NHS patients who cannot afford private health care and thus have no choice but to accept the increased waiting time. Misuse would occur because doctors would be treating patients in a way which fails to respect them as persons and does not pay sufficient regard to their health care needs. They would be prioritising their own interests by choosing to spend a greater amount of their time working within the more profitable private model, and would make a deliberate choice not to provide as good a service to NHS patients.

160 See the allegation made against doctors by the private health insurance industry in Australia in 2013, e.g. John Rolfe, 'Specialists accused of charging different rates based on what a patient looks like' *news.com.au* (31 March 2013), at http://www.news.com.au/lifestyle/health/specialists-accused-of-charging-different-rates-based-on-what-a-patient-looks-like/news-story/7bb4e0778da692f8110ac99cd7949974 accessed 20 November 2019.
161 Rupert Neate, 'GMC concerned about doctors exploiting coronavirus fears' *The Guardian* (London, 22 March 2020).
162 Although contrast the views of a medical professional based in the UK: private medicine 'encourages doctors to make decisions on the basis of profit rather than need. When confronted with a choice between two treatment pathways in equipoise – one that earns the doctor no money and the other with a fat fee attached – that conflict is stark': Dean 2015: 1.
163 Or see Wertheimer's example of a car rescue service: Wertheimer 2011: 210.
164 In the GP context, see Denis Campbell, 'Fears of "two-tier NHS" as GPs allow fee-paying patients to jump the queue' *The Guardian* (London, 8 February 2017). There is also a concern that private providers can put pressure on local or regional health services when they withdraw from or cancel contracts early, thereby having a negative effect on patients: British Medical Association 2017:5.
165 Dean 2015: 1.

There are reasons to be cautious about these claims, however, and, even if they are correct, to avoid over-generalising. It is not doctors who set waiting lists in the NHS,[166] and doctors working for the NHS must undertake a minimum amount of hours in order to be full-time salaried NHS medical professionals and accrue all the associated benefits.[167] Also, it is more likely to be systemic failings that are negatively affecting the patient experience of NHS health care and treatment rather than the fact that some NHS doctors are involved in private health care. In the current climate in which there is a shortage of medical professionals in the NHS, we should not preclude doctors from working in both the NHS and private practice as Dean advocates,[168] unless there is persuasive evidence that NHS patients' experiences of health care and the doctor-patient relationship are directly and negatively affected by this.

Finally, given the commercially driven market, we should not ignore the potential for exploitation that exists within private health care at the macro level.[169] At the organisational level, private health care providers might exploit their consumers, or their insurers, if they charge some more than others for the same treatment,[170] or if the rates that they charge far exceed their costs.[171] Such exploitation may, in fact, have little or no bearing upon the doctor-patient

---

166 See the text accompanying nn.86–88.
167 The standard working week is 40 hours for a full-time NHS consultant, for instance. NHS doctors must also declare all private practice (where, what and when) to their relevant organisation. See NHS England 2017: 23.
168 Dean 2015. We also note Guy's observation that NHS doctors have been engaging in private practice from the outset of the NHS, with this being permitted under the National Health Service Act 1946, s 5: Guy 2019: 482.
169 The response to the COVID-19 pandemic has provided exploitative opportunities at the macro level, such as taking advantage of the availability of vaccinations on the NHS for free. Following the start of the UK's vaccination programme in December 2020, it was reported in January 2021 that a firm (said to be a property investment company) sent emails to GPs' surgeries in East Anglia, reportedly describing itself as a 'private medical company' that was wishing to provide vaccinations to its 'front-line staff as soon as possible'. The Hackney Health Trust offered £5000 per vaccination as a donation to the surgery or an individual staff member for any unused COVID-19 vaccinations: Peter Stubley, 'Property Firm Apologises for Offering £5,000 "Donation" to Skip Vaccine Queue', *The Independent* (London, 10 January 2021).
170 Although outside of our focus here, there is also an interesting question about whether patients with private health care insurance are exploited by other private patients who take advantage of unnecessary health care, thereby leading providers to charge higher premiums and 'shifting the costs of their medical care to others' (see Wertheimer 2007: 247). In a national survey in the US, in which 2000 physicians across specialities participated, patient pressure/request was cited by 59 per cent of respondents who considered resources were being overused, with the lead researcher commenting that 'unnecessary medical care is a leading driver of the higher health insurance premiums affecting every American': see Chanapa Tantibanchachai, 'In survey, doctors say unneeded medical care is common, driven by fear of malpractice' *The Hub* (6 September 2017), at https://hub.jhu.edu/2017/09/06/unneeded-medical-care-hopkins-survey/ accessed 20 November 2019.
171 In the US context, see Cooper and others 2015.

relationship, especially if the patient remains unaware that she is making higher contractual payments in comparison to others, or if it is her insurance provider who bears this cost. But such practice could still constitute exploitation and the end result could be that private patients incur increased insurance premiums for their health care.[172]

In sum, notwithstanding the shift towards a more consumerist model under the NHS that we noted previously, the doctor-patient relationship in private health care continues to be a more commercialist model. However, this does not alter the fact that patients are dependent on medical professionals for their health care. They may have more choice concerning which doctors to be reliant upon, but dependency remains. We explore the matter of whether patients in a publicly funded health care system are vulnerable to exploitation in the next chapter.

6) Situating exploitation within philosophical medical ethics

We use the term 'philosophical medical ethics' to refer to academic discourse on medical ethics involving theories and principles, a discourse which is not intended to regulate the medical profession, thereby differentiating it from professional regulatory medical ethics (which we subsequently turn to below).[173] That said, theories and principles in the medical ethics literature can be reflected in professional medical ethics. An obvious symmetrical example can be found in the professional ethical duty that doctors owe to their patients not to cause them harm, and the presence of non-maleficence as one of the four principles of biomedical ethics espoused by Beauchamp and Childress.[174]

We focus our attention here on medical ethics as opposed to the broader bioethical literature. In the latter, there is a growing body of work that centres on exploitation and medical research, some of which we turn to in chapter 4. However, there is no one theory of medical ethics which concentrates on exploitation exclusively. Rather, almost all approaches to medical ethics can be utilised to condemn exploitation, as we shall now briefly demonstrate. Beauchamp and Childress's principlism offer a useful starting point here. As Wertheimer observes, whilst avoiding exploitation is not presented as an explicit principle under Beauchamp and Childress's four principles of biomedical ethics – autonomy, beneficence, non-maleficence and justice[175] – 'many violations of these

---

172 We also note that where private providers are commercial companies, they 'will have fiduciary obligations to shareholders that may, in some circumstances, be in conflict, or be perceived to be in conflict with doctors' obligations to patients. There may be occasions where, in order to reduce costs, private providers may restrict, limit or reduce services in ways that, in the views of doctors, may put patients at risk of harm': BMA 2017: 5.
173 See Foster and Miola 2015: 507.
174 Beauchamp and Childress 2013: chapter 5.
175 Ibid. The four principles are grounded in the common morality, on which, see Brazier and Ost 2013: chapter 7.

principles also involve exploitation'.[176] Much will depend on context, but the cases of doctor-patient exploitation that we have considered in this chapter have shown how a doctor's exploitation of their patient is extremely likely to cause the patient harm, and almost all of these cases involved a breach of autonomy.[177] In the previous chapter, we noted that injustice is the measure of the wrongfulness of exploitation for some commentators,[178] and we connected the moral right to equality which exploitation can sometimes breach with the principle of justice. Turning to beneficence, however, an overly paternalistic doctor might claim that they are bringing good to the patient by pressurising him to agree to treatment that is in his best medical interests, as David's doctor does in Jansen and Wall's scenario.[179] But whilst the principle of beneficence might give some limited scope for sanctioning an instance of exploitation where a doctor acts for her own ends of getting the patient to agree to treatment which is in that patient's best medical interests, such a paternalistic approach sits uncomfortably with the contemporary doctor-patient model.[180]

Undertones of Kantian moral philosophy and duty-based ethics lie behind each of Beauchamp and Childress's four principles. This brings us next to deontology, which centres upon the doctor's duties to the patient. As Garbutt and Davies have put it, the ethics of relationships between doctors and patients 'are intrinsically on a deontological footing – they are about how one person should treat another'.[181] Deontology requires that the doctor's duty towards any particular patient cannot be placed below any other consequentialist concern, such as the common good. Rather, the doctor's central concern when acting is how she ought to act towards her patient instead of what the consequences of her actions will be. This sits comfortably with a process-based account of exploitation such as ours, which is concerned with the way in which one party interacts with the other rather than the outcome of the interaction, and centres upon misuse as wrongful behaviour. Deontology's condemnation of a doctor's exploitation of their patient is also reflected in Garbutt and Davies' view of the significance of this approach for doctors: the 'deontological ethic is important in giving doctors their motivation to do good by and for each patient they meet. It is an ethic that values the particularity of each individual patient. In this ethic the patient is an end in themselves, and not a means towards anything else.'[182]

---

176 Wertheimer 2007: 247.
177 There is one case where this is less definitive: see the text accompanying nn.44–46. And specific analysis of whether autonomy was breached in the excessive benefit cases we discuss in the text accompanying n.161 would be required.
178 Such as Feinberg 1988: 199.
179 See text accompanying n.23.
180 Paternalism as a broader ethical theory might justify some limited form of exploitation in this regard, but we do not address this here given that we are considering philosophical medical ethics in the context of contemporary medical practice and are focused upon adult rather than child patients.
181 Garbutt and Davies 2011: 267.
182 Ibid: 268.

Consequentialism, or utilitarianism, in contrast, is focused upon the consequences of one's actions. Put simply, favourable consequences cause the act to be morally good, unfavourable consequences mean that it is morally bad.[183] There are two predominant approaches to assessing the morality of an action. Act utilitarianism determines the morality of each action in relation to the favourable or unfavourable consequences that emerge from that action; whereas according to rule utilitarianism, an act is right if it is carried out in accordance with a rule when following this rule will generally have good consequences. Following rules such as 'it's wrong to steal', for instance, is much more likely to lead to favourable consequences for all rather than unfavourable consequences.[184] Applying this to the scenario involving David and his doctor, an act utilitarian would weigh up all the good and bad consequences that flow from this act for David. If the good consequences outweigh the bad, the doctor's exploitation could be condoned. For a rule utilitarian, a failure to follow the rule that a doctor should not exploit his patients would lead to bad consequences, negatively affecting the doctor-patient relationship and challenging the public's trust in the medical profession. Thus, the morality of behaviour that can be perceived to be exploitative is derived from the outcome(s) of that behaviour, rather than an intrinsic duty to treat patients in particular way.[185]

We have already shown that, in a publicly funded health care system such as the NHS, it is impossible to ignore utilitarian concerns:

> In modern complex healthcare systems such as the UK NHS the needs of the system, in terms of its survival as a coherent entity, are rapidly becoming as large as those of the patients in the consulting room. This larger system is unavoidably utilitarian, having to make the best use it can of finite resources.[186]

Our earlier discussion also highlighted the difficulty of achieving a balance between deontological and utilitarian concerns in such a system. We agree with Dorr Goold and Lipkin that 'each physician in a managed care organization should primarily be an advocate for individual patients. This is not to say that physicians should ignore the cost implications of their decisions ... merely that their primary responsibility as practitioners should be for the care of their patients.'[187] However, the pressure of targets and incentives such as the prescribing incentive scheme for GP practices offered by Oxfordshire CCG,[188] means that this may well be easier said than done.

---

183 'Utility, or the Greatest Happiness Principle, holds that actions are right in proportion as they tend to promote happiness, wrong as they tend to produce the reverse of happiness': Mill 1996: 7.
184 For Mill, e.g. the principle of utility is a tool for generating secondary moral principles (or rules), like 'don't steal', which promote general happiness: ibid: 25–27.
185 See, generally, Brody 1981.
186 Garbutt and Davies 2011: 267.
187 Dorr Goold and Lipkin 1999: S30.
188 See text accompanying n.124.

Rather than centring upon duties to others, or the consequences of actions, virtue ethics emphasises moral character as the key feature underpinning the right ethical approach.[189] Agent-based accounts of virtue ethics consider the motivation for acting: if the motivation behind the act is good, then the act is good.[190] Such an approach highlights the need for doctors to be motivated to act in the interests of the patient rather than their own self-interest. But how do we define what constitutes a virtue? In Murdoch's view, 'anything which alters consciousness in the direction of unselfishness, objectivity, and realism is to be connected with virtue'.[191] This may well offer a means of identifying virtues such as unselfishness and honesty, and clearly points in the direction of condemning exploitative behaviour. However, we could envisage a situation involving exploitative behaviour where two virtues are in conflict. How should we address this dilemma? If, for instance, we return once more to the scenario involving David and his doctor, David's doctor would claim that he is acting because of a good motivation: he is seeking to benefit David by serving his best medical interests. But his approach undermines the virtue of respecting David's autonomy. Applying Aristotle's version of virtue ethics,[192] the way to resolve this apparent conflict would involve an exercise of practical wisdom to find the solution.[193] A proper understanding of what each virtue demands should reveal that there is no conflict between them.[194] It is self-indulgent and unsympathetic to ignore David's autonomy and manipulate him into agreeing to the course of action that the doctor considers to be in his best medical interests and, overall, he is not benefitted. David's autonomy should also be respected by fully informing him and allowing him to make his own choice.

Turning next to feminist medical ethics, initially, the predominant concern for feminist critiques of medicine and health care was about reproductive medicine and assisted reproductive technologies, with calls for recognition that these are not gender-neutral matters.[195] Significantly, feminist medical ethics draws attention to power disparities in relationships and patriarchal societal norms, alongside oppressive practices in medicine and health care, and the vulnerabilities

---

189 An 'ethics of virtue thinks primarily in terms of what is noble or ignoble, admirable or deplorable, good or bad, rather than in terms of what is obligatory, permissible, or wrong': Slote 2001: 4.
190 Agent-based virtue ethicists may focus more subjectively upon the motivations of the particular agent: ibid, or, conversely, and more objectively, upon whether the act is one that a virtuously motivated agent would perform: Zagzebski 2004: 160.
191 Murdoch 1971: 82.
192 Aristotle and others 2009.
193 Ibid: Book 6.
194 Indeed, Aristotle rejected the idea that conflict between virtues could occur.
195 Sherwin 2008: 23: 'few non-feminist ethicists step back to consider how pursuit of such a technology-driven, reproduction-based health agenda will ultimately affect the health of most humans on the planet. Their rights-based analysis considers only what, if any, protection is owed the immediate participants involved in these practices, and questions of social justice are rendered invisible.'

of patients in medicine and research.¹⁹⁶ Attention has been paid to the issue of exploitation, such as the exploitation of women in reproductive research,¹⁹⁷ and Ganguli Mitra and Biller-Andorno's conceptualisation of exploitation in global interactions related to health as taking advantage of vulnerabilities embedded within existing structural injustices.¹⁹⁸ Their contention that bioethics must explore exploitation and vulnerability within a discourse of 'both macro- and micro-fairness'¹⁹⁹ is an important one that we pay attention to in chapters 4, 6 and 7. A consideration of consensual exploitation informed by feminist medical ethics would construct autonomy as patriarchal; it would explore the contextual, relational settings in which patients exercise autonomy.²⁰⁰

Philosophical medical ethics acknowledges the potential for exploiting patients and offers explanations for how exploitation can occur and mechanisms through which it can be avoided. Furthermore, feminist medical ethics, for example, offers a means of providing a rich contextual analysis of exploitation in the doctor-patient relationship. However, we should not expect theories of medical ethics to capture what exactly is wrong about doctors exploiting their patients, since these theories are designed to be widely applicable, to guide medical professionals in their ethical decision-making and encourage such decision-making in all their interactions with their patients. Thus, for instance, whilst Beauchamp and Childress's four principles might catch exploitation, they are necessarily broad in nature and so cannot effectively convey the specific wrong of exploitation in the same way that they cannot convey, for example, the specific wrong of coercion. Indeed, a frequent criticism mounted against the principle that one should do no harm to others is that it is overbroad and can be overinclusive.²⁰¹ And whilst it may be true that the principle of autonomy is often violated through a doctor's exploitation of her patient, this is only one aspect and effect of such exploitation.

Keeping with the example of principlism, it may be possible to narrow the scope of the four principles to make them more directly focused on exploitation; in fact, Beauchamp and Childress have argued that the principles can lose their abstractness by being narrowed in order to fit particular contexts.²⁰² But we do not advocate tailoring existing theories of medical ethics in this way, or creating a specific theory directed at exploitation. This seems unnecessary when existing theories of medical ethics already offer various alternative frameworks in which to situate exploitation, and, as is hardly surprising, an application of almost all of these theories condemns exploitation. However, as our analysis in

---

196 See Rogers and others 2012a; Rogers and Ballantyne 2008.
197 Tremain 2006.
198 Ganguli Mitra and Biller-Andorno 2013.
199 Ibid: 97.
200 Mackenzie and Soljar 2000. On patriarchal autonomy and women's exercise of autonomy, see Ells 2003.
201 Consider, e.g. Dan-Cohen's critique of JS Mill's harm principle, as applied to the matter of criminalisation: Dan-Cohen 2002: 153.
202 See, e.g. Beauchamp 2010: 45–46.

this and the previous chapter demonstrates, exploitation in the doctor-patient relationship is a variant of harmful behaviour that warrants specific attention. Beyond the broader frameworks of philosophical medical ethics, there are other ways of directing doctors' attention to the matter of exploitation specifically, as we discuss below and in our concluding chapter.

We note one final matter here. In more recent years, philosophical medical ethics has turned its gaze from its traditional concentration on doctor responsibility to paying increasing attention to *patient* responsibility. This change of focus raises interesting questions about how the matter of patients exploiting doctors should be dealt with by philosophical medical ethics. In the literature that has begun to address patient responsibility, authors have pondered on, for example, what exactly patients should bear a responsibility for, and to whom this responsibility is owed.[203] Whilst it would be contentious to argue that patients must be held to the same professionally directed ethical code as doctors, that they are 'equal moral agents',[204] we have shown in this section that the foundations of the theories and principles in philosophical medical ethics can be found in moral philosophy of broader application, and should be considered in the wider societal context. In some of the literature on Beauchamp and Childress's principlism, for instance, wider connections have been drawn with society, with Gillon perceiving the four principles as 'a common set of moral commitments'[205] and liberalism being mooted as a sympathetic political framework in which the principles can be placed.[206] It may, therefore, be reasonable to suspect that at least some of the reasons to oppose doctors' exploitation of patients would also apply to exploitation perpetrated by patients.

7) Professional medical ethics and exploitation

Regulatory medical ethics underlines and expresses the value of trust in the medical profession.[207] Trust and other values assert what health care professionals should be held accountable for.[208] The preamble to the GMC's *Good Medical Practice* states that 'you must make care of the patient your first concern',[209] with the use of the word 'must' meaning that this is presented as an overriding

---

203 See, e.g. Brazier 2006; Coggon 2012; Cummins Gauthier 2005; Draper and Sorell 2002; Miles 2019; Ost and Biggs 2016.
204 Brazier and Ost 2013: 209. See also Ost and Biggs 2016.
205 Gillon 1986: 175. And see the 'virtue of moral responsibility' proposed by Cummins Gauthier 2005.
206 Brazier and Ost 2013: 221–222.
207 See also Hall 2005: 156.
208 Turoldo and Barilan 2008: 115.
209 General Medical Council 2013b. See also General Medical Council 2013b: 4(1) and 5(5). The correlative duty under the American Medical Association's Code of Medical Ethics is that '[a] physician shall, while caring for a patient, regard responsibility to the patient as paramount' (Principle VIII).

duty.[210] It goes on to state that 'good doctors work in partnership with patients and respect their rights to privacy and dignity. They treat each patient as an individual.'[211] Thus, this core guidance for doctors has clear deontological underpinnings.[212]

The risk of the doctor putting her own self-interest before the patient's interests, and the potential that this has to undermine trust, is a key area of focus for regulatory ethics. The American case of *Moore* v. *Regents of the University of California* offers a good example where such behaviour involved exploitation.[213] Here, the doctor used the cells from the patient's spleen without his permission in potentially lucrative research involving the development of biotechnological products. It was held by the Supreme Court of California that the doctor had possessed a personal interest unrelated to the patient's health that could have affected his professional judgment.[214] A failure to inform the patient of such an interest (economic or research-related) could give rise to a legal action for failing to obtain the patient's informed consent prior to medical procedures, or breach of a fiduciary duty.[215] The patient could thus state a cause of action for lack of informed consent to the use of his tissue for the research, *and* for breach of fiduciary duty.[216] It was stated in the majority judgment that 'the law already recognizes that a reasonable patient would want to know whether a physician has an economic interest that might affect the physician's professional judgment ... "the patient's interests and desires are the key ingredients of the decision-making process"'.[217]

Regulatory ethics emphasises that competing interests have the potential to undermine trust.[218] The position is that doctors must avoid being influenced by any self-interest when providing health care and treatment to patients.[219]

---

210 General Medical Council 2013b: [5]. The GMC is given the power to provide advice to medical professionals on standards of professional conduct and performance and medical ethics under s.35 of the Medical Act 1983.
211 General Medical Council 2013b: 4[2].
212 See also Garbutt and Davies 2011: 267.
213 793 P. 2d 479 (1990).
214 '[A] physician who treats a patient in whom he also has a research interest has potentially conflicting loyalties ... The possibility that an interest extraneous to the patient's health has affected the physician's judgment is something that a reasonable patient would want to know in deciding whether to consent to a proposed course of treatment': ibid, 484.
215 Ibid, 485.
216 Ibid, 497. Subsequent US cases have indicated that there is a reluctance to recognise a fiduciary duty upon doctors to disclose financial incentives: see *Pegram* v. *Herdrich* 530 US 211 (2000); *Neade* v. *Portes* 739 N.E.2d 496 (Ill.2000). But note the analysis in Sperling 2017.
217 Ibid, 483 and 484 (quoting *Barber* v. *Superior Court*, 147 Cal. App. 3d 1006 (1983).
218 BMA 2017: 2.
219 See, e.g. the American Medical Association's *AMA Code of Medical Ethics* Opinion 1.1.1: 'The relationship between a patient and a physician is based on trust, which gives rise to physicians' ethical responsibility to place patients' welfare above the physician's own self interest or obligations to others'.

GMC guidance clearly states the duty incumbent upon doctors not to allow any financial or commercial interest in an organisation providing health care 'to affect the way you prescribe for, advise, treat, refer or commission services for patients',[220] and the BMA reminds doctors that although they 'may wish to recommend treatments and assessments, they must not put pressure on patients to participate because of the financial benefits that they receive'.[221] Similarly, other specific GMC guidance states that:

> You must be open and honest with your patients about any such interests that could be seen to affect the way you [advise, treat them etc] ... You must not try to influence patients' choice of healthcare services to benefit you, someone close to you, or your employer.[222]

Of course, to be effective in directing doctors away from the temptation to put their own interests before their patients and to foster a culture of openness between individual doctors and their patient,[223] and the profession and the public more broadly, this guidance needs to be upheld. This is a matter that we discuss in our concluding chapter.[224]

Regulatory medical ethics also makes it clear that doctors should not accept anything from particular patients to avoid the temptation of giving these patients preferential treatment over other patients and to avoid exploiting patients' kindness for their own ends: 'you must not ask for or accept – from patients, colleagues or others – any inducement, gift or hospitality that may affect or be seen to affect the way you prescribe for, treat or refer patients or commission services for patients. You must not offer these inducements.'[225] This latter prohibition captures exploitation by way of inducement, such as that which occurred in *Norberg* v. *Wynrib*[226] (access to a drug that the patient was addicted to in exchange for sexual favours). Whilst not a case involving inducement, the actions of Dr Andrea McFarlane offer a recent example of a GP taking advantage of a patient's kindness in violation of regulatory medical ethics in the UK. She was found to have committed serious professional misconduct having accepted

---

220 General Medical Council 2013b: 24[78].
221 BMA 2017: 6.
222 General Medical Council 2013a: [14] and [15].
223 We note that transparency and accountability are also commonly called for in philosophical ethics. See, e.g. Katz and others 2003. Cf. Sperling 2017. Disclosure also appears to be what patients desire, according to a UK-based study. Participants stated that disclosure 'would be of benefit to the patient *and* doctor as patients would be fully informed and able to choose to access this service; and the doctor would clearly not be appearing to deceive patients for financial gain': Gill and others 2012: 35 (emphasis in original).
224 Chapter 7, section 3.
225 General Medical Council 2013b: 24[80]. See also BMA 2017: 6.
226 [1992] 2 SCR 226. See the discussion in chapter 5, part 1, text accompanying n.61.

a series of gifts and sums of money totalling over £117,000 from 'an elderly, vulnerable (but capacitated) patient' with whom she had developed a 'special friendship'.[227] We return to this case briefly in our final chapter.[228]

Again, connected to self-interest, doctors are also told by the GMC that 'you must not express your personal beliefs (including political, religious and moral beliefs) to patients in ways that exploit their vulnerability'.[229] The abortion context offers an example of how this could occur. Let's say that a doctor with strong religious values is approached by a young teenage girl in the early stages of pregnancy who desires an abortion that is opposed by her parents. The doctor takes advantage of the girl's weakness (her mental distress, her fear of upsetting her parents) and misuses her, failing to respect her as a person by pressuring her not to abort out of the doctor's own self-interest (her belief in the immorality of abortion).

In highlighting how professional regulatory ethics proscribes such exploitative behaviour, we are not suggesting that the doctor-patient relationship is special in having such stringent professional regulatory ethics; the legal profession has this too, for instance.[230] However, the fact that behaviour that constitutes a key ingredient of exploitation – acting for one's own ends – is prohibited by the medical profession's regulatory ethics (indeed the GMC's central guidance), emphasises how exploitation is considered to violate the ethos of the doctor's professional relationship with her patients.

8) What about the law?

Thus far we have said very little about the law. It is not our purpose to say much here either, since we cover the way in which the law responds to particular types of exploitation in our subsequent case study chapters. But reflecting more broadly upon the way in which the law categorises exploitation in the doctor-patient relationship, it is notable that there are no specific criminal law offences or civil wrongs directed towards exploitation *per se*, or within the particular context of the doctor-patient relationship. However, and as we discuss in subsequent chapters, some instances of exploitation would breach

---

227 General Medical Council, 'Meeting of the s40A Panel to Consider the Case of Dr Andrea McFarlane held on 15 January 2019', [12.1], at https://www.gmc-uk.org/-/media/documents/mcfarlane-publication—15-january-2019_pdf-79194802.pdf accessed 9 March 2020.
228 See chapter 7, n.55.
229 General Medical Council 2013b: 18[54].
230 See the Solicitors Regulation Authority Standards and Regulations, at https://www.sra.org.uk/solicitors/standards-regulations/ accessed 24 July 2020 and the Bar Standards Board Handbook, part 2, at https://www.barstandardsboard.org.uk/the-bsb-handbook.html accessed 24 July 2020.

86   *Exploitation, doctors and patients*

criminal and/or civil law,[231] with perhaps the most obvious being certain instances of sexual exploitation that would constitute sexual offences.[232]

As demonstrated by the examples provided in this and other chapters, the types of wrongful exploitation that might occur in the context of the doctor-patient relationship are many and varied and this poses a real challenge for achieving a 'one size fits all' legal response.[233] We leave our assessment of whether there is a need for a wider criminal offence or tort of exploitation, and the difficulties of such a broad-brush approach, to our final chapter.

What we highlight here is that, for those patients whose relationship with their doctor is situated within private health care, the law of contract can also catch forms of exploitative behaviour perpetrated by the doctor. The protection from certain forms of exploitative behaviour provided to private patients comes through several established contract law doctrines, such as the presumption of undue influence.[234] As noted by La Forest J in a Canadian case, 'the doctrines of duress, undue influence, and unconscionability have arisen to protect the vulnerable when they are in a relationship of unequal power … on grounds of public policy, the legal effectiveness of certain types of contracts will be restricted or negated'.[235]

Looking first to undue influence, in contract law and 'evolved from the courts of equity',[236] the doctrine of undue influence regulates transactions made in the context of a relationship of trust and influence,[237] such as is presumed to exist between doctor and patient.[238] If a patient enters into a contractual agreement or makes a gift to her doctor because a relationship of undue influence exists

231 Offences directed specifically at exploitation only exist regarding children (sexual offences under the Sexual Offences Act 2003 ss.48–50), prostitution (Sexual Offences Act 2003, s.53(A), and human trafficking (Modern Slavery Act 2015, s.2).
232 We say *certain* instances here since problems are encountered at law where the sexual activity in question is deemed to be 'consensual' (on which, see chapter 5, part 2). A further non-sexual example of exploitation caught by the criminal law is a case 'without legal precedent in criminal law', where surgeon Simon Bramhall branded his initials on the organs of two patients undergoing transplant surgery was charged with assault by beating and assault occasioning actual bodily harm. He admitted the counts of assault by beating and his not guilty pleas to assault occasioning actual bodily harm were accepted. See Ost 2019; Ost 2020.
233 See also Collins 2015: 53–54.
234 Collins also notes the way in which contract law doctrines can tackle exploitation: ibid: 259.
235 *Norberg* v. *Wynrib* [28] and [34] (La Forest J).
236 Beginning in *Huguenin* v. *Baseley* (1807) 14 Ves 273; Bell 2007: 556. A narrower version of the doctrine is also applied in the law of probate.
237 Chen-Wishart 2006: 202; Bell 2007.
238 See *Goldsworthy* v. *Brickell* [1987] 2 WLR 133; *Dent* v. *Bennett* (1839) 4 Myl & Cr 269, 277 (Lord Cottenham LC) : 'when I find an agreement so extravagant in its provisions, secretly obtained by a medical attendant from his patient of a very advanced age, and carefully concealed from his professional advisers and all other persons, and have it proved that the habits, views, and intentions of the testator were wholly inconsistent with those provisions, I cannot but come to the conclusion that the medical attendant did obtain it by some dominion exercised over his patient.'

between them, then the patient's consent is vitiated.[239] Undue influence vitiates consent because 'in each case of undue influence we are essentially concerned with a superior party who wrongfully provides an ordinarily free ... person with what appears to be a reason for doing what the influencer desires'.[240] As Birks puts it, 'undue influence consists in unconscionable exploitation of influence'.[241] In the land law case of *Thompson* v. *Foy*, involving an informal agreement between parties to transfer property, it was said of undue influence that 'the critical question is whether or not the influence has invaded the free volition of the [person] to withstand the influence'.[242] If the patient could show that her acquiescence can only be explained on the basis that it was procured through undue influence rather than there being 'good and sufficient reasons' for this acquiescence, then the criteria for presumed undue influence should be met.[243] Moreover, since the doctor-patient relationship has been cited as an example of a relationship in which the existence of trust and confidence is presumed in the context of equitable doctrine (an irrebuttable presumption), this gives rise to an evidential rebuttable presumption of undue influence in contract law.[244] It is also significant that there appears to be some judicial appetite for limiting the scope of undue influence to instances where the influence is used exploitatively by a person considered to be in authority by the exploited person,[245] thereby further demonstrating the connection between this doctrine and exploitative behaviour.

---

239 See, e.g. *Bank of Credit and Commerce International SA* v. *Aboody* [1990] 1 QB 923 (albeit outside the doctor-patient context). Whether undue influence is enough to vitiate consent in tort law (the tort of battery) when an inducement is offered in a relationship involving an imbalance of power is yet to be settled, as we discuss in chapter 5, part 2, section 2.i.
240 Bigwood 1996: 511.
241 Birks 2004: 34
242 [2009] EWHC 1076 (Ch), [101] (Lewison J).
243 See *Royal Bank of Scotland* v. *Etridge* [2001] UKHL 44, [30]; cf. *U* v. *Centre for Reproductive Medicine* [2002] EWCA Civ 565 [20] (Hale LJ) (although note that this case involved a nursing sister and patient rather than a doctor-patient relationship).
244 *Royal Bank of Scotland* v. *Etridge* ibid, [18], [157]. Although, as Bell observes, and as alluded to in the text accompanying the previous footnote, a party in a relationship that gives rise to this evidential presumption 'may be forced to prove misconduct, for undue influence will only be presumed if there is something unusual about the impugned transaction': Bell 2007: 557. See also *Royal Bank of Scotland* v. *Etridge*, [24]; Bell 2007: 562 and, for criticism, see Haughey 2012: 144–147. Even if the doctor-patient relationship had not been recognised as one involving trust and confidence, thereby giving rise to the rebuttable presumption of undue influence, actual undue influence could still be found. Because actual undue influence must be proven by the claimant, there would need to be evidence that the doctor had overtly persuaded the patient in order to establish that she did what she did because of the doctor's undue influence (as was established by the claimant in *Bank of Credit and Commerce International SA* v. *Aboody*).
245 See *R* v. *Attorney General for England and Wales* [2003] UKPC 22, [21] and [24] (Lord Hoffman): 'Undue influence has concentrated in particular upon the unfair exploitation by one party of a relationship which gives him ascendancy or influence over the other ... the question is whether the nature of the transaction was such as to give rise to an inference that it was obtained by an unfair exploitation of that relationship.'

88 *Exploitation, doctors and patients*

Whilst undue influence appears to be the most apposite doctrine to capture certain forms of exploitative behaviour perpetrated by a doctor upon a patient in private health care, two other contract law doctrines are also worth highlighting. Back in 1976, Waddams argued that unconscionability should be recognised as a general principle of contract law, related to the unreasonableness of the agreement.[246] Described by Wertheimer as the contractual version of economic exploitation,[247] unconscionability is still a 'fledgling' doctrine.[248] Whilst more commonly applied in the United States, Canada, Australia and New Zealand,[249] the doctrine has its roots in English common law and an eighteenth-century case in which it was said that the courts could invalidate a contract 'such as no man in his senses and not under delusion would make on the one hand, and as no honest and fair man would accept on the other'.[250] Rather than operating in relationships of trust, the doctrine essentially targets victimisation: a situation where the stronger party to the contract is aware that the other party is at a disadvantage and uses this to their own advantage.[251] Finally, there is the doctrine of economic duress, which can operate where the claimant makes a wrongful threat or exerts pressure that 'was operative in inducing the defendant to enter into the contract'.[252] The claimant is 'precluded from enforcing the contract by virtue of the wrongdoing principle'.[253] Citing Lord Scarman, Chen-Wishart states that:

> 'the classic case of duress is ... not the lack of will to submit but the victim's intentional submission arising from the realisation that there is no practical choice open to him'. Where this results from the defendant's illegitimate pressure, the law does not ascribe the normal responsibility it would to the victim's consent. [That] consent is deemed to be vitiated.[254]

Phang has noted that economic duress is 'very similar to [actual] undue influence', and has drawn connections between all three of the doctrines noted here.[255] They all operate where unequal power exists between the parties to a contract, and reveal 'two factually related, but conceptually distinct, possible

---

246 Waddams 1976: 375.
247 Wertheimer 1987: 40.
248 Phang 2009: 570.
249 Enman 1987.
250 *Earl of Chesterfield* v. *Janssen* (1750) 28 Eng. Rep. 82, 100. See also *Evans* v. *Llewellin* (1787) 1 Cox CC 333. For a discussion of more recent cases where the doctrine appears to have been applied, see Greenfield and Osborn 1992.
251 See the Privy Council's judgment in *Hart* v. *O'Conor* [1985] AC 1000, 1024.
252 Smith 1997: 354.
253 Ibid: 372. And see the quotation from Smith in the text accompanying n.256, which presents wrongdoing as a concern that underlies this area of contract law.
254 Chen-Wishart 2006: 206 (citing Lord Scarman in *Universe Tankships Inc of Monrovia* v. *International Transport Workers Federation (The Universe Sentinel)* [1983] 1 AC 366, 400).
255 Phang 2009: 570–571. See also Waddams 1976: 387.

concerns: a concern for wrongdoing and a concern for autonomy'.[256] We consider whether the protection from exploitative behaviour that contract law doctrine (namely undue influence) might offer to patients receiving private health care should be extended beyond the contractual context in our concluding chapter.

9) Exploitation in the doctor-patient relationship: a special example of exploitation that violates the ethos of a distinctive intimate and confidential professional relationship

> You feel violated, because somebody's put you to sleep, got into your body and done things that you didn't consent to, and you trusted, wholeheartedly, and they're a monster.[257]

When exploitation occurs in intimate and confidential professional relationships, we have argued that it is especially wrongful. Indeed, it can be seen as a *violation*, and this is the term that we have used throughout this chapter. Violation is defined by the Cambridge English Dictionary as 'an action that breaks or acts against something, especially a law, agreement, principle, or something that should be treated with respect'.[258] We tend to describe something as a violation when it infringes something fundamental; the term is frequently used when referring to human rights breaches, for instance. The use of such a strong term in our context is appropriate because it conveys the significance of a doctor's exploitation; violation is bound up with the taking advantage of (using) and misuse of a patient. We have explored how the doctor-patient relationship is one in which trust is so fundamental, and have presented the doctor's duty not to act out of self-interest as a fiducial duty. The doctor's access to the patient's body and mind is unmatched when compared with other professional relationships. Vulnerability is often an issue because the patient is ill or has a concern about their health, and a power imbalance is a core feature of this relationship. Taking advantage of and misusing the weaker party for one's own ends in the doctor-patient relationship is particularly indicative of the wrongfulness associated with exploitation that we presented in the previous chapter.

Exploitation in the doctor-patient relationship is, therefore, a special, prime example of exploitation that violates the ethos of the professional relationship. More specifically, it is a violation of the patient's trust, of the doctor's fiducial duties, and of professional medical ethics that is condemned by philosophical medical ethics. Doctors have a fundamental role-based obligation not to exploit their patients. And the particular context of the doctor-patient relationship means that the more

---

[256] Smith 1997: 343. We note that Smith was referring specifically to duress here, but consider that these concerns can be seen across the three doctrines.
[257] Paterson Inquiry 2020: 80. See also statements from other patients of Paterson which also speak to the violation of the intimate doctor-patient relationship at 30 and 61.
[258] See *Cambridge Dictionary* (Cambridge University Press 2019), at http://dictionary.cambridge.org/dictionary/english/violation accessed 20 November 2019.

powerful party's exploitation of the weaker party is almost certain to be normatively harmful. As we explored in the previous chapter, it is always going to amount to a violation of a moral right where the exploited person is treated solely as means to an end, a right that we presented as a universal right. And failures to respect privacy, autonomy or the right to equality of treatment are also likely to amount to violations of moral rights. All these are rights that are highly likely to be possessed by patients in the context of doctor-patient relationship, as demonstrated by the real-life cases and fictional scenarios explored here and in the previous chapter.

But is exploitation in the doctor-patient relationship a *special* example of exploitation in intimate and confidential professional relationships? Whilst we return to this issue in our concluding chapter, we emphasise one point in particular here. It is arguable that, albeit to a lesser degree, relationships between lawyer and client and clergyperson and parishioner also reflect the elements of trust, reliance, fiducial duties, imbalance of power and the vulnerability of the weaker party. However, there is one crucial component that sets the doctor-patient relationship apart from other intimate and confidential professional relationships: health, the concern which lies at its core. For 'the doctor-patient relationship is remarkable for its centrality during life-altering and meaningful times in persons' lives, times of birth, death, severe illness, and healing'.[259]

Those of us who experience a lifetime of good health are remarkably lucky. In the contemporary societies of developed countries, the individual who never receives any form of health care or treatment from birth to death is a rarity if, indeed, such an individual exists. Our health, whether good or bad, shapes our lives and our life experiences. Good mental and physical health enables our interaction with others, ensures our capacity to work and socialise, and to develop and maintain meaningful personal relationships. Ill-health can have a negative impact upon all of the above. It can isolate us, confine us, paralyse us, and cause our relationships with others to break down.[260] Sometimes, because of societal reactions to certain diseases and conditions, we are stigmatised by our ill-health, with attitudes towards AIDS in the 1980s being an obvious case in point. If ill-health is long-term and in the form of a chronic condition, it can significantly reduce our quality of life. Thus, the primary concern at the heart of the doctor-patient relationship is profound and all-inclusive in terms of its relevance for each and every one of us. Doctors' exploitation of their patients is especially wrongful and patients' interests are more likely to be set back by such exploitation because their health (and trust)[261] is vested in this intimate and confidential, special relationship.

---

259 Dorr Goold and Lipkin 1999: S27.
260 See Fineman 2010: 268: 'should we succumb to illness or injury there may be accompanying harm to or disruption of existing employment, economic, or family relationships. These harms are not located in the body itself, but in the interruption or destruction of institutional or social relationships.'
261 'Because trust arises and gains its strength from conditions of vulnerability, trust in physicians has an inherent basis in the universal condition of illness and the nature of medical care': Hall 2005: 159.

4 Patient vulnerability and exploitation

Those who are vulnerable may be more prone to exploitation in the sense that we have used it in this work: namely as wrongful exploitation related to taking advantage of and misusing another person for one's own ends. Consequently, alongside exploitation, vulnerability is an important concept within our analysis, having already featured in the previous two chapters.[1] It was, for example, referred to in our discussion of the doctor-patient relationship, where we drew on Archard's explanation of the characteristics that a typical relationship of power possesses:

> The first is an ethos of intimacy, closeness, trust, openness, and confidence. The second is the relative dependence and *vulnerability* of the client. The third is the esteem, respect, and admiration which the client has for the professional.[2]

However, defining vulnerability and its impact on individuals (especially patients), is an intricate, multifactorial process that is often imprecise. In this chapter, we consider what it means to be vulnerable, and highlight the complexities involved if a society strives to both respect autonomy and diminish vulnerabilities. We then proceed to assess the role of vulnerability in some specific health care situations. Patients who participate in medical/clinical research are often regarded as uniquely vulnerable, and there are numerous examples of abuse and exploitation in this context.[3] We therefore examine the relationship with vulnerability in this context, including the matter of whether those who conduct medical research might also possess certain vulnerabilities. Then, we build on our discussion of the patient in

---

1   See, particularly, chapter 2, section 2, i, ii and iv–vii, section 3; chapter 3, sections 1, 4 and 9. The significant connection that we draw between exploitation and vulnerability is compatible with the Kantian liberal account of exploitation we present in chapter 2. See Formosa 2014 and n.50. We note that we are not suggesting that there is an *inevitable* connection between vulnerability and exploitation: see further Macklin 2003: 472–473.
2   Archard 1994: 98 (emphasis added), cited earlier in chapter 2, section 1.
3   Some of which include the Tuskegee study in the United States, the New Zealand cervical cancer study and the Perinatal AZT Trials in Africa: Jones 1981; Coney 1988; Wendland 2008.

public and private health care settings in the previous chapter to question whether vulnerability is an issue in the case of patients who can avail themselves of private health care. Such patients may, because of their more financially secure position and likely social status, be perceived to be in a stronger position vis-à-vis the doctor. However, for private health care patients who access cosmetic services, for instance, social pressure to conform to looking a particular way is highly influential and can shape the way a person regards their body and impact upon their body image. Therefore, using the more consumer-orientated setting of cosmetic surgery as an exemplar of private health care, we assess the relationship between vulnerability and potential exploitation further, exploring whether those who might be susceptible to such pressure seek out cosmetic and body-altering surgery. In concluding the chapter, we assess whether all patients are vulnerable to exploitation and draw attention to potential vulnerabilities in all aspects of health care.

Vulnerability is a term used in many and various situations with subtly different implications. For example, the *Oxford English Dictionary* describes a person who is vulnerable as 'in need of special care, support, or protection (esp. provided as a social service) because of age, disability, risk of abuse or neglect etc.'.[4] This common sense kind of approach is also reflected in the NHS guidance on safeguarding vulnerable adults who are regarded as at risk of sexual, physical, psychological, discriminatory, financial and domestic abuse.[5] By contrast, the *Collins English Dictionary* describes being vulnerable as 'capable of being physically or emotionally wounded or hurt', 'open to temptation, persuasion, censure … liable or exposed to disease, disaster, etc',[6] which incorporates other factors that may be relevant in the doctor-patient relationship, particularly the potential for the doctor (and/or the researcher in the medical research context) to be vulnerable to persuasion or temptation, which will be discussed later. Goodin reflects this view, explaining that to be vulnerable is often relational, so that although all are potentially susceptible to harms, a person's interests are more likely to be threatened in relationships where the ability to protect those interests is diminished.[7] The doctor-patient relationship is an obvious example. By contrast, treating all as vulnerable, or identifying specific groups as vulnerable may render the concept less effective in protecting individuals, by disguising the specific risks that some persons may be exposed to.[8]

We are keen to avoid stereotypical ideas of vulnerability that imply weakness,[9] victimhood, helplessness and dependence, in favour of an understanding that,

---

4   OED Online at https://www.oed.com/view/Entry/224872?redirectedFrom=vulnerable& accessed 1st June 2019.
5   NHS, *Abuse and Neglect of Vulnerable Adults*, at https://www.nhs.uk/conditions/social-care-and-support-guide/help-from-social-services-and-charities/abuse-and-neglect-vulnerable-adults/ accessed 5 January 2021.
6   *Collins English Dictionary* at https://www.collinsdictionary.com/dictionary/english/vulnerable accessed 1 June 2019.
7   Goodin 1985.
8   Macklin 2003; Luna 2009.
9   Fineman 2019: 342.

although there is a potential for vulnerable persons to exhibit these traits, that is often merely a *potential*. The impulse to treat all potentially vulnerable individuals as weak and in need of protection is, therefore, not an appropriate response in contemporary health care, where good therapy should be delivered via a partnership between each patient and their doctor. With this in mind, we now turn to explore theoretical understandings of vulnerability in more detail.

1) What does it mean to be vulnerable?

In contemporary society, independence and the expectation that each individual is competent, self-determining and autonomous is the default position, with vulnerability framed as an exception. However, alternatively, vulnerability has been described as '*the* primal human condition',[10] on the basis that 'the term "vulnerable", used to connote the continuous susceptibility to change in both our bodily and social well-being that all human beings experience, makes it clear that there is no position of invulnerability – no conclusive way to prevent or avoid change'.[11] On this construction, all humans are equally vulnerable all the time, since change is an inevitable constant in life, and is always disruptive. Nevertheless, it also seems clear that every individual is subject to vulnerabilities that are specific to themselves due to their own circumstances and environment, as well as the universal vulnerabilities that relate to the human condition. It is unclear, however, how far these vulnerabilities can be encapsulated within the liberal subject traditionally conceived of by the law.

Exploring these ideas, Fineman draws on Butler's work[12] in the development of her thesis on the vulnerable subject, which she uses to provide a theoretical perspective to understand disadvantage and inequality.[13] Fineman considers that inequalities within society result in vulnerabilities that cannot be addressed in a system founded upon the idea of the rational, self-interested individual who bears rights enforceable by law: the archetypal liberal subject. In her view, therefore, the ideology that underpins liberal legal theory and reveres individual autonomy and self-determination in health care law, should be replaced with an understanding of *universal* vulnerability.[14] She regards the strength of this vulnerability approach as lying in its ability to provide 'an independent universal approach to justice, one that focuses on exploring the nature of the *human* rather than the rights, parts of the human rights trope'.[15] Here, the human aspects are regarded as 'universal and constant, inherent in the human condition'[16] and emphasised through the life experiences of the individual and their particular circumstances.

---

10 Fineman 2017: 142 (emphasis in original).
11 Ibid.
12 Butler 2004.
13 Fineman 2008.
14 Fineman and Grear 2013.
15 Fineman 2013: 13 (emphasis in original).
16 Fineman 2008: 1.

Embedded in this theory is the expectation that universal vulnerability can be overcome by political and institutional support that enables individuals to prosper; Fineman calls for vulnerability to be acknowledged as an inherent human characteristic, arguing that political discourse should be reorganised in response.

Vulnerability is fundamental to bioethics, which locates protection from harm at its core, with moral responsibilities flowing from this.[17] More specifically, Fineman's approach has been embraced by some authors in relation to bioethics,[18] which, it is argued, can be enriched by recognising the embodied and embedded qualities of the human subject within the social environment that create inevitable dependence in others.[19] Similarly, in the bioethical context, ten Have refers to vulnerability as the state of being susceptible to harm, potentially incorporating a limited ability to recover from that harm or to adapt to it.[20] These notions would indicate that in health care, individual patients are likely to be especially vulnerable and in need of protection. However, somewhat counter to this approach, as noted above, bioethics and health care law have traditionally located individual autonomy and self-determination at the centre of the doctor-patient relationship, using the concept of informed consent to strengthen and protect the interests of patients.[21] Fineman regards autonomy as a 'myth' in the unequal relationship of power between doctor and patient.[22] Yet while we acknowledge that consent is an imperfect mechanism in many regards,[23] we are concerned that foregrounding vulnerability in the way Fineman suggests has the potential to both introduce paternalism and remove control from the patient. In the doctor-patient relationship, the dynamic between vulnerability and autonomy is complex,[24] especially where one is concerned to maximise patient self-determination and avoid paternalism. It is because of this that we steer away from the notion of the universal vulnerable subject as our starting point, beginning instead with the concept of *potential* vulnerability. It has been acknowledged that the inequality of power in the doctor-patient relationship can exacerbate patients' inherent vulnerabilities,[25] leading to disadvantage and, inevitably, poor health has the potential to exacerbate vulnerability. Thus, Fineman's analysis, based on the corporeal frailty that

---

17 See, e.g. Rogers and others 2012b.
18 See, for instance, Thomson 2018: 1209.
19 Fineman 2014: 318.
20 ten Have 2016.
21 See, e.g. *Montgomery* v. *Lanarkshire Health Board* [2015] UKSC 11.
22 See, e.g. Fineman 2010: 263. We note that Fineman does not reject the value of attaining autonomy. That is, she does not advocate the 'casting aside autonomy, but rather that we realize that as desirable as autonomy is as an aspiration, it cannot be attained without an underlying provision of substantial assistance, subsidy, and support from society and its institutions, which give individuals the resources they need to create options and make choices.' (Fineman 2010: 260). It is the liberal conception of individual autonomy that Fineman is especially critical of.
23 See chapter 5, part 1, sections 3.i and 3.ii and part 2, section 1.
24 As we discuss further in the next section.
25 Pilnick and Dingwall 2011.

is experienced by all, clearly underpins and reinforces general understandings of the impact of ill-health on individual vulnerability. It does not, however, explain why the impact of this vulnerability is more profound on some than others.[26] Differences that may be inherent in the individual play a crucial role here, due to their own resilience, or situation, in response to the social and economic circumstances or relational/relationship environment within which a person exists. In the following section, we develop the argument that only by considering autonomy *alongside* vulnerability can we appreciate these differences and thereby oppose and overcome susceptibilities to exploitation.

What follows includes a discussion of the relationship between vulnerability and autonomy in the context of health care. It focuses on the legal and ethical aspects of patient decision-making and is informed by established legal principles, medical ethics and feminist philosophy.

2) Illness, vulnerability and (diminished) autonomy

Vulnerability as a universally recognised concept intuitively arises in the context of health care, where the state of vulnerability describes a person who may be at increased risk of harm or lacks the capacity (mental or physical) to protect themselves from harm. The law attempts to protect such persons – indeed all patients – from such potential harm by ensuring that medical decision-making is conducted within acceptable ethical and legal standards. Generally, this means that patients are provided with information upon which to base their decisions about whether or not to agree to treatment,[27] or to opt for one approach to treatment over another, which is believed to ensure that patients are exercising their autonomy. In this way, respect for individual autonomy has given rise to understandings that patients have legal rights to consent to any touching that interferes with their bodily integrity, and if a patient is unable to consent to such interference, medical touching is only legitimate if legally authorised

---

26 We acknowledge that universal vulnerability theory does recognise that the level of vulnerability which an individual experiences is particular to that individual: 'while all human beings stand in a position of constant vulnerability, we are individually positioned differently. We have different forms of embodiment, and also are differently situated within webs of economic and institutional relationships. As a result, our vulnerabilities range in magnitude and potential at the individual level. Vulnerability, therefore, is both universal and particular; it is experienced uniquely by each of us.': Fineman 2010: 268–269. However, this still begins from the starting point of indistinguishable vulnerability: that we are all automatically vulnerable, *per se*.

27 Including any 'material risks involved in any recommended treatment' and 'any reasonable alternative or variant treatments. The test of materiality is whether, in the circumstances of the particular case, a reasonable person in the patient's position would be likely to attach significance to the risk, or the doctor is or should reasonably be aware that the particular patient would be likely to attach significance to it.' *Montgomery* v. *Lanarkshire Health Board* above, n.21, [87].

through a mechanism such as best interests.[28] Yet even a patient with demonstrable decision-making capacity may be vulnerable,[29] and the fact that a patient appears to act autonomously does not guarantee that they have done so wholly voluntarily,[30] or that they have not been exploited as 'one person's liberation is another's enslavement, and the reverse'.[31]

A further reason to challenge the claim that all patients should be empowered to protect and champion their own interests by exercising their autonomy is that if vulnerability is a universal and constant characteristic, it must surely function *prior to* autonomy and, if it does, it clearly has the capacity to undermine, or even prevent, autonomy from operating.[32] Autonomy, therefore, seems to be dependent on vulnerability in a way that may challenge the legal reliance on autonomy as a mechanism to evidence self-determination. Furthermore, it is clear that unless it is certain that the patient fully comprehends the implications of what is proposed by their doctor, simply imparting relevant information about a diagnosis or procedure to a patient does not assure an autonomous decision.[33] As Moore and Miller explain, a vulnerable person is one who experiences *diminished* autonomy due to either their own physical or psychological frailties, or inequalities as a result of disparities of status. They may consequently 'lack the ability to make life choices, to make personal decisions, to maintain independence, and to self-determine',[34] hence, in relation to care, vulnerability is often associated with dependence[35] and the need to be cared for.

Butler has explored ideas of vulnerability and its associated ethical implications for the actions of others who may be involved in caring for, or otherwise assisting, those who need support. She refers to this kind of caring situation as 'precariousness' and, for her, the potential for such vulnerability generates ethical obligations, duties, to ameliorate suffering as far as possible, and also to redress the inequalities that exploit vulnerability.[36] As we have discussed, Goodin explains that exploitation is a violation of this ethical duty to protect the vulnerable,[37] a view that we have problematised in chapter two.[38] But where that vulnerability is created by particular social circumstances that have created special responsibilities, which clearly applies to the doctor-patient relationship, we are more sympathetic to his view.

What is questionable, however, is whether the special responsibilities to protect the vulnerable in the context of the doctor-patient relationship and health

---

28 Coggon 2016: 405.
29 Spiers 2000.
30 Chapter 6, e.g. offers an analysis of undue influence that may remain hidden.
31 Englehardt 2001: 284. On consensual exploitation, see our discussion in chapter 2, section 3.ii.
32 Coyle and Atkinson 2019: 279.
33 Miola 2006; General Medical Council 2008.
34 Moore and Miller 1999: 1034.
35 Kittay 1999; Kitty and others 2005.
36 Butler 2004.
37 Goodin 1985.
38 See chapter 2, section 2.iv, text accompanying nn.46–54.

care can be addressed by the prioritisation of autonomy. According to ten Have, 'vulnerabilities ... are consequences of power differences and inequalities within the cultural and social environments that have been created'[39] and, in this context, individual agency cannot necessarily overcome the harms produced in environments that result in disadvantages, disparities and inequalities, including those caused by exploitation. Similar issues have been shown to apply in the context of race in health care and the doctor-patient relationship.[40] Although we should be mindful of the limitations of attempts to overcome harms caused through disadvantages and inequalities by way of prioritising individual agency, we concur with Anderson that:

> a liberal society's commitment to the protection of autonomy obligates it to do what it can to diminish vulnerabilities that undermine autonomy, including many institutional and cultural conditions that subtly constrain the development, maintenance, and exercise of autonomy.[41]

In considering the question of whether it is possible to 'reconcile obligations to protect vulnerable persons with obligations to respect autonomy',[42] one important parallel that can be drawn relates to the relational dimensions that both phenomenon share. Offering a relational conceptualisation of autonomy that we are sympathetic to, Anderson refers to autonomy competencies which include:

> the ability to appreciate what activities one finds genuinely worthwhile, to figure out how to realize one's ends, to step back from one's felt convictions, and to actually carry out one's intentions in the face of temptations. There are thus many dimensions along which autonomy is developed and exercised, including interpretive, deliberative, critical, and executive capacities. In this sense, being autonomous is like being able to find one's way through the woods: you have to discern where you want to go, figure out how to get there, persevere through the brambles, and occasionally stop to ask yourself whether the trip is worth the effort. [This conception of autonomy] conceptualizes these competences as importantly social or intersubjective.[43]

He goes on to assert that these competences are developed through interpersonal interaction and often applied in both the formation and maintenance of relationships.[44] Mackenzie supports the view that, especially when understood relationally, autonomy need not necessarily be seen in opposition to vulnerability[45]

---

39 ten Have 2016: 132.
40 Stone 2002.
41 See also Anderson 2013: 135.
42 Macklin 2012: 64.
43 Anderson 2013: 137.
44 Ibid: 138.
45 Mackenzie 2013.

and should therefore be respected and encouraged. For her, a focus purely on human (corporeal) vulnerability is dangerous because it can result in social relations, institutions and policies that are 'objectionably paternalistic', and whilst acknowledging vulnerability generates moral obligations to assist and protect, those obligations must also operate to respect and encourage autonomy if paternalism and exploitation are to be avoided.

This may not be reflected in health care generally, however, when vulnerability tends to be attributed to specific groups who are regarded as particularly susceptible to exploitation, such as research participants, the dying and those lacking mental capacity. But locating vulnerability as a status relevant only to specific groups means that vulnerability is regarded as exceptional and other than the norm. It also fails to respect the individual qualities and needs of the group members[46] that would be protected by acknowledging vulnerability alongside autonomy.[47] In turn, this precautionary, or paternalistic, approach can result in the violation of autonomy and the exclusion of individuals within those populations from aspects of health care from which they, and others, might benefit.

For these reasons, we advocate that *potential* vulnerability should logically form part of the assessment of each patient's needs and desires when determining how best to maximise their autonomy, but ought not to be regarded as automatically preventing them from reaching their own decisions, or being capable of so doing. For if autonomy is not properly supported, it can 'function to compound rather than ameliorate the vulnerability of persons or groups [it is] designed to assist'.[48] This is particularly problematic if a more libertarian (as contrasted to relational) approach to autonomy results in only limited representation of choice in circumstances where vulnerable persons are not fully appraised of the options available to them, or if the consequences and potential impacts of choices made are poorly understood. It thus seems to us that the relational nature of autonomy means that autonomy alone is adequate but not sufficient to protect the interests of vulnerable subjects, particularly when that vulnerability goes beyond the inherent frailties of all humans and is compounded by situational aspects such as poor health, dependence and social pressures. We explore this further in the next sections, which focus on medical research and specific medical treatments offered in the private sector.

In sum here, our position is that autonomy should be restored and enhanced as much as possible, *alongside* a recognition of vulnerability[49] in the context of all aspects of health care, in order to oppose and overcome susceptibility to exploitation. And, in our view, viewing vulnerability and autonomy as compatible in this way is not at odds with our Kantian liberal account of exploitation. As Formosa notes, 'nothing in Kant's account of autonomy implies that being a

---

46 See also Formosa 2013: 92
47 Clough 2017.
48 Mackenzie 2013: 34.
49 See also Hall 2018.

dependent and vulnerable being is incompatible with being autonomous ... So there is no reason why vulnerability cannot play an important role in Kantian ethics.'[50]

To illustrate how we might recognise both vulnerability and autonomy in practice, and following on from this theoretical assessment of the role of vulnerability in health care and its relationship with exploitation, we now turn to discuss vulnerability in medical research, as an example of a specific situation where vulnerability *may* play a role alongside the need to respect autonomy. We follow this by considering whether particular vulnerabilities are generated in interventions typically offered in privately funded health care settings, to further demonstrate ways in which specific situations might heighten the potential for exploitation.

3) Vulnerability in medical research

Medical research has long been regarded as suspicious and potentially exploitative,[51] and these impressions have only been compounded by well-documented examples of abuse and exploitation, including the Nazi atrocities in the Second World War, and numerous instances of unethical research practices throughout the twentieth century.[52] The Nuremberg Code[53] and subsequent Declaration of Helsinki,[54] first published in 1964, were designed as a foil to such unethical and exploitative research practices on largely socially disadvantaged persons, such as the financially insecure, people who were captive or incarcerated, and those lacking mental capacity. However, following the publication of an influential paper in 1967[55] it was soon apparent that abuses were still occurring, which quickly led to further guidance in the US, known as the Belmont Report.[56] This was probably

---

50   Formosa 2014: 94–95. Formosa explains that autonomy based on Kant's account of rational self-government is 'a fragile achievement that comes in degrees and is never fully secure. It constitutes an ideal ... When we achieve this ideal, we are free from domination by other people and our own desires and emotions': Formosa 2014: 94. Although we support a relational approach to autonomy rather than one that is based on Kantian ethics in this chapter, we would argue that a relational conceptualisation of autonomy can undoubtedly recognise that individuals can be dependant and vulnerable (see, e.g. Hall 2018), and that this recognition is in keeping with our account of the way in which exploitation – taking advantage of and misusing another person for one's own ends – can have a wide-reaching impact on the exploitee.
51   Brazier 2008.
52   Lederer 1995; Shamoo and Resnik 2003; Michael Evans, 'Porton Down guinea-pigs get apology' *The Times* (London, 18 January 2008); Godlee and others 2011.
53   Nuremberg Code (1947) 1996.
54   World Medical Association (1964) 'Declaration of Helsinki: Ethical Principles for Medical Research Involving Human Subjects' (1964, updated 2013) at https://www.wma.net/what-we-do/medical-ethics/declaration-of-helsinki/ accessed 10 January 2021.
55   Beecher 1966.
56   National Commission for the Protection of Human Subjects of Biomedical and Behavioral Research 1979.

the first document to implicitly consider vulnerability *per se* as requiring special consideration when obtaining consent from potential research participants. The report made recommendations for the practice of medical research based on three fundamental ethical principles: respect for persons, including their autonomy; beneficence, whereby the risk of harm is minimised in favour of potential benefits; and justice to ensure that the burdens of research are fairly distributed and participants are not exploited. In line with most concerns about vulnerability, the guidance aimed to reduce potential harms to research participants while simultaneously enhancing individual autonomy. Similar guidance has also been published, and repeatedly updated, in the UK,[57] adopting the same guiding principles. Dedicated legal regulation of medical research is rather scant in the UK, being largely limited to instruments rooted in the EU, and specific sections of the Mental Capacity Act 2005[58] relating to research involving adults who lack the capacity to give a valid consent. The extensive ethical guidance available generally forms the basis of the professional regulation that shapes the extent of clinical responsibility.

On the whole therefore, there is clear and detailed guidance available about the ethical conduct of research with those specific groups that are regarded as particularly vulnerable, and regulatory controls and ethical review processes are designed to ensure that such research participants are properly protected.[59] A great deal has been written about the conduct of research involving specific vulnerable populations, such as those with cognitive impairments and children, who are generally regarded as lacking decision-making capacity.[60] However, here we are more concerned about the *potential* vulnerabilities of participants who are able to give informed consent, but may still be vulnerable to exploitation. It is important to reiterate that being vulnerable is not a blanket term, it may be inherent or situational. Potential participants may be vulnerable because of the situation they find themselves in due to their health status, or because they are socially disadvantaged and therefore disempowered. Both groups are at risk of exploitation, which tends to suggest an objective and external reality when contrasted with actually being vulnerable, and indicates a subjective and experiential state.[61]

In essence, our concern is for self-determining autonomous participants who may simultaneously be vulnerable to risks that they are ostensibly prepared to take. For instance, some medical students report their experience of participating in research caused them to regard themselves as guinea pigs, which seems to imply that they went through the experience feeling disempowered or even captive or

---

57 For instance, the General Medical Council (GMC) publishes general ethical guidance on the conduct of research: General Medical Council 2013c, and most of the Royal Colleges also publish their own guidance regarding research relating to their own specialisms.
58 Primarily ss.30–34.
59 Regulation (EU) No536/2014 Of the European Parliament and the Council on Clinical Trials on Medicinal Products for Human Use, and Repealing Directive 2001/20/EC, specifically Articles 31 and 32.
60 Bracken-Roche and others 2017; Ivanova and others 2017.
61 Clarke and Driever 1983.

enslaved, despite having decision-making capacity.[62] Such an impression is likely to be based on the fact that their involvement was largely predicated on financial necessity, suggesting that they would not have participated had they not been students. Without wishing to perpetuate stereotypical assumptions about researchers or research participants, it is therefore likely that all actual and potential research participants are potentially vulnerable to exploitation, but that some (those with no other hope,[63] the socially and financially disadvantaged,[64] and those in Third World countries,[65] for example) may be *more* vulnerable to exploitation and abuse.

Regulatory instruments and ethical guidance enshrine consent and autonomy at the centre of guidance on the conduct of research, in order to protect the interests of research participants. Nevertheless, participants need to balance complex risks in the same way that patients do before consenting to treatments. It may therefore seem odd to consider research participants as especially vulnerable, but there is an important distinction to be drawn. Where patients are receiving treatment or diagnostic interventions, the aim is that they will receive health benefits. By contrast, research participants, who may also be patients, are involved with interventions that generally aim to benefit others and will be exposed to risks due to the uncertain outcomes of participating in medical research. Here, as will be explained, autonomy alone may not be sufficient to protect the interests of research participants. Hence, as we argued in the previous discussion, vulnerability ought to be considered in tandem with autonomy to protect against exploitation. We advocate this position because, while autonomy can be evidenced through the mechanism of consent, both intellectually and formally, the consent given may not be legally or ethically adequate if the participant has been unduly influenced by the researcher or the beguiling potential benefits of the research project.[66]

There are numerous reasons why patients participate in research. The participant patient may agree to the research for entirely altruistic reasons: a desire to do good or give back to the system that has supported them in their illness. Alternatively, they may view their involvement in research as potentially so beneficial to their health that they are prepared to take any risks involved and be blind to any potential hazards. Such a situation could arise, for instance, in trials of interventions often perceived as life-saving, such as chemotherapy drugs or xenotransplantation. Even though the results of properly designed research trials are unknown, and sometimes unknowable, because the interventions are untried, there is often a perception that a new treatment or procedure is likely to be an improvement on current practice,[67] especially if there is no existing

---

62 Mandeville 2006.
63 Fovargue 2013.
64 Typically, students (especially medical students), and the unemployed or those on low wages.
65 Nuffield Council on Bioethics 2002.
66 Mngadi and others 2017. For our discussion and explanation of undue influence, see chapter 3, text accompanying n.240 and chapter 6, section 4.
67 Wendler 2008.

treatment. Indeed, in relation to xenotransplantation, which, in the absence of an alternative, would likely be regarded as life-saving treatment, the Nuffield Council on Bioethics has observed that 'the offer of such a procedure in itself puts pressure on patients to accept – and may distort judgement.'[68]

All research involving seriously ill or dying patients has the potential to raise such issues, but it is important that research involving these groups is conducted so that treatments that might prove to be beneficial can be developed for future patients. The centrality of informed consent is stressed in these situations so that autonomy is maximised, however, it is clear that autonomy can be compromised where people are in pain, weary of life or clinging to hope.[69] When there is little or 'no other hope',[70] participating in research may be regarded as an opportunity that is simply too promising a proposition to turn down,[71] despite the reality that treatments being trialled are unproven, may not work or may be less effective than existing interventions, and that the patient may be in a control group. In many ways, the offer of participation in research in these situations may seem to exhibit characteristics of undue inducement.[72] And outwith such situations, there can be structural factors which can also exacerbate a potential participant's vulnerability to inducements. In their analysis of the CAPRISA[73] 008 trial involving access to unlicensed HIV prevention technology in South Africa, Mngadi et al discuss one participant's concealment of significant clinical information that would have made her ineligible for the study. Her situational circumstances, including her husband's suspected infidelity, made her vulnerable to HIV infection, thereby constituting strong motivational factors to participate. The authors note:

> Her poor financial status and consequent dependency on her partner exacerbated by an unplanned pregnancy, the risk of intimate-partner violence, inability to negotiate condom usage, especially during pregnancy and the direct personal benefit of access to HIV prevention and ancillary care. The combination of these factors may potentially have constituted, for this participant, an undue inducement.[74]

The participant's involvement in the CAPRISA study potentially put her health and the health of her foetus at risk, thereby illustrating that participation in a medical trial may hold out the prospect of a 'desirable good' that is irresistible in its context and can result in poor judgement.[75] However, notwithstanding their final statement in the quotation above, it is interesting to note that the

---

68 Nuffield Council on Bioethics 1996: para 7.7.
69 Morse 2000.
70 Fovargue 2013: 183.
71 Fox 1998.
72 Mngadi and others 2017. On inducements, see chapter 5, part 1, section 3.i.
73 Centre for the AIDS Programme of Research in South Africa.
74 Mngadi and others 2017: 827.
75 Ibid: 825.

authors conclude that there was no undue inducement to participate in this case 'because inducements typically concern only financial incentives'.[76] We would challenge this conceptual limitation of inducements to financial incentives: our detailed analysis of inducements in the subsequent chapter presents the alternative argument that an individual's decision-making can be distorted and, in some cases their consent can be impeded, by incentives other than financial ones.[77] Moreover, the assumption that financial inducements are suspect because they can encourage a person to place financial interests over welfare interests has been critiqued.[78] The focus on monetary incentives in medical research no doubt stems from the fact that there is much work on the influence of such incentives on potential participants' decisions as to whether to enrol in medical research.[79] Yet, and although it has been acknowledged that not all inducement is undue,[80] there is limited material on the impact of this kind of vulnerability on autonomy and decision-making.[81] Furthermore, the matter is surely complicated because the question of whether an inducement is undue is inevitably subjective.[82]

Clearly the motivation of research participants is complex, and consent is a useful mechanism in striving to maximise autonomy. But, returning to research participants who are seriously ill or dying, in order to avoid exploitation, there needs to be careful consideration of the *special* vulnerability of such participants alongside consent, with an explicit assessment of the possible impact of situational vulnerability relating to the patient's particular health status. For this reason, we advocate that the details of good ethical practice ought to be enshrined in law. More specifically, it should be a requirement that information about the research is given by a person independent of the clinical team involved in medical care, and that the patient be given time, at least 24 hours, to consider whether they wish to proceed. In addition, once information has been provided and the time period for consideration has lapsed, if the patient is inclined to proceed, their motivation for participating should be assessed. None of this should be regarded as implying that vulnerable research participants are being deliberately exploited, or that those who do consent to participate are not capable of making a reasoned decision. Instead, these measures are designed to ensure, as far as possible, that vulnerability is not a driver behind any consent given.

We address one final matter here, turning the tables to recognise that situational pressures can impact on those who conduct medical research as well as potential

---

76 Ibid.
77 See chapter 5, section 3.i.
78 'Why should we assume that individuals' material interests do not outweigh their present and future physical welfare interests …? The rewards received will, likely, substantially impact on their own or their family's quality of life, and thus the exchange is not obviously and invariably a "bad bargain"': Price 2013: 529
79 See, for instance, Wertheimer 2011: 149–156.
80 Emanuel 2005; Wertheimer 2011: 149–156.
81 See, e.g. Almeida and others 2007; Ballantyne 2008.
82 Macklin 1981.

participants. Despite the raft of ethical guidance, both national and international, unethical and exploitative research practices still seem to occur with alarming regularity, although thankfully the occasions when deliberate misconduct occurs are infrequent. Although rare, well-publicised examples of research misconduct and fraud, such as McBride's falsification of research on birth defects and Wakefield's discredited work on MMR and autism, have been influential in the regulation of medical research designed to limit the possibility of misconduct.[83] Nevertheless, researchers are sociopolitical beings who respond to pressures and motivations associated with personal and professional development that may lead them to compromise the interests of participants,[84] either intentionally or unconsciously. Academic careers are structured around the ability to perform and publish research, which can provide an incentive to perform research of dubious scientific efficacy. Alternatively, researchers may feel pressure to conduct types of research that involve vulnerable individuals and populations because the potential benefits are great, or act compassionately out of concern to do the best for their patients.

In turn they may become vulnerable to the risk of perpetrating exploitation due to emotional stresses associated with conducting such research:

> Questions of exploitation, or 'using' others tend to arise as you become immersed in research and begin to rejoice in the richness of what you are learning. You are thankful, but instead of simply appreciating the gift, you may feel guilty for how much you are receiving and how little you are giving in return.[85]

Vulnerability is inherently relational, so can be regarded here as a two-way street,[86] whereby both the research participant and the researcher are susceptible to influences that could be regarded as 'undue'. Researchers themselves may, therefore, become vulnerable to powerful influences that could be brought to bear by participants keen to participate in research. Or the researcher may be so focused on getting the project completed that they ignore the fact that the participant is taking risks, perhaps because they are overly sympathetic to the participant's plight and thus overlook the potential harms and uncertain outcomes due to the pressure exerted by the participant. Thus, in our view, alongside researchers' potential physical vulnerabilities, it is imperative that research ethics committees also give due regard to potential emotional vulnerabilities that researchers can face.[87]

---

83 Ragg 1993; Godlee and others 2011.
84 McNeill 1993.
85 Glesne and Peshkin 1992: 112.
86 Henderson and others 2004.
87 Whilst researchers' emotional vulnerabilities have been discussed in other disciplines (e.g. education: Howard and Hammond 2019; ethnographical research: Sikic Micanovi and others 2020; consumer research: Hamilton and others 2006; and in qualitative research more broadly: Duffy 2008), the potential situational vulnerabilities of medical researchers have been subjected to less scrutiny. For one example, see Laar 2014.

In sum, applying the lens of vulnerability is useful with regard to medical research, in helping to ensure that additional scrutiny is imposed on research projects that involve individuals who may be vulnerable to particular harms or exploitative practices through their potential involvement in research. However, it should also be acknowledged that the potential for vulnerability is not just limited to participants, but extends to researchers also. And greater scrutiny is required of what exactly can give rise to vulnerabilities in medical research to avoid a sweeping approach that fails to both give due regard to maximising autonomy and to be mindful of the factors that can exacerbate a participant's vulnerability to exploitation.

4) Vulnerability in privately funded health care

In the publicly funded NHS, the health care system is regulated by organs of the state such as the GMC, rather than the quasi-contractual approach that typifies the private health care sector. That said, on the face of it, it should make no difference to a patient's treatment whether they are treated in the public NHS system or in the private sector in the UK. Care should be determined and offered on the basis of the patient's best interests and delivered according to clinical need. But in practice this may not be the reality. Patients who use the private sector could feel more able to demand particular treatments or approaches and use their financial authority to obtain the treatments they desire rather than using the public sector. For instance, in an aforementioned[88] study of private patients published in 1996, Wiles and Higgins demonstrated that, at that time, respondents opting for private care were concerned that paternalism still existed in the NHS and would restrict their autonomy, whereas they could be more assertive in the private sector.[89] However, some choices may not be in the best interests of the individual patient, particularly if autonomy gives way to choices that may be heavily influenced by social or relational pressures.[90] We thus focus on patients in the private sector rather in a publicly funded health service here, to illustrate that having more choice does not necessarily remove vulnerability and could exacerbate it.

Although not specifically in the context of medical treatment, Fineman is sceptical about the value of choice, arguing that 'choice trumps any perceived inequality and justifies maintenance of the status quo',[91] by which she means that a person may *appear* to have been empowered by being offered a choice and then to have exercised their autonomy by expressing a preference, but that appearance can mask a different reality whereby the choices are limited and the outcomes are predetermined and not necessarily beneficial. Also, Wiles and Higgins concluded

---

88 See chapter 3, section 5.ii.
89 Wiles and Higgins 1996.
90 Christman 2009.
91 Fineman 2004: 41.

after analysing their data that choice and patient demand did not necessarily drive treatment decisions in the doctor-patient relationship. They opine that 'the cold and detached nature of market exchanges'[92] does not characterise the actual relationship between doctor and patient. Rather, the power imbalance remains since the doctor retains greater knowledge of the body and intimate aspects of care. Nevertheless, it seems that the more consumer-oriented attitude of patients in the private sector does have an impact on the kinds of treatment that patients receive, and that some patients may be potentially vulnerable to seeking treatment that is risky and unnecessary. To illustrate this point, we focus on a specific area where patients may turn to the private sector even though they would generally rely on NHS treatment for routine care: cosmetic surgery.

Whilst not necessarily being a treatment sought in response to an illness or medical condition, cosmetic surgery is a medical procedure that is one of the most commonly sought in the private health care sector. We are concerned that some patients seeking cosmetic surgery may be vulnerable to accepting treatments offered, or indeed demanding treatments, because of social and cultural pressures, pressures which can create unrealistic expectations about how one *should* look. Griffiths and Mullock have referred to the 'normalisation of surgical enhancement' and the perception of cosmetic surgery as a 'lifestyle choice'.[93] They conceptualise the motivation(s) for cosmetic surgery as 'an intersubjective and embodied process that takes place in a consumerist environment', with the latter being shaped by the particular culture and society in which the person lives.[94]

Women in particular face cultural pressures to look a certain way, pressures that are exacerbated by social media; and it remains the case that women more commonly have cosmetic surgery compared to men.[95] Cultural pressures are all the more omnipresent for adolescents. McHale has discussed the increase in demand for procedures such as lip enhancement for teenagers and the role that media representations have played in fuelling this rise. She provides Queensland as an example of a jurisdiction that has placed legal prohibitions on cosmetic procedures for minors as a consequence of clinicians' concerns about the impact that the 'body beautiful' and 'beach' culture were having on adolescents particularly.[96] In the case of surgeries such as breast enhancement, Zuckerman has noted that because breast implants typically last for ten years, an adolescent who has such surgery will need repeated surgeries throughout her life.[97] She also questions whether 'adolescents who want to improve their appearance rationally consider the risks', arguing that 'teenagers are often oblivious to the well-documented long-term health consequences of smoking, tanning, and other risky behaviours, and are likely to pay even less attention to the risks of

---

92 Wiles and Higgins 1996: 353.
93 Griffiths and Mullock 2018: 220–221.
94 Ibid: 223.
95 Ibid; Pereira and others 2018: 2.
96 McHale 2015.
97 Zuckerman 2005: 253–254.

cosmetic surgery, making informed consent difficult'.[98] While this might be true of some adolescents and could thus be a potential vulnerability that needs to be considered, we would be cautious about applying a broad-brush approach that would assume that *all* teenagers who seek to improve their appearance are unable to appreciate and understand the risks of cosmetic surgery.[99] In addition, we have critiqued the use of the concept of rationality when it comes to decision-making.[100]

That said, when faced with patients who are vulnerable to accepting procedures that they can access through private health care, but which they do not need for therapeutic, health-related purposes, what it means to respect the patient is muddied if it is unclear whether we are, and should be, respecting autonomy, and/or respecting best interests. There is a real risk of cosmetic surgery essentially acting as a sticking plaster for serious psychological issues related to body image and self-worth that some women and adolescents who seek these procedures may have. Griffiths and Mullock question the legally legitimating rationale for permitting cosmetic surgery[101] where patients might be vulnerable because of self-image issues since, for example, whilst breast enhancement as a treatment for psychological issues regarding self-image may have therapeutic aspects, 'it does nothing to treat the possible psychological causes for the lack of self-worth and it harms physical health via the surgery'.[102] Zuckerman draws attention to the risk that where a teenager's desire to change her appearance is fuelled by an eating disorder,[103] this may go undetected, pointing to body dysmorphic disorder (BDD) as an example, which has an average onset of 16 years of age.[104] Notably, a connection has been drawn between BDD and 'Snapchat

---

98   Ibid.
99   It seems to us that such an approach shares a synergy with that reflected in the High Court judgment in *R (on the application of) Quincy Bell and A v. Tavistock and Portman NHS Trust and others* [2020] EWHC 3274 (Admin), which concerned the use of puberty-suppressing drugs for those aged under 18 who experience gender dysphoria. The court held that for teenagers aged between 13 to 16, 'there will be enormous difficulties in a child under 16 understanding and weighing up this information and deciding whether to consent to the use of puberty blocking medication. It is highly unlikely that a child aged 13 or under would be competent to give consent to the administration of puberty blockers. It is doubtful that a child aged 14 or 15 could understand and weigh the long-term risks and consequences of the administration of puberty blockers': [151].
100 See chapter 2, section 2.vi; chapter 5, part 1, section 3.i, n.84.
101 In the UK, cosmetic surgery is considered to fall within the medical exception to an offence against the person under the Offences Against the Person Act 1861 (ss.18, 20 and 47), because the patient consents to a procedure that constitutes 'proper medical treatment': *R v. Brown* [1994] AC 212, 258 HL; Lewis 2012.
102 Griffiths and Mullock 2018: 227.
103 There are numerous reports of eating disorders being on the rise in teenagers and children and the COVID-19 pandemic appears to have contributed to this. See, e.g. Yohannes Lowe, 'Hospital admissions for children with eating disorders rise by a third in England' *The Guardian* (London, 29 December 2020); Petkova and others 2019.
104 Zuckerman 2005: 255.

dysmporphia', a phenomenon that the media has reported on over recent years,[105] which involves patients (particularly millennials) requesting procedures to make them look more like their filtered selfie.[106] The cosmetic doctor reported to have coined the term Snapchat dysmporphia is quoted as stating that:

> The danger is when [a filtered selfie] is not just a reference point, but it becomes how the patient sees themselves, or the patient wants to look exactly like that image. Filtered selfies especially can have harmful effects on adolescent[s] or those with BDD because these groups may more severely internalise this beauty.[107]

What is more, the contemporary popularity of 'cosmetic surgery tourism'[108] can generate additional vulnerabilities. A driving force behind cosmetic surgery tourism is the fact that such surgery costs less outside of the UK,[109] with Poland and the Czech Republic being favoured choices for certain procedures such as breast augmentation, for example.[110] A consequence of this international availability is that such surgery is now more accessible to those who would previously not have been wealthy enough to afford it.[111] But this gives rise to potential vulnerabilities that could be exploited, since as, Griffiths and Mullock note, it is often harder to check the reputation and safety records of clinics based outside of a patient's own country.[112] And where 'cosmetic surgery tourists' pay for package deals prior to travel, this may cause them to be reluctant to cancel the procedure if they begin to have misgivings about it.[113]

Because of our concerns, we have much sympathy for Latham's call for a relational autonomy approach involving 'constructive dialogue between a patient and her surgeon'. Besides providing information to ensure fully informed consent, this would require feminist counselling designed to 'build self-trust and recognise structural oppression; professional self-awareness and ideally an institutional

---

105 See, g. Anna Davies A 'People are getting surgery to look like their Snapchat selfies' BBC 3 news report (19 April 2018), at https://www.bbc.co.uk/bbcthree/article/9ca4f7c6-d2c3-4e25-862c-03aed9ec1082 accessed 7 January 2021; Chelsea Ritschel, '"Snapchat dysmorphia": Teenagers are getting plastic surgery to look like selfie filters' *The Independent* (London, 6 August 2018); Ellie Hunt, 'Faking it: how selfie dysmorphia is driving people to seek surgery' *The Guardian* (London, 23 January 2019).
106 'Applying filters to photos allows oneself to smooth the skin, widen the eyes, narrow the jawline, plump the lips, and flatten the nasolabial folds, among countless other edits, with the click of a button': Cristel and others 2021: 123.
107 Ritschel, n.105.
108 Pereira and others 2018.
109 Ibid: 3.
110 Griffiths and Mullock 2018: 221; ibid: 3.
111 Albeit not during the period of travel restrictions imposed during the COVID-19 pandemic in 2020 and 2021.
112 For a discussion of the research findings on complications arising from cosmetic surgery procedures undertaken abroad, see Pereria and others 2018: 3–6.
113 Griffiths and Mullock 2018: 229.

commitment to work against damaging social and cultural pressures', in order to assess 'whether the reasons for surgery are in fact socially constructed'.[114] We also support Zuckerman's call for the screening of potential teenage patients via psychological testing in order to ensure that they have the maturity to reach decisions about such surgery.[115] We are doubtful that the potential vulnerabilities we discuss above can necessarily be properly addressed through information giving and consent in the commercial sector. It is surely unrealistic to expect the cosmetic surgeon (and indeed all clinicians working in the private sector) to impart value-free information about elective procedures they are selling.[116] For this reason, we argue that the feminist counselling and screening that Latham and Zuckerman advocate should occur *prior* to information giving and consent sessions and be conducted by independent counsellors and mental health professionals.

It is a positive development that current key professional guidance in the UK has taken account of the need to recognise that some patients who seek cosmetic surgery may be vulnerable. The GMC requires doctors offering cosmetic surgery to address any vulnerability, directing that 'when you discuss interventions and options with a patient, you must consider their vulnerabilities and psychological needs. You must satisfy yourself that the patient's request for the cosmetic intervention is voluntary.'[117] The Royal College of Surgeons advises that surgeons should 'make attempts to identify the psychologically vulnerable patient and, where they have concerns, be prepared to avoid or defer operation pending psychological assessment.'[118] And the college states there should be 'a cooling off period of at least two weeks between the stages to allow the patient to reflect on the decision' to [e]nsure that consent is obtained in a two-stage process'"[119]

The standards expected of cosmetic surgeons by the professional bodies as set out above are still not legal requirements, however, even after the highly critical Keogh review of the regulation of cosmetic practice recorded a failure to prioritise patients' well-being and safety in the UK.[120] And, more recently, the effects of the COVID-19 pandemic and 'lockdowns' may also be playing a role in limiting protection that professional regulations offer.[121] Griffiths and

---

114 Latham 2008: 449 and 448.
115 Zuckerman 2005: 254.
116 Holm 1997:157; Zuckerman 2005: 254.
117 General Medical Council, 2016b: [19].
118 Royal College of Surgeons 2016: 9.
119 Ibid: 11.
120 Department of Health and Social Care 2013.
121 In 2020, BAAPS (British Association of Aesthetic Plastic Surgeons) reported on a survey revealing that numerous non-BAAPS clinics were not requiring a cooling off period, or face to face consultations, and warned that 'unscrupulous' providers were 'coercing vulnerable patients' : see BAAPS, 'Post-pandemic panic – BAAPS issues a stark warning to the public: "Don't fall victim to unscrupulous providers selling surgery as a post-lockdown quick fix"' (5 October 2020), at https://baaps.org.uk/about/news/1824/postpandemic_panic_baaps_issues_a_stark_warning_to_the_public_dont_fall_victim_to_unscrupulous_providers_selling_surgery_as_a_postlockdown_quick_fix accessed 10 January 2021.

Mullock have called for 'much tighter regulation and sufficiently informed consent for all non-therapeutic cosmetic surgery'.[122] In light of the guidance from the GMC and the Royal College of Surgeons of England referred to above, they offer the cautious opinion that 'we may anticipate a marginally better regulated collection of cosmetic surgery providers in the UK'.[123] Although we support their call for tighter regulation, globalisation means that the additional protection these existing regulatory revisions and any future reform to introduce corresponding legal requirements might provide will not necessarily be offered to patients seeking more affordable cosmetic surgery beyond the UK.[124] This highlights that fact that situational vulnerabilities which are the result of a person's social and cultural environment cannot be resolved through regulation without also tackling the social and cultural representations which play such a contributory role in the motivation to seek treatment in the private sector that is often not required for therapeutic, health-related purposes.

Whilst we only have the space to consider a further example briefly, fertility treatment offers a further instance of a treatment that is commonly offered in the private sector and can involve procedures that are risky or of limited efficacy. For several years, it has been reported that some IVF clinics are 'over-selling or mis-selling adjunct therapies'[125] at extra cost, which those who are desperate to achieve a pregnancy may be prepared to accept, or even demand.[126] Examples of such add-ons include assisted hatching[127] and intrauterine culture.[128] Yet the evidence to support claims by fertility clinics that these add-on treatments offer a way of increasing the chances of a live birth is 'poor or non-existent'.[129] Consequently, the Human Fertilisation and Embryology Authority has published regularly updated guidance to fertility patients which includes a traffic light rating for various add-ons, with a red rating meaning there is no evidence

---

122 Griffiths and Mullock 2018: 227.
123 Ibid: 226.
124 Ibid: 228.
125 Harper and others 2017: 486. 'It didn't really sink in, when the doctor described this as cutting edge, that that meant experimental': Sharon Begley, 'From assisted hatching to embryo glue, most IVF "add-ons" rest on shaky science, studies find' *STAT* (Boston, 5 November 2019).
126 Begley, ibid; Pamela Mahoney-Tsigdinos, 'The big IVF add-on racket' *New York Times* (New York, 12 December 2019); Harper and others 2017; Wilkinson and others 2019.
127 Breaching the patient's zona pellucida with the aim of encouraging implantation of the embryo, usually via a non-contact laser: Harper and others 2017: 488.
128 Following the collection and preparation of eggs and sperm, the fertilised eggs are placed in an intrauterine device that is inserted into the patient's womb. It remains there during the initial stages of embryo development for several hours and then, on removal, the embryos are placed into an incubator until ready to be transferred back to the patient's womb: HFEA, 'Treatment add-ons' at https://www.hfea.gov.uk/treatments/treatment-add-ons/ accessed 9 January 2021.
129 Harper and others 2017: 486. Well-designed, high-quality randomised controlled trials continue to be considered the best evidence of efficacy of additional fertility treatments: Wilkinson and others 2019; Harper and others 2017: 489.

to show that the treatment can increase the chances of a live birth and/or that it is unsafe. Both assisted hatching and intrauterine culture have red ratings and thus should only be offered in a research setting.[130]

We agree with Harper et al that the legal requirement of informed consent is not enough in itself to prevent fertility clinics from mis-selling 'add-ons', especially where patients have also been influenced by inaccurate explanations of reproductive failure presented in the media.[131]

But we would also draw attention to the potential vulnerability that some patients seeking fertility treatment will possess to accepting any additional treatment because of the strength of their desire for a child. For, if IVF add-ons are recommended on the basis of a possible increased chance of success,[132] it is almost inevitable that the patient will choose to accept them. This reflects Fineman's views, quoted above; that is, it may *appear* that a patient is being offered a choice and thereby empowered, but the reality is that when a fertility doctor informs a patient who is desperate to have a child and has already invested emotionally and financially in numerous unsuccessful rounds of IVF, that 'they have one more thing you can try, it gives you hope'.[133] The outcome – that the patient will say yes – is predetermined.

There is an interesting question as to whether offering add-ons to patients whose fertility treatment has been unsuccessful amounts to exploitation. A fertility doctor quoted in one news article expresses the view that add-ons are offered with good intentions to patients when all else has failed: 'sometimes, when you're down to your last hurrah … you want to throw everything you've got at it'.[134] This raises the matter of whether, returning to our account of exploitation, patients are being misused and whether doctors are acting for their own ends in such circumstances. Much would depend on whether the fertility doctor's desire to 'throw everything you've got at it' stems from a wish to serve the patient's interests by exhausting every possible means of achieving a live birth, or from a more self-serving reputational purpose that would be fulfilled through achieving the same outcome. And even if it is the former, thus indicating that there may not be exploitation,[135] we would question the view that offering an add-on treatment with an unproven success rate is in the interests of a patient who would surely be so desperate at this stage, since there is a vulnerability here that is at risk of being taken advantage of.

---

130 HFEA, n.128.
131 Harper and others 2017: 486.
132 Success rates appear to be the most important factor behind which fertility clinic patients choose. See, e.g. Lass and Brindsen 2001. See also chapter 3, n.75.
133 Begley, n.125.
134 Ibid.
135 Whether exploitation occurs would require further analysis of the specific interaction between doctor and patient, involving detail that we do not have here. See, e.g. our consideration of Jansen and Wall's scenario involving David in chapter 3, text accompanying n.23.

To conclude, it is both inaccurate and dangerous, in our view, to characterise *all* patients who seek health care and treatment in the private sector as vulnerable. It is inaccurate because the ability to pay can empower some patients. It is dangerous because such a characterisation may invoke paternalism and protectionism which are not, in themselves, necessarily harmful, but should be avoided as the default position. However, more contemporary accounts of vulnerability, such as Fineman's, can help explain why patients in the private sector may be vulnerable and might be exploited and how, as sociopolitical beings who are relationally autonomous, we face pressures and motivations that could cause some to become the manipulators or the manipulated.[136]

5) Potential vulnerabilities in all aspects of health care and exploitation

In identifying a particularly pernicious kind of vulnerability, Goodin highlights 'morally unacceptable vulnerabilities and dependencies which we should, but have not yet managed to, eliminate'.[137] The vulnerabilities that can exist in the doctor-patient relationship and all aspects of health care, and can result in exploitation, offer examples of such pernicious kinds of vulnerability.

Furthermore, whilst we should recognise that ill-health can exacerbate vulnerability, we must also be cognisant of the fact that vulnerability can exist in all aspects of health care. It is notable that although cosmetic surgery and fertility treatment are both treatments offered through the health care system, what is being treated in both cases is not necessarily regarded as an 'illness'. But this does not mean that patients, or clients, accessing such treatments are not vulnerable to exploitation. Moreover, Fineman's approach to vulnerability can help explain why both patient and *doctor*[138] (or medical researcher) might be vulnerable to exploitation.

We reiterate our position, however, that it is not appropriate to make assumptions regarding groups and vulnerability in health care. We should not assume, for instance, that simply being a research participant makes one vulnerable. Indeed, it is worth noting that in some circumstances, research participants are potentially advantaged when compared to NHS patients. For example, the Declaration of Helsinki requires that patients in a control group should be provided with the 'best proven treatment' yet in the NHS, patients cannot be assured of receiving such treatment due to resource constraints.

Being mindful of actual and potential vulnerabilities helps shed light on situations and circumstances in which exploitation is more likely to occur and which society can then endeavour to guard against. And we have argued that it is crucial to support and maximise autonomy alongside assessing potential

---

136 ten Have 2016.
137 Goodin 1985: 203.
138 See also chapter 1, n.17; chapter 5, part 2, section 4; chapter 6, section 3.

vulnerability in order to tackle vulnerabilities and susceptibilities to exploitation. Thus, in the context of medical research involving potential participants who are seriously ill or dying, we have advocated for the creation of legal requirements pertaining to the provision of information about the research by an independent person. We have called for a minimum time period before the decision as to whether to participate can be made, as well as an assessment of the person's motivation should they wish to participate. Similarly, the situational vulnerabilities that can be possessed by patients seeking cosmetic surgery in the private sector cause us to support calls for stricter (legal) regulation to protect vulnerable patients. Having identified the potential vulnerability that some patients seeking fertility treatment will possess to accepting any adjunct treatments because of their desperate desire for a child, we have expressed concerns that there is a real risk that offering such treatments with an unproven success rate is not in the best interests of such a patient and may amount to exploitation.

To conclude, what we have sought to do in this chapter is to emphasise that we should not assume that a particular person will be vulnerable. Rather, building on Fineman's universal vulnerable subject approach, we have foregrounded the notion of universal *potential* vulnerability, especially in the dual contexts of ill-health and the doctor-patient relationship.

5 Sexual exploitation in the doctor-patient relationship

PART 1: SEXUAL BOUNDARY BREACHES AND SEXUAL EXPLOITATION

Sexual misconduct perpetrated by doctors is seemingly not uncommon[1] and, as we explore in this chapter, some such misconduct can involve sexual exploitation. This is despite the strict position in regulatory medical ethics that doctors should never breach sexual boundaries with their patients, with any such violation being considered a serious breach of professional duty and the Hippocratic oath.[2] Writing in the 1990s regarding the UK, Smith found that sexual misconduct had been a significant matter for the GMC and the courts for some time, highlighting a 'leading case' from 1961 on such 'improper relationships',[3] and providing evidence of the common occurrence of a breach of this professional duty.[4] Subsequent research revealed that 19 of the 36 cases against psychiatrists decided by the Professional Conduct Committee of the GMC between January 2000 and November 2004 related to sexual misconduct, thereby demonstrating that 'sexual misconduct was the major issue for serious professional misconduct (SPM) hearings at the GMC for psychiatrists'.[5] Reporting in 2005, the Kerr/Haslam inquiry considered that it could be assumed that sexual activity between health professionals and their patients is vastly underreported.[6]

Moving forward to 2013–2014, it was reported that 90 doctors were investigated by the GMC for having an inappropriate relationship or making inappropriate advances to a patient.[7] At a similar time, a report prepared for the

---

1   See, e.g. Subotsky and others 2010: 1; Bismark and others 2020: Galletly 2020.
2   See also Wertheimer 1996: 159
3   Smith 1994: 40–41; *De Gregory* v. *GMC* [1961] AC 957. See also *GMC* v. *Spackman* [1943] AC 627.
4   Smith 1994: 8–9 (sexual behaviour was the third highest category of cases before the GMC between 1989–1990).
5   Subotsky 2010: 71. See also n.27.
6   Department of Health 2005: 617, para 30.14. On this inquiry, see the text accompanying nn.47–49, n.140 and part 2 of this chapter, n.47.
7   Davies 2015.

GMC explored data involving 103 cases where doctors were suspended or erased from the medical register in 2014 by a Medical Practitioners Tribunal Service (MPTS) Panel for matters related to a doctor's working life.[8] Fifteen of these cases involved inappropriate relations with patients of a sexual nature, including 'engaging in consensual (sexual) relationships with patients, touching patients inappropriately, sexual assault and sexually motivated examinations'.[9] Other data has revealed that 222 requests for advice on sexual misconduct involving doctors were received by the National Clinical Assessment Service between October 2012 and mid-October 2017.[10] Further research conducted by Searle et al examined 633 fitness to practise cases brought against doctors between 2014–2016. Charges for sexual misconduct amounted to 92 of the multiple charges brought in these cases.[11] In the subsample of 24 cases that the authors conducted in-depth thematic analysis upon, 16 cases involved misconduct against patients rather than colleagues, and involved multiple incidents against single and multiple patients, leading the authors to suggest that 'such behaviours were not impulsive'.[12]

Notwithstanding Searle et al's suggestion, we should not assume that all sexual boundary breaches committed by doctors are deliberate. The Council on Ethical and Judicial Affairs of the American Medical Association (AMA) has observed that:

> the emotions of admiration, affection, and caring that are a part of the physician-patient relationship can become particularly powerful when [the doctor] is experiencing intense pressures or traumatic or major life events. The usual professional restraint exhibited by physicians may falter under such profound emotional influences, resulting in the transformation of sexual attraction into sexual contact.[13]

In such circumstances, a sexual boundary breach is not the result of a deliberate and calculated choice made by the doctor to take advantage of the relationship of power and trust with the patient. But it is also undoubtedly the case that, in part, the occurrence of sexual boundary breaches and exploitation is due to the unique way in which the doctor-patient relationship readily furnishes

---

8   On the MPTS, see chapter 3, n.95.
9   Harris and Slater 2015: 4 and 29.
10 Rimmer 2018. The same medical news report also cited data acquired from the GMC that 18 doctors were erased from the medical register in the UK for sexual assault or rape between 2014–2017 (it was not specified whether the victims were patients or other health care professionals).
11 Searle and others 2017: 9, 11.
12 Searle and others 2017: 21. A more recently reported Australian study examining data related to all health practitioners registered in Australia between 2011–2016 (724,649 health practitioners) found that regulators received 1507 notifications of sexual misconduct involving 1167 practitioners. 25% of these notifications concerned alleged sexual relationships and 75% related to sexual harassment or assault: Bismark and others 2020.
13 Council on Ethical and Judicial Affairs 1991: 2741.

opportunities for sexual exploitation.[14] We have already noted that the patient is required to grant the doctor unparalleled access to her body and mind, in comparison to other intimate and confidential professional relationships.[15] As Schneider and Phillips observe, 'the nature of the doctor-patient relationship involves some unique situations. Patients are often partially nude, genital examinations are sometimes necessary, and patients may justifiably raise sexual matters in conversation.'[16]

Our overall aims in this chapter are to assess whether all sexual boundary breaches perpetrated by doctors are exploitative; to explore, in particular, cases involving inducements to engage in sexual activity; to investigate the relevance and contentiousness of consent; and to evaluate the current legal response to sexual exploitation in the doctor-patient relationship. Because this is a large and complex task, to assist the reader we have separated the chapter into two parts. In this, the first part, we begin by considering how significant the matter of gender is, before proceeding to outline the zero-tolerance position taken to sexual boundary breaches by professional regulatory ethics. Next, we critically assess whether a zero-tolerance approach is always appropriate. We assess just how significant the issue of consent is when assessing whether a sexual boundary breach is exploitative. Connected to consent, our particular focus is the way in which sexual exploitation can be facilitated through an inducement available because of the doctor's professional role which can impede the patient's consent or distort the patient's decision-making. And is it ever possible for sexual boundary breaches to be non-exploitative if patients consent to sexual activity with their doctors absent any kind of inducement or coercion?

1) Is gender an issue in sexual boundary breaches?

When a doctor engages in sexual behaviour with a patient, this is commonly referred to in the professional and academic literature as a sexual boundary breach, which can be defined as follows: '[a] breach of sexual boundaries occurs when a healthcare professional displays sexualised behaviour towards a patient or carer. Sexualised behaviour is defined as acts, words or behaviour designed or intended to arouse or gratify sexual impulses or desires.'[17] It is important to note that there are greater opportunities for sexual boundary breaches to occur involving female patients because of the medical attention paid to the female (reproductive) body:

> Medical surveillance related to the female reproductive tract includes cervical smears, breast examinations, and check-ups related to pregnancy and

---

14 See Tschan 2013: 132; Wertheimer 1996: 160.
15 See chapter 3, section 2.
16 Schneider and Phillips 1997: 675.
17 Council for Healthcare Regulatory Excellence 2008a: 3. And see Penfold 1998: 19.

childbirth. In addition, the processes of menarche, menstruation, and menopause attract medical attention such as pharmacological interventions … Women are regularly and repeatedly placed in positions of physical exposure in the clinical setting, exacerbating power inequalities in the relationship, and increasingly feelings of vulnerability. Men are not subject to the same frequency and intensity of medical surveillance of their reproductive organs or processes.[18]

The reported cases and research tend to reveal a significant gender issue: sexual boundary breaches are being instigated, by and large, by older male doctors against their younger female patients.[19] Where doctors who acknowledged sexual contact with their patients specified their and their patient's sex in one study, it was found that 89% of breaches occurred between a male doctor and female patient.[20] A more recent wide-scale literature review revealed, similarly, that the majority of reported sexual boundaries breaches involve a male doctor and female patient,[21] and of the 90 doctors who were investigated by the GMC in 2013–2014 for such alleged breaches, 91% were male.[22] Furthermore, notably, all the doctors involved in sexual cases that led to suspension or erasure by a MPTS Panel in 2014 were male.[23]

Numerous authors have focused upon the inequality of power in the doctor-patient relationship and have sometimes coupled this with the sexual imbalance of power between a male doctor and female patient. For example, Daniels et al argue that: 'under no professional circumstances can a woman be an equal consenting partner in the relationship. This causes women to feel abused and to suffer psychologically'.[24] The authors of a New Zealand study draw attention to the power of a male-dominated medical profession, juxtaposed against the vulnerability of a 'predominantly female patient population'.[25] However, they note that this power and vulnerability is assumptive[26] and neither they, nor Daniels et al, provide any evidence to substantiate the claims of ever-present female vulnerability. There are cogent reasons for being sensitive to the environment and circumstances of the doctor-patient relationship that can make female

---

18   Rogers and Ballantyne 2008: 50–51.
19   Cohen and others 1995: 171; Council on Ethical and Judicial Affairs 1991: 2742. The vast majority of the 38 sample reported cases presented in the final report of the Task Force on Sexual Abuse of Patients involved male doctors and female patients: College of Physicians and Surgeons of Ontario 1991: 63–69.
20   Gartrell and others 1992: 140. 6% of cases occurred between female doctors and male patients, 4% between male doctors and male patients, and 1% between female doctors and female patients. See also Bismark and others 2020.
21   Halter and others 2007: 7, 60 and 70.
22   Davies 2015.
23   Harris and Slater 2015: 35.
24   Daniels and others 1995: 287.
25   Eyres White and others 1994: 391–392.
26   Ibid.

patients vulnerable, as outlined by Rogers and Ballantyne in the quote above. But we should be wary about over-generalising that all female patients are vulnerable. They might be vulnerable to sexual exploitation in some fields in medical practice more than others, psychiatry,[27] for instance. But studies have also shown that, albeit less frequently, sexual exploitation does occur where the doctor is female[28] and the patient is male, or where they are of the same sex.[29] There is an interesting question here about whether the sexual imbalance of power can be more powerful than the female doctor's professional power in her relationship with male patients,[30] and the occurrence of sexual exploitation in same sex scenarios suggests that sexual exploitation in the doctor-patient relationship is not reducible to being only a gender issue. In a broader context of sexual abuse of power beyond the doctor-patient relationship, Buchhandler-Raphael posits that 'professional, institutional, and economic vulnerability is gender-neutral ... power may be equally abused across gender lines. Victims of sexual abuse of power may also be males who are situated in disadvantageous positions that make them vulnerable to abuse.'[31] Such a model of vulnerability reflects the position that we adopt in this work, which does not begin from the premise of assumed vulnerability. That said, the fact remains that because these breaches tend to occur in contexts where the doctor is male and the patient is female, we need to be mindful of this as a potential dimension of the inequality of power between the parties in such cases.

2) Professional ethics and regulation: a 'zero-tolerance' approach

The stance taken by professional regulatory ethics to sexual boundary breaches is stark and absolutist. The GMC states that doctors 'must not pursue a sexual or improper emotional relationship with a current patient'.[32] This strict position appears to be followed through to the sanction stage in the GMC's regulatory response: erasure rather than suspension tends to be the more likely sanction

---

27   According to the CHRE, the medical specialities which have the highest reported occurrence of sexual boundary breaches are psychiatry, general practice and obstetrics and gynaecology: Council for Healthcare Regulatory Excellence 2008b: 3. In Australia between 2011–2016, notifications of sexual relationships were more frequent for psychiatrists, psychologists and GPs: Bismark and others 2020. See also the text accompanying n.133.
28   See *Ontario (College of Physicians and Surgeons of Ontario)* v. *Sundaralingam*, 2019 ONCPSD 11 for an example of such from Canada. On female health care professionals engaging in sexual misconduct within the context of a relationship, see Millbank 2020a.
29   See Phillips and Schneider 1993; Schneider and Phillips 1997; CHRE 2008b: 14.
30   See also the studies referred to in part 2, section iv concerning the unwanted sexual behaviour of male patients.
31   Buchhandler-Raphael 2010b: 135. See also Buchhandler-Raphael 2010a: 433.
32   General Medical Council 2013d: para 4.

in proven cases brought before MPTS panels.[33] In a similar vein, according to the AMA:

> Romantic or sexual interactions between physicians and patients that occur concurrently with the patient physician relationship are unethical. Such interactions detract from the goals of the patient-physician relationship and may exploit the vulnerability of the patient, compromise the physician's ability to make objective judgments about the patient's health care, and ultimately be detrimental to the patient's well-being ...[34]

The Medical Council of New Zealand has gone so far as to describe a doctor's sexual impropriety and transgressions as sexual abuse,[35] and the Canadian Task Force on Sexual Abuse of Patients has presented a similar classification.[36] Notably, the regulatory and legal response to sexual boundary breaches is particularly strict in Canada following a high level of professional and societal attention paid to this issue over a number of years. The Protecting Patients Act 2017 construes as sexual abuse any sexual activity with a patient, no matter if consensual, and anyone who has been a patient for up to a year after the cessation of the professional relationship is defined as a patient. A doctor who commits sexual acts with a patient or encourages a patient to commit sexual acts faces the mandatory revocation of his license.[37]

A zero-tolerance approach[38] is thus clearly evident in the regulatory response to sexual boundary breaches in numerous countries. Arguments supporting such an approach have been explored by Cullen, and include that because of the relationship of trust involving inequality between the parties, patients cannot give valid consent to sexual contact; that sexual contact between doctor and patient is 'almost always harmful to patients';[39] and that because there would be unacceptable consequences if sexual boundaries were breached, no sexual contact should be allowed.[40] As Cullen argues, however, each of these arguments is challengeable.

---

33 Harris and Slater 2015: 30. For one such example, see MPTS, 'Record of Determinations – Fitness to Practise Panel: Dr Navin Zala', 9 June 2015, GMC reference number 2266446 (copy on file with authors).
34 American Medical Association 2016: opinion 9.1.1.
35 Medical Council of New Zealand: 1994. See now Medical Council of New Zealand 2004: paras 7–10.
36 College of Physicians and Surgeons of Ontario 1991: 12. According to the Task Force, 'Sexual activity between a patient and a doctor always represents sexual abuse': College of Physicians and Surgeons of Ontario 1991: 259–260.
37 Protection of Patients Act 2017, Schedule 2 s.51(5).
38 'Zero Tolerance is the *only* philosophy consistent with protecting the public, the goal of self-regulation of Physicians.' College of Physicians and Surgeons of Ontario 1991: 16 (emphasis in original).
39 See, e.g. Fahy and Fisher 1992.
40 Cullen 1999.

First, some authors have contended that the inequality of power in the doctor-patient relationship will *always* affect the patient's emotional capacity and ability to give real consent,[41] as is reflected in the final report of the Task Force on Sexual Abuse of Patients from Canada.[42] However, such claims assume that this is a certainty without proof, in other words, that there can *never* be any cases where a patient can give real consent to sexual contact with their doctor.[43] In section 3, we critically assess whether we should construe *all* sexual activity between doctor and patient as sexual abuse and/or exploitation because the patient's consent can never be deemed real, thereby justifying a zero-tolerance approach.

Secondly, there is evidence that patients have suffered harm as a consequence of sexual contact with their doctors and that the sexual context of the exploitation, the private, intimate nature of the behaviour, makes it especially harmful and difficult to disclose. For instance, in 2000, GP Clifford Ayling was convicted of indecently assaulting ten female patients by inappropriately touching their breasts or gynaecological organs.[44] His patients felt defiled[45] and reported that they felt unable to remove themselves from his exploitative, abusive behaviour and were then unable to disclose what had occurred.[46] As a further example, at least 67 of psychiatrist William Kerr's patients complained of his sexualised behaviour between 1965–1980s.[47] According to their accounts, during appointments or unscheduled domiciliary visits, Kerr would 'allegedly expose himself and "invite" patients to perform sexual acts (often of masturbation or oral sex) upon him, sometimes suggesting that this was part of their treatment. A number of patients also alleged that full sexual intercourse took place.'[48] Similarly to Ayling's victims, Kerr's victims were left confused and experienced feelings of guilt that prevented them from making official complaints against him.[49] In the report of the Task Force on Sexual Abuse of Patients, patients:

---

41 See Coleman 1988 and the discussion in section 3.ii.
42 'Due to the position of power the physician brings to the doctor-patient relationship, there are NO circumstances – NONE – in which sexual activity between a physician and a patient is acceptable'. College of Physicians and Surgeons of Ontario 1991: 12 (emphasis in original).
43 See also Cullen 1999: 484.
44 Department of Health 2004a: 17 [2.5], [2.6].
45 According to one patient's police statement, she felt 'dirty and abused', 'sexually abused and defiled'. Ibid: 63 [3.167].
46 For instance, 'I can't just ring somebody up to say my doctor's done this. It's not the done sort of thing.'; 'I did not voice my concerns at the time because, as a patient, I felt I should trust my doctor.'; 'I was young and inexperienced and I had nothing to compare this treatment to.'; 'I did not make a complaint, because although I found these examinations unpleasant, I did not realise that they were unnecessary. Ayling was the only doctor I had visited for contraceptive advice': Ibid: 109–110 [4.3], [4.4].
47 Department of Health 2005: 7.
48 Ibid: 7–8.
49 Ibid.

reported that the experience was devastating and left them emotionally scarred. They reported symptoms that included nightmares, feelings of guilt, shame and humiliation, fear or distrust of men, and inability to develop and maintain intimacy ... Others told us that manipulation and betrayal of their trust by their doctor hurt them much more than the sexual act itself.[50]

In a similar vein, following its study of relevant research, the Council on Ethical and Judicial Affairs of the AMA commented that 'victims have been reported to experience guilt, severe distrust of their own judgment, and mistrust of ... physicians'.[51] It is this breach of trust that thus plays a significant part of the wrong done.[52]

We should be cautious, however, about assuming that *all* sexual contact that takes place between doctors and patients 'is almost always harmful' and exploitative. As Cullen notes, whilst empirical evidence exists to demonstrate that some patients have been harmed, in the form of case reports and small studies involving patients and psychotherapists,[53] there has been no large-scale survey with a sample size that is representative of patients who have experienced sexual contact with their doctors.[54] Spiegel et al recognise, rightly, that patients can suffer serious mental harm because of a doctor's sexual abuse. However, whilst they also accept that patients may be harmed by having (consensual) sexual contact with a doctor, and could henceforth find it difficult to have trusting future relationships with doctors,[55] they argue that 'there is no evidence to suggest that harm following a failed relationship with a health professional is any different to that resulting from the break up of a relationship with a non-health professional'.[56]

---

50 College of Physicians and Surgeons of Ontario 1991: 59. The list of harms provided by the CHRE include traumatic stress disorder and distress, major depressive disorders, suicidal tendencies and emotional distrust, failure to access health services when needed and relationship problems: Council for Healthcare Regulatory Excellence 2008b: 15.
51 Council on Ethical and Judicial Affairs 1991: 2742.
52 Trust 'explains why some immoral acts are especially egregious when done by doctors': Rhodes 2001: 498 (and see 499). Schulhofer draws attention to the impact of the doctor's abuse of trust and sexual exploitation potentially being more significant in the contexts of health care and treatment involving 'emotional exposure' (providing the example of infertility treatment) and 'physical exposure', because of the vulnerabilities that such contexts can create: Schulhofer 1998: 235.
53 See, e.g. the studies referred to by Fahy and Fisher 1992.
54 Cullen 1999: 483. Note also the Council on Ethical and Judicial Affairs' observation that 'most research has been based on patients who have initiated disciplinary action against physicians or on patients whom subsequent psychiatrists or therapists have identified as being harmed by the sexual contact with a physician. Patients not harmed by sexual contact with a physician may have escaped the attention of researchers': Council on Ethical and Judicial Affairs 1991: 2742–2743.
55 'Many patients cease to be able to trust doctors or health care providers again [and] may avoid further medical care': College of Physicians and Surgeons of Ontario 1991:14.
56 Spiegel and others 2005: 27.

Finally, it is undoubtedly true that there would be at least some unacceptable consequences if sexual boundaries between doctors and patients were breached. But is this enough to justify the conclusion that *no* sexual contact should be allowed? As Cullen observes, this argument 'should be treated with caution for it does not require strong empirical evidence, may rest on vague concerns and prejudices, and cannot specify the probability of the unacceptable consequences predicted'.[57] Nonetheless, he concludes that the risk of unacceptable consequences may be enough to justify a precautionary regulatory response of zero tolerance since 'this stance protects the public from real harms that are known to occur in at least a proportion of cases where sexual contact occurs between doctors and patients'.[58] Whilst we agree that there is a need for a precautionary regulatory response, in the following section, we suggest that there is an alternative to a complete zero-tolerance response that should still protect the public from harm and maintain public trust in the medical profession.[59]

3) Can a 'zero-tolerance' approach be justified because all sexual boundary breaches are exploitative?

The quote from Daniels et al in section 1 draws on a possible connection between gender and consent, and raises the broader contextual question of *when* the presence of consent should impact on the assessment of whether a sexual interaction between doctor and patient is exploitative. On the face of it, the presence of some level of choice and consent can make the question of the existence of wrongful exploitation more normatively challenging. However, we have already argued that wrongful exploitation can still occur in cases where the exploited person consents to the exploitative behaviour.[60] We now explore this issue further in the particular context of sexual exploitation. First, we consider cases where consent is provided, but the validity of this consent can be questioned because of a coercive or irresistible inducement that a doctor can offer by virtue of his professional role, followed by cases where the sexual behaviour is consensual and there is no inducement. An underlying issue that we address is whether doctors always misuse patients, even when they engage in consensual sexual behaviour with them.

i) Consent and coercive or irresistible inducements to provide medical treatment or services

Their position of power in being able to provide their patients with something that they need (or perceive that they need) for their health/welfare can enable doctors

---

57 Cullen 1999: 485.
58 Ibid: 485.
59 See the end of section 3.
60 See chapter 2, section 3.ii.

to carry out sexual exploitation. Although not all cases of sexual exploitation perpetrated by doctors on their patients will involve this element, there are prominent examples of such exploitation, like the Canadian case of *Norberg* v. *Wynrib*.[61] That case involved a patient, Laura Norberg, who was addicted to Fiorinal, a drug available on prescription. She had been obtaining this drug from numerous doctors who subsequently refused to prescribe it when her addiction became apparent. She then approached Dr Morris Wynrib, who, after realising that she was addicted, said that if she was 'good to him', he would 'be good' to her and pointed upstairs to where he lived above his office. She understood the implication that he would supply her with the drug in exchange for sexual favours. Unable to acquire the drug elsewhere, Norberg provided Wynrib with sexual favours to gain access to Fiorinal on numerous occasions. As a consequence of this, Norberg testified at Wynrib's trial for sexual assault, negligence, breach of fiduciary duty and breach of contract,[62] that she felt humiliation, shame and a loss of dignity.[63]

Taking account of the way in which Laura Norberg was induced to consent, we present two scenarios here to demonstrate how a patient's ability to give free consent might similarly be questioned because the doctor uses the doctor-patient relationship to exploit the patient by offering inducements related to their professional role. As with Laura Norberg, both scenarios feature a situation where the patient stands to gain something from the exploitation:

Scenario 1
A consultant states she will move a seriously ill child's operation up on the waiting list if the child's father, who is also her patient, engages in sexual activity with her. He does not wish to do so, especially since he is married. However, he is desperate for his son to have his operation as soon as possible and so agrees.

Scenario 2
For a genuine medical reason, a patient asks her GP for a sick note which she needs urgently. The GP states that he will only write her a sick note if she touches herself intimately in front of him. She reluctantly agrees, as he tells her she is unlikely to get another appointment with an alternative GP in the practice for at least a week (which he knows to be untrue).

The doctors in our scenarios have misused their patients by taking advantage of their particular vulnerabilities, whether this is a desire to see their child made better sooner, or a need to utilise the services that only a GP can provide access to. The unequal status of the parties, and the doctors' power, bring into question the validity of the patients' consent.[64] In both our scenarios, and Laura Norberg's

---

61 1992 CarswellBC 155, [1992] 2 SCR 226.
62 *Norberg* v. *Wynrib* [1988] 6 WWR 305.
63 Ibid, [57]. We explore the grounds on which Norberg brought legal claims against Dr Wynrib after she overcame her addition in: part 2, section 2.i and ii and section 3.
64 See generally Eskridge 1995: 55.

case, the doctors have acted in a way that has interfered with the patients' exercise of control over the state of affairs.[65] We contend that both our doctors have interfered with their patients' moral right to freedom of choice to engage in sexual activity, and thus the patients have been wronged. The doctors' behaviour may also have a negative impact upon interests that are vital to the patients' well-being. Neither of our patients wished to engage in sexual activity.[66] Both could experience feelings of guilt or shame as a result. Consequently, in our view, the behaviour of our hypothetical doctors constitutes wrongful exploitation that is likely to set back the patients' interests. In addition, the consultant's actions in *Scenario 1* may also set back the health of other seriously ill children who were ahead on the waiting list, and thus need the operation more urgently. In this way, the doctor is not only exploiting the patient's father but, because she is not authorised to make the offer, she is also acting against an established professional and ethical duty (her duty of care to her other patients) and harming the interests of others.

Inducement is an important aspect of the exploitation in the two scenarios we have presented; it is significant that the doctors are able to exploit the patients, and benefit from this exploitation, by offering them something that they want but which they believe they would otherwise not receive. The first question to consider here is whether these exploitative offers can be described as coercive and could, thereby, invalidate consent. We follow Mappes's caution against *assuming* that an offer is automatically coercive because it is 'extremely enticing or seductive'[67] without more careful analysis. Likewise, we should avoid assuming that offers, because of their nature, can *never* be coercive. Hill provides an account of offers as non-coercive which does not start from such an assumption, but, rather, seeks to differentiate exploitation involving the making of an offer from coercion based on choice versus compulsion:

> Exploitation is distinguished from coercion or duress in that coercion inevitably occurs in the context of a threat which serves to reduce the number of available options open to the actor. Exploitation, however, characteristically involves a situation in which the actor is presented with an *offer* that represents an additional alternative to the choices previously available … the decision to pursue the proffered choice is precisely that – a *decision* made by the actor. Because it is a decision and not a compelled act, the choice springs from internal motives and is not imposed by forces outside the agent … an offer

---

65 Lamond 1996: 233. We proceed to discuss whether the patients' consent is invalidated, or their decision-making is distorted, shortly.
66 On willingness to engage in sexual relations, see Buchhandler-Raphael 2010b:115–116 (although we note that we do not necessarily agree with her position that there is *non*-consent in all cases involving sexual abuse of power where B does not desire the sexual activity – see part 2 of this chapter, text accompanying nn.38–39)
67 Mappes 1985: 213. Although note Held's contention that 'as an inducement to accept an offer approaches a high level, it approaches coercion proportionately': Held 1972: 57. See also the discussion in chapter 4, section 3 regarding inducements to participate in medical research.

that creates an additional alternative can never render an action less free or voluntary than the action which would otherwise have been performed ...'[68]

Thus, Hill would presumably conclude that the doctors in our scenarios exploit their patients but do not coerce them, since they present them with offers. Following Hill's analysis, therefore, our doctors do not invalidate their patients' consent by the particular exploitation that they perpetrate. However, as we see it, further analysis is required here. It might, in fact, only be true that an offer cannot be coercive *provided* that rejecting the doctors' offers would not place the patients in a worse situation than that which they were in prior to the offers being made. Hill proceeds to say: 'coercion *worsens* the actor's situation. An offer, on the other hand, can be rejected without making the offeree's situation any worse than it was *ex ante*.'[69] Notably, there is a difference between *Scenarios 1* and *2* that could reveal that the latter is, in fact, coercive. According to Price, 'whilst coercion usually consists of a positive action such as a threat, it can also occur where one threatens *not to benefit* another person where there is a *duty* to provide such a benefit'.[70] And Wertheimer's position is that 'proposals are properly understood as coercive only when they can be cast as threats by reference to B's moralized baseline'.[71] This occurs when A proposes 'to make B worse off relative to where B has a right to be vis-à-vis A'.[72] The father in *Scenario 1* has no right to expect that the consultant place his son higher up on the waiting list; the consultant's offer to do this in exchange for sexual activity with the father does not make him worse off than his moralised baseline, and, thus, it would not count as a coercive offer invalidating consent. In contrast, as the GP in *Scenario 2* has an obligation to provide the patient with a sick note because she has requested one for a genuine medical reason, the GP proposes to make her worse off than her moralised baseline;[73] the doctor is depriving the patient of something she is actually entitled to, unless she does as he asks.[74] Similarly, Laura Norberg was entitled to be offered

---

68 Hill 1994: 660 (emphasis in original).
69 Hill 1994:662–663 (emphasis in original). See also Schulhofer 1998: 120.
70 Price 2013: 531 (emphasis in original) (citing Wilkinson 2003: 92 in support).
71 Wertheimer 2003: 173.
72 Ibid. And see Wertheimer 1987: chapters 12 and 13; Knight 2012: 143–147; Schulhofer 1998: 120.
73 Wertheimer recognises that his view on what can constitute coercion, which we adopt here, 'is frequently rejected' (Wertheimer 2003: 167). However, as Hill notes, it is only 'a *slight* majority [that] adhere to the view that an offer can never be coercive': Hill 1994: 663 (emphasis added).
74 Following Price's and Wertheimer's analysis, it would not make a difference if the patient remains unaware that she is entitled to this sick note as, regardless of her lack of awareness, her moralised baseline has still been affected by the fact that the doctor has threatened not to provide this note when he has a duty to provide it. It would make a difference, however, if she were not entitled to the note since then the doctor's proposition does not make her worse off than her moralised baseline. Thanks to Grant Lamond for causing us to reflect on this.

appropriate treatment to overcome her addiction (as she later did) and thus, in breaching his duty towards her, Dr Wynrib caused her to be worse off than her moralised baseline.[75]

In addition, it is possible to draw parallels with *Scenario 2* and the offence of blackmail, since one of the elements of blackmail is that the threat is made with a view to generating a gain for the blackmailer,[76] and one of the justifications for criminalising blackmail is that the victim is coerced into doing something that would ordinarily require his valid consent.[77] Lamond presents blackmail as 'a crime which rests upon the moral wrong of ... interfering with [another's] personal autonomy without his valid consent'.[78] Whilst in the context of blackmail, it is the use of coercive threats that invalidates consent, in *Scenario 2*, it is the coercive inducement – the offer of a much desired option – which makes the patient worse off than her moralised baseline and could thereby nullify her consent.[79] It must surely be true that 'like a threat [a coercive] offer is a proposal which alters the context in which the other makes their choice with a view to making non-compliance unattractive'.[80] Bogart goes so far as to contend that one may act *non-voluntarily* if 'there are overpowering factors favouring one course over others'.[81] What is more, there is also a similarity between the

---

75 As Lamond explains, rather than a moralised baseline, some of the literature uses a statistical baseline (that is, what *would be expected* to occur otherwise) when assessing whether a person is worse off. On this basis, it might be contended that Laura Norberg was actually made no worse off by Dr Wynrib's proposal, because she would not have been able to obtain Fiorinal from any other doctor aware of her addiction (Lamond 2013: 845; see also Westen 2004: 217–221). However, we are following the literature which adopts a moral baseline as the comparator, that is, what *ought* to occur otherwise (see, e.g. Wertheimer 1987: 217–221). This is because, in drawing attention to what the doctor ought to have done/provided, this approach better reflects our conception of exploitation and its focus on the way in which A treats B.
76 See s.21 Theft Act 1968.
77 Lamond 1996: 232–233.
78 Ibid: 216. More broadly, Collins has also drawn attention to a further similarity between exploitation and blackmail: 'like exploitation, blackmail has the tendency to be a hidden wrong which is unlikely to be widely reported by vulnerable victims': Collins 2015: 100–101.
79 See also Archard 1998: 55–60 on the question of whether offers can coerce and invalidate consent.
80 Archard 1998: 55. And see Held's view that 'if the degree of inducement is set high enough in the case of seduction, there may seem to be little difference in the extent of coercion involved [compared to a threat]'. Held 1972: 58.
81 Bogart, 1995: 162. See also Mappes 1985: 215–216. In contrast to Bogart, we choose not to use the notion of voluntariness, agreeing with Westen that '"voluntariness" is ambiguous. It can be used in a purely factual sense to refer to any conscious exercise of will on a person's part, regardless of how wrongfully pressured a person may be to exercise his will in a certain way ... Or alternatively, "voluntariness" can also be used in a legally conclusory fashion to refer to such additional conditions as are necessary to transform a subject's conscious and willed acquiescence to conduct into a criminal defense on the actor's part.': Westen 2004: 179. As will become apparent, our preference is to refer to what we see as the more specific language of *manipulated* or *compromised consent*.

blackmailer and the exploiter in *Scenario 2*: the GP here has created a situation that is unwelcome to the patient[82] (that she will not get a sick note for at least a week) in order to induce her to choose what she perceives to be a less unwelcome option (touching herself intimately in front of him).

Turning back to *Scenario 1*, although the offer made is not coercive and thus it is harder to argue that it invalidates the patient's consent, it may still distort his decision-making. Wertheimer states that:

> What I call *seductive offers* can also compromise B's competence to consent. A makes a seductive offer when A's proposal contains such great short-term benefits that it causes B to excessively discount the long-term costs and to make a decision that does not serve her long-term interests.[83]

The concerns about their health that patients are experiencing (or, in our patient's case, the health of his son) may make them more susceptible to such seductive offers, and less able to weigh up the effect of their decisions on their longer-term interests. According to Price:

> decision-making may sometimes be compromised as a result of the vulnerability of the individual ... In particular, suffering and need may cause one to move toward a decision out of desperation rather than deliberateness and adherence to personal values and life choices which serve their core/critical interests.[84]

Our patient in *Scenario 1* acts out of desperation rather than deliberation: his desire for his seriously ill son to have his operation quickly means that he is unlikely to act in a way that serves his long-term, core interests, nor to consider the psychological consequences of guilt, for instance. A real-life example here could also illustrate what might amount to an irresistible offer. Douglas Shelton, a gynaecologist who practised in Amarillo, Texas, was subject to a hearing in 2015 following allegations that he had offered free fertility treatments in exchange for sex and to 'naturally inseminate' a woman who desired to have a child.[85]

---

82 On blackmail and the creation of an unwelcome situation, see Lamond 1996: 219.
83 Wertheimer 2007: 251 (emphasis in original). And see Price 2013: 535; Hill 1994: 665–666; Archard 1998: 55–60; Feinberg 1986: 343.
84 Price 2013: 550–551. We note that the word 'rational' precedes 'decision-making' in Price's original wording. We have expressed discomfort about using this word elsewhere (see chapter 2, section 2.vi), and thus choose not to include it in the extract that we have quoted here. In our view, it is decision-making *per se* that is clouded.
85 Mollie Bryant, 'Medical board holds closing arguments in Shelton hearing' *Amarillo Globe-News* (Amarillo, 27 December 2014), at https://www.amarillo.com/article/20141227/news/312279813 accessed 6 April 2019. See also Mollie Bryant, 'Judges push sanctions in doc's ethics case' *Amarillo Globe-News* (Amarillo, 3 April 2015), at http://amarillo.com/news/latest-news/2015-04-03/judges-push-sanctions-docs-ethics-case accessed 6 April 2019.

His licence to practice was subsequently revoked.[86] Such an offer, if made to a woman who desperately desires a child, and if it provides the only means of achieving this (because she cannot afford the fertility treatment, for example), could be irresistible.[87] Again, there is a real risk that a patient in such a situation acts out of desperation rather than making a choice after due consideration of the long-term consequences of the decision.

Without the doctors' irresistible inducements, there is nothing to suggest that the patients in this real-life example, or our *Scenario 1*, would have agreed to engage in the sexual activity that occurred. Whilst the offer may enhance their freedom by enlarging their options, once they are offered something which could benefit their ill child or fulfil their desire for a child, it would be extremely difficult for them to exercise this freedom by rejecting the offers, notwithstanding the undesired condition attached. In such circumstances, their choices are 'severely constrained by [their] needs'.[88] We refer to what the doctors do as *compromising*, or *distorting* the patients' decision-making, because they intrude upon the factors affecting their patients' choices, introducing distracting, irresistible influences into their deliberations and 'taking ... power over [their patients'] choice situation'.[89] Whilst this does not nullify consent, it does strongly suggest that the consent given is *minimal*.[90] The exploiters are deliberately taking advantage of their patients' vulnerabilities to these offers for their own, as opposed to the patients', interests. Thus, it is these inducements which make the exploitation especially objectionable and wrongful. This is coupled with the fact that, in *Scenario 1*, the doctor is enabling the patient to gain an illicit advantage; aiding and abetting him to obtain something to which he is not entitled. But we are more likely to excuse this patient for accepting the offer because every parent would, of course, wish to see their seriously ill child made better sooner and might struggle to resist this incentive.[91]

Looking again at both our scenarios, we also note that although the patients in *Scenarios 1* and *2* have received a benefit from the situation, this does not

---

86 Mollie Bryant, 'Board revokes Amarillo doc's license' *Amarillo Globe-News* (Amarillo, 10 July 2015), at http://amarillo.com/news/local-news/2015-07-10/gynecologist-loses-license accessed 6 April 2019.
87 See chapter 4, section 4 for a discussion of the vulnerability of patients in this kind of situation.
88 Mappes 1985: 215.
89 See generally Greenspan 2003: 159 and 160.
90 For further discussion, see part 2 of this chapter, text accompanying nn.23–39. These seem to be instances of what Archard describes as 'manipulated consent': Archard 1998: 64–65.
91 See generally Rudinow 1978: 347, n.12. We are grateful to Grant Lamond for this observation. To pre-empt the possible criticism that we have deliberately chosen a scenario where it is harder for the patient to say no because his child's health is at stake, we argue that it would also be difficult for the patient to resist if his own health was at issue (that is, if it was his own operation for a serious illness that the consultant says she will move up the list).

detract from the fact that they have been exploited.[92] In both cases, the doctors have failed to respect their patients as reasoning agents.[93] Moreover, even if the patient's right to give valid consent in *Scenario 2* has not been interfered with, and the patient's decision-making process in *Scenario 1* has not been distorted (and we believe that both have occurred), their moral rights not to be treated merely as a means have been violated here and this also constitutes misuse, a wrong against them. Whilst designed to apply to manipulation in a broader context, Rudinow's explanation of the wrong committed seems especially apt:

> To attempt to manipulate someone is to elicit his behavior without regard for – and with a will to interfere with – his operative goals. Insofar as a person regards the selection of goals as rightfully within his sphere of autonomy and the freedom to pursue his goals as a prima facie right, it is little wonder that he finds attempts to manipulate him objectionable. So it is ... that being manipulated is so frequently assimilated to being used, treated instrumentally ... as a means rather than an end.[94]

Finally, on the issue of inducements and consent, we are not arguing that *any* inducement to engage in sexual behaviour that a doctor provides by offering medical treatment or services is going to be coercive or irresistible to the patient; whether the inducement offered invalidates consent, or distorts the patient's decision-making depends upon the patient's situation and the offer being made. Consider the real-life Australian case of Fabian Baez, a cosmetic surgeon who offered to provide a patient with a free Botox procedure in exchange for sexual favours.[95] There is a clear indication in the case report that the patient was psychologically vulnerable, with Dr Baez having commented in the patient's medical notes during earlier consultations that she had bipolar affective disorder; was 'very manic', continuing 'with drug abuse', feeling 'depressed'; and that he had counselled her about 'weight gain and "magic treatments"'.[96] Such vulnerabilities could well have compelled the patient to accept the doctor's offer, thereby distorting her decision-making. Now envisage the same situation, but involving a patient who possesses no such psychological vulnerability. It may be that the only reason that the patient consented to the sexual activity with a cosmetic surgeon in this second version was to obtain the procedure that she desired. Hence, the surgeon would still have acted exploitatively because he took advantage of

---

92 Consider, e.g. how a patient may benefit from being involved in a medical trial of a new drug that improves his condition, but is still exploited if his doctor obtains his consent by taking advantage of his desperate desire to be made better. See chapter 4, section 3.
93 Greenspan 2003: 159.
94 Rudinow 1978: 347.
95 *Health Care Complaints Commission v. Dr Baez* [2014] NSWCATOD 3. The judgment is at http://www.caselaw.nsw.gov.au/decision/54a63cd63004de94513db887, accessed 9 April 2020.
96 Para 90.

(used) the patient and took advantage of her desire to have the surgery.[97] He would have misused her, failing to respect her as a person (and a patient) by treating her in a demeaning way, as a sexual object. But this would not amount to an irresistible inducement.[98]

Thus, to conclude here, sexual boundary breaches are exploitative where doctors proffer coercive and irresistible inducements to provide medical treatment or services in exchange for sexual favours. In such cases, there is reason to consider that patients' consent is nullified, or that their capacity to engage in undistorted decision-making has been compromised. A zero-tolerance approach towards such breaches is, therefore, surely justifiable. And, as we explored directly above, sexual boundary breaches involving inducements can also be exploitative on our account of exploitation even if the inducement is *not* irresistible, but exploitation in such cases does not occur due to the violation of a patient's right to give valid consent or exercise an uncompromised decision-making process. Rather, exploitation lies in the doctor's misuse of the patient, his treatment of her merely as a means to an end. Consequently, we contend that *a zero-tolerance approach is justified in any situation where the doctor provides an inducement, and especially when the inducement invalidates consent (where it is coercive) or distorts the decision-making process (where it is irresistible)*. This is because, in the context of the doctor-patient relationship, the very existence of an inducement to engage in sexual activity in exchange for medical treatment or services signifies a doctor's misuse of a patient rather than treating her as a person.

ii) *Consensual cases where there is no inducement*

> With respect to the doctor-patient relationship ... special relationships between the [patient] and [doctor] should alert [us] to the possibility that apparent consent is not genuine; however, the existence of a particular relationship is not determinative of the presence or absence of consent.[99]

> In relationships characterised by power and dependency, the relationship with the defendant may become so important to the victim that it becomes difficult to express or even make an independent choice.[100]

These quotations suggest different approaches to the matter of whether a patient's consent to sexual activity with their doctor can ever be real. The position that

---

97 See also Feinberg 1988: 201–202. We are not thinking here of a woman who is vulnerable because her desire to have surgery is influenced by psychological issues related to body image and self-worth that are compounded by cultural pressures to look a certain way. See our discussion in chapter 4, section 4.
98 In contrast, a case where, for instance, the patient had a distorted perception of her appearance that compelled her to seek such procedures (see chapter 4, section 4) and was unable to otherwise pay for them, would again involve a psychological vulnerability that could be taken advantage of to compel the patient to agree.
99 *Norberg* v. *Wynrib*, see n.61, [133] (Sopinka J). Note also Price's view that 'vulnerability is not in itself a sufficient condition for an invalid consent': Price 2013: 550.
100 Allen 1996: 58.

the existence of a 'power dependency' relationship should always cause us to question the validity of the patient's consent is taken by Allen (the author of the second quote above) and Coleman.[101] And, in the specific doctor-patient context, Halter et al warn that 'patients are not in a position to give valid consent to sexual involvement with health professionals as they are bound into the unequal relationship in which they have real need'.[102] But are these authors correct to say that the inequality of power in this intimate and confidential professional relationship means that the patient' consent can *never* be genuine? And is there a legitimate argument that a doctor who engages in sexual activity with a patient *always* exploits that patient? To reiterate, we see exploitation as the taking advantage of (using) and misuse of a person, for one's own ends. There will always be cases involving sexual boundary breaches where the patient is vulnerable, this vulnerability is taken advantage of, and the doctor misuses the patient for his own sexual gratification. And there will be cases where a doctor is able to take advantage of (use) a patient because of the very fact that she is his patient. That is, although the doctor does not exert any pressure or manipulation, or offer any inducement, the patient consents because it is *her doctor* who makes sexual advances.[103] We must also be sensitive to the fact that, because of the setting, the doctor-patient relationship facilitates the opportunity to engage in sexual activity that would not otherwise have occurred (for instance, the circumstance of the patient undressing for an examination).

However, instances of non-exploitative sexual activity between doctor and patient can occur. Say that the patient consents to sexual activity without any inducement or coercion, but the doctor-patient relationship was the necessary precondition for the sexual activity because the individuals would not otherwise have met or known each other. Consider, for example, a scenario where a patient, Jake, sees and approaches a hospital doctor who treated him recently, Dr Jones, at a pub one night. They are mutually attracted to each other and, ultimately, spend the night together. They both desire to be in a romantic relationship with each other. Whilst Jake would not have approached Dr Jones that night if he had not already known him (due to him treating him at hospital), the setting in which the interaction between them that leads to the sexual activity and potential sexual relationship is non-professional, and Dr Jones does not utilise his professional relationship to facilitate this interaction. A scenario somewhat similar to this was presented to 89 members of the public[104] participating in a UK-based study on the standards expected of doctors.[105] Reasons that participants gave for seeing this as acceptable behaviour included that the relationship had 'started outside of the doctor's

---

101 Allen 1996; Coleman 1988.
102 Halter and others 2007: 7.
103 For instance, 'a patient [sleeps] with her therapist because he is her ... therapist': Archard 1994: 95.
104 The study involved a purposively selected sample 'in order to ensure that diversity of views and experiences among the population of interest were captured': Gill and others 2012: 5 and 6.
105 Ibid: 41.

professional environment which further removed it from the doctor's professional life', and that the doctor was not a GP, or otherwise long-term doctor of the patient.[106] But participants also expressed the view that 'the onus should be on the doctor to ensure they ceased to have a professional, medical relationship with the patient if their relationship became personal'.[107] Moreover:

> If the scenario was changed and the doctor and patient became close during a hospital stay and started dating immediately, this was less acceptable. Participants felt that here the lines between personal and professional relationships were being blurred as both were occurring at the same time.[108]

Interestingly, a stricter view was taken by the majority of GPs involved in an American study, with only 15% considering dating current patients outside of the professional consultation to be appropriate.[109] Further, 94% of doctors in a study by Gartrell et al, 'opposed sexual contact with current patients',[110] and 91% of doctors considered sexual relations with patients to be inappropriate in a study by Regan et al.[111]

Doctors and patients can, on occasion, enter into genuine relationships of affection.[112] In these circumstances, should we conclude that the doctor has exploited the patient *merely because of* a pre-existing doctor-patient relationship? If the doctor has not set out to take advantage of a vulnerability possessed by the patient and does not misuse him by treating him solely as a means to an end or violating his right to autonomy, we argue that it is much harder to demonstrate wrongful exploitation. There may thus be some limited instances where a more pragmatic, as opposed to zero-tolerance, approach to sexual boundary breaches is required. We could also alter the scenario we presented above so that Jake is a former patient of Dr Jones, having been treated by him over a year ago. For those members of the general public who participated in the UK-based study referred to above, personal

---

106 Ibid: 22. The report containing the study's findings does not provide figures regarding the percentage or number of participants who expressed these views.
107 Gill and others 2012: 24. Members of the general public who participated in an earlier UK-based study reported in 2006 considered consensual sexual relationships with patients to be minor misdemeanours that should not lead to the doctor's erasure from the Medical Register: Chisholm and others 2006: 38 and 72.
108 Gill and others 2012: 23. These views appear to reflect those of GP participants in an earlier New Zealand study, who considered sexual relationships with patients to be unhealthy because of the imbalance of power, and because they could consciously or unconsciously use their knowledge of the patient for their own purposes: Eyres White and others 1994: 390.
109 Coverdale and others 1994. And only 9% considered sexual contact with a current patient outside the professional consultation to be appropriate.
110 Gartrell and others 1992: 141.
111 Regan and others 2010: 550. We note here that there is always a risk that medical professionals involved in studies exploring perceptions and experiences of sexual boundary breaches may have conscious or unconscious bias towards responding in a 'socially desirable' way: Coverdale and Turbott 1997: 339.
112 See also Council on Ethical and Judicial Affairs 1991: 2743: Puglise 2000: 349; Schulhofer 1998: 230–231, 234, 236 and 239.

relationships with former patients were considered to be acceptable: 'all of the groups felt that it would be acceptable for a doctor to have a relationship with a previous patient as long as that relationship had not come about following an abuse of the trust or commenced while the patient was still under their care'.[113] In the study by Gartrell et al involving medical professionals, 63% considered sexual contact between doctor and patient permissible if 'treatment had stopped and the patient had been referred to another physician'.[114] This was also the view taken by nearly 50% of GPs, and more than 50% of all doctors in other medical specialities, in Coverdale et al's study.[115] No detail is provided in the studies as to whether participants expressed a view upon the reason for ending the professional relationship, but, notably, the position taken in the GMC Guidance is that doctors 'must not end a professional relationship with a patient *solely* to pursue a personal relationship with them'.[116] The broader position that the regulatory body adopts regarding personal relationships with former patients starts from the premise that such relationships 'may ... be inappropriate'.[117] This will depend upon how long ago the professional relationship ended;[118] the nature of this relationship; whether the former patient was particularly vulnerable[119] and whether they still are vulnerable;[120] and whether other members of the former patient's family are still under the doctor's care.[121] The GMC advises that the doctor 'must consider these issues carefully before pursuing a personal relationship with a former patient'.[122]

---

113 Gill and others 2012: 23.
114 Gartrell and others 1992: 142.
115 Coverdale and others 1994. See also Coverdale and Turbott 1997: 337: the majority of medical students in this subsequent study considered sexual contact between a GP and a former patient to be appropriate (80% of 65 students who had been given a three-hour session on ethical issues regarding sexual boundaries, and 68% of 76 students who took the survey prior to the session). Notably, this percentage decreased when the doctor's speciality was psychiatry. See n.133.
116 General Medical Council 2013d: [7] (emphasis added).
117 Ibid: [8].
118 In the Task Force on Sexual Abuse of Patients's view, 'A two-year time lapse after the last professional (doctor-patient) contact before sexual involvement is appropriate'. College of Physicians and Surgeons of Ontario 1991: 20. The current policy position of the College is that there should be a minimum one-year period after termination: College of Physicians and Surgeons of Ontario 2008: 4.
119 We turn to the issue of vulnerability in the text accompanying nn.130–137.
120 See also Council for Healthcare Regulatory Excellence 2008b: 16.
121 General Medical Council 2013d: [8](a-d).
122 Ibid: [8]. Parallel guidance from the AMA is framed around the doctor's behaviour and its effects: American Medical Association 2016: opinion 9.1.1: 'sexual or romantic relationships between a physician and a former patient may be unduly influenced by the previous physician-patient relationship. Sexual or romantic relationships with former patients are unethical if the physician uses or exploits trust, knowledge, emotions, or influence derived from the previous professional relationship, or if a romantic relationship would otherwise foreseeably harm the individual.' Centring on the same issue of influence, the CHRE in the UK states that 'sexual relationships with any former patient ... will *often* be inappropriate, however long ago the professional relationship ended. This is because the sexual relationship may be influenced by the previous professional relationship, which will often have involved an imbalance of power.': Council for Healthcare Regulatory Excellence 2008b: 16 (emphasis added).

A further consensual sexual relationship that we might wish to adopt something other than a zero-tolerance approach towards is that which occurs between doctor and patient in remote rural locations. Some of the members of the public who participated in the UK-based study adopted a more 'pragmatic' approach in the case of '[doctors who] lived in rural areas or who were registered at small family GP practices, whereby they accepted that it may be inevitable or at least likely that a doctor might go on to date a patient'.[123] It is also worth bearing in mind that a strict zero-tolerance approach is at risk of preventing GPs in rural locations from having any romantic relationships, with the effect that medical professionals might be discouraged from seeking employment in such remote rural settings.

Some hard lines have to be drawn. In our opinion, and taking into account the views expressed by members of the general public discussed above, the current zero-tolerance regulatory approach should be modified so that whilst the default position is that sexual boundary breaches are generally unethical and inappropriate, certain consensual sexual relationships between doctor and patient that are instigated outside of the professional interaction *could* be permissible. Our suggested approach here focuses on sexual relationships rather than one-off sexual interactions between doctors and patients because we are not wishing to advocate a regulatory position that would give the impression that breaching sexual boundaries with patients for sexual gratification can be ethical. Our proposal is that consensual sexual relationships between doctor and patient occurring outside of any professional interaction *could* be permissible, but only provided that there is no:

- continuing professional relationship with the patient[124] (that is, the doctor must refer the patient to another medical professional);[125] or
- instigation of an intimate relationship where the patient or former patient is vulnerable, such as where the doctor is, or was, the patient's psychiatrist; or
- instigation of an intimate relationship during the professional encounter, or through any exploitative behaviour.

As we see it, on our first requirement, it would be difficult to present a compelling case for reform to a strict zero-tolerance approach that would permit doctors to continue the professional relationship with a patient to whom they become sexually involved with outside the professional context. For:

---

123 Gill and others 2012: 23. See also Coverdale and Turbott 1997: 339; Goldie and others 2004: 483.
124 We are also open to the possibility of including the patient's close relation here. Note the GMC's guidance that 'you must not use your professional relationship with a patient to pursue a relationship with someone close to them. For example, you must not use home visits to pursue a relationship with a member of a patient's family': General Medical Council 2013d: [6]. For reasons of space, we cannot explore this further, however.
125 Reflecting the view of the Council on Ethical and Judicial Affairs 1991: 2743: 'before initiating a dating, romantic or sexual relationship with a patient, a physician's minimum duty would be to terminate his or her professional relationship with the patient.'

regard for the physician's needs or gratifications may interfere with efforts to address the needs of the patient. At the very least, the emotional factors that accompany sexual involvement may affect or obscure the physician's medical judgment, thus jeopardizing the patient's diagnosis or treatment.[126]

We also advocate the continuation of a zero-tolerance approach where the professional relationship has ended, but the sexual relationship was brought about during the professional interaction, as reflected in our third requirement. In such a situation, the doctor *knowingly* runs the risks identified by the Council on Ethical and Judicial Affairs above. Terminating the professional relationship does not alter this. That our restrictions can encompass former patients is reflected here and in our second requirement. We do not include reference to a point in time from which an intimate relationship with a former patient could be permissible, since we concur with the Council on Ethical and Judicial Affairs that rather than the crucial factor being the amount of time that has passed, 'the relevant standard is the potential for misuse of emotions derived from the former professional relationship'.[127] For even where the professional relationship has ended, initial sexual contact may have occurred 'as a result of the use or exploitation of trust, knowledge, influence, or emotions derived from the former professional relationship'.[128] Thus, the prohibition should continue to apply to relationships that occur following an initial sexual boundary breach facilitated by inducement, for example, which we have argued would amount to exploitation of the patient.[129]

On our second requirement and the issue of vulnerability, our proposal involves a more nuanced approach than one of simply assuming that all patients have an automatic, inherent vulnerability because of their ill-health.[130] Rather, it recognises the potential for vulnerability and that some patients are more susceptible to sexual exploitation because of their circumstances. This tallies with the GMC's advice to doctors that:

> some patients may be more vulnerable than others and the more vulnerable someone is, the more likely it is that having a relationship with them would be an abuse of power and your position as a doctor;[131]

---

126 Ibid: 2743.
127 Ibid: 2744.
128 And see ibid.
129 See section 3.i. See also the Australian Health Practitioner Regulation Agency's guidance, which states that whether sexual activity with a former patient amounts to sexual misconduct depends, in part, on 'the means by which sexual activity was established (for example, whether a practitioner used information obtained during a treating relationship to contact a patient and commence sexual activity)': Australian Health Practitioner Regulation Agency and National Board 2020: para 2.6.
130 See generally Dunn and others 2008: 244 and our discussion in chapter 4, section 2.
131 General Medical Council 2013d: [11].

and that:

> some patients are likely to be more vulnerable than others because of their illness, disability or frailty, or because of their current circumstances (such as bereavement or redundancy).[132]

We provide the specific example of the vulnerability of a current or former patient where the doctor is their psychiatrist. This is in line with the particular concern expressed by professional bodies regarding doctors in this speciality engaging in sexual relationships with patients, whether or not the professional relationship is current.[133] In one such case which occurred in Canada, psychiatrist Nagi Ghabbour began a romantic relationship with his former patient who had displayed strong romantic feelings for him during therapy appointments, one month after their professional relationship had ended. She had been seeing him for anxiety and depression following marital difficulties and work-related stress and Ghabbour's diagnoses included a major depressive illness, adjustment disorder with depressed mood and dependent and borderline traits. He also documented suicidal ideation at numerous sessions, sometimes noting that he viewed this as a serious concern.[134] Having accepted his admission that he had committed professional misconduct, the panel of the Discipline Committee of the College of Physicians and Surgeons of Ontario chose to remove his license to practise. The panel referred to the patient's 'profound vulnerability'[135] and the

---

[132] Ibid: footnote to [11].

[133] See, e.g. ibid: [12]: 'Pursuing a relationship with a former patient is more likely to be (or be seen to be) an abuse of your position if you are a psychiatrist'; College of Physicians and Surgeons of Ontario 2008: 5 'when the physician-patient relationship involves a significant component of psychotherapy, sexual relations with the patient is likely inappropriate at any time after termination'. See also Department of Health 2005: 23. The majority of medical students who had been given a three-hour session on ethical issues regarding sexual boundaries in one study considered sexual contact between a psychiatrist and a former patient to be inappropriate (65% of 65 students): Coverdale and Turbott 1997: 337. We have noted above (n.27) that besides psychiatry, general practice and obstetrics and gynaecology are the other specialisms with the highest reported occurrence of sexual boundary breaches. However, we have not included these alongside psychiatry in our proposed criteria because the latter can be distinguished given that research illustrates that psychiatric patients are more emotionally and mentally vulnerable to sexual boundary breaches. This is because of the intimate nature of the professional therapeutic relationship and the risk of sexualised transference 'whereby a patient's feelings about significant relationships are transferred onto the patient's feelings and may be acted out towards the therapist/healthcare professional) and counter-transference (where the therapist's feelings about significant relationships are triggered by, and may be acted out in, the relationship with the patient)': Council for Healthcare Regulatory Excellence 2008b: 11. See further Hook and Devereux 2018 on 'adverse idealised transference'. See also Schulhofer 1998: 213–216 and chapter 10.

[134] *Ontario (College of Physicians and Surgeons of Ontario) v. Ghabbour*, 2017 ONCPSD 38.

[135] Ibid, 14.

existence of 'an intense psychotherapeutic relationship that endured for many months',[136] emphasising that:

> When there is a deep intimate one-sided exchange of personal information as occurs in ongoing psychotherapy, this inherently sets up a deep trust in the doctor by the patient. This trust causes a great vulnerability in the patient and an exceptional power imbalance of lasting and enduring impact.[137]

As we see it, in other cases, a zero-tolerance approach to consensual sexual relationships occurring outside of the professional context where the professional relationship is then discontinued and where there is no inducement or particular vulnerability is inherently paternalistic towards the patient. What we suggest is the adoption of a 'first-hand, subjective, account of vulnerability' in respect of such cases that engages meaningfully with the patient's experience, as Dunn et al have called for in the broader context of protective interventions regarding vulnerable adults.[138] Hence, we begin with a default position of inappropriateness and state that consensual sexual relationships occurring outside of the professional context *could* be permissible rather than *would* be permissible. Whether or not a particular case could be permissible requires consideration of the patient's situation and experience to ascertain whether or not she was, or is, vulnerable to sexual exploitation. We do not think it unreasonable to require doctors to engage in such an assessment; surely any doctor who seeks to respect as a person the patient with whom he is considering a personal relationship with, and to act in a way that does not breach professional ethics, would wish to reassure himself of the patient's free choice to enter into a consensual sexual relationship? Further, in order to ensure consistency in regulation and an objective assessment of the situation, we propose that it is a requirement that doctors who have satisfied themselves that the patient is not vulnerable, and that the other proposed criteria do not apply, must approach an adequately constituted GMC ethics committee trained to deal with the particular issues raised by sexual boundary breaches to have their case reviewed. We propose such ethical scrutiny because we consider this necessary to safeguard public trust.

Should we go further than this in diluting the current zero-tolerance position? We could, for instance, start from a premise which reflects Spiegel et al's pragmatic view that sexual boundary breaches still occur notwithstanding the zero-tolerance regulatory position.[139] They call for guidance on how to handle

---

136 Ibid, 10.
137 Ibid, 9. For a UK example also involving a psychiatrist, see MPTS, 'Record of Determinations – Medical Practitioners Tribunal: Dr Osborne', 11 February 2016, GMC reference number 6079770, at http://cchr.org.uk/wp-content/uploads/2017/03/Dr_Adam_OSBORNE__11_February2016.pdf accessed 9 March 2020.
138 Dunn and others 2008: 251 and see 247.
139 Spiegel and others 2003: 840.

sexual feelings towards patients to be included in medical students' education.[140] The authors suggest that to encourage reflection on the dangers of crossing professional boundaries and being sexually intimate with patients, students should be invited to discuss a number of factors that a doctor should consider before initiating an intimate relationship with a patient. These would include an assessment of factors that are parallel to those we propose above,[141] albeit notably absent the question of whether instigation of an intimate relationship

---

[140] Ibid. Similarly, Searle et al have argued for reinforcing the need to maintain the sexual boundaries 'in induction and ongoing training' (Searle and others 2017: 33; see also Halter and others 2007: 6; White 2003), and the lack of clarity on sexual boundary breaches and criminal behaviour was highlighted by the Kerr/Haslam inquiry (Department of Health 2005: 786, [36.53]). In fact, the CHRE recommended that 'training on sexual boundaries should be an *essential* part of the healthcare curriculum' back in 2008 (Council for Healthcare Regulatory Excellence 2008b: 2 (emphasis added), see also the view of the Medical Education Working Group of the Institute of Medical Ethics, as stated in Stirrat and others 2010: 57). Yet, although students are prohibited from using their position to pursue a sexual relationship with a patient, and failing to keep appropriate boundaries in behaviour is cited as an example of failing to demonstrate good medical practice in the GMC's guidance for medical students (General Medical Council 2016a: [65], [81]), there is no specific requirement that medical students receive training on avoiding sexual boundary breaches. Rather, medical schools 'have considerable autonomy in deciding what is taught where and when' and sexual boundaries training could be taught in a number of different parts of the curriculum, such as ethics and law and clinical skills development (Council for Healthcare Regulatory Excellence 2008b: 2, 11). Within one of our own universities, for instance, sexual boundaries training is included in modules covering the ethical dimensions of medicine at the Medical School at Lancaster University. Whilst this flexible approach means that medical schools can decide where sexual boundaries training fits best in their curriculum, the risk is that it may be more likely to be overlooked when it is not recognised as 'belonging' within, and being an integral part of, a particular area. We do recognise that it is difficult to assess the extent to which such training actually influences and changes behaviour: 'no examples have been found of assessment and evaluation tools that are capable of determining how far training has actually prevented sexual boundary transgressions which might otherwise have occurred' (Council for Healthcare Regulatory Excellence 2008b: 10 and see Coverdale and Turbott 1997: 338). This is perhaps unsurprising given the sensitive nature of the behaviour in question: would doctors be willing to profess that they experienced sexual feelings towards a patient that they would have acted on had they not received sexual boundaries training? And how would they know for sure that they would have acted on such feelings without this training? However, even in the absence of such an evaluation tool, there is a clear impetus for the inclusion of sexual boundaries training in undergraduate medical education and beyond as part of a doctor's post-registration education and continuing professional development (Council for Healthcare Regulatory Excellence 2008b: 12; Anderson Spickard and others 2008). Indeed, 'many students and healthcare professionals feel they have not received adequate training in this area' (Council for Healthcare Regulatory Excellence 2008b: 5).

[141] Namely, an assessment of: the extent to which the patient is 'emotionally or medically dependent on the doctor'; whether the patient's partner, child or close relative is being treated by the doctor; what the consequences will be for the patient and/or the doctor on termination of the relationship; and whether 'the patient's feelings of attraction towards the doctor arise from transference': Spiegel and others 2003: 841. On transference, see above, n.133.

occurred during the professional encounter, or through any exploitative behaviour.[142] They also suggest that students deliberate on whether the doctor-patient relationship should be terminated, asking to what extent 'the doctor's loss of authority and objectivity [will] impair the doctor/patient relationship'?[143] The final suggested matter for consideration is whether the doctor should consult a colleague or mental health professional about the possible impact of the romantic relationship.[144]

Utilising the factors that Spiegel et al suggest be taken into consideration, we could fashion a more attenuated regulatory approach to doctors' sexual boundary breaches that starts from the same default position presented in our suggested approach above – that such breaches are generally unethical and inappropriate – but does not rule out initiating an intimate relationship *during* a professional encounter between doctor and patient, nor demand particular reflection on whether the relationship might have been brought about through exploitative behaviour on the doctor's part. Such an approach would also bestow discretion upon doctors to continue the professional relationship. Having reflected on the identified factors, the doctor could decide whether a) it would be ethically appropriate to initiate the intimate relationship in question and b) whether she should end the professional relationship with the patient. The latter question could be asked regardless of whether the answer to the first question is yes or no: even if the doctor decides it would not be appropriate to embark on the sexual relationship, she may be of the view that feelings of intimacy with the patient have started to develop to the extent that the professional relationship has already been compromised and/or that continuing the professional relationship would be risky.[145]

Thus, this more attenuated regulatory response would amount to a 'generally no but not never' approach to sexual boundary breaches, coupled with a 'generally yes but not never' approach to the question of whether the professional relationship between doctor and patient should be ended. This would be to adopt a more flexible stance on the hard line that we drew above regarding the continuation of the doctor-patient relationship; ending the professional relationship *might well* be the ethically correct thing to do, but the doctor could continue this relationship if she or he was satisfied that it will not be (greatly) impaired by the romantic association with the patient.

We would, however, resist a further attenuated, more self-regulatory approach such as this for two primary reasons. First, whilst we do not doubt that the

---

142 That Spiegel and others do not include considering whether the relationship is instigated through exploitative behaviour is surprising given that one of the accepted factors they present regarding when sexual boundaries should never be breached (according to medical ethics), is where the doctor acts exploitatively: Spiegel and others 2003: 840.
143 Ibid: 841.
144 Ibid.
145 See also Council on Ethical and Judicial Affairs 1991: 2743 and American Medical Association 2016: opinion 9.1.1.

majority of doctors considering initiating an intimate relationship with a patient would conclude that they are likely to be conflicted and consequently end the professional relationship, it is possible that some will conclude that there will be no impairment to the latter, or that the level of impairment which they foresee is not ethically problematic. We argue that an alternative to a zero-tolerance approach *must* demand that any professional relationship is terminated. This is in line with the views expressed by the regulatory bodies,[146] participants from the general public and medical professionals in the studies noted above, and avoids a conflict between the doctor's duty of care to the patient in his professional capacity and his emotional attachment to the patient. It also takes into account the risk of endangering public trust in the medical profession that could occur if patients are aware that some doctors are treating patients whom they are personally involved with, and may, as a consequence, treat them preferentially. What is more, it would surely be difficult, if not impossible, for a doctor who is experiencing or is beginning to experience feelings of affection for a patient to look at the situation objectively.[147] Whilst we recognise that the same argument can be raised against our proposed approach, our requirement of review by a GMC ethics committee is directed towards alleviating this concern. Under a more diluted approach such as Spiegel et al's, where consulting a colleague or mental health professional is optional rather than a requirement, some doctors may choose not to do so.[148] They could make this decision because of fearing, for instance, that if they discuss the situation with another medical professional, she might conclude that the professional relationship would be impaired and then inform the relevant regulatory body if the doctor does decide to initiate the romantic relationship.

Secondly, this self-regulatory approach offers too much room for doctors' discretion. It would be harder for doctors' sexual boundary breaches to be regulated consistently and there would be less certainty amongst medical professionals as to what is and what is not ethically and professionally acceptable behaviour. Patients could perceive a threat to the professional nature of the doctor-patient relationship,[149] thereby risking a loss of trust in the medical profession. It would thus be safer to reject the elements of discretion and to adopt an approach that

---

146 E.g. 'A physician must terminate the patient-physician relationship before initiating a dating, romantic, or sexual relationship with a patient': American Medical Association 2016: opinion 9.1.1.
147 See also Cullen 1999: 485; Millbank 2020b: 214. In the aforementioned case of *Ontario (College of Physicians and Surgeons of Ontario)* v. *Ghabbour* (n.134), the doctor appeared to remain unaware of how his own feelings were impacting on his professional care of his patient.
148 Or approach a colleague who they consider could be more sympathetic to their case: Galletly 2020.
149 Albeit we note that a minority of patients may actually welcome this: see part 2 of this chapter, section 4, and Ost and Biggs 2015.

involves hard lines which should not be crossed, with medical professionals (and patients too) being aware of what these boundaries are in advance.

In sum here, our discussion in chapter 3 revealed that the imbalance of power that continues to exist in the doctor-patient relationship has been moderated by the patient-centred, autonomy-led contemporary model of the doctor-patient relationship. In this environment, we should be prepared to scrutinise whether there can be defensible exceptions to a zero-tolerance approach in situations such as that of the doctor in a rural area, or the doctor who desires a romantic relationship with someone who is a former patient.

Finally, we return to the issue of consent. The question of consent is bound up in sexual behaviour and sexual exploitation. A lack of consent, impeded consent or a distortion of the decision-making process caused by the doctor's behaviour *exacerbates* the sexual exploitation. But consent is not necessarily the *crucial determinative* issue when it comes to exploitation. Rather, it is misuse, often by way of taking advantage of a vulnerability, that lies at the heart of such behaviour. Inducement is indicative of misuse, of a failure to treat the patient as a person. Where there is no inducement and the sexual activity is consensual, we have proposed a cautious dilution of the zero-tolerance approach. As we now turn to explore, the vexatious issue of consent is a fundamental aspect of the criminal law on sexual offences, with the consequence that this law only applies to certain instances of sexual exploitation perpetrated by doctors upon patients.

5 Sexual exploitation in the doctor-patient relationship

PART 2: THE APPROPRIATE LEGAL RESPONSE TO SEXUAL EXPLOITATION

In this part, we consider how doctors' sexual exploitation of their patients is dealt with at law in England and Wales, paying special consideration to a gap in the criminal law through which sexual exploitation where a doctor proffers inducements could fall, and suggesting how this gap might be plugged. The significance of the matter of consent at law remains an important part of our focus. Moving next to the potential remedies that the civil law may offer, and finding this law wanting, we draw upon the approaches taken in Canada and Australia. In particular, we consider the significant Canadian case of *Norberg* v. *Wynrib*[1] and the advantages of tackling such exploitation through the law of fiduciary obligations. Our final concern is to recognise the existence of the reverse situation, where patients initiate sexual activity. Can such behaviour be exploitative of doctors? We then bring part 2 to a close by drawing some conclusions from our analysis in this chapter.

1) Assessing the scope of the criminal law in England and Wales and plugging a gap

The criminal law's increased intervention into health care matters indicates that the legislature, judiciary and, to a broader extent, society generally, sometimes consider it necessary to subject doctors' and other health care professionals' conduct to more than just ethical, regulatory and civil law restraints in order to protect patients from harm and the effects of serious wrongdoing.[2] That said, given the level of seriousness that is called for in order for wrongful behaviour to be criminalised, and the severe repercussions for the accused upon a guilty plea or conviction, there must be a sufficient public interest to criminalise the wrong in question.[3] Husak has

---

1   1992 CarswellBC 155, [1992] 2 SCR 226.
2   See Ost and Erin 2007; Brazier and Ost 2013.
3   See generally Duff 2007.

proposed internal constraints that must be satisfied for criminal laws to be justified, which dictate, inter alia, that they must involve non-trivial harm, the criminalised behaviour must be wrongful and those who advocate criminalisation should bear the burden of proof.[4] With this in mind, initially (and briefly), we note how the current criminal law would capture sexual exploitation perpetrated by doctors *without* consent. We then turn to explore, in more depth, how the criminal law would respond to sexual exploitation where consent is given, but we have reasons to consider that the patients' consent has been impeded because of an inducement.[5] Such exploitation may give rise to a more than trivial risk of causing patients to suffer significant psychological or physical harm and can, therefore, be seen to be *prima facie* wrongful.[6] We set out our reasons for contending that this type of exploitation can also constitute a *public* wrong below.[7]

Where sexual activity occurs between a doctor and a patient without the patient's valid consent, the doctor's behaviour is criminalised under the current criminal law under the Sexual Offence Act 2003 (SOA). The relevant offences would be rape, assault by penetration, sexual assault or causing sexual activity.[8] We do not consider the criminal law's response to such sexual exploitation without consent further, since the intervention of the law on sexual offences in such cases is wholly appropriate.[9] But what of cases such as those we discussed in part 1 of this chapter, where consent has been given but there has been an inducement? Could the doctors in our scenarios have committed the offence of sexual assault (*Scenario 1*), or of causing sexual activity (*Scenario 2*)? The criminal law's regulation of sexual activity revolves around the absence of consent. The definition of consent is provided under s.74 of the SOA: 'a person consents if he agrees by choice, and has the freedom and capacity to make that choice'. Thus, at issue in cases of sexual

---

4   Husak 2008: chapter 2. The other internal constraint Husak proposes is that the relevant punishment must be deserved.
5   For reasons of space, we are precluded from considering the way in which the criminal law would intervene in cases of sexual exploitation involving a doctor's observation/recording of a patient's private, intimate acts, as in our *Dr X* and *Mr Y* scenario and the real-life case of Dr Nikita Levy who took intimate, explicit photographs of his unknowing patients (see the text accompanying nn.34 and 35 in chapter 3). However, we note the applicability of the voyeurism offence under s.67 of the Sexual Offences Act 2003 (SOA), on which, see Gillespie 2008b. See also n.75 on possible civil law remedies.
6   Madden Dempsey and Herring, 2007: 479.
7   See the text accompanying nn.61–70.
8   Ss.1–4. We note that there are also a cluster of offences where *Y* and *X* are in a relationship of care and *X* has a mental disorder impeding choice, and where: *Y* sexually touches *X*; engages in sexual activity in *X*'s presence; causes or incites sexual activity by *X*; or causes *X* to watch sexual activity (s.42(3) SOA). A relationship between a doctor and patient would be recognised as a relationship of care for the purposes of these offences (s.42(3)). Sexual activity and behaving in certain sexual ways with children is also criminalised where the adult is in a position of trust with the child, such as being the child's doctor (Ss. 16–19 and 21(4)).
9   This is not to say that the law of rape is flawless, by any means. But we leave analysis of its gendered character to others who have offered powerful critiques. See, e.g. MacKinnon 2005.

exploitation perpetrated by doctors upon their patients such as those in our two scenarios, is whether the patients can be shown to have agreed by choice.

There are evidential and conclusive presumptions which establish non-consent under the SOA. The evidential presumptions operate[10] when:

- the defendant uses violence or causes the complainant to fear that immediate violence would be used against them or another person;
- the complainant was, but the defendant was not, unlawfully detained at the time;
- the complainant was asleep or unconscious at the time;
- the complainant would not have been able to communicate to the defendant whether he consented due to the complainant's physical disability;
- anyone administers to or causes the complainant to take, without the complainant's consent, a substance capable of causing or enabling the complainant to be stupefied or overpowered at the time.

The conclusive presumptions[11] apply either where the defendant intentionally deceived the complainant as to the nature or purpose of the act; or intentionally induced the complainant to consent by impersonating a person known personally to the complainant. None of the evidential or conclusive presumptions appear to apply in the scenarios we presented in the previous section and so, although we have provided reasons to argue that the patients' consent or their ability to engage in undistorted decision-making has been impeded, non-consent cannot be established for the purposes of the criminal law.[12] Whether our patients have consented would, therefore, be a matter for a jury, applying the general definition of consent under s.74. The SOA offers no guidance on how to assess whether a person 'agrees by choice' and has 'the freedom and capacity to make that choice'. This has been the subject of academic criticism, with Horder observing that 'freedom of decision-making may be greater or less, depending on the impact of any deception, threats, or other perceived pressures, and the question is what degree of impairment should be taken to mean that any apparent consent was not free'.[13] For Elliott and de Than, 'the use of ambiguous concepts of freedom and choice leaves the definition [under s.74] extremely vague'.[14] Case law has, so far, only offered guidance in specific contexts.[15] Thus, 'freedom of consent'

---

10 SOA, s.75
11 SOA, s.76.
12 See also Law Commission 2016: 78–79, [3.164]. On the limited protection that the criminal law provides to our sexual autonomy, see Schulhofer 1998: 101.
13 Horder 2019: 363. See also ibid: 79, [3.165]; Finch and Munro 2006.
14 Elliott and de Than 2007: 238.
15 For instance, according to the Court of Appeal decision in R v. Jheeta [2007] EWCA Crim 1699, the pressure that the defendant placed on the complainant to have intercourse with him by a fabricated, 'complicated' and 'unpleasant' scheme meant that she did not consent ([29]). The element of the defendant's deceit as to the reality of the situation may have played a role in the judgment (see [28]), which might suggest that the doctor's deception as to the situation in Scenario 2 could be used to make the case that there is no consent. See also R v. McNally [2013] EWCA Crim 1051.

may not be easily measured, and the circumstances in which the legislature deemed that an individual does not give free consent to sexual activity do not cover the situations that are reflected in our inducement scenarios and the real-life case involving gynaecologist Douglas Shelton as previously discussed, for instance.[16] Whilst it remains possible that a jury *might* decide that the consent given does not meet the requirements of s.74, we cannot say with any confidence that the behaviour of the doctors is criminalised under the SOA given the existence of ostensible consent.[17]

The fact remains that in both our scenarios, the patient is in a relationship of trust with the doctor, which has been exploited by the doctor to illicit agreement to engage in sexual activity. The patients' trust makes them vulnerable to this exploitation.[18] As in the case of Clifford Ayling's patients, they are disempowered by the circumstances within which they find themselves, and the knowledge of this has enabled the doctor to exploit their vulnerability to coercive or seductive offers of medical services in exchange for sexual favours. Their vulnerability to this form of exploitation is 'situational and socially constructed' rather than lying in any of their own 'personal characteristics or weaknesses'.[19] And the impact of any consequential harm is likely to be made worse because of the relationship of trust.[20] For instance, note again Laura Norberg's testimony that she felt humiliation, shame and a loss of dignity because of her doctor's actions.[21]

The doctors are able to induce the patients to consent by using their more powerful position to turn the patients' circumstances to their advantage. And where:

> the [doctor] has any undue control or influence over the [patient] ... then it can be legitimately questioned whether a [patient] is truly able to give full, knowing and considered consent. Our objection to accepting that the [patient's] consent is genuine is undoubtedly connected to the way in which it has been obtained by the [doctor's] manipulation of power and exertion of control or influence ...[22]

---

16 See Knight 2012: 144: 'Within English law, as far as offers and inducements are concerned, the decision in [R v. *Olugboja* [1981] 1 All ER 443] and the SOA 2003 make clear that anything goes. From simple economic gains ... to clearly immoral offers which may be difficult to resist given the circumstances, in law positive inducements independent of any other considerations will not vitiate consent.'
17 What is more, the criminal law in England and Wales is not alone in leaving grey areas into which fall cases where the validity of consent is questionable, but the fact that consent exists means that the behaviour does not constitute an obvious criminal wrong. See, e.g. Buchhandler-Raphael 2010b on the criminal law in the US.
18 See also Collins 2015: 154; Searle and others 2017: 22-23.
19 Buchhandler-Raphael 2010b: 135. Although perhaps in the case of the patient in *Scenario 1*, we might say that being the parent of a child is more of a personal characteristic that gives rise to vulnerability in respect of what happens to that child, the situational context of relying upon the doctor to make one's seriously ill child better plays a crucial role in creating the patient's vulnerability to the doctor's offer.
20 Council on Ethical and Judicial Affairs 1991: 2743; Rhodes 2001: 499.
21 See part 1, n.63.
22 Gillespie and Ost 2016: 176 (wording revised to our specific context). The existing literature on undue influence recognises that doctors have the power to wield such influence. See Quinn and others 2010: 11, 14.

Thus, although the presence of consent would seemingly place the behaviour outside the criminal law, we have reason to doubt the efficacy of the minimal consent that has been given. This is because such compromised consent is essentially 'permission or authorization to engage in sexual acts ... which is given [because of an inducement/undue influence rather] than the complainant's positive willingness'.[23] As we see it, this is a significant matter of impaired consent that is not tackled by the evidential and conclusive presumptions which establish non-consent to sexual acts under the SOA.

It seems apposite at this point to confront head-on the fact that the matter of consent is thorny and evasive, as the discussion throughout this chapter evidences. Moreover, the criminal law's preoccupation with consent in the context of sexual offences has long been critiqued as failing to address the asymmetries of power in human relationships.[24] This could lead to the argument that we should look to an alternative, less polemic peg on which to hang the wrong, perhaps abandoning the focus on consent altogether. Indeed, this is the way that Schneebaum chooses to approach what she conceptualises as sex in authority relations (SAR) offences. In her view:

> Many SAR cases do not conform to any of the *categories* of nonconsent traditionally recognized under common law ... certain SAR cases involve fraud, and others involve coercive threats, but many SAR cases ... do not include these elements. The typical scenario described in these cases is of two mature partners who engage in sexual relations with no explicit threat or fraudulent claims by the offender and with no expression of nonconsent by the victim ... The leap from assuming unwanted sexual conduct to concluding *nonconsensual* sexual contact is unfounded. It ends up transforming consent into a psychological experience, which makes significant the victim's inner will (or lack thereof) in sexual contact.[25]

Just as we do, Schneebaum recognises that SAR cases involving offers raise an 'interesting question' which existing sexual offence models do not tend to answer. Her solution is to place them within her proposed offence model revolving around abuse of authority,[26] for she contends that it is '*abuse of authority*' rather than consent that lies at the crux of SAR offences and which should thus be the 'conceptual focal point'.[27] We agree with Schneebaum that SAR cases do share this element, and that this is a part of the wrong which is committed. However, the problem

---

23 We have used Buchhandler-Raphael's wording here (with some modification to fit our context): Buchhandler-Raphael 2010b: 83.
24 See, e.g. Ehrlich 2015; Buchhandler-Raphael 2011. See also Lacey 1998: 60: 'an abstract notion of non-consent as the core of rape provides a distorted or (at the very least) partial representation of the real wrong of rape, in that it displaces the embodied and affective aspects of the offence'.
25 Schneebaum 2015: 361–362 (emphasis in original).
26 Ibid: 383, n.182.
27 Ibid: 349 (emphasis in original). For her, the perception should be one of 'the complainant's submission as subservient compliance within an authority relation': ibid: 376.

with placing all SAR cases into such a category is that although this categorisation reflects one commonality which they all share – an abuse of authority – it neglects to convey all of the wrong in cases which involve inducements.[28] As we have expressed above, in these cases, part of the wrong is the way in which the doctor's offer is designed to compromise the patient's decision-making. Paying attention to the manipulation of the 'victim's inner will'[29] in the sexual activity emphasises the doctor's deliberate ploy to obtain the patient's acquiescence, his wrongful act of unduly influencing the patient for his own purposes.[30]

In contrast to Schneebaum, Buchhandler-Raphael maintains a focus on (non-) consent. She presents cases in which sexual activity occurs in a relationship of unequal power at the instigation of the person in a position of power as involving *non-consent*.[31] On her conceptualisation:

> Sexual abuses of power… share some distinctive features: first, the perpetrator engages in unilateral sexual conduct with another person by exploiting that other person's body for the purposes of his own gratification, arousal or sexual pleasure, and against the will of that other person … Second, submission to unwanted sexual acts is not obtained by consent, but rather, by intimidation and coercive pressures stemming from the disparities of power between the parties, which induce mere acquiescence.[32]

She goes on to argue that there is no consent where 'the circumstances indicate that there was such an abuse of the power disparity between the parties that the weaker party was not in a position to choose freely, because she perceives that withholding permission is not an option … [there is thus] a non-physical overwhelming of the free will.'[33] Adopting Buchhandler-Raphael's approach can lead to a legal model that would catch sexual exploitation when the patient's consent has been obtained through coercion and, potentially, any sexual activity occurring in a relationship of unequal power which involves an abuse of power.[34] This position would seem analogous with the aforementioned Canadian law. Recall that the law in that jurisdiction considers a doctor's sexual activity

---

28 Or, indeed, those involving threats or fraud. As the quote from Schneebaum above reveals, the analysis in her article extends to SAR cases that involve threats or fraud. Schneebaum conceives of such cases as falling within her conceptualisation of SAR, whilst also potentially amounting to sexual offences where there is non-consent: ibid: 348 n.11, 383.
29 Above, n.25.
30 We thus disagree with Schneebaum that SAR offences are not 'concerned with personal autonomy' or 'the rights of individual victims': Schneebaum 2015: 381. Some SAR cases, such as those involving threats or offers, are concerned with both autonomy and rights.
31 Buchhandler-Raphael 2010b.
32 Ibid: 79.
33 Ibid: 119.
34 Some caution is required here, because Buchhandler-Raphael's conceptualisation captures coercive *inducements* as well as coercive threats, but would not appear to apply to inducements without 'coercive pressures': ibid: 79, 121–122.

with a patient to be sexual abuse, no matter if consensual.[35] And in relation to the offence of sexual assault under the Canadian Criminal Code, there is no consent where 'the accused induces the complainant to engage in the activity by abusing a position of trust, power or authority'.[36] By way of a further example, under Texas's Penal Code, and with the notable inclusion of an element of exploitation, a sexual assault occurs without the consent of the other person where 'the actor is a mental health services provider or a health care services provider who causes the other person, who is a patient or former patient of the actor,

---

35 See part 1 of this chapter, the text accompanying n.37.
36 S.273.1(1)(2)(c). Moreover, there is also no consent to an assault (including sexual assaults) where the complainant submits because of an exercise of authority (s.265(3)(d)). Although 273.1(1)(2)(c) is little used (Buchhandler-Raphael 2011: 174), the following offer examples of case law where this provision has been utilised. In *R v. Snelgrove* 2019 SCC 16 (involving an on-duty police officer and an intoxicated woman who he gave a lift home from a bar and subsequently had sex with), the Supreme Court confirmed what had been stated in *R v. Hogg* (2000), 148 C.C.C. (3d) 86 (Ont. C.A.) [17] that s.273.1(2)(c) is directed to 'the protection of the vulnerable and the weak and the preservation of the right to freely choose to consent to sexual activity'. Moreover, the Supreme Court confirmed that 'inducing consent by abusing the relationships set out in s. 273.1(2)(c) does not imply the same kind of coercion contemplated by s. 265(3)(d) of the Criminal Code, which speaks to consent obtained where the complainant submits or does not resist by reason of the "exercise of authority"' [3] (Moldaver J). *R v. TD* 2019 ONSC 3761 illustrates the application of s.273.1(2)(c) to a personal relationship. The provision was applied to a husband in 'the particular context of [his wife's] immigration circumstances' [71]. In sentencing the accused in the Ontario Superior Court of Justice, Howard J held that 'within the context of s. 273.1(2)(c) ... [the accused] abused his position of trust and power when he threatened to withdraw the complainant's immigration sponsorship application for his own personal sexual gratification and for no reasonable justification or excuse.' [22]. In *Re ATU, Local 113 and Toronto Transit Commission* 2018 CarswellOnt 12619, involving a workplace supervisor and an employee, it was noted that 'Just as a woman in a rape situation might succumb to threats of violence, so too may an employee succumb to an abuse of workplace power by a supervisor. Accordingly, consent to sex must be distinguished from acquiescence or compliance or attempted appeasement ... He did not need to make any forceful or power statement to her, his supervisory position alone provided him with all the accoutrements of power that she, as an employee, subject to his control and direction would be immediately aware of... she was a single mother with three children and her job ... Thus any conduct on her part must be viewed not only in the context that I have described but also from the point of view of [her] vulnerability.' [135], [138] (O.B. Shime Member, Ontario Arbitration). As a final example, in *R v. Kilian* 2018 ABQB 273, the accused was a therapist treating the complainant. He used the therapeutic relationship to normalise physical contact. He touched her sexually four times, two times after she had said no and the other two times without warning. The trial judge in the Alberta Court of Queen's Bench found that 'Dr. Kilian used [his] position to make Ms. M depend on him and believe that he was her lifeline. He groomed her for sexual activity by introducing sexual dialogue in their sessions and by normalizing physical contact, first through tapping and then through healing touch. He exploited the power imbalance between them to impose sexual acts upon her, and to induce her to engage in sexual activity. She was not a willing participant. She complied because she trusted him and needed to preserve a therapeutic relationship on which she depended.' [104] (Antonio J).

to submit or participate by exploiting the other person's emotional dependency on the actor'.[37] However, although modifying the non-consent presumptions under the SOA to include such a presumption offers a similar way to address the issue of minimal, or compromised, consent, we do not advocate going down this route. Whilst consent can be nullified where coercion (including coercive offers), is involved in sexual exploitation,[38] in the case of seductive but non-coercive inducements, we are not contending that there has been *no* consent to sexual activity. The patient has given some form of consent, but it is compromised.[39] To present these cases as involving non-consent is, therefore, inaccurate.

An alternative and a more appropriate means of tackling the issue, as we see it, would be to introduce a new offence which takes implicit account of the existence of impaired consent, but avoids framing the matter around the difficult conundrum of consent and focuses, instead, on what *causes* the sexual activity to take place.[40] An offence that revolves around the existence of the undue influence and an abuse of trust would provide a fuller and more accurate reflection of the situation and the wrong.[41] We have in mind a new abuse of trust offence that could look something like the following:

1. Whilst in a position of trust, A intentionally causes a relevant sexual act to occur through exploiting[42] B by exercising undue influence.[43]
2. A relevant sexual act is where:

---

37. Texas Penal Code § 22.011(b)(9).
38. See the discussion above in part 1 of this chapter, text accompanying nn.79–81.
39. And see Law Commission 2016: 203, [8.7]: 'it could be argued that there is an intermediate class of case, in which [B's] consent should be regarded as flawed rather than non-existent: for example, if it was obtained by ... improper pressure. Such cases, on this argument, do not deserve to be stigmatised in the same way as a non-consensual sexual offence but should not escape liability altogether.'
40. 'In those cases in which we suspect that consent it merely apparent, rather than asking whether permission to engage in sexual acts was given, the key question we must ask instead is this: *Why* was permission given?': Buchhandler-Raphael 2010b: 104 (emphasis added).
41. And we explain why we have opted for an abuse of trust (rather than authority) conceptualisation below, see pp. 150–154.
42. We do not think that using the word *exploiting* in the wording of the proposed offence gives rise to ambiguity, or the need for a definition of exploitation, since the offence proceeds to state what exploitation is for the purposes of this offence: exercising undue influence. In chapter 3, section 8, we noted that undue influence is a legally workable concept, as evidenced by its existing legal usage in the law of contract. Thus, the proposed offence provides an explanation of exploitation particularly directed to the wrong we have in mind, thereby according with Collins' assertion that, 'wrongful interpersonal exploitation must be disaggregated into a number of wrongs', with legal certainly only being achievable 'by focusing on the type of offence': Collins 2015: 53–54. See chapter 7, section 4.ii, for our analysis of the difficulties that would by posed if exploitation were to be utilised as a (broad) category of legal wrong.
43. Whilst it reflects the terminology we have adopted elsewhere in this work, in referring to the alleged perpetrator as A and the alleged victim as B, we are also following the convention laid out in the SOA.

a *A* does anything sexual[44] to, or with *B*, or;
b *B* does anything sexual to, or with, *A* or;
c *A* causes or incites *B* to do anything sexual to herself or himself or another.

The label of (criminal) wrongdoing attached to this behaviour would thus be one of an abuse of trust rather than abuse of authority or power as in Schneebaum's and Buchhandler-Raphael's models.[45] We accept that it is difficult to choose which wrong – the abuse of trust or the abuse of authority – should be at the crux of the offence. However, as we see it, whilst abuse of authority is undoubtedly an element of the wrong, and an imbalance of power continues to be a characteristic of the doctor-patient relationship,[46] labelling the offence as one of abuse of authority does not convey the doctor's breach of a, if not *the*, fundamental characteristic on which the doctor-patient relationship is based. As we explained in chapter 3, trust is one of the most integral elements in the doctor-patient relationship and it is thus, in our view, the most appropriate peg on which to hang the offence.[47] Although, as the Law Commission has noted in the context of the misconduct in public office offence,[48] 'the boundaries of "trust" are very hard to draw',[49] notably, the relationship of trust that we are centring on here involves the same variant of trust that the Commission has identified as being vested in a public office holder. This is trust in a '"strong sense", involving a duty of acting selflessly and in the exclusive interests of a person or purpose.'[50] Thus, *A* would be in a position of trust where he has a

---

44 A definition of 'sexual' is already provided under s.78 of the SOA as follows: 'penetration, touching or any other activity is sexual if a reasonable person would consider that (a) whatever its circumstances or any person's purpose in relation to it, it is because of its nature sexual, or (b) because of its nature it may be sexual and because of its circumstances or the purpose of any person in relation to it (or both) it is sexual'.
45 We note that the categorisation of sexual exploitation of members of the public by police officers is also conceptualised as 'abuse of position for a sexual purpose' in professional inspection reports. Abuse of position for a sexual purpose is defined as 'any behaviour by a police officer ... whether on or off duty, that takes advantage of their position as a member of the police service to misuse their position, authority or powers in order to pursue a sexual or improper emotional relationship with any member of the public': Her Majesty's Inspectorate of Constabulary and Fire & Rescue Services 2019: 5.
46 See chapter 3, section 4.
47 Note also one of the guiding principles stated in the Kerr/Haslam Inquiry report that there should be 'a recognition that trust between patient and doctor is of central importance. Insofar as it has been damaged by the allegations [of sexual exploitation and abuse] made in recent years, including the allegations (whether true or not) listed in this Report, then every effort should be undertaken to restore that trust.' Department of Health 2005: 19. Schulhofer highlights how doctors 'exercise exceptional influence because they have special claims to their clients' trust': Schulhofer 1998: 229.
48 A common law offence, the elements of which can be found in *Attorney General's Reference No 3 of 2003* [2004] EWCA Crim 868.
49 Law Commission 2016: 70, [3.122].
50 Ibid.

duty to act in the interests of B, who is in a position of vulnerability in relation to A's position. We say more on trust below. The *mens rea* would be exercising undue influence to bring about the occurrence of a sexual act when knowingly in such a position of trust.

Thus far, we have made the case for our proposed offence being particularly apt for such sexual exploitation in the doctor-patient relationship. However, whilst we have contended that wrongful exploitation in the doctor-patient relationship is a special example of exploitation in intimate and confidential professional relationships,[51] when it comes to the criminal law's response to sexual exploitation, it would be contentious to argue that creating a new abuse of trust offence should extend only to this particular relationship involving trust and an imbalance of power. Albeit in relation to sexual exploitation perpetrated by an adult upon a young person, one of us has argued, with Gillespie, that it is not helpful to focus on a list of certain defined relationships/positions of trust to criminalise sexually exploitative behaviour.[52] To do so is to leave unregulated numerous relationships involving trust and an imbalance of power in which exploitation could occur.[53] Take, for example, the relationship between lawyer and client, which has been described as 'one of ultimate trust'.[54] It surely would not be right if a solicitor who induces a client to engage in sexual activity by making an irresistible or coercive offer that impedes the client's choice to engage in this activity, commits no offence (provided the jury is satisfied that consent has been obtained), whereas a new offence catches the same behaviour instigated by a doctor. True, we may wish the judge to reflect on the particular severity of exploitative behaviour by virtue of the specific relationship in determining the level of sentence imposed upon a guilty plea or conviction. However, at the criminalisation stage, should the criminal law not apply to all professionals who act in a sexually exploitative way in intimate and confidential professional relationships of trust?[55]

An abuse of trust offence, which centres upon impeding choice through A's influence, creates room for a consideration of factors that could compromise consent (such as coercion) or the ability to engage in an undistorted decision-making process (such as seductive inducements), but that

---

51 See chapter 3, especially sections 1, 2 and 9.
52 Their focus being abuse of trust offences designed to protect 16 and 17-year-olds under the SOA: ss.16–24.
53 Gillespie and Ost 2016. See also the CHRE's concern about misconceptions that sexual boundary breaches are more serious if perpetrated by certain groups of professionals: Council for Healthcare Regulatory Excellence 2008b: 17.
54 *Re Piatt* 191 Ariz. 24, 951 P.2d 889 (Ariz.1997), 891 (Martone J), Supreme Court of Arizona. And see Schulhofer 1998: chapter 11.
55 And, indeed, we recognise that the implications of our analysis and proposed new offence extend beyond professional relationships to personal relationships involving trust and an imbalance of power (see chapter 7, text accompanying n.142, and Gillespie and Ost 2016). However, our discussion here is necessarily limited by the focus of this book.

are less likely to be enough of an invasion to consent to mean that the person's acquiescence falls outside the vague definition of consent under the SOA. Consequently, the criminal law would be able to respond to Lacey's critique that:

> violation of trust, infliction of shame and humiliation, objectification and exploitation find no expression in the legal framework, albeit that they surface with increasing insistence ... at the sentencing stage. Why should it be that the contemporary criminal law dealing with sexuality has such an oblique relationship with social attitudes about ... what is wrong with or abusive about certain forms of sexual behaviour?[56]

Uprooting the traditional placing of consent as the pivot also removes the potentially powerful and distorting effect that the jury's worldview perceptions and social norms on consent and rape can have.[57] As Buchhandler-Raphael observes, 'juries make decisions about culpability based on the social norms they hold regarding the boundaries between legitimate and illegitimate sexual practices, and on how they define consent to sex'.[58] Instead, through our proposed offence, attention remains focused on what the 'culpable perpetrator' does to induce B's acquiescence, rather than 'scrutinizing [B's] behaviour and responses'.[59]

In respect of our proposed offence, factors indicative of undue influence could include coercive and irresistible inducements, thereby extending to behaviour such as that of the doctors in *Scenarios 1* and *2*. And we note that the concept of inducement is not unfamiliar to the criminal law on sexual offences, with the existence of offences relating to involving a person with a mental disorder in sexual activity where an inducement is used to obtain the person's agreement to the activity.[60]

We suggest that a strong argument can be made for the existence of a sufficient public interest to criminalise this particular wrong of sexual exploitation involving the impeding of consent or distortion of the patient's decision-making process through a breach of trust. Again, we keep our focus upon sexual exploitation in the doctor-patient relationship here, but the arguments that we now make could also be made in respect of such exploitation in other relationships of trust and unequal power. First, if society does not

---

56 Lacey 1998: 54. On consent being bound up with social contexts and conventions, see Westen 2004: 68.
57 Finch and Munro 2006; Ellison and Munro 2009.
58 Buchhandler-Raphael 2010b: 144.
59 Buchhandler-Raphael 2011: 195.
60 SOA, ss.34–37. In the Explanatory Notes accompanying the SOA, it simply states in relation to these offences that 'an inducement might be A promising B presents of anything from sweets to a holiday' (Sexual Offences Act 2003 Explanatory Notes: note 67). We also note the concept of undue influence's longstanding history in the laws of equity and contract. See chapter 3, section 8; Quinn and others 2010: 97–98.

denounce such harmfully exploitative behaviour, we would fail to recognise both the extent of the wrong suffered by the individual and the significance attached to the ethical responsibility to treat individuals as ends in themselves rather than solely as a means to an end.[61] In an earlier chapter, adopting Uniacke's analysis, we presented this wrong as a violation of the right not to be treated merely as an object.[62] We would also fail to address the harm caused to victims, noted earlier to include guilt, humiliation, shame and a loss of dignity that is exacerbated by the breach of trust. Framing the offence as one of an abuse of trust thus acknowledges the trust placed in the doctor on a public and private level to act in the patient's interests, and the abuse of trust label also draws attention to what makes the wrong especially harmful for patients.[63] Thus, the justification for considering this wrong as an abuse of trust that should attract criminal liability is the patient's situational and socially constructed vulnerability[64] in relation to the doctor's position, which is indicative of a relationship of trust in a strong sense.[65] The trust the patient vests in the doctor plays a significant role in making the patient vulnerable to exploitation. As the Law Commission has stated, when carrying out their professional role, doctors may be expected:

---

61 And, to utilise Tadros's terminology, this behaviour should ignite the public's moral indignation (warranting communication through criminal sanction) because of the manifestation of 'the kind of vice that displays a failure to have proper regard for a significant interest of others': Tadros 2005: 83.

62 See chapter 2, s.3(iii). For rights violations as justification for criminal laws generally, see Simester and von Hirsch 2011. It could also be argued that the doctor violates the patient's right to sexual integrity by his behaviour. This violation could be defined as an 'invasion of self and the psyche' (Buchhandler-Raphael 2010a: 424–425) through compromising the patient's decision-making by presenting a seductive offer which causes her to agree to sexual activity that she does not desire, and does not serve her core interests. We note that besides such conceptualisations of sexual integrity as a privacy right, there are other conceptualisations (see, e.g. Westen 2004: 149–150). For instance, Lacey has drawn attention to feminist literature in which 'integrity embraces both physical integrity and the affective sense in which access to bodily or sexual integrity also depends on a host of social and psychic conditions [such as] conditions of respect for differently embodied subjects ... respectful relationships as conditions internal to human integrity.' And, importantly, she adds that '[a] recognition of the value of integrity invites the incorporation of implications of sexual abuse such as shame, loss of self-esteem, objectification, dehumanisation': Lacey 1998: 64–65. Lacey advocates 'rethinking the idea of autonomy as integrity': Lacey 1998: 65, which could thus open the door to a right to autonomy that encompasses sexual integrity. Although space precludes us from exploring this further, this more explicitly embodied conceptualisation of sexual integrity seems especially apt in its recognition of the types of harms described by patients who have been sexually exploited by their doctors.

63 See part 1 of this chapter, text accompanying nn.50 and 52. See also Council for Healthcare Regulatory Excellence 2008b: 16.

64 Buchhandler-Raphael 2010b: 135.

65 Law Commission 2016. 82 [3.181].

to put the public's interests before their own. Alternatively, [they] may be considered to be in a position of public trust because they are able, by virtue of their position, if they choose to do so, to exercise influence over people otherwise dependent on them, such as a patient ... not only is [B] in a position of 'vulnerability' (either absolutely or in relation to [A]) but [A] also has a professional duty to respect and safeguard those in that position. Exploiting that vulnerability for sexual advantage is a breach of trust (both [B's] trust and the trust of the public) ...[66]

As such, the kind of exploitative behaviour we have considered amounts to a public wrong that should concern society and be condemned, since it contravenes defining values that society recognises as fundamental and that the state endeavours to safeguard to ensure the good of its citizens:[67] 'it undermines a basic assumption of interpersonal trust' that patients place in their doctors.[68] Notably, its nature reflects a type of behaviour that the Law Commission considers could justify a new offence.[69] And criminalisation of such behaviour is not without precedent: it is a wrong that the criminal law already recognises in the context of relationships with children and adults with mental disorders.[70]

Secondly, it is not only a matter of society recognising the public wrong committed; it should also be acknowledged by the doctor. Leaving the doctor and patient in the particular case to deal with the conduct as a private wrong through the civil law does not encourage the doctor to reflect upon the broader normative implications of their wrongful conduct. Concluding that the matter should be resolved privately also involves an assumption that the exploitee is able to overcome the imbalance of power between the parties, enabling him to be in a position to make the exploiter right her wrong. It is dangerous, and unrealistic, to make such an assumption when a relationship of unequal power continues to exist, as it could in the doctor-patient relationship.

Even in these circumstances, however, it is likely that some will counter that criminalisation is unnecessary because alongside potential civil law remedies that we discuss shortly, such matters can be adjudicated through public

---

66 Law Commission 2016: 60 [3.76], 82 [3.182]. See also Buchhandler-Raphael 2010b: 87–88: 'when perpetrators who represent [the healthcare profession] induce victims' unwanted submission through abuse of their power, the institution itself is abused. Such abuse may damage the institute's reputation by compromising its integrity and the public's trust in it.'
67 See Duff 2007: 86 and 143; Husak 2007: 135–137; Law Commission 2016: 82 [3.183]; Marshall and Duff 1998: 20.
68 Greenspan 2003: 164 (albeit on manipulation more broadly).
69 With the Law Commission suggesting that the new offence could be 'sexual exploitation of a vulnerable person for whom D has responsibility', or 'exploitation of a position to facilitate a sexual relationship': Law Commission 2016: 82–83 [3.182], 203 [8.3], 204 [8.10].
70 Under ss.16–19 and 38–41 of the SOA.

hearings by the MPTS, following the investigation of complaints by the doctors' professional regulatory body, the GMC. Yet a counterargument is that the serious and public nature of the wrong committed demands that the doctor should be judged by a jury of lay persons, rather than a panel comprised of other members of the medical profession and some lay members who have been both chosen and trained by the GMC. And there are also questions regarding the appropriateness of the sanctions for professional misconduct. Searle et al's aforementioned thematic analysis of fitness to practise cases involving doctors' sexual misconduct led the authors to conclude that 'given the severity of the impact [the victims' reported mental harm], from a lay perspective it is surprising that a range of sanctions are applied, from being struck-off, to placement on restrictive practice, or suspension'.[71] What is more, the GMC's primary concern is with the doctor's fitness to practise,[72] and it is not necessarily straightforward for the public to access the findings of fitness to practise hearings.[73] Reform to the adjudication of fitness to practise cases that occurred in 2012 was, in part, the result of what had been a growing public distrust with the willingness and ability of the GMC to adequately deal with serious cases of misconduct and abuse of power.[74] Additionally, whilst it is self-evident that the criminal law is concerned with public condemnation, the central function of the criminal justice system, that justice is seen to be done in response to a serious wrong, cannot be overstated. Hence, we maintain our conviction that, where a doctor violates the sexual boundaries with a patient and obtains the patient's consent through undue influence, this exploitative behaviour should be clearly criminalised.

2) Possible civil law remedies in England and Wales

Our argument above supports the criminal law's intervention where there is no consent to sexual contact, or where there is consent, but the doctor's exploitative behaviour means that the patient's consent is invalidated (because of a coercive inducement) or her decision-making has been distorted (because of an irresistible inducement). It could be contended, however, that our concern that cases falling into the latter category are not definitely caught by the criminal law is less significant if there is an alternative, appropriate legal avenue for addressing such exploitation. In this section, we explore actions potentially available under the civil law to catch cases of sexual exploitation involving contact with a

---

71 Searle and others 2017: 24, 29.
72 Davies 2007: 74–77.
73 Ibid, at 77–78. See the description of the availability of data in Chamberlain 2016: 4 (n.17).
74 Irvine 2006; Department of Health 2007; General Medical Council 2011; Chamberlain 2017: 12.

patient's body under the torts of battery and negligence.[75] We briefly consider non-consensual cases, before turning to the more challenging cases that are, on the face of it, consensual.

i) Battery

Where the doctor's exploitative behaviour has involved contact with the patient's body without his or her consent, a possible civil law action is for one of the torts of trespass to the person: battery. Since harm is constituted by the unconsented to touching, it would be unnecessary to establish the existence of any damage beyond this. Where consent has been given, a battery could still have been committed if the patient was deceived as to the nature and quality of the act by the doctor; this could vitiate consent.[76] Even where no such deception exists, English case law suggests that it might still be possible for consent to be deemed less than real because of the doctor's power in the relationship. We should, however, exercise some caution here because the case in question, *Freeman* v. *Home Office*,[77] relates to a doctor-patient relationship in the particular setting of a prison. Freeman, a prisoner, had consented to the injection of prescribed drugs by a prison medical officer, but he claimed that this consent was not real because he was in the defendant's custody. Notably, at first instance, the judge stated that the power exercised by a doctor in a prison setting to influence a prisoner's situation and prospects meant that the court

---

75 We do not have the space to consider in detail whether there would be a civil law remedy for sexual exploitation involving a doctor's observation and/or recording of a patient's private acts for sexual gratification (and see n.5). In short, whilst the development of the tort of breach of confidence relating to surreptitiously acquiring private information could offer a remedy (see *Tchenguiz* v. *Imerman* [2010] EWCA Civ 908, [68]), it is unlikely that there would be any remedy under the tort of misuse of private information. This is because the tort requires the wrongful *disclosure* of private information (*Campbell* v. *MGN* [2004] UKHL 22, [12]) or of intentionally inflicting harm (following the Supreme Court's rejection of the inference of intention from recklessness in *Rhodes* v. *OPO* [2015] UKSC 32). Also, for reasons of space, we do not explore the potential applicability of the Protection from Harassment Act 1997 (PFHA), because it requires a *course* of conduct: the conduct must occur on at least two occasions (PRHA s.7(3)(a); *Lau* v. *DPP* [2000] 1 FLR 799, [15]). In cases where the doctor's sexual exploitation occurs more than once, the PFHA could catch 'oppressive and unreasonable' conduct (*Thomas* v. *News Group Newspapers Limited and another* [2001] EWCA 1233, [30] (Lord Phillips MR)). However, the conduct must be calculated in an objective sense to cause alarm or distress (*Dowson* v. *Chief Constable of Northumbria Police* [2010] EWHC 2621 (QB), [142]; *AMP* v. *Persons Unknown* [2011] EWHC 3454 (TCC)), and unless a doctor perpetrated exploitation for reasons pertaining to her or his self-interest in causing the patient alarm or distress, it would be difficult to see how this requirement could be made out.
76 *Appleton* v. *Garrett* (1997) 34 BMLR 23 and, under the criminal law, *R* v. *Tabassum* [2000] 2 Cr App R 328 and s.76 of the SOA 2003.
77 *Freeman* v. *Home Office* [1984] QB 524.

should examine what might seemingly appear to be real consent.[78] We return to *Freeman* below, but look first to case law elsewhere to see how at least some members of the judiciary may be prepared to question the genuineness of a patient's consent in the context of exploitative sexual activity between doctor and patient.

In the afore-discussed case of *Norberg* v. *Wynrib*, three judges in the Supreme Court of Canada found for Laura Norberg on the basis that Dr Wynrib committed a sexual assault against her under the tort of battery. La Forest J found that the imbalance of power in the parties' relationship could place a constraint upon the patient's freedom to consent.[79] In answering the question of whether Laura Norberg had given legally effective consent to a sexual assault under the tort of battery, and alluding to contract law, as we will shortly discuss, La Forest J applied a two-step process. First, it was necessary to ascertain whether an inequality of power existed between the parties. Dr Wynrib's medical knowledge and his authority to prescribe drugs meant that an imbalance of power was indeed apparent. Secondly, it had to be determined whether exploitation had occurred. La Forest J found that Dr Wynrib's behaviour was exploitative because he had taken advantage of Norberg's drug addiction, her vulnerability, in pursuit of his own interests. He thus concluded that meaningful consent was absent.[80]

Grubb supports La Forest J's finding that consent was absent in the context of Norberg's drug addiction, which he considers likely to have deprived her of the ability to give consent to sexual activity.[81] But does the added ingredient of this vulnerability set this case apart from others in which there is an inducement to partake in sexual activity in a relationship of unequal power? We have noted that there is no equivalent criminal law provision in this jurisdiction to that under Canadian criminal law which holds that no consent is obtained to sexual activity where the complainant is induced to consent by the abuse of a position of trust, power or authority.[82] Could tort law better accommodate a more multifaceted understanding of consent, recognising that consent can be compromised by a coercive or irresistible inducement? Using the *Freeman* case as persuasive authority, Grubb argues that '[tort] law would scrupulously examine the actual relationship between a doctor and patient to ensure that the patient's consent is not involuntary due to undue pressure, inducements etc'.[83] The approach undertaken by the Court of Appeal in that case does indeed indicate that, where inducement in a dependent relationship is present, this

---

78 However, he found no grounds to suggest that 'the plaintiff's capacity to consent was overborne or inhibited in any way': ibid, 535 and 542–543.
79 *Norberg* v. *Wynrib*, above n.1, [27]. Gonthier and Cory JJ concurred with his judgment.
80 Ibid, [49].
81 Grubb 1995: 109.
82 See section 1, text accompanying n.36.
83 Grubb 1995: 109.

could be enough to vitiate consent.[84] That said, both the judge at first instance and the Court of Appeal held that the significant influence a prison doctor exerts over an inmate was not enough to vitiate consent. Given this, Allen cites the *Freeman* case to support his contention that, in professional relationships involving an unequal balance of power, any pressure stopping short of force or threats would be insufficient to make consent less than real in cases of sexual exploitation.[85]

As we see it, Grubb's interpretation is the most persuasive and we support this position by drawing a parallel with undue influence under contract law.[86] As we discussed in chapter 3, undue influence is a doctrine that vitiates consent.[87] In the doctor-patient relationship, because of the doctor's superior power, where he exerts his influence to provide the patient with a reason to do what the doctor desires,[88] then the criteria of either actual or presumed undue influence[89] applied under the doctrine could be met. Notably, there is case law in which the doctor-patient relationship has been recognised as the kind of relationship of trust and influence that undue influence requires,[90] and the argument that a patient's relationship with her doctor is one which should give rise to presumed undue influence has received academic support from Pattinson.[91] Moreover, the doctrine of undue influence has its origins in the law of equity, and both contract and tort law draw from equitable doctrine. Whilst we recognise that contract and tort are different branches of the civil law of obligations, judicial support for the position that they should be harmonious is reflected in La Forest J's reference to the relevance of undue influence in *Norberg*.[92] He also considered that the availability of the unconscionability doctrine to address the issue of voluntariness in contract law 'provides insight into the issue of consent [in tort law]: for consent to be genuine, it must be voluntary'.[93] In his view, principles developed

---

84 At 555 (Sir Stephen Brown LJ). Although we note that the Court of Appeal dismissed the plaintiff's appeal.
85 Allen 1996: 62.
86 See also Pattinson's call for the application of the doctrine of undue influence in cases involving consent to medical treatment: Pattinson 2002.
87 Although cf. Sopinka J's view quoted in n.102 below.
88 Our rewording of Bigwood 1996: 511.
89 See chapter 3, section 8, text accompanying nn.243–244.
90 See *Goldsworthy v. Brickell* [1987] 2 WLR 133; *Dent v. Bennett* (1839) 4 Myl & Cr 269; Bell 2007: 261.
91 Pattinson 2002.
92 [28] and [34]. Undue influence is a concept that has also been given legal recognition in the context of the High Court's exercise of its inherent protective jurisdiction in *Re SA (Vulnerable Adult with capacity: Marriage)* [2005] EWHC 2942, [79]: 'A vulnerable adult who does not suffer from any kind of mental capacity may nonetheless be entitled to the protection of the inherent jurisdiction if he or she is, or is reasonably believed to be, incapacitated from making the relevant decision by reason of such things as constraint, coercion, undue influence or other vitiating factors.' (Munby J) See also *A Local Authority v. DL, RL and ML* [2010] EWHC 2675 (Fam).
93 *Norberg v. Wynrib*, see n.1, [29] (La Forest J).

in contract law regarding the vitiation of consent in unconscionable transactions 'provide a useful framework for this evaluation'.[94] And it was this framework that provided him with the two-step process which we refer to above.[95]

As our discussion of the criminal law has shown, however, the question of what counts as a valid consent is notoriously tricky, and it has yet to be confirmed whether offering an inducement in a relationship involving an imbalance of power vitiates consent under tort law.[96] Notably, numerous judges involved in the *Norberg* case in different courts considered, contrary to La Forest J, that Laura Norberg *did* give voluntary consent.[97]

What is more, the tort of battery only communicates in broad terms the wrong that is committed in cases where the doctor engages in sexual contact with the patient without consent, or impedes consent by inducing the patient to engage in sexual contact. A battery is unconsented to touching (a violation of the right to bodily integrity)[98] and, whilst it 'carries connotations of intentional wrongdoing and harm',[99] it fails to convey the doctor's violation of trust and wrongful exploitation within a dependent relationship,[100] the breach of duty to act in the patient's best interests rather than her own self-interest.[101] We recognise that this might be dealt with through an award of aggravated damages, but this, the essence of the wrongful exploitation committed by the doctor, is not the essence of the tort.

And, finally, whilst we have supported the argument that the tort of battery could extend to consensual activity where consent is arguably vitiated, this would involve a manipulation of the essence of the tort beyond cases involving deception as to the nature and quality of the act. When rejecting La Forest J's analogy with consent in tort law and the unconscionability doctrine in contract law in *Norberg*, Sopinka J drew attention to the difference between: 1) a finding

---

94 Ibid. Note that Sopinka J disagreed that it was appropriate to draw a parallel between how unconscionability and voluntariness could operate in contract and tort, finding there to be 'a fundamental difference' between the two legal contexts: 'In the former, the court may refuse to recognize the validity of a transaction voluntarily entered into by reason of the unfair use of power by the strong against the weak. In the latter, the court is asked to saddle a party with damages for a wrong inflicted on the plaintiff.' [135].

95 We also note that the concept of undue influence would not be alien to health care law. It has been utilised when finding a patient's decision to be ineffective in the health care law context, albeit not in a case involving an action for battery against a medical professional: *Re T (Adult: Refusal of Treatment)* [1993] Fam 95 (CA). It was also raised (albeit not established) in *U v. Centre for Reproductive Medicine* [2002] EWCA Civ 565.

96 See also Birks 2004: 37: 'undue influence may be a [tortious] wrong in aggravating circumstances. *That is largely unexplored territory*' (emphasis added).

97 *Norberg v. Wynrib*, see n.1, [42] (referring to the trial judge and Court of Appeal judges) and [133] (Sopinka J).

98 Scanlon 2009: 74.

99 Kennedy 1986: 113.

100 And see *Norberg v. Wynrib*, see n.1, [64] (McLachlin J).

101 See also Tan 1997: 252.

of no consent, and 2) a finding that consent was given but the context in which it was given means that there is reason to be concerned about the agreement.[102] The wrong of battery – unconsented to touching – seems an obvious fit for the former, but less so for the latter.

ii) *Negligence*

An action for negligence might be envisaged if the doctor's sexual exploitation can be connected to a breach of a professional duty towards the patient (say it occurs under the guise of treatment, for instance). Or a looser connection between sexual exploitation and negligence could be drawn. Take the behaviour of Dr Wynrib: Sopinka J connected Wynrib's sexual exploitation of Laura Norberg to his failure to treat her appropriately for her drug addiction and recommend her for a drug addiction programme.[103] His breach of duty was held to relate to 'the obligation of a physician to treat the patient in accordance with standards in the profession'.[104]

Where there is no link between the exploitation and the doctor's duty to treat, it might be possible to frame a negligence action around the doctor's breach of his broader professional duty to promote the patient's general health,[105] because of the likely consequence that the sexual exploitation will cause psychological harm. It would not matter that the doctor's exploitation was deliberate rather than inadvertent; negligence liability is simply ascribed based upon a failure to meet an expected standard of conduct.[106] However, such a framing relies upon an entirely novel conception of the professional legal duty which has, until now, been firmly secured to the tasks that a doctor undertakes in the deployment of her or his professional skills. Judicial appetite for extending the duty of care in negligence in this way may not

---

102 In his view, under the doctrine of unconscionability in the law of contract, 'the issue is not consent but whether it was fairly obtained ... the weight of academic and judicial opinion is that the doctrine of unconscionability operates to set aside transactions even though there may have been consent or agreement to the terms of the bargain. It is not that this doctrine vitiates consent but rather that fairness requires that the transaction be set aside notwithstanding consent.': *Norberg* v. *Wynrib*, see n.1, [29] (Sopinka J), [135] and [136].

103 See Sopinka J's judgment in *Norberg* v. *Wynrib*.

104 *Norberg* v. *Wynrib*, see n.1, [149] (Sopinka J). Given that engaging in sexualised behaviour with a patient is 'in no way, shape, or form rendering a professional service', we agree with Puglise that pursuing this avenue for legal redress is an attempt to 'fit inappropriate conduct into a type of action which cannot legally or logically support it'. Puglise 2000: 328.

105 See Allen 1996: 69. And we note too that intertwining a doctor's sexual exploitation of his patient with his inappropriate treatment is also tenuous: see Puglise 2000: 328. Puglise's article offers a persuasive critique of the way in which courts in the United States have broadened the remit of medical malpractice to cases involving sexualised behaviour where the doctor and patient relationship has involved 'counselling matters'.

106 Gearty 1989: 223.

be forthcoming. We also note that in any case involving consensual sexual exploitation, the doctor might raise the defence of *volenti non fit injuria*, or contributory negligence.[107] Whilst Sopinka J did not allow consent to vacate Dr Wynrib's professional duty,[108] this was regarding his specific duty to treat according to accepted medical standards rather than a broader duty to promote the patient's health.

To conclude this section, we have reason to be cautious that a civil law remedy for patients who have been sexually exploited by their doctors in cases other than those involving non-consent exists. However, even if we could manipulate the contours of the tort of battery through the application of undue influence, it is questionable whether this would be the most apposite means of dealing with sexual exploitation in the doctor-patient relationship. Thus, the case for creating a new criminal offence remains compelling. But there is one other area of law that could potentially offer an additional route to tackle doctors' sexual exploitation of their patients.

3) The fiduciary approach under Canadian and Australian law

In chapter 3, we highlighted the symmetry between, on the one hand, the doctor's professional and ethical obligations to avoid an abuse of trust and power and to act in the patient's best interests rather than their own self-interest, and on the other, the essential elements of the fiduciary duty.[109] Elsewhere, one of us has explored in greater detail the potential that the law of fiduciary obligations might offer to catch sexual exploitation by doctors, and we revisit this analysis here.[110] Fiducial obligations arise in the law of equity in recognised fiduciary relationships, such as that between trustee and beneficiary.[111] They involve the bestowal of a power to one party (the fiduciary) over the other's (the beneficiary's) legal or practical interests regarding property or confidential information, for instance. The obligations limit the fiduciary's power to acting only on the beneficiary's behalf, in the beneficiary's interests. Beyond this, there is less clarity regarding the theory of liability upon which fiduciary accountability rests.[112] In the courts in various jurisdictions, attention has been drawn to different elements of power, vulnerability and reliance as the justification for the existence of these duties, and judges have applied tests based on discretion and reasonable expectation when finding that fiduciary duties exist.[113]

---

107 See Harper 2001: 196.
108 Sopinka J's judgment in *Norberg* v. *Wynrib*, see n.1, [153] and [156].
109 See chapter 3, section 3.
110 Ost 2016.
111 Bartlett 1997: 195.
112 Flannigan 2004: Miller 2011: 237, 239.
113 Flannigan 2004. Flannigan analyses Canadian and Australian cases, finding tests based on discretion; reasonable expectation and vulnerability; power; and reliance.

The protection of relationships considered valuable by society is a traditional rationale for recognising fiduciary obligations,[114] and Commonwealth courts elsewhere have been willing to find fiduciary obligations in the doctor-patient relationship.[115] Indeed, according to McLachlin J, in *Norberg*, 'the doctor-patient relationship shares the peculiar hallmark of the fiduciary relationship – trust, the trust of a person with inferior power that another person who has assumed superior power and responsibility will exercise that power for his or her own good and only for his or her good'.[116] Breach of a fiduciary duty constituted Laura Norberg's final claim against Dr Wynrib, and McLachlin and L'Heureux-Dubé JJ considered this claim to be made out. These Justices adopted an approach to fiduciary law that recognised and protected the patient's 'personal interest in obtaining professional medical care *free of exploitation for the physician's private purposes*'.[117]

Recognition of fiducial obligations thus occurred in the specific context of sexual exploitation in the doctor-patient relationship in the *Norberg* case. Elsewhere, their existence has been considered in contexts where doctors profit at their patients' expense,[118] or place themselves in a position where their own interests conflict with their patients',[119] and we consider this broader potential relevance of fiduciary law in our concluding chapter. It may be particularly challenging to call for legal recognition that doctors possess such obligations in England and Wales, however, as there appears to have been judicial reluctance to accept such a proposition since the latter part of the last century. In an *obiter* statement in the House of Lords judgment in the case of *Sidaway*, Lord Scarman stated that 'there is no comparison to be made between the relationship of doctor and patient with that of solicitor and client, trustee and cestui qui trust or the other relationships treated in equity as of a fiduciary character'.[120] But we should bear in mind the different context in which this very limited judicial consideration of whether the doctor-patient relationship should be recognised as fiduciary occurred. Whilst noting that there are some similarities between the sexual exploitation of patients by their doctors and the context of the *Sidaway* case (a failure to

---

114 Chamberlain 2016: 227.
115 Canada (*Norberg* v. *Wynrib*), Australia (to a more limited degree in *Breen* v. *Williams* (1996) 186 CLR 71), New Zealand (*Smith* v. *Auckland Hospital Board* [1965] NZLR 191) and the US (*Moore* v. *Regents of the University of California* (1990) 793 P. 2d 479).
116 *Norberg* v. *Wynrib*, see n.1, [65]. See also the Supreme Court of Washington's judgment in *Lockett* v. *Goodill* 430 P.2d 589 (Wash 1967), 591.
117 Ibid, [74] (emphasis added).
118 See, e.g. *Moore* v. *Regents of University of California*.
119 In the New South Wales Court of Appeal decision in *Breen* v. *Williams* (1994) 35 NSWLR 522, 569-71. And see the High Court of Australia's judgment in this case (*Breen* v. *Williams* (1996) 186 CLR 71 [14] (Brennan CJ)).
120 *Sidaway* v. *Board of Governors of the Bethlem Royal Hospital and the Maudsley Hospital* [1985] AC 871, 884.

inform the patient of inherent risks involved in a particular medical procedure), one of us has emphasised elsewhere that there are more distinctions. Not least of these is that an action in negligence is more apt and recognised by the courts in failure to inform cases, which can often be the result of negligent incompetence.[121] In contrast, unless it becomes clear that the tort of battery recognises that undue influence vitiates consent (and even then, this would only offer a source of legal redress where there has been touching with some form of acquiescence), we have shown that there is no neat or obvious form of legal redress for doctors' sexual exploitation under tort law. The provision of redress under fiduciary law in such cases would thereby '[offer] a meaningful, alternative cause of action for interactions that create implicit dependency and peculiar vulnerability'.[122]

There may be a more positive judicial reception to recognising the doctor-patient relationship as a fiduciary one in the particular context of sexual exploitation. As we have discussed above, the effects of the power imbalance and abuse of trust in the doctor-patient relationship are heightened in the context of sexual exploitation. Focusing on sexual exploitation by doctors would reflect a fact-based approach to finding fiduciary obligations, in contrast to a status-based approach that could give rise to the broader legal recognition of the doctor-patient relationship as fiduciary.[123] We concur with Sopinka J that the latter conceptualisation of the doctor-patient relationship *at law* would be inappropriate: 'the relationship between a doctor and his or her patient is ... of [a] hybrid genre';[124] whilst some duties in the doctor-patient relationship are fiduciary, others are not. Some of the doctor's legal duties towards the patient (the duty to meet the standard of care in treatment, for instance), are more appropriately conceptualised as deriving from the doctor's professional duty of care. However, although we do not advocate legal recognition of the relationship as fiduciary in totality, we are supportive of a wider legal conceptualisation of fiduciary obligations in the doctor-patient relationship beyond the sexual exploitation context, *provided* that the doctor's fundamental duty not to act out of self-interest is at stake. This is where recognised fiducial accountability at law for exploitative behaviour is called for, as we argue in our concluding chapter.

---

121 Ost 2016: 225–226. Whereas, as noted in *Bristol and West Building Society* v. *Mothew* [1996] 4 All ER 698, 712 (Millett LJ), 'breach of fiduciary obligation ... connotes disloyalty or infidelity. Mere incompetence is not enough'.
122 Rotman 2011: 925.
123 These different approaches are explained elsewhere: see Bartlett 1997: 196; Miller 2011: 270–272 for criticism.
124 *Norberg* v. *Wynrib*, see n.1, [147] (Sopinka J).

4) Sexual exploitation in the doctor-patient relationship: patients' sexual exploitation of doctors, the complexities of consent and some final thoughts on the appropriateness of a strict zero-tolerance approach

> [Dr Wynrib] argues that [Laura Norberg] exploited the weakness and loneliness of an elderly man to obtain drugs. While Dr. Wynrib, no doubt, had vulnerabilities of his own, it seems to me that the determining factor in this case is that he instigated the relationship – it was he, not [Laura Norberg], who used his power and knowledge to initiate the arrangement and to exploit her vulnerability. [Dr Wynrib's] argument *might be more persuasive if it had been [Laura Norberg] who had suggested that she would exchange sex for drugs.*[125]

Drawing the threads together from parts 1 and 2, we end this chapter recognising that doctors too can be sexually exploited by their patients. We noted at the outset that the intimate nature of the doctor-patient relationship exacerbates its susceptibility to feelings of sexual attraction and boundary breaches. This is also true for patients as well as doctors.[126] And whilst the power imbalance between doctor and patient may make it more likely that it is the doctor who is the initiator of a sexual boundary breach, this does not preclude the patient from being the one who makes the first move or, indeed, being the sexual harasser.[127] This is evidenced by research findings which reveal that sexual harassment of doctors by patients is far from unusual.[128] In one study, for instance, 77% of female doctors who participated had experienced some form of sexual harassment from a patient,[129] and in another, unwanted sexual contact from patients was experienced by 75% of psychiatric trainees.[130] In a further study, female family doctors expressed concerns about male patients sexualising the professional encounter and referred to 'frequently encountered' sexual harassment.[131]

The nature of the doctor-patient relationship also offers patients the opportunity to blackmail their doctors in relation to sexual boundary breaches. We have in mind here situations such as where there has been a boundary violation

---

125 *Norberg* v. *Wynrib*, see n.1, [87] (La Forest J) (emphasis added).
126 Council on Ethical and Judicial Affairs 1991: 2742.
127 See Council for Healthcare Regulatory Excellence 2008b: 18.
128 See, for instance, Bratuskins and others 2013; Viglianti and others 2018.
129 See Phillips and Schneider 1993. See also Farber and others 2000; Denis Campbell, 'Infatuated Patients use Facebook to stalk doctors' *The Guardian* (London, 28 October 2012).
130 Morgan and Porter 1999.
131 Cohen and others 1995: 172 and 175. We note that this study only involved family doctors who had recently graduated, and the authors thus note that the results may not be generalisable to the broader family doctor population. A similar caution applies to Morgan and Porter's study, ibid.

initiated by the patient and the patient threatens to allege that the activity was not truly consensual (by saying they felt they had no choice but to do what the doctor wanted because of the power imbalance, for example). Or, such as where there was no boundary violation, but the patient threatens to allege that there was. In one of the studies referred to above, male family doctors in Canada expressed concern about sexual abuse allegations by patients.[132] There are obvious, serious implications for a doctor's professional reputation and a likely negative impact on his personal life, where he is in a personal relationship, because of the nature of such an allegation. The doctor's position (the vulnerability of his professional reputation and personal life) could constitute a weakness that the patient can take advantage of. For instance, one case reported in a news article involved a complaint to the GMC from a patient that her GP had a sexual relationship with her. This was denied by the doctor and, following a six-month investigation by the GMC, he was cleared of wrongdoing.[133]

The occurrence of patient-initiated sexual boundary breaches and the potential for blackmailing a doctor should make us mindful that the identity of the doctor as the (sexual) exploiter in the doctor-patient relationship should not be assumed. The intimate, confidential nature of this special relationship could encourage patients who do not appreciate the significance of maintaining boundaries for the protection of the professional relationship to initiate sexual contact,[134] and can offer the opportunity to unscrupulous patients to sexually exploit their doctors.

To conclude this chapter, consent and the way in which consent is obtained can be relevant to the question of whether sexual activity between a doctor and patient is exploitative. But consensual sexual activity can still be exploitative if the doctor misuses the patient by, for example, offering her medical services as an inducement to engage in sexual activity which does not amount to a coercive or irresistible inducement, but, nonetheless, fails to respect her as a person. In large part, much of the ethical conundrum revolves around consent, and thorny issues regarding this concept are also apparent in the legal context. In particular, the ambiguity regarding what constitutes free and valid consent for the purposes of criminal and civil law is not easily resolved. Looking to the criminal law's response to sexual exploitation in the doctor-patient relationship,

---

132 Cohen and others 1995: 172.
133 See Campbell, n.129.
134 We note that the doctor's professional and ethical responsibility in such cases is to take action to avoid not breaching the sexual boundaries, as the words of Lord Denning in *De Gregory* v. *GMC* (part 1 of this chapter, n.3) make clear: 'It was said that Mrs Round set her cap at Dr de Gregory and that he was caught in a spider's web. Mrs Round indeed admitted that she deliberately set out to seduce Dr de Gregory and succeeded in her efforts. Assuming this to be true, it could afford him no answer ... The doctor must resist temptation, not succumb to it.' (966). See also Council for Healthcare Regulatory Excellence 2008b: 19; *Ontario (College of Physicians and Surgeons of Ontario)* v. *Ghabbour* (part 1 of this chapter, n.134), 15.

we have advocated the creation of a new abuse of trust offence which would operate where a doctor exercises undue influence by way of a coercive or irresistible inducement, for example. Our assessment of potential civil law actions is that where a patient has given consent to sexual activity with her doctor, there is no guarantee that an action in battery or negligence will be applicable. Given its fit with the nature of the doctor's professional duty not to act out of self-interest, and its easier applicability to cases involving consent when compared to battery, we have argued that fiduciary law could offer an additional avenue to the criminal law to address a doctor's sexual exploitation of his patient. Where a sexual boundary breach occurs with consent and there is no inducement or other form of exploitation, we do not consider legal intervention to be appropriate. Such breaches should continue to be dealt with via professional regulation. But we have called for something other than a strict zero-tolerance approach in cases where a genuine, mutually desired and pursued sexual relationship occurs outside of the professional doctor-patient relationship, when the patient is not vulnerable to exploitation, and there is no continuing professional relationship between the parties.

6 Assisted dying and exploitation

This chapter offers our final case study, exploring the risk of exploitation in the context of assisted dying. Both of us have examined and critiqued the law in England and Wales on assisted dying and considered options for reform in earlier work.[1] Thus, there is no substantive coverage here of the broader debate for and against assisted dying, and related ethical issues. Instead, our focus is more specific. Exploitation plays a significant role in the background to the assisted dying debate, especially as a rationale for maintaining the current prohibition on assisted dying. However, whilst the looming threat of abuse,[2] of exploitation of the vulnerable, is frequently raised in response to calls that this jurisdiction should allow some form of assisted dying,[3] there is less analysis of what this actually means and *how* patients might be exploited were assisted dying to be permitted.

To address this analytical gap and apply our account of exploitation to groups of patients often deemed to be vulnerable in the assisted dying debate – namely, older adults;[4] the terminally ill; those with chronic illnesses; those who are incurably ill with serious degenerative conditions; and disabled patients[5] – we centre our attention on how patients' perceptions that they are a burden, and their desire to die, might be exploited. We necessarily move beyond the

---

1   Biggs 2011; Biggs 2001; Brazier and Ost 2013: chapter 5; Ost 2010; Ost 2007.
2   As an aside, it is of interest that the common discourse within the assisted dying debate is framed around the concepts of abuse and the slippery slope more than the concept of exploitation. See, e.g. Battin and others 2007: 591. However, as we explore in this chapter, what lies at the heart of these concerns is the ways in which vulnerable individuals might be exploited.
3   See later, text accompanying nn.17 and 47. For an example of such concerns in the press, see Richard Edwards, 'Assisted suicide law "will threaten elderly"' *Daily Telegraph* (London, 29 August 2009); Martin Beckford, 'Fearful elderly people carry "anti-euthanasia cards"' *The Telegraph* (London, 21 April 2011).
4   Whilst recognising that there is an ambiguity about the age at which someone becomes an 'older adult', we have chosen to use this term rather than others such as 'the elderly', 'senior citizens' or 'aged' because it is more contemporary and seems a less negatively loaded, more respectful term. For an interesting discussion on the best term to use when referring to people in later life, see Joe Pinsker, 'When does someone become "old"?' *The Atlantic* (Washington DC, 27 January 2020). See also Fineman 2012: 89–90.
5   See the text accompanying nn.63–65.

doctor-patient relationship because of the nature of this exploitation and the identity of potential exploiters, exploring whether relatives and society (in a jurisdiction where assisted dying is permitted and made available via a publicly funded health service) exploit those who seek an assisted death. As we shall see, whether or not their loved ones exploit patients by supporting and encouraging them in their desire to have an assisted death, and whether or not a society exploits patients through offering assisted death, will depend upon the purpose of offering or supporting an assisted death, and whether (mis)use occurs for the assistor's/society's own ends. We also reflect on the possibility of doctors who are prepared to consider assisting a patient's death being exploited by the patient or the patient's relatives before, finally, considering how the law might respond to the risks of exploitation that we have highlighted.

1) The danger of relatives or carers[6] exploiting the patient's perception that they are a burden

A systematic review of end of life studies published in 2007 found that the perception that they are a burden on their relatives (hereafter the burden perception) is 'a culturally pervasive phenomenon' that can affect patients towards the end of life.[7] The review's authors reported that 'the few available studies on end of life care indicate that it is a common concern for people with advanced disease',[8] with 65% of participants in one American study considering they were a burden to their families and 77% being distressed about burdening others in a Canadian study.[9] The authors also refer to a Japanese study in which the burden perception was identified as a major reason for the desire to die expressed by patients who had died of cancer in 42% of cases, and a minor reason in 16% of cases.[10] Furthermore, the burden perception can often be a reason for individuals requesting an assisted death in jurisdictions where assisted dying is permitted.[11] Whether or not this burden perception is an accurate reflection of the reality of the situation, where it is known that a person seeking an assisted death holds this perception, this gives rise to an obvious exploitation opportunity for someone in a personal relationship with that person who has reason to benefit from their death. In Richman's (modified) words, '[assisted] suicide is a relief or

---

6   In considering the risk of such exploitation in this chapter, we do not seek to underplay the difficult task that carers face, and their conflicting responsibilities. See further Biggs 2007.
7   McPherson and others 2007: 117.
8   Ibid: 117-118.
9   Ibid: 118.
10 Ibid: 121.
11 Ibid: 121. See also Roest and others 2019: 11. According to data from Oregon, 44.8% of patients who received an assisted death under the Death with Dignity Act between 1998–2018 stated that being a burden on family, friends and caregivers was an end of life concern for them. See Oregon Health Authority 2019: 12. See Biggs 1998 for consideration of how female older adults, in particular, may experience the burden perception.

escape from pain, but it [can also be] a sacrifice – to relieve others of pain. It is the suicide which is assisting the assister.'[12]

In England and Wales, a jurisdiction where assisted suicide is prohibited,[13] 'the potential for indirect coercion or undue influence' in assisted dying was highlighted by the Court of Appeal in the *Conway* case.[14] In dismissing Mr Conway's appeal against the Divisional Court's refusal to make a declaration that the law prohibiting assisted suicide constitutes a disproportionate interference with the right to respect for private life under Article 8 of the European Convention on Human Rights, the Justices referred to expert evidence, reports and public briefings such as that from the Association for Palliative Medicine. In its briefing, among the reasons provided for opposing the legalisation of assisted suicide, the association warns that 'coercion, real or imagined, may be undetectable and feeling burdensome is a prominent and rising reason for requesting assisted suicide'.[15] Such concerns clearly played a part in the Court of Appeal justices' concurrence with the Divisional Court judgment that the statutory scheme proposed by Mr Conway, which would have permitted some instances of assisted suicide, would be 'inadequate … to protect the weak and vulnerable'.[16] Such concerns are far from new, and have played a notable part in blocking a series of attempts to enact legislation to permit assisted suicide through failed Private Members' Bills between 2013–2016.[17] The burden perception was

---

12 Richman 1987: 58.
13 Under s.2(1) of the Suicide Act 1961, it is an offence to commit an act capable of encouraging or assisting the suicide or attempted suicide of another, with the intention to encourage or assist.
14 *R (on the application of Conway)* v. *The Secretary of State for Justice* v. *Humanists UK, Not Dead Yet (UK), CNK Alliance Ltd* [2018] EWCA Civ 1431, [160].
15 Association for Palliative Medicine, 'Public Briefing on the APM's Position on Assisted Suicide', July 2015, at https://apmonline.org/wp-content/uploads/2015/07/AS-Full-briefing-final.pdf accessed 9 June 2020, p.2.
16 Ibid, [24].
17 The first of these, the Assisted Dying Bill prepared by Lord Falconer, was introduced in the House of Lords during the 2013–2014 parliamentary session (Assisted Dying Bill [HL] Bill 2013–2014). The session was prorogued without the bill getting beyond its first reading. When reintroduced at the 2014–2015 parliamentary session, the bill reached committee stage but, again, made no further progress before the end of that session (Assisted Dying Bill [HL] Bill 2014–2015). The Assisted Dying (no 2) Bill 2015–2016, sponsored by Rob Marris, was presented to the House of Commons during the 2015–2016 session, but moved no further after it did not pass its second reading debate on 11 September 2015. Finally, Lord Hayward's Assisted Dying Bill was introduced in the House of Lords during the 2016–2017 session of Parliament, but did not get beyond the first stage of progress before the session was prorogued (Assisted Dying Bill [HL] Bill 2016–2017). We have not recorded every single instance of the burden perception being raised as a concern in the debates on these bills in the list that follows, but the length of this list of examples should convey the prominence of the issue: HC Deb 11 September 2015, vol 599, cols 663–665, 669–670, 677, 689, 702–703, 705, 708, 710, 718, 720; HL Deb 18 July 2014, vol 755, cols 789, 792, 793, 797, 802, 806, 809, 816, 831, 841, 851, 860, 869, 886, 891, 901, 916; HL Deb 7 November 2014, vol 756, cols 1860, 1862, 1866, 1901, 1922, 1929, 1937, 1948. See also HC Deb 23 January 2020, vol 670, cols 191WH, 195WH, 202WH and 203WH. At the time of writing, the Assisted Dying Bill [HL] 2019–2021 received its first reading on 28 January 2020 (HL Deb 28 January 2020, Vol 801), but the date of its second reading is still to be announced.

directly recognised by Lord Bingham in the earlier case of *Pretty* v. *DPP*: 'it is not hard to imagine that an elderly person, in the absence of any pressure, might opt for a premature end to life if that were available, not from a desire to die or a willingness to stop living, but from a desire to stop being a burden to others'.[18] This statement followed Lord Bingham's reference to the exact same caution expressed by the House of Lords Select Committee on Medical Ethics in 1994.[19] More recently, in the *Nicklinson* case, the 'vulnerability to pressure of the old or terminally ill' was stated to be a 'formidable problem'.[20]

Alongside case law jurisprudence such as *Pretty*, *Nicklinson* and *Conway* involving a series of unsuccessful human rights challenges to the legal prohibition on assisted dying, the Director of Public Prosecution's (DPP's) prosecutorial policy on assisted suicide[21] sets out the public interest factors that tend towards, and mitigate against, prosecution. This policy followed the DPP's earlier published decision not to prosecute the parents and family friend of Daniel James (a young man who was left tetraplegic following a rugby accident and who sought and obtained an assisted death in Switzerland). The policy and the decision both speak to the real possibility of exploitation and the exercise of undue influence over the patient. Factors in favour of prosecution in the DPP's policy include that 'the suspect was motivated by the prospect that he or she or a person closely connected to him or her stood to gain in some way from the death of the victim', and that the 'suspect pressured the victim to commit suicide'.[22] Part of the explanation for the decision not to prosecute Daniel James's parents who accompanied him to Switzerland, or their friend who helped organise and fund the trip, was that it was clear that:

> Daniel was a mature, intelligent and fiercely independent young man with full capacity to make decisions about his medical treatment whose determination to commit suicide was not in any way influenced by the conduct or wishes of his parents ... although Daniel was vulnerable in many senses, he was *not vulnerable to manipulation* by his parents or the family friend.[23]

The DPP's statement here that Daniel James was considered to be 'vulnerable in many senses', notwithstanding the clear recognition that he possessed capacity and was independent of mind, is notable. The reasons for finding vulnerability

---

18   *Pretty* v. *DPP* [2001] UKHL 61, [29].
19   House of Lords Select Committee on Medical Ethics 1994: [239].
20   *R (Nicklinson)* v. *Ministry of Justice* [2014] UKSC 38, [228] (Lord Sumption).
21   CPS, *Policy for Prosecutors in Respect of Cases of Encouraging or Assisting Suicide*, February 2010, updated 16 October 2014, at http://www.cps.gov.uk/publications/prosecution/assisted_suicide_policy.html accessed 9 April 2020. The DPP was required to publish this policy by the House of Lords' judgment in *R (on the application of Purdy)* v. *DPP* [2009] UKHL 45.
22   Ibid, 11.
23   CPS/DPP, *Decision on Prosecution – The Death by Suicide of Daniel James*, 9 December 2008, [32] (emphasis added). The decision is no longer available to access on the CPS website, but the text can still be found at http://www.bedeutung.co.uk/magazine/issues/3-life-death/starmer-prosecution-suicide-daniel-james/, accessed 9 April 2020.

presumably rest with Mr James' corporal situation, his paralysis and the serious physical disability that this caused, and his strikingly younger age in comparison with patients typically associated with assisted dying.[24] That said, no assumption was made that *simply because* Daniel was deemed to be a vulnerable individual, he would have been manipulated into requesting an assisted death. A similar approach is reflected in the case of *Re Z (Local Authority: Duty)*,[25] involving an adult deemed to be vulnerable under statutory law.[26] Z, who had an incurable degenerative brain disease, wished to have an assisted death in Switzerland but needed her husband to make the necessary arrangements and accompany her. In discharging the injunction that had been obtained by the local authority to prevent her husband from removing her from the jurisdiction, Hedley J was in no doubt that Z possessed the capacity to make her own decisions, had not been influenced by any family members and that the burden perception was not a concern. Notably, he stated that the presumption of legal capacity could have been rebutted if either of these elements had been present.[27] Thus, Hedley J did not automatically conclude that Z was vulnerable to exploitation simply by virtue of her categorisation as vulnerable under statutory law.

In contrast to this lack of manipulation in the Z and Daniel James cases, it is notable that 82% of doctors who participated in a study in Oregon expressed concern that patients who considered themselves to be a burden might feel pressured by others to request assisted suicide.[28] In their study of complex cases of assisted dying, Snijdewind et al highlight relational complexities that affected the assisted dying process.[29] One of their findings relates to 'the importance of the role of relatives in the process of [assisted dying]. The process is not only influenced by the physician and the patient but also should be seen as a triangle [between] physician, patient, and relatives.'[30] This relational complexity could give rise to exploitation and, indeed, the authors question whether we should 'be worried about relatives gaining *too much* influence over the course of the process'[31] of assisted dying. Elements that we have identified as playing an important role in enabling exploitation in the doctor-patient relationship also feature here, in these personal relationships. First, trust that loved ones

---

24 We note too that the current version of the Code for Crown Prosecutors, (of which an earlier version was referred to by the DPP in his published decision, ibid), states that 'the circumstances of the victim are highly relevant' and that a decision to prosecute should be influenced by how vulnerable the victim's situation is and the level of the '*perceived* vulnerability of the victim': Crown Prosecution Service 2018: 4.14(c) (emphasis added). For further consideration of the issue of deemed vulnerability, see section 2, text accompanying nn.63–66.
25 [2004] EWHC 2817 (Fam).
26 Law which imposes duties on local authorities, such as the Local Authority Social Services Act 1970, s.7.
27 At [13]. See also *Re L (No 2)* [2012] EWCA Civ 253 [65].
28 McPherson and others 2007: 123.
29 Snijdewind and others 2014: 1129.
30 Ibid: 1130.
31 Ibid: 1132 (emphasis added).

are acting in their interests makes patients vulnerable to undue influence and exploitation of the burden perception by their relatives. Secondly, there may also be a relationship of unequal power, especially in cases where the patient is physically incapacitated and/or is dependent on their relative for their daily needs.[32] Of course, a key difference is that this is a personal rather than a professional relationship and, as we will explore, this may make any such exploitation harder to bring to light.

One key matter to consider here is whether the doctor-patient relationship acts, or could act, to decrease the risk of exploitation being exacted by relatives or carers if some form of assisted dying is permitted. As discussed in chapter 3, the current doctor-patient relationship model prioritises patient autonomy. Does this mean that any decision a patient makes to request an assisted death will be carefully scrutinised to ensure that it is a true reflection of her autonomy, or is there a danger that, provided there is no obvious reason to rebut the presumption that the patient possesses capacity, her exercise of free will could be assumed? The doctor's role and the level of protection that the doctor-patient relationship offers to the patient's autonomy will be critical, as will environmental factors related to, for example, the quality of palliative and social care provided, as we explore further below.

To set the scene for this more detailed exploration, and to tease out the nature and levels of exploitation that might be exacted by relatives, it may be helpful to consider the following two scenarios in the context of a jurisdiction which permits assisted dying:

Scenario 1
The adult children of an incurably ill man both wish to relieve themselves of the burden that they consider he imposes on their lives. They make it clear to their father that they are struggling to continue caring for him. They know that the medical treatment he is receiving is no longer alleviating his pain and that he has recently started to consider the option of an assisted death, and begin to drop hints that this might be the best option for all of them. They gather information about having an assisted death and leave this around the house for him to find. Both place emphasis on the amount of pain that he is experiencing and ask him how he is able to bear this. During a family argument, the son says that if he really loved them, he would stop putting them through this. His daughter tells him that she is struggling to look after her family and spend time caring for him each day and doesn't

---

32 For an example of concern expressed in Parliament about the risk of pressure from relatives standing to gain, see HC Deb 23 January 2020, vol 670, col 199WH. Alongside any physical incapacity or dependency, Formosa explains how intimate relationships can give rise to 'deferential vulnerabilities, since we can be under pressure to defer to our intimates' wishes, and allocational vulnerabilities, since intimates are monopoly providers of something that we need, namely, *their* love, affection, and friendship.': Formosa 2013: 106 (emphasis in original).

know how much longer she can continue doing both. When their father informs them that he is going to request an assisted death, they both express relief and tell him that he is doing the right thing. In giving his reasons for requesting an assisted death to his doctor, with his children present, he tells her that he is in a great deal of pain and no longer wishes to be a burden to his children.

Scenario 2
A terminally ill, older adult perceives herself to be burden to her son and tells him that her main reason for wishing to have an assisted death is to relieve him of his caring responsibilities towards her. Her son does in fact consider her to be a burden, although he does not express this to her, as he does not wish to cause her further distress. He is aware that part of his motivation for supporting her in her desire for an assisted death is to fulfil his own ends: the relief of the burden she has become to him. When they both explain her reasons for desiring an assisted death to her doctor, they make no reference to the burden perception, but base her wish on unbearable suffering.

The daughter and son exact overt pressure in *Scenario 1*, pushing their father into requesting an assisted death. Since there is no indication of any mental incapacity or a condition affecting cognitive ability such as dementia, their father must surely be aware of their view that he is a burden – they make no effort to disguise this – and they undoubtedly take advantage of (use), and misuse him, for their own ends. They take advantage of his vulnerability, his feelings of guilt and love for them, and their manipulation is wrought through a process over time.[33] The exploitation could be consensual, if the father is aware of his children's manipulation, or he may remain unknowing that the pressure they are putting him under is intentional and wrought in order to achieve their own ends. His children perpetrate a more blatant form of exploitation, although this does not mean that it will be obvious to the doctor, especially if she does not speak to the patient alone, without the presence of his family.

The question of whether exploitation occurs in *Scenario 2* is more ethically challenging. The son is not suggesting an assisted death, or pressurising or unduly influencing his mother into requesting an assisted death. He does not tell her that her burden perception is correct. But he does support her wish for an assisted death, partly for his own ends. Does this mean that he takes advantage of his mother? If his main motivation is relieving himself of the burden that she is causing him, then he is utilising her desire to die for his own purposes and

---

33 See also Quinn and others 2017: 167 for a discussion of the tactics that can be used by the undue influencer. Note Hall's view that '… a person's ability to act autonomously is diminished where family members express hostility towards the person, making her feel that she is a burden, and undermining her value.': Hall 2018: iv.

taking advantage of her vulnerability (her burden perception). However, what if his main motivation in supporting her decision is to respect her wishes, even though he is aware that this main motivation is accompanied by a more selfish desire? There would be no clear-cut misuse if he acts primarily to respect her autonomy, since he would not be treating her solely as a means to his ends or taking advantage of her vulnerability. The fact that he does not raise the burden perception with the doctor may be indicative of a decision that this should remain hidden due to a concern that it might not be a legally accepted reason for desiring an assisted death. But he could have been motivated to make this decision for either of the two reasons discussed above (selfless or selfish). In sum, *Scenario 2* involves an overtly expressed burden perception by the patient and, indeed, this could be an instance where 'the decision to die may be the ill-person's form of therapy for the suffering and burdened' son,[34] but it is unclear whether the relative utilises the exploitation opportunity that this raises. There is no apparent undue influence, as occurs in *Scenario 1*, to direct us towards the presence of exploitation.[35] Moreover, it is highly doubtful that the burden perception would be uncovered by the doctor if it is not disclosed and the patient's case based on unbearable suffering is convincing.

Scenario 2 reveals some of the complexities involved in identifying exploitation of the burden perception if assisted dying is permitted, and we will return to this in the context of undue influence in the final section of this chapter. On the other hand, it is possible that individuals might be more likely to be exploited by family members or others and suffer an unwanted, unlawful concealed assisted death where there is *no* legal regulation of assisted dying other than blanket criminalisation. As put by Finkelstein:

> At the moment, you can press your relative to commit suicide, as long as you don't get caught doing it. The investigation into the pressure that has been placed on the deceased doesn't take place until after [they] are gone. By which point it is a little late.[36]

Thus, if a form of assisted dying were to be permitted, more safeguards could be put in place to protect against undue influence and assess whether the burden perception exists. Later in this chapter, we will present a possible model to assist doctors in identifying the existence of undue influence, and in detecting and discussing the burden perception with patients and relatives.

There is one final matter that we wish to highlight here, which is related to the pressure that relatives might exact. The findings of studies involving the

---

34 Richman 1987: 63.
35 See the further discussion in section 4, and also the general discussion of the concept of undue influence and how it might be identified in that section.
36 Daniel Finkelstein, 'This suicide law will not turn us into killers' *The Times* (London 9 September 2015).

experiences of Dutch doctors could expose a potential *converse* exploitative situation. Some of the Dutch GPs interviewed in a study by de Boer et al reported that, when they were prepared to grant the patient's request for an assisted death in principle, they had encountered counterpressure from relatives strongly opposed to assisted dying. Indeed, '[one] GP decided ultimately to not grant the [assisted dying] request because she did not want to "give [the patient's] wife an unacceptable problem and huge grief to [his] children," but was left with the feeling "we could have saved [the patient] from dreadful weeks"'.[37] According to a doctor in another study, in one case of assisted dying that he was involved in, 'I told [the patient] I wouldn't perform euthanasia if I didn't get the feeling that her children could cope with it.'[38] In a further study involving Dutch GPs, some respondents highlighted that, for them, the need to have family members' agreement can be essential in order to comply with a patient's request for an assisted death.[39]

This reluctance to go against the relatives' wishes could be felt even more strongly by the patient. In cases where the patient's relatives do not wish her to have an assisted death and she already considers herself to be a burden to her loved ones and desires what is best for them, this desire could be exploited. That is, her relatives could take advantage of her emotional sense of obligation to them, exacting pressure to persuade her out of having the assisted death that she desires to avoid any potentially guilty feelings that they would feel over not having done enough to prevent her from having an assisted death. It is noteworthy that this converse exploitative situation has received scant attention.[40] This may be due to the distinct possibility that conceiving of such behaviour as exploitative is controversial, owing to the strong presumption that desiring and encouraging a person to live when they want to die is a positive thing to do.[41] Whilst we accept that our conceptualisation of such behaviour as wrongful goes against the grain, if a relative exacts undue influence as we have suggested here, then there is misuse by way of taking advantage of the patient's vulnerability (their love and sense of obligation), in order to achieve that relative's own ends. Thus, on our account, exploitation would occur.

37　de Boer and others 2019: 427.
38　Snijdewind and others 2014: 1129.
39　ten Cate and others 2017: 727.
40　To our knowledge, it has not been the subject of any detailed, explicit analysis in the existing literature. The matter was raised in a BBC2 documentary by Louis Theroux, *Choosing Death*, aired on 18 November 2018 and available for UK TV licence holders at https://www.bbc.co.uk/iplayer/episode/b0bshjrp/louis-theroux-altered-states-2-choosing-death accessed 9 June 2020. In this documentary, in response to a question about whether there was any pressure from his family, a 74-year-old man with stage 4 pancreatic cancer in California stated that he would have opted for an assisted death two weeks earlier, but for wanting to support his daughter.
41　We are grateful to Alexandra Mullock for encouraging our reflection on this point.

2) The risk that a society which permits assisted dying exploits those who no longer wish to live because of their burdensome situation

If a society permits assisted dying in at least some cases where patients are experiencing such a burdensome situation that they consider death to be a better option than continuing to live, would this society be exploiting patients by taking advantage of this situation?[42] This question has been considered briefly by Mayo and Gunderson. They conclude that no exploitation occurs because:

> Exploitation involves using a person for the exploiter's own benefit by taking advantage of his or her misfortune. But ... society is not 'making the offer' of a quick and easy death *in order to* use terminally ill patients for ends which the terminally ill could not, as rational persons, accept.[43]

---

42 Whilst a matter that is beyond the remit of this monograph, we note the related question of whether right-to-die organisations such as Dignitas (operating in Switzerland) exploit the terminally and incurably ill by offering them an assisted death. Where such organisations operate on a not-for-profit basis, no economic benefit is accrued from their provision of an assisted death. However, it could be argued that *some* benefit is gained through any (successful) case of assisted dying that occurs via the relevant organisation – especially where publicised – by way of furthering the organisation's cause. We note the not guilty verdict in a case brought against Ludwig Minelli, founder of Dignitas, on charges of profiteering from patients (see 'Dignitas Boss Found not Guilty of Profiteering', Swissinfo.ch, 1 June 2018, at https://www.swissinfo.ch/eng/assisted-suicide-_dignitas-founder-found-not-guilty-of-profiteering/44160762 accessed 9 April 2020, and Justin Huggler, 'Founder of Swiss assisted suicide organisation on trial for profiteering from his clients' *The Telegraph* (London, 18 May 2018). Legal developments in Germany which had prevented the operation of assisted suicide clinics are also worthy of note. A revision to the German Criminal Code that was enacted by the Bundestag (the German Parliament) in 2015 (s.217), continued the toleration of assisted suicide for altruistic reasons, but prohibited assisted suicide as a professional service. Thus, doctors, organisations or private individuals were unable to prescribe or sell drugs to end a person's life: see generally Friere de Andrade Neves 2018. In 2019, the law was challenged by patients, doctors and clinics which had been operating in Germany, such as Sterbehilfe Deutschland ('Germany reopens painful debate on assisted suicide', France24, 16 April 2019, at https://www.france24.com/en/20190416-germany-reopens-painful-debate-assisted-suicide accessed 9 April 2020). In February 2020, Germany's highest court (the Federal Constitutional Court) ruled that this prohibition violates patients' rights: Federal Constitutional Court, Press Release No. 12/2020 of 26 February 2020, at https://www.bundesverfassungsgericht.de/SharedDocs/Pressemitteilungen/EN/2020/bvg20-012.html accessed 2 June 2020. Following this ruling, concerns regarding society sanctioning the offering of assisted suicide as a service were voiced by members of the Bundestag and the introduction of a cross-party draft bill in the Bundestag in January 2021, which would provide a system of regulated lawful assisted suicide, has been met with calls for assisted suicide for payment to be an offence. See Christopher Schuetze, 'German Court overturns ban on assisted suicide' *The New York Times* (New York, 26 February 2020); Elliot Douglas, Assisted Suicide: German government seeks to regulate practice' DW, 29 January 2021, at https://www.dw.com/en/assisted-suicide-german-government-seeks-to-regulate-practice/a-56384539 accessed 4 April 2021.

43 Mayo and Gunderson 1993: 333 (emphasis in original).

Thus, in Mayo and Gunderson's view, the reason for there being an absence of exploitation is that there is no taking advantage of misfortune, since the purpose in providing the requested death is not one of use for society's own ends which 'rational persons' could not accept. Mayo and Gunderson also appear to attach significance to the (lack of) role that society plays in bringing about the burdensome situation that the patient experiences, noting that allowing an assisted death in such a case 'does not create the burdensome situation which later becomes a reason for self-willed death. Rather it turns a burdensome situation into a reason for self-willed death by providing that option.'[44]

First, we agree with the principle that no exploitation occurs where there is no taking advantage of, for the exploiter's own ends: indeed, these elements form part of our conception of exploitation. We also concur that exploitation can often (but not always) involve the exploiter gaining a benefit. However, the point at which we take issue with Mayo and Gunderson's explanation is the seeming need for the ends being those which 'rational' persons could not accept. This is not a necessary part of our account of exploitation and we have expressed concern about the use of the concept of rationality in demarcating exploitation earlier.[45] Secondly, whilst it is not an element of our account of exploitation (as with the issue of benefit), we agree that if a society plays a causative role in creating the person's burdensome situation and then gains in some way by offering a means of resolving this situation, this is much more indicative of a graver form of exploitation (provided that the essential elements of exploitation are made out). But it is also necessary to evaluate whether it is correct to conclude that the aspects alluded to by Mayo and Gunderson are *not* made out where a society offers assisted dying.

Crudely put, any society gains an economic benefit from an assisted death which brings an end to what would otherwise be a continued cost of expensive medical care and treatment to the public purse.[46] However, this benefit, in and of itself, does not indicate that a society *exploits* those who avail themselves of an assisted death. That said, the very existence of this benefit means that the reasons for offering the option of an assisted death in a society in which the health care service is publicly funded will fall under scrutiny. This is the major challenge for any proposed law reform to permit assisted dying in the context of the NHS: any government that seriously proposed such reform would undoubtedly struggle to get legislation through, because critics would argue that the hidden, underlying motivation was to reduce NHS costs. Indeed, just about every parliamentary debate in Westminster that has ever taken place on assisted dying speaks to the

---

44 Ibid: 332.
45 We argued that whilst the exploitee's state of mind can sometimes be relevant in terms of misuse, it should not be a defining element of exploitation because ambiguity surrounds the concept of rationality (see chapter 2, nn.71–73).
46 At least on the face of it: see n.79.

potential exploitation of vulnerable patients – who are most commonly presented in the debates as being older adults and individuals with disabilities[47] – within the NHS in order to save costs. Take, for instance, Baroness Sherlock's contribution during the debate which preceded the second reading of the Assisted Dying Bill [HL] Bill 2014–2015 in the House of Lords: 'I … worry about where the interests of the state lie. If the state or its agents cannot kill people or help them to die then it must treat them and it must care for them, and that will always be more expensive.'[48] In the same debate, Baroness Nicolson referred to:

> the cash-strapped, overworked NHS. I do not want our trusted NHS to turn from being the National Health Service into the national death service—the change that this Bill offers … Do not use my taxes on the proposed state death department, with its inevitable growth in records of hits and misses, of targets and bonuses for each bed emptied …[49]

The contemporary shape of the NHS only serves to exacerbate such concerns. In a previous chapter, we noted how the move towards integrated delivery of publicly funded health and social care in England and Wales risks continuity of care taking second place to efficiency in delivery, and that this move was motivated, in part, by the desire to reduce costs.[50] Alongside this, Veitch has recently drawn attention to the way in which the privatisation and marketisation of the NHS is having a negative impact on patients accessing health care services, and leading to the abuse of patients.[51] He explains that the first impact is occurring because the wide use of private finance initiative (PFI) contracts to construct hospitals means that a significant part of the NHS budget is spent on repaying the capital and interest of these arrangements, causing there to be less money for health care services and consequent cutbacks. The abuse of patients has taken place due to the poor performance and limited monitoring of contracts by private companies to whom the delivery of NHS health care is outsourced.[52] Veitch concludes that:

---

47 For instance, explicit references to the disabled being at risk were made during the House of Commons debate on assisted dying in 2020: HC Deb 23 January 2020, vol 670, cols 191WH and 196WH and in HC Deb 11 September 2015, vol 599, cols 677, 678 and 708. There is explicit reference to older adults as vulnerable in, for instance, HC Deb 11 September 2015, vol 599, cols 664, 665, 669, 670, 677, 697, 703 and 708.
48 HL Deb 18 July 2014, vol 755, col 888.
49 Ibid: col 827. See also: HC Deb 11 September 2015, vol 599, cols 677, 705, 708, 713; HL Deb 18 July 2014, vol 755, cols 788, 797, 802, 809, 824–825, 826, 866, 889; HL Deb 7 November 2014, vol 756, cols 1908, 1949; HC Deb 23 January 2020, vol 670, col 188WH.
50 See chapter 3, section 5.i.
51 Veitch 2019: 288 and 291.
52 He gives the example of a private provider's running of the Winterbourne View hospital in England, to demonstrate this (Veitch 2019: 291 and see Department of Health 2012).

whether private consortia supplying finance as part of PFI schemes or private healthcare providers, it is the confidence of market players that the state is increasingly careful to sustain, something that results in the prioritising of obligations to finance over those associated with the healthcare of patients.[53]

Similar cost-saving concerns exist in some of the US-orientated literature. For instance, Wolf points to 'the general danger of assisted suicide being encouraged and embraced as a cost-saving measure', in part because a significant proportion of health care expenditure is spent on older adults.[54] Cases in which it is reported that older adults in the US have been advised to request an assisted death as a cheaper option have attracted worldwide attention. In 2015, the example of a patient in Oregon was raised by an MP opposed to the legalisation of assisted dying in England and Wales.[55] Barbara Wagner was a 65-year-old woman (thus on the younger side of 'older adult')[56] with lung cancer in Oregon, whose health plan provider would not pay for medication prescribed by her doctor that had an 8% chance of extending her life by four to six months. When she said that she would not pay for this medication herself, her provider advised her of her other options, one of which was an assisted death under the law in Oregon.[57] Whilst a different health care system of managed care exists in the US,[58] the fact that the (mis)reported[59]

---

53 Veitch 2019: 292.
54 Wolf 1996: 465–466. See also Garzino 1997: 559.
55 HC Deb 11 September 2015, vol 599, col 660 (Edward Leigh, MP).
56 See Pinsker, n.4.
57 See the explanation of her case provided by Rob Marris, MP, at HC Deb 11 September 2015, vol 599, col 660, which challenges the 'urban myths' generated by sensationalist media coverage.
58 Through which health care is provided by organisations that perform the functions of both insurer and health care provider, 'thus marry[ing] the insurer's cost-consciousness with the provider's mission of patient care' (Wolf 1996: 460). Garzino explains that these organisations 'share one essential characteristic. They receive capitated payment, a fixed amount of money per year for each person who becomes a member of their group. This capitated payment features means once a person is enrolled in a managed-care group, management's focus is on controlling health-care costs rather than increasing revenues. If the total expenses of caring for a given patient are below the fixed annual premium, then the managed-care group will keep the difference as its profit for providing cost-effective care': Garzino 1997: 548.
59 Media reports inaccurately suggested that an assisted death was the only other option presented to her and/or failed to explain the extremely limited chances of the success of the medication in question (it was likely to be ineffective in 92% of cases, with serious side effects). This meant that it fell under Ms Wagner's health care provider's policy of not covering the costs of treatment deemed futile, with 'futile' meaning any treatment that does not have at least a 5% chance of five-year survival. For examples of such misreporting, see Wesley Smith, '"Right to die" can become a "duty to die"' *The Telegraph* (London, 20 February 2009); Marilyn Golden, 'Too many flaws in assisted suicide laws' *The New York Times* (New York, 10 April 2012); Christopher Hale, 'There's nothing progressive about physician-assisted-auicide' *Time* (New York 14 October 2015). The case was originally reported in Susan Donaldson James, 'Death Drugs Cause Uproar in Oregon', *ABC News* (30 September 2008).

Wagner case was presented as a warning of the 'market forces' that would come into play if assisted dying were permitted in England and Wales demonstrates that cost-reduction-based arguments are broadly applicable to any health care system in which cost effectiveness is a primary consideration.

Notably, the same cost-reduction-based argument could be made in respect of withdrawing life-sustaining treatment from patients with prolonged disorders of consciousness (PDofC). It has been estimated, for instance, that health care for a patient in the vegetative state costs in the region of £100,000 a year.[60] Although the significant amount of resources and expenditure has been observed by the judiciary in cases involving patients with PDofC such as the vegetative state,[61] this has never formed part of the legal rationale for withdrawing life-sustaining treatment, which centres on the matter of the patient's best interests.[62] However, this very absence in judicial reasoning could well spur on those concerned about the exploitation of those groups of individuals who are deemed to be vulnerable – alongside older adults and individuals with disabilities,[63] other groups referred to include the terminally ill[64] and those with serious degenerative or chronic conditions[65] – who are considered most likely to avail themselves of an assisted death.[66] Garzino observes that economic considerations are 'conspicuously absent' from

---

60 Formby and others 2015.
61 In the seminal case of *Airedale NHS Trust* v. *Bland* 1 All ER 821, involving a patient in the vegetative state, Lord Mustill commented, at 896, that 'the large resources of skill, labour and money now being devoted to Anthony Bland might in the opinion of many be more fruitfully employed in improving the condition of other patients, who if treated may have useful, healthy and enjoyable lives for years to come.' Also in the House of Lords, see Lord Browne-Wilkinson, at 879, and, in the Court of Appeal, see Sir Stephen Brown, at 795–796, and Hoffmann LJ, at 833.
62 See also Samanta and Samanta 2018: 649. The matter of resources was raised by a medical expert witness in the case of *W* v. *M* [2011] EWHC 2443 (Fam), [205], involving a patient in the minimally conscious state. She commented that 'whilst it should not weigh substantially ... in comparison with M's best interest, there are considerable costs to the State of maintaining her in the best possible condition minimise to distress and discomfort. Given that resources are limited, this inevitably means that expenditure ... (which could amount to £1m or more over the remainder of her life) results in deprivation of healthcare funds available for other patients, in whom they could potentially make a real and substantial to quality of life.' However, as the issue of the cost did not relate to the patient's best interests, it was not addressed by the court.
63 See n.47 and n.70.
64 See, e.g. HC Deb 11 September 2015, vol 599, cols 669, 693 and 718.
65 See n.70. We note that the cases of *Pretty*, *Purdy* and *Conway* were all brought by individuals with serious degenerative conditions, although all three would have objected to being perceived as vulnerable to exploitation by virtue of their conditions. They also felt that those who were caring for them might be vulnerable, not least to prosecution: see particularly the cases of *Pretty* and *Purdy*.
66 Wolf 1996: 473–477. Other groups perceived to be vulnerable to exploitation might be any of those whom there are social biases against. Back in 1987, Richman listed 'social biases against the ill, the disabled, the elderly, and the poor', for instance (Richman 1987: 63). However, note the research findings cited in n.71.

the US case law which is sympathetic to physician-assisted suicide and, consequently, this 'makes it difficult, if not impossible, to fully address the underlying economics of the physician-assisted suicide decision'.[67] Thus, when coupled with more recent developments in withdrawal of life-sustaining treatment cases in England and Wales that now enable treatment to be discontinued without court approval when all parties are in agreement,[68] a parallel could be drawn which would warn of the slippery slope in allowing medical behaviour that leads to patients' deaths without tackling economic considerations head-on.

In a society in which the need to reduce NHS costs has entered the public consciousness, there is also a danger that those who request an assisted death could experience the burden perception as a consequence of pressure from an external (as opposed to a more personal, familial) source. That is, they may feel indirect pressure to request an assisted death because they perceive that their long-term and continuing health care costs are tying up resources that could be better used elsewhere.[69] In the *Nicklinson* case, Lord Sumption alluded to the:

> particularly acute [difficulty] in the case of ... 'indirect social pressure'. This refers to the problems arising from the low self-esteem of many old or severely ill and dependent people, combined with the spontaneous and negative perceptions of patients about the views of those around them... There is a good deal of evidence that this problem exists, that it is significant, and that it is aggravated by negative modern attitudes to old age and sickness-related disability... The legalisation of assisted suicide would be followed by its progressive normalisation, at any rate among the very old or very ill. In a world where suicide was regarded as just another optional end-of-life choice, the pressures which I have described are likely to become more powerful ...[70]

It is thus significant that such 'powerful' pressures have not been shown to impact on 'vulnerable' groups according to a study which explored data from both the Netherlands and Oregon. The authors did not find any heightened risk that older adults or people with non-terminal physical disabilities or chronic non-terminal illnesses were being 'especially heavily targeted ... pressured, manipulated or forced to request physician-assisted dying'.[71] These findings

---

67 Garzino 1997: 551.
68 See *An NHS Trust* v. *Mr Y (by his litigation Friend, the Official Solicitor) and another* [2018] UKSC 46.
69 A matter considered recently by Shaw and Morton 2020: 68.
70 [228]. See also Richman 1987: 61.
71 Battin and others 2007: 594. Similarly, no heightened risk was found for: women, uninsured people, the poor, racial and ethnic minorities and people with low educational status, minors and mature minors and patients with psychiatric illnesses. The only heightened risk detected was for individuals with AIDS: Battin and others 2007: 594–596, although the reasons as to why this might be are not explored in the article.

support Collins's claim that 'it is right to challenge the notion that older persons are automatically vulnerable'.[72] Further significant findings have emerged from research regarding older adult victims of financial exploitation and other forms of maltreatment. Those who were financially exploited tended to possess *fewer* potential indicators of vulnerability such as communication problems, cognitive confusion and dependency on others, and the typical characteristics of victims differed depending on the maltreatment in question.[73]

What is more, there are also potentially damaging effects of applying blanket labels to certain groups in society, as encapsulated in the Law Commission's caution against equating disability with vulnerability in the context of hate crime:

> It is true that many disabled people, by reason of a range of factors including poverty and social exclusion, find themselves in vulnerable situations. However, to call a person vulnerable conflates their situation with their identity. This is problematic [because] it evokes a damaging misperception of disabled people as weak and in need of paternalistic protection ...[74]

The blanket label of vulnerability also engenders assumptions of 'sameness' that fail to take account of the uniqueness of different disabilities and differing levels of mental impairment experienced by those with the same disabilities, for instance.[75] Similarly, Fineman has highlighted that in the case of older adults, 'the negative assumptions revolve around capacity and capability, with images of the elderly as inevitably in "need" due to assumed physical and mental limitations'.[76] Therefore, it is important to avoid making automatic assumptions of vulnerability in the assisted dying debate that can be both inappropriate and offensive, and can compound vulnerability.[77] However, even if there were greater awareness of the research findings that contest conceptions of assumed and heightened vulnerability, we strongly suspect that the concerns about exploitation of older adults, individuals with terminal, serious degenerative and chronic illnesses, and those with disabilities would remain, both because of the frequency in which they are raised and because of the gravity of the predicted effects.[78]

As we see it, the most effective way to tackle such cost-reduction-based concerns is to be open from the outset that permitting assisted dying *might* reduce NHS

---

72 Collins 2015: 159.
73 Jackson and Hafemeister 2010: 287–290.
74 Law Commission 2013: 2.151.
75 See, e.g. Holland and Kydd 2015.
76 Fineman 2012: 75. See also Pritchard-Jones 2016. On blanket vulnerability assumptions regarding the involvement of older adults in the context of research, see Pachana and others 2015.
77 Mackenzie 2013: 34; chapter 4, section 2.
78 See also Battin and others 2007: 591.

costs.[79] However, it should be made absolutely clear in any legislation permitting some form of assisted dying that this should *never* be *the*, or indeed *a*, reason for acting on a patient's request for an assisted death. In our view, this should take the form of an unambiguous statement that it is a necessary condition of a lawful assisted death that cost-effectiveness is not the purpose for which the assisted death is provided.[80] This would then mean that any assisted death provided with this purpose would be unlawful, regardless of whether the other conditions have been met. If this condition, a statutory duty, is breached by a health provider or any individual working for that provider then they would act ultra vires and the individual could also face prosecution for murder.[81] In addition, a prosecution for corporate manslaughter[82] *might* be brought against the health provider.[83] It would need to be proven that the way in which the senior management of the

79 Empirical evidence would be needed to measure the costs involved in providing assisted dying (such as consultations, prescription writing and the cost of a drug that does not usually have long shelf life), against the costs of the ongoing medical treatment and care for a patient who requests an assisted death, the latter of which will of course differ depending on the patient's particular condition. A cost comparison calculation would also depend on how many of the population would request and be granted an assisted death. Although now some time ago, Emanuel and Battin found that the likely savings on total health care spending in the United States 'can be predicted to be very small — less than 0.1 percent': Emanuel and Battin 1998. More recently, Shaw and Moreton have argued that there are economic arguments in favour of legalising assisted dying which, although they should not be the primary reason to legalise assisted dying, are 'supplemental facts that should not be neglected.' Shaw and Moreton 2020: 69. However their quality-adjusted life years (QALYs) based analysis does not include consideration of the economic costs involved in providing assisted death.

80 Cf. s.4(5) of the Mental Capacity Act 2005: when determining what is in a person's best interests where the treatment in question is life-sustaining, the relevant person 'must not, in considering whether the treatment is in the best interests of the person concerned, be motivated by a desire to bring about his death.' Whilst one of us has argued previously that this provision is 'meaningless' (see Brazier and Ost 2013: 157, n.207), this is in relation to the specific application of this provision to the withdrawal of life-sustaining treatment, where the only purpose behind withdrawing treatment is, surely, to bring about death.

81 One further possibility might be the tort of misfeasance (or criminal offence of misconduct in public office). It would be necessary to prove that the individual concerned acted in bad faith, either knowingly beyond his powers or in a way that was inconsistent with his duties. And he must have known that in so acting, he would be likely to injure the claimant (as per the second version of tort defined by Lord Steyn in *Three Rivers D.C. Bank of England (No. 3)* [2003] 2 AC 1 (HL), 190). The individual concerned would also need to be a public officer, defined in *R v. Whitaker* (1914) KB 1283: 'a public office holder is an officer who discharges any duty in the discharge of which the public are interested, more clearly so if he is paid out of a fund provided by the public'. This might thus encompass a health care professional working for the NHS, but would be a matter for judicial assessment. Nurses working in a prison have been held to be public officers whether directly employed by the prison service or by a private company contracted by the prison service (*R v. Cosford* [2013] EWCA Crim 466). For analysis of the tort of misfeasance, see Murphy 2012.

82 Under s.1 of the Corporate Manslaughter and Homicide Act 2007.

83 NHS Foundation Trusts can be considered corporations under s.25 of the Corporate Manslaughter and Homicide Act 2007, since they are public bodies which are incorporated by statute.

provider managed or organised its activities was a substantial element in a gross breach of duty (to provide a lawful assisted death and/or to act in the patient's best interests), and that this breach was an operating cause of death that made more than a minimal contribution to the patient's death.[84] If greater certainty as to the applicability of a criminal offence is required, then a specific offence could be created under the legislation permitting assisted dying, which would be committed by a provider, director or senior individual – a 'controlling mind' of the provider –[85] in any case where they knowingly provide assisted death for cost-effectiveness purposes.[86]

We also suggest that legal regulation of assisted dying could better ensure closer scrutiny of the care and treatment of vulnerable patients. Regulation before the event would, in and of itself, offer a means of scrutinising the assisted dying process (and the involvement of others within this process) that does not currently exist given the illegality of assisted dying. Consider that criminal investigations occur after the event and can be made more difficult where the death has occurred outside of this jurisdiction. Dignity in Dying[87] has reported that more than 350 Britons have used the services of Dignitas to obtain an assisted death. According to the organisation, 'under the current law, if someone were a victim of malicious or coercive behaviour during an assisted death overseas, it would unlikely be detected by UK authorities'.[88]

Any legislation permitting assisted dying through a publicly funded health care system would thus certainly need to include careful regulation, involving close scrutiny, of the way in which vulnerable patients are treated and cared for. It is notable that such close scrutiny has sometimes been lacking in the context of publicly funded health care systems operating in jurisdictions where assisted dying is not permitted. One of the most powerful examples of serious failings which lead to the lives of over 450 patients being shortened occurred at the Gosport War Memorial Hospital in England, between 1989–2000. The Gosport Independent Panel report reveals the administration of drugs (especially diamorphine) when not clinically indicated, and the inappropriate use of anticipatory prescribing of diamorphine, with the effect of shortening life. Whereas a large number of the patients and their relatives understood admittance to the hospital was for rehabilitation or respite care, patients 'were, in effect, put on a terminal care pathway'.[89] Failings lay with, inter alia, nursing

---

84 R v. Hughes (2014) 1 Cr App R 6.
85 Such as the false or misleading information offence under s.92 of the Care Act 2014.
86 For reasons of space, we must leave aside the question of whether the creation of such an offence could be justified on criminalisation principles. See Collins 2015: chapter 5 for a comprehensive analysis of the principles that would require consideration.
87 The most prominent campaigning organisation for the legalisation of assisted dying (formerly the Voluntary Euthanasia Society, 1935–2006) in the UK.
88 See Dignitas, 'Every eight days a Briton travels to Dignitas for help to die. The absence of an assisted dying law forces dying people to take drastic measures to control their death', available at https://www.dignityindying.org.uk/why-we-need-change/dignitas/ accessed 9 April 2020.
89 Gosport Independent Panel 2018: Forward.

staff, doctors, regulatory bodies and the bodies within the criminal justice system,[90] and occurred in a culture in which whistle-blowers were (then) not well protected.[91] The panel's report is replete with examples of a failure to communicate with patients' relatives[92] and inadequate record-keeping, and demonstrates that there was no evidence of effective monitoring of the effects of drugs administered.[93] According to the report there was:

> no planning for end of life care with patients' families[.] The absence of any reference to the psychological needs of individuals, or discussion about their condition, anxieties and fears, suggest a lack of awareness of end of life care, a lack of regard for individual wishes, needs or concerns and a failure to provide an opportunity for patients to express their worries.[94]

In short, 'there was a disregard for human life'.[95] It thus seems that continuous communication with both patients and their families is a fundamental aspect of good, individualised patient care focused on the patient's needs, as well as being an important means to assist in detecting the existence of a burden perception and/or undue influence. We would also draw attention to Colburn's emphasis on the need to ensure the availability of a number of other factors related to palliative and social care in his analysis of voluntariness: 'access to adequate pain management, support for independent life and decision-making, and adequate support for carers'.[96] The availability of these factors could help prevent the occurrence of the burden perception and/or undue influence. On this point, it is notable that the codification of the Dutch law on assisted dying occurred alongside a drive to improve the provision of palliative care as part of national health care policy.[97] Therefore, requiring good communication and improved palliative and social care, coupled with strict regulation, could offer a way of countering claims that vulnerable patients would be exposed to exploitation if assisted dying were to be offered through a publicly funded health care system due to an underlying motivation of reducing costs. Moreover, if assisted dying did, in fact, reduce NHS costs, any cost savings could be deployed on palliative care and social care. Of course, we recognise that in a climate of austerity, including cuts to social care and a limited NHS budget, achieving all of this will be challenging to say the least. But opinion polls consistently demonstrate public support for a better-funded NHS, and social care cuts have been

---

90 Ibid: [12.11].
91 Ibid: [12.42].
92 See, e.g. ibid: [3.8] and [3.10]
93 Ibid: [3.27–3.28].
94 Ibid: [3.32].
95 Ibid: [12.11].
96 Colburn 2020: 319.
97 See, e.g. Gordijn and Janssens 2004.

castigated.[98] What is needed is the political will and determination to bring about the changes outlined here.

3) The possible exploitation of the doctor who is willing to consider offering assistance

> Doctors can come under enormous pressure from relatives and from their own emotions to hasten the death of a patient whom they believe to be suffering too much.[99]

In our exploration of sexual exploitation in the doctor-patient relationship, we highlighted the fact that doctors, too, can be vulnerable to exploitation by their patients. In the context of assisted dying, we should be mindful that the impact of playing a crucial role in the process of an assisted death can make doctors vulnerable. Clark and Kimsma have drawn attention to '(the philosophical and psychological) vulnerabilities a physician faces by agreeing to assist in ending a life'[100] and studies have shown that doctors 'have emotional (28%) or burdensome (25%) feelings and … experience general discomfort in 42% of all cases of life-termination, and especially in the case of euthanasia (75%)'.[101] Where doctors are experiencing such feelings, they may be more susceptible to pressure or manipulation to carry out the assisted death. Such pressure could come from the patient himself, as alluded to in the following accounts from doctors in the Netherlands, where assisted dying is lawful:[102]

> Perhaps at some point there was some sort of moral pressure. The moment [the patient] said: 'If you won't perform [assisted dying], I might go to a railway line or climb a high building.'

---

98 See, e.g. Denis Campbell, 'NHS privatisation would be "political suicide", says thinktank' *The Guardian* (London, 1 February 2018); Matthew Smith, 'Majority of people would support raising National Insurance to fund the NHS', YouGov, 12 January 2017, at https://yougov.co.uk/topics/politics/articles-reports/2017/01/12/majority-people-would-support-raising-national-ins accessed 5 June 2020; Matthew Smith, 'Half of Britons support raising taxes to support the NHS' YouGov, 13 November 2019, at https://yougov.co.uk/topics/politics/articles-reports/2019/11/13/half-britons-support-raising-tax-fund-nhs accessed 5 June 2020. On social care cuts, see, e.g.: The King's Fund, 'Older people are paying the price for cuts to social care', 15 September 2016, at https://www.kingsfund.org.uk/press/press-releases/older-people-social-care-cuts accessed 5 June 2020; Patrick Collinson, 'Social care: Why are we "beyond the crisis point"?' *The Guardian* (London, 12 December 2016); Joe Gammie, 'Thousands of old and disabled people could be impacted by social care cuts, report says' *The Independent* (London, 26 June 2019).
99 11 Sep 2015: Column 656 Assisted Dying (No. 2) Bill HC, second reading, column 679 (Liam Fox, MP).
100 Clark and Kimsma 2004: 65.
101 van Marwijk and Haverkate 2007: 609.
102 Under the Termination of Life on Request and Assisted Suicide (Review Procedures) Act, passed in 2001.

> [The patient] said something like: 'I want [an assisted death]; soon I'll no longer be able to handle [the disease] and you can't let me down.'[103]

At the very least, these demands amount to pressure. And, where a doctor has a close professional relationship with her patient and desires to respect her patient's autonomy, the patient may be able to take advantage of this professional virtue which makes his doctor more susceptible to being coerced into providing an assisted death, even when she is not wholly comfortable in so doing. The elements of exploitation following our account (taking advantage of and misuse for one's own ends) would thus be made out.

Pressure or manipulation could also emanate from the patient's relatives, as reflected in findings from one study:

> Physicians frequently mentioned feeling pressured by the patient or the relatives to perform [assisted dying]. The latter most often happened when the patient was no longer able to express his/her request.[104]

In Roest et al's thematic analysis of research on the involvement of family members in euthanasia practice in the Netherlands, some doctors reported experiencing pressure from relatives in a number of studies. Although not a huge percentage, it is still notable that in one of these studies, 13% of the doctors who participated had experienced pressure from relatives during the assisted dying decision-making process.[105] For one doctor interviewed in another Dutch study, the pressure stemmed from both the patient and his partner: 'The patient says: "I want it [euthanasia] now, or else I will hang myself from the bridge," to which the partner of the patient reacts by saying: "he will do it for real"'.[106]

In the following, final, section, we suggest how consideration could be paid to the possibility of the doctor being pressurised and, potentially, exploited. We will propose that this should be one of the matters that is explored as part of a process of review before an assisted death can occur.

4) How the law and practice might respond to the potential for exploitation: Identifying undue influence and the burden perception

Our earlier discussion has demonstrated that there are real risks regarding undue influence and the burden perception that need to be addressed within any jurisdiction in which some form of assisted dying is permitted, or is to be permitted. One

---

103 Snijdewind and others 2014: 1130. See also de Boer and others 2019: 427.
104 Ibid: 1130. See also van Marwijk and Haverkate 2007: 611–612.
105 Roest and others 2019: 14. See also de Boer and others 2019.
106 de Boer and others 2019: 427.

more extreme way to address the risk of undue influence is to exclude the availability of an assisted death whenever the person who expresses a desire for an assisted death has been influenced *in any way* by others. Such an approach can be seen in a proposed amendment to Lord Falconer's second Assisted Dying Bill put forward during the 2014–2015 parliamentary session. The amendment stated that, inter alia, any applicant would have 'capacity commensurate with a decision to end his or her own life and a clear, settled, informed and voluntary intention to do so *if he or she … is not the subject of influence by, or a sense of obligation or duty to, others*.'[107]

But this would go too far. It is difficult, if not impossible, to envisage a situation where a patient who has personal relationships is not influenced in some way by the views of their loved ones. The 'large majority' of patients in one Dutch study made their requests for an assisted death 'in the context of both familial and societal relationships',[108] for instance. Indeed, doctors have a 'keen awareness' of familial influence in assisted dying requests in the Netherlands.[109] However, not all such influence constitutes exploitation, and would 'simple persuasion'[110] not be an expected (and acceptable) factor in any such relationship?[111] It is also notable that the reference to acting out of 'a sense of obligation or duty to, others' in the proposed amendment would additionally have prevented instances of assisted dying where the burden perception is part of the patient's rationale for requesting an assisted death, even where there is no exploitation. We consider whether the burden perception should be a legitimate reason for requesting an assisted death in such circumstances later, but at this juncture, we note that if it is not, this would give rise to a distinction with the law on the capacitous person's refusal of treatment, or request that treatment be withdrawn. For, where a person requests that life-sustaining treatment be withdrawn, they can do so on *any* ground, including that they consider themselves a burden to their loved ones, provided that they have capacity.[112]

Returning to the matter of influence, in our view, focusing on the notion of *undue* influence would be a better way to address the risk of exploitation.

---

107 List of Marshalled Amendments to the Assisted Dying Bill 6, 6 November 2014, Amendment 65 (proposed by Lords Carlile, Darzi and Harries) (emphasis added).
108 Norwood 2007: 159.
109 Kimsma and van Leeuwen 2007: 367.
110 Bell 2007: 564.
111 As recognised at law many years ago in *Hall* v. *Hall* (1868) LR 1 P&D 481. See also Collins 2015: 205–206. For our analysis of relational autonomy and vulnerability, see chapter 4, section 2.
112 The test for establishing a lack of capacity is set out under the Mental Capacity Act 2005, ss.2(1) and 3(1): due to an impairment of or disturbance in the functioning of their mind or brain, a person is not able to make the decision for themself because they cannot understand information, or retain information, or use or weigh information, or communicate their decision. In a case that preceded this statutory law, *B* v. *An NHS Hospital Trust* [2002] EWHC 429 (Fam), Dame Butler Sloss stated: 'if the patient is capable of making a decision whether to permit treatment and decides not to permit it his choice must be obeyed, [even] if on any objective view it is contrary to his best interests. A doctor has no right to proceed in the face of objection, even if it is plain to all, including the patient, that adverse circumstances and even death will or may ensue' [24].

Whilst we recognise that undue influence lacks a definitive definition,[113] it is not a concept that is new to the law, or to fields such as psychology, sociology and criminology.[114] Earlier in this work, we alluded to Birks's definition that 'undue influence consists in unconscionable exploitation of influence',[115] with the critical question identified at law as being 'whether or not the influence has invaded the free volition of the [person] to withstand the influence'.[116] In applying the concept of undue influence to our case study of sexual exploitation in the doctor-patient relationship, we identified the factors of coercive and irresistible inducements[117] as being capable of distorting the exploitee's decision-making.

There are also statutory examples that we can look to which include legal definitions of undue influence, a number of which are designed chiefly to protect consumers in contract law. For instance, under regulation 7 of the Consumer Protection from Unfair Trading Regulations 2008 (CPRs), undue influence is defined as 'exploiting a position of power in relation to the consumer so as to apply pressure, even without using or threatening to use physical force, in a way which significantly limits the consumer's ability to make an informed decision'.[118] Turning away from contract law, the US state of California's Welfare and Institutions Code (which includes provisions designed to protect the welfare of those with disabilities and older adults) defines undue influence as 'excessive persuasion that causes another person to act or refrain from acting by overcoming that person's free will and results in inequity'.[119] A list of factors is then provided that should be considered in determining whether undue influence has occurred (although there is no requirement that *all* of these factors be present in order for undue influence to be found):[120]

- the *victim's vulnerability* (evidence of which may include, but is not limited to, 'incapacity, illness, disability, injury, age, education, impaired cognitive

---

113 Bell 2007: 556; Quinn and others 2010: 2. See also chapter 7, section 4.iii.a.
114 A point well made by Quinn and others 2017: 158. See also chapter 5, part 2, text accompanying n.60.
115 Birks 2004: 34. See chapter 3, text accompanying n.241. Note also the explanation offered in the Supreme Court of Canada case, *Geffen* v. *Goodman Estate* [1991] 2 SCR 353, 377 (Wilson J): 'It seems to me ... that when one speaks of "influence" one is really referring to the ability of one person to dominate the will of another, whether through manipulation, coercion, or outright but subtle abuse of power. To dominate the will of another simply means to exercise a persuasive influence over him or her.'
116 *Thompson* v. *Foy* [2009] EWHC 1076 (Ch), [101] (Lewison J).
117 See chapter 5, part 2, text in paragraph accompanying n.60.
118 CPRs, regulation 7(3). Note also the definition of undue influence in contract law codified in California's Civil Code, which states that undue influence occurs: (1) In the use, by one in whom a confidence is reposed by another, or who holds a real or apparent authority over him, of such confidence or authority for the purpose of obtaining an unfair advantage over him; (2) in taking an unfair advantage of another's weakness of mind; or, (3) in taking a grossly oppressive and unfair advantage of another's necessities or distress. (Cal. Civil Code § 1575 (1872)).
119 § 15610.70.
120 As observed by Plotkin and others 2016: 346.

function, emotional distress, isolation, or dependency, and whether the influencer knew or should have known of the alleged victim's vulnerability');
- the *'influencer's apparent authority'* (evidence of which can include, inter alia, their status as a family member, a care provider or a health care professional);
- the *influencer's tactics or actions* such as the use of coercion[121] or affection, controlling the victim's 'necessaries of life' or 'interactions with others'; and
- the *'equity of the result'*, evidence of which can include 'any divergence from the victim's prior intent'.[122]

We will now use this undue influence model as our basis for assessment, with a few modifications. First, we concur with Plotkin et al that the influencer's knowledge of the alleged victim's vulnerability, which appears in the *victim's vulnerability* factor above, is more appropriately placed within the *influencer's tactics or actions* factor,[123] because it speaks more to the influencer's behaviour than the victim's status. Secondly, regarding the *victim's vulnerability* factor, we would add *potential* to reflect the approach we have taken consistently through this work that we should avoid drawing assumptions of automatic vulnerability because of a person's disability, age, etc. Thirdly, in relation to the same factor, given what the aforementioned studies have revealed about the prominence of the burden perception for patients nearing the end of life, we would also include explicit reference to the influencer's taking advantage of this perception. This perception might relate to feeling one is a burden to one's family and/or the state. Fourthly, we suggest that the final factor should be removed and replaced. Whilst the *equity of the result* may well have real resonance in cases involving challenges to wills and trusts,[124] it does not sit as comfortably in our context and is likely to be more difficult for a doctor to assess.[125] However, the existence of a factor such as 'any divergence from the victim's prior intent' could be possible evidence of undue influence, of the decision to request an assisted death not being truly voluntary/involving impaired voluntary decision-making, and is more likely to be an issue that a doctor can assess.

For instance, the patient could be devoutly religious and have said previously that she has always intended to follow God's will regarding when she dies, but

---

121 Coercion is also referred to in part of the definition of a prohibited aggressive commercial practice under the CPRs. Such a practice 'significantly impairs or is likely to significantly impair the average consumer's freedom of choice or conduct ... through the use of ... coercion or undue influence': CPRs, regulation 7(1)(a).
122 §15610.70(a)(1), (2), (3) and (4) (emphasis added). These four factors reflect the defining features most commonly found in the existing literature on undue influence. See Quinn and others 2010: 11–12.
123 Plotkin and others 2016: 348.
124 This definition of undue influence and the list of factors is also employed by the California Probate Code (§ 86).
125 'Assessment of this factor includes matters of fact and opinion that are generally outside the range of expertise of the [mental health professional]'. Plotkin and others 2016: 349.

now says that she is tired of life and wishes to have an assisted death. Whilst this may be a genuine change of mind, without any element of undue influence, the fact that the patient's newly stated intent is so starkly different to her previously stated intent might be an indication that she has been affected by some form of influence which warrants further exploration. Thus, the modified assessment of undue influence model we are adopting comprises of the following elements:

- the alleged *victim's potential vulnerability* (evidence of which may include, but is not limited to, incapacity, illness, disability, injury, age, education, impaired cognitive function, emotional distress, isolation or dependency);
- the alleged *influencer's apparent authority* (evidence of which can include, inter alia, their status as a family member, a care provider or a health care professional);[126]
- the alleged *influencer's tactics or actions* such as the use of coercion[127] or affection, controlling the alleged victim's 'necessaries of life' or 'interactions with others', and using their knowledge of the alleged victim's burden perception and/or vulnerability;[128]
- the *desire to have an assisted death is inconsistent* with the alleged victim's prior intent.

We can see how this model might play out by returning to our two earlier scenarios (see p. 172), exploring whether the elements in the adapted model above are present and, if they are, whether they would be apparent to the doctor. Looking to *Scenario 2* and the first three elements of the modified undue influence model, whilst her age, illness and burden perception might make the patient vulnerable and her son could be deemed to be in a position of authority because of their family relationship, there is no apparent influence (undue or otherwise) exacted. There are no actions or tactics employed by the son involving coercion or affection in order to pressure his mother to request an assisted death. Indeed, it is a desire not to cause his mother further distress that prevents him from confirming her burden perception. All we have is a desistance from discouraging her from requesting an assisted death. There is nothing in the scenario to suggest that the son is controlling his mother's 'necessaries of life' or her

---

126 Unaltered from the Californian statutory provision.
127 On coercion, we can look to the explanation of undue influence in the form of coercion in the historic probate law case of *Hall* v. *Hall* (1868) LR 1 P&D 481, 482 (Sir James Wilde): 'Importunity or threats, such as the testator has not the courage to resist, moral command asserted and yielded to for the sake of peace and quiet, or of escaping from distress of mind or social discomfort, these, if carried to a degree in which the free play of the testator's judgment, discretion or wishes, is overborne, will constitute undue influence'.
128 This element of taking advantage of a weakness is reflected somewhat in one of the factors that will be taken into account in deciding whether a practice is aggressive under the aforementioned CPRs: 'the exploitation by the trader of any specific misfortune or circumstance of such gravity as to impair the consumer's judgment, of which the trader is aware, to influence the consumer's decision' (CPRs, regulation 7(2)(c)).

interactions with others. Finally, there is no indication that the fourth element of an inconsistency in intent is present. Thus, applying this model, this does not appear to be a case of undue influence.

If we apply this model to *Scenario 1*, considering the first element of the alleged victim's vulnerability, whilst we should avoid making the assumption that the father is vulnerable simply by virtue of his suffering from an incurable illness, he is in a degree of pain notwithstanding medical treatment. This should alert us to the fact that he may be more susceptible to manipulation, depending on the level of pain he is in. He says that it is 'a great deal of pain' to his doctor, although there is a question about how accurate this statement is – does he overemphasise this, presenting it as the primary reason for requesting an assisted death in order to play down the significance of the burden perception in his reasoning? Even if the degree of pain he is actually in does not make him vulnerable to manipulation, the expression of this burden perception to his doctor should be indicative of his possible vulnerability in this regard. The second element of the alleged influencers' apparent authority is present, given his children's status as close family members and their caring role. Whether the doctor will be aware of this caring role is not clear. The third element is certainly present, with tactics of coercion and the daughter's and son's exploitation of their father's affection. They also use their knowledge that the medication he is receiving is no longer relieving his pain. However, the undue influence perpetrated in *Scenario 1* 'occurs behind closed doors without witnesses',[129] in common with most instances of undue influence. Finally, regarding the fourth factor, this may not be present here as there is no clear indication that the patient's desire to have an assisted death is inconsistent with his prior intent, although the scenario states that he has only *recently* started to consider the option of an assisted death.

Even if the fourth element is not in evidence, the model strongly points to the existence of undue influence in *Scenario 1*. However, the difficulty lies in detecting this undue influence. Requiring that the patient be seen alone, away from relatives, could enable some more visible/apparent instances of undue influence and the burden perception (in cases where it is not initially declared by the patient) to be discovered. But it is highly unlikely that all instances will be detected through such one-to-one interactions between doctor and patient, as highlighted by a palliative care consultant in an expert report[130] given in evidence in the *Conway* case: 'detecting coercion depends crucially on the relationship and a working knowledge of a person's family or forensic objectivity, a characteristic that is not routinely part of doctors' training'.[131] Moreover, according to Quinn et al, 'assessing for undue influence requires focusing on a *process* that has taken place over time … the constant in undue influence situations is psychological

---

129 Quinn and others 2010: 2.
130 Provided for Care Not Killing, a UK-based organisation opposed to any legalisation of assisted dying.
131 See n.14, [162].

manipulation.'¹³² This point is also well made, more broadly, by Rudinow: 'To describe some piece of behavior as manipulative is usually to diagnose or interpret it, to say of the behaviour something which calls for support by reference to details of the history and contextual surroundings of the behavior.'¹³³

It is in relation to the challenge of uncovering such psychological manipulation that an important contrast between the ways that primary health care is delivered in this jurisdiction and the Netherlands is significant. Dutch doctors (and it is primarily GPs who are involved in assisted dying)[134] generally speak more often with the patient's family members about the patient's end of life decision than doctors in other European countries,[135] and euthanasia practice in the Netherlands involves 'a dialogue between doctors, patients and families'.[136] A doctor commonly schedules a family meeting after a patient's initial requests for an assisted death, with such meetings offering the doctor valuable insights into the patient's decision-making process. For instance, in one case discussed by Norwood, the family meeting alerted the doctor to the validity of the patient's request for an assisted death because she was unable to talk much about her request in front of her family.[137] Where there is a question about the authenticity of the request, Norwood reports that the common practice is to pause the process and only continue if, or when, firmer evidence of the request meeting the necessary requirements exists.[138] It thus seems more likely that the presence of undue influence would be detected by doctors in the Netherlands than in England and Wales (and, indeed, elsewhere), because of a stronger, more long-standing communicative relationship[139] with patients and their closest relatives and the Dutch practice of 'euthanasia talk'.[140]

---

132 Quinn and others 2017: 159 (emphasis in original).
133 Rudinow 1978: 346.
134 ten Cate and others 2017: 273: 'in 2014, 88% of [assisted dying] cases were performed by a GP'. See also Jansen-van der Weide and others 2005: 1704; de Boer and others 2019: 425.
135 Roest and others 2019: 12. See also ten Cate and others 2017: 727.
136 Norwood 2007: 142.
137 Ibid: 148–150. We note that the case in question was not one in which there was any indication of undue influence; there were other reasons to suggest that the patient's euthanasia request was not genuine (ibid: 154).
138 Ibid: 155–156.
139 According to one study involving interviews with 33 GPs, 'many respondents mention that for them it is important to have a good relationship with the patient in order to perform [assisted dying]' (ten Cate and others 2017: 727). See also Clark and Kimsma 2004: 63: 'Our discussions with Dutch physicians turned in a unanimous report that, *if* the doctor is going to participate in [assisted dying], a personal relationship was an absolute necessity ... to some extent a personal relationship not only better meets the depth of the experience but also allows the physician to be more fully convinced of the patient's real wishes and convictions.' (Emphasis in original.)
140 'Euthanasia talk is based on a relatively flat power differential where all are encouraged to participate in the dialogue, reflecting on how they feel about the request for euthanasia' (Norwood 2007: 151).

Whilst the level of communication and interaction between doctors, patients and patients' families would necessarily need to change if the law in England and Wales were to be altered, the difficulty in uncovering undue influence is, undeniably, one of the greatest challenges that exploitation via undue influence poses. It would be unrealistic to expect that the distinctive approach of Dutch general medical practice could simply be transplanted into the delivery of primary health care in England and Wales. The former exists as part of a larger cultural practice of *overleggen*, a fundamental aspect of Dutch social life involving consultation, group communication and consensus building that is not mirrored in England and Wales.[141] How, then, might we increase the likelihood that instances of undue influence will be detected?

According to the latest version of the Assisted Dying Bill in England and Wales, the attending doctor and an independent doctor must be satisfied that, inter alia, the patient has a 'clear and settled intention [to] end their own life which has been reached voluntarily, on an informed basis and without coercion or duress'.[142] One means to assist in detecting any coercion or duress could be through the creation and utilisation of a screening tool, such as that developed by Quinn et al for professionals working in adult protective services.[143] This screening tool is consistent with the definition of, and factors related to, undue influence under the Californian statutory model discussed above. It requires the user/assessor to work through a tick box assessment comprised of four sections that reflect the four elements of the statutory undue influence model. Thus, for instance, under 'Client's Vulnerability', there are factors such as 'developmental disability', 'depends on others for help or care' and 'emotional distress (such as grief, anxiety, fear, depression)'. If the assessor does not find any of the listed factors present, they can tick 'other' (and then specify what), or 'no apparent vulnerability'. There is space in each section for the assessor to give an example of the factor they have ticked and/or provide comments. The tool is accompanied by instructions to assist in its completion, including a list of examples of the different factors.[144] In the final summary section of the tool, the assessor ticks which (if any) of the four elements are present. Details are then provided regarding further steps that can be taken including, for example, 'capacity assessment' and 'interviews with friends, family, neighbors or professionals'.[145]

Using such a tool would enable a broader assessment involving consideration of the patient's relationship with relatives or carers which the doctor would

---

141 Ibid: 150. The Dutch practice of *overleggen* does not always guarantee shared decision-making between doctor and patient, however, and the Dutch government reported in 2018 that it was focusing on improving shared decision-making as part of a move towards outcome-based health care. See Ministry of Health, Welfare and Sport 2018.
142 [HL] Bill 2019–2021, clause 3(3)(c).
143 Quinn and others 2017: 182–185.
144 Ibid: 183–185.
145 Ibid: 184.

not normally have knowledge of, thereby increasing the chances of detecting a process of undue influence. It would also help achieve a consistent and shared approach to assessing undue influence.[146] It would be unrealistic to expect the patient's doctor to have the expertise to provide a full assessment through such a screening tool, however, and consideration should be given to the involvement of another medical professional who is a mental health expert in this assessment. As noted by Plotkin et al, mental health professionals can claim expertise on the issue of victim vulnerability as it pertains to mental impairments, emotional distress and/or dependency.[147] And the 'subjective perspective and experience of the alleged victim (with regard to the apparent authority of the alleged influencer) … may require [a mental health professional's] expertise to assess'.[148]

Whilst supporting the involvement of a mental health professional in such an assessment, Plotkin et al recommend that mental health professionals should 'refrain from opining on the state of mind or actions of the alleged influencer (*except* as to how such actions may affect the victim emotionally, and whether the influencer knew or should have known of the victim's vulnerability)'.[149] Given the purposes of the assessment through the screening tool (whether the patient's free will has been overcome and their request for an assisted death is the result of 'excessive persuasion'), then this is surely correct. In fact, this approach is reflected in Quinn et al's tool, which is directed to considering whether certain tactics or actions on the part of the alleged influencer exist and *have impacted on* the victim. That is not to say that the issue of the alleged influencer's culpability should not be a matter for the law that is external to the assisted dying process,[150] however, a matter to which we return below.

Following the use of the screening tool, the assessment could go before a panel for review.[151] The panel could meet with the doctor to discuss the case and, at this point, to also check that the doctor has not felt under pressure from the patient or her family to agree to an assisted death. Alternatively, or in addition to this, there could be a requirement at this stage to obtain a court order before proceeding further in any case where an assisted death remains the patient's wish and the assessment has found no undue

---

146 Ibid: 160.
147 Plotkin and others 2016: 348.
148 As also recognised in ibid: 348–349.
149 Ibid: 349 (emphasis added).
150 Indeed, one of the further steps that may be taken after the use of the screening tool is to '[contact] law enforcement to discuss the case' (ibid: 184). The exercise of undue influence can lead to civil or criminal action under Californian law if it is an element of financial elder abuse, which occurs when, inter alia, a person takes the real or personal property of an elder or dependent adult through undue influence (Welfare and Institutions Code, §15610.30). Financial elder abuse is thus a cause of action that can, for instance, invalidate trust documents: *Lintz v. Lintz* (2014) 222 Cal.App.4th 1346.
151 Who this panel should be comprised of would have to be determined, but we do not have the space to consider this here.

influence. The latter would not be dissimilar to the latest version of the Assisted Dying Bill, which would make it necessary to obtain an order from the High Court to include confirmation that the person has a voluntary, clear, settled and informed wish to end his or her own life, in order for an assisted death to occur.[152]

There is an important question to be asked about whether the screening tool should be designed to rule out an assisted death in any case where the burden perception is apparent, or whether it should *only* lead to this conclusion where there is an indication that the burden perception has been taken advantage of by the influencer. As we see it, the crucial issue would be whether, in cases where the burden perception exists, there has been misuse. If there is no taking advantage of the burden perception, then (absent other factors which amount to misuse) there is no exploitation. Thus, the *mere existence* of the burden perception should not preclude an assisted death, provided whatever necessary legal criteria has been met.[153] Such a position is reflected in the Dutch approach to assisted dying: Kimsma and van Leeuwen's review of four studies revealed that whilst doctors are aware that the burden perception can exist within the 'mix of many motives' for an assisted dying request,[154] they focus on the medical and statutory criteria that render an assisted death lawful, criteria which include that the request is voluntary and well-considered and the patient is experiencing unbearable suffering.[155] There would, consequently, be a cause for concern about compliance with this criterion where a burden perception has been taken advantage of, so that there are questions about the true, voluntary nature of the request, or where there is a burden perception, but no apparent unbearable suffering.[156] However, provided the doctor is satisfied that the patient is experi-

---

152 [HL] Bill 2019–2021, clause 1(2)(a).
153 See also McLean 2007: 54.
154 Although in seeming contrast to this, and notwithstanding what we have discussed above regarding the stronger, more long-standing relationships that Dutch doctors have with patients and their close relatives, Roest et al's analysis of the existing Netherlands-based studies leads them to raise the question whether 'physicians recognize family-related reasons or social-relational origins of suffering, and whether patients feel free to speak about it when they have an explicit request for [an assisted death]'. Roest and others 2019: 16.
155 Kimsma and van Leeuwen: 2007: 368–369. This is not to suggest that applying the Dutch 'law's rather abstract and openly formulated criteria' is necessarily straightforward (ten Cate and others 2017: 726). The criterion can be found in s.2 of the statutory law referred to in n.102.
156 It is interesting to note the finding that the presence of the burden perception occurs most commonly in cases where patients' requests for an assisted death are *refused* rather than granted in the Netherlands (Jansen-van der Weide and Onwuteaka-Philipsen 2005: 1699). Rather than this evidencing doctors' concerns that the burden perception is present, however, this may indicate that in cases where this is presented as an important reason for requesting an assisted death, doctors have cause to question the satisfaction of the unbearable suffering criterion (see Jansen-van der Weide and Onwuteaka-Philipsen 2005: 1701).

encing unbearable suffering, the mere presence of the burden perception would not, in itself, render an assisted death unlawful.[157]

Detecting the burden perception is not going to be easy in some cases, as we demonstrated earlier through *Scenario 2*. In the words of Lord Sumption in the *Nicklinson* case:

> I very much doubt whether it is possible in the generality of cases to distinguish between those who have spontaneously formed the desire to kill themselves and those who have done so in response to real or imagined pressure arising from the impact of their disabilities on other people.[158]

Similarly, we are not suggesting that assessing whether undue influence has occurred will be an easy task. Indeed, like the broader matter of exploitation, 'undue influence remains a complex problem, subject to ambiguities and nuances'.[159] That said, as we noted above it is not a concept which is alien to the law. Where undue influence is detected, there should be a legal sanction which would also serve as a symbolic message that the use of pressure or manipulation to persuade another person to request an assisted death will not be tolerated. We are of the view that a law that permits assisted dying but also seeks to address the potential for exploitation which could be wrought through the exercise of undue influence should include a specific offence that would be committed where B requests an assisted death as a result of A exercising undue influence over B. This offence would be somewhat akin to the current offence of assisted suicide,[160] but, whereas the latter can be committed by an individual without any element of bad faith, a crucial difference would be the necessary,

---

157 We note that McPherson et al's systemic review found that 'polls indicate that over one-third of the general public [in various jurisdictions] believe the burden perception is an acceptable reason to provide assisted suicide': McPherson and others 2007: 123. For a brief argument *against* the burden perception being a legitimate ground for an assisted death, see C Foster, '"Being a burden": An illegitimate ground for assisted dying', at http://blog.practicalethics.ox.ac.uk/2017/09/being-a-burden-a-illegitimate-ground-for-assisted-dying/ accessed 9 April 2020. Cf. Rob Marris, who presented the Assisted Dying (no 2) Bill 2015–2016: 'it is patronising and wrong to say that someone should be denied the choice because one factor in their decision making is that they would feel that they are a burden. They should have the choice': HC Deb 11 September 2015, vol 599, col 661.
See also similar views, expressed by Baroness Warnock and Lord Layard during the debate which preceded the second reading of the Assisted Dying Bill [HL] Bill 2014–2015: HL Deb 18 July 2014, vol 755, cols 830–831, 894–895. Notably, studies have shown differences of opinion among GPs, consulting doctors and review committees as to whether the burden perception could be considered to constitute 'unbearable suffering'. See Roest and others 2019: 15.
158 *Nicklinson*, [228].
159 Plotkin and others 2016: 350.
160 See n.13.

exploitative element of undue influence in the offence that we have in mind. It might be worded as follows:

> A person commits an offence where he or she intentionally does an act capable of encouraging or bringing about the assisted death of another person through exploiting that other person by exercising undue influence.[161]

Concluding this chapter, whilst we have moved our attention away from the doctor as exploiter in the professional doctor-patient relationship, exploitation in personal, caring relationships by way of taking advantage of the patient's burden perception and exercising undue influence shares significant characteristics: the abuse of trust and power. And such exploitation can remain hidden because of the power imbalance and more evidential uncertainty. We have emphasised the relational triangle that exists between the patient, her relatives and her doctor as the crucial framework in which exploitation can play out, and through which exploitation could be detected by a doctor who is able to scrutinise the dynamics of the patient's personal relationship with their relatives. The modified version of the undue influence model that applies under Californian statutory law, and a screening tool based on this model, offer a lens through which to assess wrongful behaviour (misuse of the patient). The means of addressing the risk of exploitation that we have focused on in this chapter can be found in: a strictly regulated model of assisted dying that demands good communication with patients and their relatives/carers; the availability of the offence we suggest above; the use of an undue influence screening tool; and improved palliative and social care to tackle the root causes of the burden perception and undue influence.

---

161 This could be accompanied by a statutory definition of undue influence which reflects the third element of our modified undue influence model (see text accompanying nn.127–128). It is the convention in the criminal law of England and Wales to refer to the defendant as *A* and the victim as B. Our comment in chapter 5, part 2, n.42 on our use of the word *exploiting* in the proposed offence there also applies here.

7 Reflecting on exploitation in the doctor-patient relationship

Our final chapter revisits the predominant themes of this work. We bring together the analysis in the preceding chapters to draw conclusions regarding commonalities that our case studies of exploitation in the doctor-patient relationship share, explicating why the matter of exploitation in the doctor-patient relationship should be brought to the fore, and highlighting why exploitation in this relationship is a special case warranting ethical and legal attention. The issue of vulnerability and its relationship with exploitation has been a constant thread weaving throughout each of the preceding chapters. Thus, we draw particular attention to the way in which examining exploitation in the doctor-patient relationship sheds light on the connections between exploitation and vulnerability, and how the theoretical framework surrounding the concept of exploitation could be enhanced by further consideration of this connection. We then turn to our evaluation of the professional medical ethics and legal responses to exploitation in the doctor-patient relationship. We assess whether enough consideration is given to the issue of exploitation in professional medical ethics, and argue that the medical ethics educational and regulatory framework should be premised explicitly upon the ethical notion of the doctor as fiduciary. We call for a mandatory focus on avoiding exploitation in the medical ethics component of medical education and continuing professional development (CPD), and for the compulsory disclosure of conflicts of interest in a central, publicly accessible register held by the GMC. Finally, we reflect on the way in which exploitation in the doctor-patient relationship is addressed under the current law, and present our suggestion as to how we might advance the legal response. Because exploitation in the doctor-patient relationship can occur in a variety of contexts and at varying levels of gravity, we argue that a 'one-size-fits-all' legal response involving the creation of a new criminal offence, for example, would be unworkable. However, taking into account the way in which perpetrating exploitation violates the doctor's fundamental duty not to act out of self-interest, we propose that careful consideration be given to the way in which the law of fiduciary obligations could be expanded to offer an apposite, cohesive legal framework for conceptualising exploitation in the doctor-patient relationship.

1) Commonalities that the cases of exploitation share and why exploitation in the doctor-patient relationship is a special case

In the first substantive chapter in this work, we sought to get to the nub of what makes exploitation wrongful. In answering this question, we presented a process-based account of exploitation that resonates with Kantian liberalism in its focus on how exploitation can both wrong and harm, and in its recognition of a (universal) moral right not to be treated solely as an object. Our conceptualisation of exploitation is most closely affiliated with the accounts of Goodin and Sample, which also recognise vulnerability and respect for persons. However, our conception is distinguishable because it centres on *mis*use (with taking advantage of another's vulnerability, for one's own ends, being a common example of misuse), rather than taking unfair advantage of, or degradation and taking advantage of basic needs. We now draw together the central characteristics that such wrongful exploitation perpetrated by doctors against their patients possesses.

i) The nature of the breach of duty and the wrong: An abuse of trust and power, and misuse through taking advantage of vulnerability

Regardless of the particular character of the exploitation perpetrated by a doctor against her patient – whether it be for sexual, research, commercial or other purposes – what lies at the core of this behaviour is a violation of the ethos of the intimate and confidential professional relationship. Doctors have a fundamental negative role-based obligation not to exploit their patients. To do otherwise is to violate professional medical ethics (which we return to later). It is also a breach of the patient's trust *and* the doctor's fiducial duty to act in the interests of her patient rather than her own self-interest.

What is more, where doctors exploit their patients, they utilise their more powerful position which exists because of the professional relationship, whether that be in publicly or privately funded health care. We have argued that, whilst the doctor's power has been somewhat diffused by the contemporary doctor-patient model, the continuation of a power imbalance is inevitable because the doctor is still the expert to whom the patient goes for advice and help. The wrong is often exacerbated because, as the cases we referred to in chapters 3, 4 and 5 reveal, a common way in which a doctor can misuse his patient is through taking advantage of a vulnerability. Whilst we have expressed caution about *assuming* that all patients are vulnerable, the existence of ill-health, or the feared existence of ill-health, is a factor that should prepare us for the greater likelihood that a patient will be vulnerable. We say more on the significance of the way in which the characteristics of the doctor-patient relationship interact with exploitation and vulnerability in the next section.

ii) Using opportunities offered by the professional role to exploit patients and the use of undue influence to facilitate exploitation

In numerous cases of exploitation that we have discussed, the intimate and confidential nature of the professional role enables doctors to exploit their patients by committing acts that patients are unaware of, or acts that they consider to be legitimate because the exploiter is a doctor committing these acts during their professional interactions. Recall, for instance, Nikita Levy's secret explicit recording of his gynaecological patients, the use of fertility doctors' own sperm in their treatment of patients, Simon Bramhall's branding of his patients' livers, Ian Paterson's provision of unnecessary surgeries to his patients, and Farid Fata's prescription of unnecessary drugs and dangerous treatments to his patients.[1]

Moreover, especially in sexual exploitation cases, the professional role can provide opportunities to facilitate intimate interactions with vulnerable patients such as Laura Norberg, which can lead to both non-consensual and consensual exploitation. But, when exploitation occurs,[2] the presence of consent does not legitimate wrongful exploitation. As we explored, the patient's consent can be impeded and her decision-making can be distorted by coercive and irresistible inducements which the doctor can offer by virtue of his professional role.[3] The relevance of undue influence as a concept, and as a conduit through which exploitation can be brought to bear, is apparent in several chapters. We are not suggesting that undue influence is present in all instances of exploitation in the doctor-patient relationship. Also, we do not seek to claim that undue influence can *only* be exercised by doctors to exploit patients, as our case study of assisted dying – through which we explored the exercise of undue influence by relatives and carers – demonstrates. However, it is notable that the doctor's more powerful position means that undue influence can be the instrument through which the patient's acquiescence to exploitative behaviour is obtained in cases of sexual exploitation, for instance (by way of inducements such as that Dr Wynrib offered to Laura Norberg), and in some instances of exploitative medical research.[4] Thus, the doctor's professional role can both be utilised to take advantage of vulnerability, and to provide coercive and irresistible inducements or otherwise exert undue influence.

iii) The damage caused to the patient because of the context of the relationship in which the exploitation occurs

Throughout this work, the cases that we have discussed reveal that patients' interests can be set back (by way of mental suffering and distress and feelings of

---

1 Cases discussed in chapter 3, sections 2 and 4.
2 As we noted in chapter 5, there can be some instances of consensual, *non-exploitative* sexual relationships between doctors and patients that occur outside the professional context (see chapter 5, section 3.ii).
3 See chapter 5, section 3.i.
4 See chapter 4, section 3.

shame) because of the breach of trust that their doctors' exploitation is entwined with. And the doctor's breach of trust can lead to the patient distrusting the medical profession more broadly. We also explored how a doctor's exploitation of a patient is almost always going to wrong the patient, constituting a violation of her moral right(s). A common violation that we highlighted is in regard to the right not to be treated solely as means to an end, with the other examples being violations to privacy, autonomy and equality rights.[5]

Exploring wrongdoing and the harm caused to patients through the lens of exploitation has revealed more about the wrong and why it is morally objectionable. Taking an example from chapter 3,[6] if a doctor provides patients with an experimental treatment without informing them of the nature of the treatment, the redress would be via professional negligence (legal or regulatory), but this does not adequately acknowledge, or compensate for, the doctor's exploitation of the patients – the doctor's misuse of them and taking advantage of their lack of awareness of the experimental nature of the treatment – and its impacts on their rights and interests. Such impacts could include violations of the moral rights to autonomy and not to be treated solely as a means to an end, mental suffering caused once the patient becomes aware of the breach of trust, and a setback to the patient's interest in health. This suggests that an alternative legal approach is required that would better address these harms, as we explore in the final section of this chapter.

At the end of chapter 3, we emphasised that the doctor-patient relationship is unique because it centres on health, a matter of profound relevance to everyone; and ill health, or fear of ill health, can make all of us vulnerable. It is the combination of this and the common aspects that we discuss in this section that makes exploitation in the doctor-patient relationship a special case. We now turn to the connection between exploitation and vulnerability.

2) What exploitation in the doctor-patient relationship tells us about the connection between exploitation and vulnerability

> It seems possible to forge new connections between vulnerability and exploitation. We may want to be concerned to understand conduct which exploitatively preys on vulnerable individuals.[7]

In this work, we have provided a Kantian liberal account of exploitation that is conducive to recognising the common relevance of vulnerability when exploitation occurs within the doctor-patient relationship. We have scrutinised how

---

5 See chapter 2, section 3.iii.
6 See the discussion of Robert Trossel's actions in offering stem cell therapy treatment in chapter 3, section 4.
7 Collins 2013: 42.

exploitation and vulnerability interact with trust and power:[8] the necessity of trust, coupled with a power imbalance, give rise to vulnerability and this enables exploitation. And the effects of the abuse of trust exacerbate the wrong of the exploitation. This has clear ramifications outwith the professional relationship that we examine, to others which also possess the elements of trust and power, such as that between clergyperson and parishioner, for example. Whilst beyond the scope of this work, our analysis suggests a clear need for introducing a new theoretical framework exploring the connection between exploitation and vulnerability in such relationships. In part, vulnerability can be present because of the fiduciary nature of these relationships,[9] since 'vulnerability is understood as arising from the structural inequality of power and dependence of the fiduciary relationship ... it is, namely, the beneficiary's vulnerability to having his interests compromised by misuse [and] exploitation ... in the fiduciary's exercise of discretionary power.'[10]

We also need to recognise the role that structural injustices and pressures can play in causing patients to be more vulnerable to exploitation.[11] In chapter 6, we noted how tackling the risk of exploitation of those seeking an assisted death through undue influence needed to be considered in conjunction with current inadequacies in palliative and social care. With this in mind, it may be inappropriate to adopt a model of responsibility that lays the blame (solely) at the feet of the exploiter in all cases. If we recall a scenario discussed in chapter 2 involving Joan and the exploitative researchers, we could, and *should*, also be asking what has made Joan poor and why she has come to be out of work, for instance. And we should be attentive to the possibility that the time and workload pressures that doctors face could make patients more likely to be vulnerable to exploitation because their interactions are rushed, thus the protection that independent professional scrutiny of a situation can offer may be lost. A doctor might not have the time, for instance, to scrutinise the reasons why a husband is suggesting that his wife's capacity to make medical decisions is diminishing. Reflecting on such matters entails consideration of a shared social responsibility to address vulnerability.[12]

---

8   See chapter 3, sections 2–4. Note Barnard's conceptualisation of trustworthiness and vulnerability as 'the twin polestars of professionalism in healthcare': Barnard 2016: 297.
9   For our analysis of fiduciary obligations, see chapter 3, section 3; chapter 5, part 2, section 3; this chapter, section 4.iii.b.
10 Miller and Weijer 2006: 428.
11 And doctors in the NHS too, since they work in a 'system where moral exploitation happens to groups not individuals because of structural phenomena built into the NHS system. All healthcare professionals are vulnerable to this by virtue of working within the system': Parker 2019: 573.
12 That said, we are not arguing here for recognition of a broad duty that Goodin would hold us all to, to protect the interests of anyone whose interests are strongly affected by our own actions and to prevent *anyone* from taking unfair advantage of that person (see chapter 2, section 2.iv). Instead, we are calling for greater social awareness of the structural pressures and injustices that can contribute to vulnerability, and acceptance that there is a shared social responsibility to tackle these factors.

In their feminist analysis of exploitation in global interactions related to health, Ganguli Mitra and Biller-Andorno refer to Young's work and her social connection model of responsibility: 'such a model entails that "all agents who contribute by their actions to the structural processes that produce injustice have responsibilities to work to remedy these injustices"'.[13]

At the same time as being prepared to tackle the structural pressures that can increase the likelihood that someone will be vulnerable, autonomy, and the protection of autonomy, are key, and we have drawn attention to the relational dimension that vulnerability and autonomy possess. We have argued that a vulnerable person is one who experiences diminished autonomy and thus, in order to address and overcome vulnerability to exploitation, restoring and enhancing autonomy should be prioritised as far as possible.[14] This played a role in shaping the approaches to tackling exploitation that we propose in the contexts of sexual boundary breaches and assisted dying in chapters 5 and 6.

We have foregrounded the notion of universal *potential* vulnerability (thereby restricting our adoption of Fineman's universal vulnerable subject approach to emphasise that whether or not a particular individual will be vulnerable is not cast in stone), and presented ill-health as a shared vulnerability which can cause *any* person to be more likely to be vulnerable to exploitative tactics. Whilst we have explored how the power imbalance in the doctor-patient relationship can be utilised to facilitate a patient's exploitation, Goodyear-Smith and Buetow have reminded us that doctors do not always possess the power to cure illnesses; indeed, on occasion, they may be unable to cure the patient's ailment and only able to relieve a degree of suffering, as epitomised in cases such as *R v. Cox*.[15] Significantly, Goodyear-Smith and Buetow contend that when doctors allow patients to give a psychosocial account[16] of their story in their interaction with them, doctors can appreciate their *own* vulnerability to illness:

> paradoxically, acknowledgement of their powerlessness and humility may be one of the most powerful things doctors do to facilitate healing in patients. This could be viewed as the strength borne from the awareness of shared weakness, a vital aspect of healing power.[17]

In the context of the contemporary shared decision-making model of the doctor-patient relationship, this raises the question of whether doctors should be encouraged to see the professional relationship as involving not only shared decision-making, but also shared vulnerability. Increased recognition of this

---

13 Ganguli Mitra and Biller-Andorno 2013: 99, quoting Young 2006: 102–103.
14 Chapter 4, section 2.
15 (1992) 12 BMLR 38, in which the doctor gave the patient a lethal dose of potassium chloride at her repeated request to end her life. Her condition (rheumatoid arthritis) was incurable and the doctor was unable to alleviate her suffering.
16 On which, see chapter 3, n.2.
17 Goodyear-Smith and Buetow 2001: 457.

shared vulnerability might facilitate the patient's healing as Goodyear-Smith and Buetow suggest, but it could also make the doctor more cognisant of the patient's situation[18] and the way in which the manner of her interaction with the patient might exacerbate any existing vulnerability that he possesses. And bearing in mind doctors' own actual and potential vulnerabilities, appropriate consideration must be given to patients as exploiters, the possibilities of which we highlighted in chapters 5 and 6,[19] and circumstances which could cause doctors' abilities to resist potentially exploitative interactions with patients to be compromised.[20]

To conclude here, whilst we agree with Collins that exploitation and vulnerability can be conceived to be 'cognate' concepts,[21] a relationship between exploitation and vulnerability should not be presumed.[22] Notwithstanding that we are highlighting the need for further research exploring the connection between exploitation and vulnerability, we chose not to include vulnerability as a component within our conceptual definition of exploitation. To recap, this is because whilst taking advantage of *B*'s vulnerability is a common characteristic of wrongful exploitation, it can also feature in instances of non-wrongful exploitation.[23] It thus fails to demarcate the distinction between non-wrongful and wrongful exploitation. As we see it, this distinction lies in the notion of *mis*use, which taking advantage of another's vulnerability can be an instance of. Beyond this issue of conceptual clarity, however, it is certainly notable that almost all the examples (factual and fictional) of exploitation that we have considered in this book involve some kind of vulnerability that is taken advantage of.[24]

Having brought together the central themes in our analysis of what exploitation in the doctor-patient relationship involves, and the significant interplay between exploitation and vulnerability in the context of this relationship, we now assess the responses to exploitation in professional ethics and law.

3) Assessing the professional response to exploitation in medical ethics education and regulatory medical ethics

In chapter 3, we reflected on the particular focus in professional regulatory ethics core guidance on doctors avoiding any self-interest when providing health care

---

18 See Barnard 2016: 297–298.
19 Chapter 5, part 2, section 4; chapter 6, section 3.
20 See chapter 5, part 1, text accompanying n.13 and p. 209.
21 Collins 2013: 42.
22 'The fact that a person is vulnerable... only means that he or she *may* need services and has a *potential* for suffering harm or serious exploitation': Law Commission 1995: 163 (emphasis in original). See also Macklin 2003: 472–473.
23 See the example of the chess player in chapter 2, text accompanying nn.13 and 108.
24 The two examples where no vulnerability is present are in chapter 2, text accompanying n.101 (the first scenario involving Sandra, which we argue does not involve *wrongful* exploitation) and chapter 5, part 1, text accompanying n.97 (involving a cosmetic surgery patient with no apparent vulnerability, although see also the text in n.98 of that chapter).

and treatment to patients, and how this emphasises that acting out of self-interest violates the very ethos of the doctor-patient relationship. Here, we consider the question of how medical ethics education and regulatory professional ethics could tackle exploitation more explicitly, whilst being mindful of the limits of such interventions, and the impossibility of eradicating exploitation in the doctor-patient relationship.[25]

The GMC stated in 1993 that medical ethics should be one of the core components of the medical curriculum,[26] and it has been a required part of the medical curriculum since 1985 in US medical schools.[27] Published in 2015, the Romanell Report explored medical ethics education in medical school and residency training in the US.[28] Part of the report's description of professionalism includes aspects that are core to not exploiting patients and the notion of a fiduciary relationship: 'using clinical knowledge and skills primarily for the protection and promotion of the patient's health-related interests, [and] keeping self-interest systematically secondary'.[29] Similarly, and again in the US, according to the Accreditation Council for Graduate Medical Education, one of the core competencies that post-doctoral fellows and physicians completing residency programmes must demonstrate is a 'responsiveness to patient needs that supersedes self-interest' and a 'respect for patient ... autonomy'[30] However, the Romanell Report states that 'there is no consensus about specific educational objectives for medical ethics'[31] in the US medical school curriculum.

In the UK, in its *Outcomes for Graduates*, the GMC presents professional and ethical responsibilities that newly qualified doctors must be able to demonstrate. Echoing the preamble to the GMC's *Good Medical Practice*,[32] the overarching outcome is that 'newly qualified doctors must make the care of patients their first concern'.[33] Acting in accordance with a number of the specific responsibilities subsequently stated would restrain doctors from exploiting their patients. Again, these responsibilities are reflective of the idea of the doctor as fiduciary. For instance, doctors should:

- 'place patients' needs and safety at the centre of the care process';[34]

---

25 The latter being a matter that we explore in the final section of this chapter.
26 General Medical Council 1993. This was followed in 1998 by a consensus statement from academics teaching medical students which presented the minimum content of ethics teaching: Ashcroft and others 1998.
27 Bickel 1987.
28 Carrese and others 2015.
29 Ibid: 744–755.
30 Accreditation Council for Graduate Medical Education 2020a: IV.B.1.a)(1)(b) and IV.B.1.a)(1)(c); Accreditation Council for Graduate Medical Education 2020b: IV.B.1.a)(1)(b) and IV.B.1.a)(1)(c).
31 Carrese and others 2015: 750.
32 See chapter 3, text accompanying n.209.
33 General Medical Council 2018b: 7.
34 Ibid:11.

- 'demonstrate compassionate professional behaviour and their professional responsibilities in making sure the fundamental needs of patients are addressed';[35]
- 'maintain confidentiality and respect patients' dignity and privacy' and 'act with integrity, be polite, considerate, trustworthy and honest';[36] and
- 'recognise the potential impact of their attitudes, values, beliefs, perceptions and personal biases (which may be unconscious) on individuals and groups and identify personal strategies to address this'.[37]

All medical schools in the UK must refer to this guidance when designing their curriculums, although the content of the curriculum is open to interpretation and will vary in emphasis, time, delivery and content in each school.[38]

Whilst this guidance gives an implicit nod in the direction of exploitation, and other guidance and regulation in specific areas, such as sexual boundary breaches,[39] can obviously apply to exploitative behaviour, there is no specific professional guidance for doctors on avoiding exploitation.[40] Nor is there any requirement from the GMC that training on avoiding exploitation be a part of medical education in the UK.

In our view, if we seek to tackle exploitation in the doctor-patient relationship head-on, an *explicit* focus on exploitation in medical ethics education[41] and professional guidance is required. This should begin from a stated premise of the ethical notion of the doctor as fiduciary, exploring what exploitation is, how it violates the ethos of the doctor-patient relationship, and what doctors can do to avoid acting exploitatively. Specific matters such as sexual exploitation,[42] undue influence, and how to deal with unsolicited gifts from a patient, such as a legacy,[43]

---

35 Ibid: 9.
36 Ibid.
37 Ibid.
38 See also Ashcroft and others 1998; Stirrat and others 2010.
39 See chapter 5, section 2.
40 Although we note that there is explicit reference to a *type* of exploitative behaviour in both the GMC's core guidance *Good Medical Practice* and its guidance for medical students, which state that personal views must not be expressed in ways that exploit patients' vulnerability: General Medical Council 2013b: 18(54); General Medical Council 2016a: [66].
41 We recognise the possibility that matters connected to avoiding exploitation could be covered in other themes in the undergraduate medical programme, such as communication skills training. Consensus guidelines in the UK related to the communication skills training theme comprise of four principles, including that the curricula should incorporate awareness of and familiarity with ethics and the law and professionalism (honesty, integrity and strong professional boundaries, for instance). See Von Fragstein and others 2008. We note that we have not been able to discuss the postgraduate medical education curriculum here, for reasons of space.
42 See our discussion of medical education in respect of sexual boundary breaches in chapter 5, part 1, n.140.
43 For discussion, see Rimmer 2019.

for example, could then be examined through a lens of students' real-life experiences to encourage reflective practice,[44] wherever possible.

It is insufficient to keep this focus within the medical education stage, however. For, as Rogers and Ballantyne note:

> It is easier to monitor doctors' technical competence than it is to monitor and assess their goodwill towards patients. Health professionals are ... taught medical ethics during their training, and their competence in at least identifying appropriate ethical behaviors can be assessed during these years. However, once they are practi[s]ing, there are no standard mechanisms for testing doctors' ongoing goodwill.[45]

The fiduciary ethical framework approach should thus also be applied to CPD, to reinforce and embed this explicit ethos throughout a doctor's practice, and to reassure the public that the fiduciary ethic is the constant attribute that doctors must possess. CPD is closely connected to revalidation. In the UK, doctors must seek revalidation every five years in order to continue to have a licence to practise. To meet the requirements for revalidation, doctors must provide supporting information which demonstrates that they 'are continuing to meet the principles and values set out in Good Medical Practice'.[46] Such information includes CPD that is tailored to the scope of the doctor's practice and needs.[47] Whilst we would not wish to prescribe a mandatory 'one-size-fits-all' content to CPD, since this would run the risk of being far less tailored and thus of lesser value, we argue that all doctors should undertake at least one compulsory CPD component on avoiding exploitation.[48] This should involve doctors reflecting on their own medical practice and interactions with patients. Continuing on from the earlier focus in medical ethics education, an exploration of how patients can be exploited could include consideration of high-profile cases of exploitation on a grand scale, such as that involving Harold Shipman and Ian Paterson, since it is the more extreme cases that have an inevitable impact on regulation of the medical profession and patient trust:

> extreme cases are more likely to become public knowledge and so directly influence public perception of the doctor-patient relationship and patients' assumptions about whether and how they should trust medical professionals ... [And]

---

44 On the advantages of such an approach, see Corfield and others 2020.
45 Rogers and Ballantyne 2008: 61.
46 General Medical Council 2018a 12, [39].
47 Ibid: 03, [5].
48 Existing modules could be reframed to fit this more explicit focus on avoiding exploitation. For instance, the American Medical Association offers its members a continuing medical education e-learning module on maintaining professional boundaries regarding sexual and romantic involvement with patients and former patients: See https://cme.ama-assn.org/Activity/5293437/Detail.aspx accessed 14 April 2020. See also Anderson Spickard and others 2008.

extreme cases act as triggers for regulatory reform; therefore, they have a direct impact on the regulation of doctors and the protection of patients.[49]

Doctors should also be encouraged to reflect on how certain types of exploitative behaviour may be perceived as being especially egregious because of contemporary concerns. The most obvious current example would be the impact of the prominence of the #MeToo movement, involving allegations of sexual harassment against professionals in numerous spheres. Whilst sexual exploitation cases involving doctors frequently attracted media interest before this, the #MeToo movement has further cemented the public interest in tackling this form of exploitation perpetrated by those acting in a professional capacity. Doctors could assess how they would identify and address a potential or actual sexual boundary breach, how this breach is, or could become, exploitative, and when they might be at greater risk of committing such a breach because of emotional problems or traumatic or major life events.[50]

At the same time, however, it is important that CPD training include less prominent, appropriately tailored examples of potentially exploitative behaviour, especially those which demonstrate how the boundaries of exploitation can be shifted by contemporary ethics and practice. We have in mind here behaviour in 'greyer' areas,[51] like a therapist including (anonymised) patient case studies in a scientific publication, or the example of a doctor taking advantage of his patient's weak condition to unduly influence him to agree to treatment that he considers to be in his best interests.[52] Prior to the emergence of the contemporary model of the doctor-patient relationship, within the traditional paternalistic model in which patient autonomy was (far) less prominent, such behaviour would have been less likely to be perceived as morally problematic.

Looking next to the matter of enforcing ethical guidance through regulation, and keeping in mind our emphasis on the ethical, fiduciary duty to act in the patient's interests and not out of self-interest, we argue that more needs to be done in the UK to ensure that guidance which directs doctors away from potentially exploitative behaviour is being adhered to. In chapter 3, we explored how professional guidance advises doctors not to allow conflicts of interest to affect their treatment and care of patients and that any such conflicts should be disclosed.[53] Yet, notwithstanding this, conflicts of interest disciplinary cases

---

49 Rogers and Ballantyne 2008: 53.
50 See chapter 5, part 1, text accompanying n.13.
51 Greyer areas, in which greater uncertainty resides, can also provide a valuable means of assessing the point at which we can say that behaviour is exploitative. As Hart once observed, 'sometimes the difference between the clear, standard case or paradigm for the use of an expression and the questionable cases is only a matter of degree. A man with a shining smooth pate is clearly bald; another with a luxuriant mop clearly is not; but the question whether a third man, with a fringe of hair here and there, is bald might be indefinitely disputed, if it were thought worthwhile or any practical issue turned on it.': Hart 1961: 4.
52 Both discussed in chapter 3, section 2.
53 See chapter 3, section 7; General Medical Council 2013a: [14] and [15].

have been reported to be prominent: 'the second highest number of GMC investigations relate to doctors acting dishonestly and unfairly, including on conflicts of interests and financial arrangements'.[54] Furthermore, it was alleged in 2015 that the GMC had not ensured this guidance was being adhered to in respect of findings from the Competition and Markets Authority's (CMA) investigation regarding a failure by doctors to declare financial interests in private health care providers.[55] The GMC took no action when presented with the CMA's findings, when it could have asked for names and then investigated the doctors concerned. Adlington et al argue that the problem lies in the regulator's approach of leaving it to doctors to choose themselves whether or not it is necessary to declare a financial interest: 'the current GMC guidance asks that doctors declare their financial interests to their patients and in their medical notes when appropriate, but it leaves the onus on doctors to decide what and where, creating a grey area that is open to exploitation'.[56] The disclosure of such interests to patients provides a means of being both transparent and accountable,[57] and there is thus a clear rationale for disclosure to be mandatory. Adlington et al critique the lack of any specific professional or legal requirement that financial interests be declared to the GMC, or the public,[58] and call for a central register including all UK doctors' financial interests that is publicly available and searchable.[59]

In our view, the GMC should act on such calls,[60] including those from the Royal College of General Practitioners in 2019[61] and the Independent Medicines and Medical Devices Safety Review in 2020,[62] for a public register in which doctors are required to list their financial interests. According to statements made by the GMC's Chief Executive in 2015, the GMC appeared open to considering the possibility of including financial interests on the Medical Register, albeit that legislation bestowing new powers on the GMC to make this a compulsory requirement would be required.[63] However, following the GMC's consultation in 2016 on whether to include additional information such as conflicts of interest

---

54 Adlington and others 2015: 1.
55 Gornall 2015: 1. Discussed in chapter 3, section 5.i. It is also noteworthy that the GMC chose not to appeal against the sanction of suspension imposed by the Medical Practitioner Tribunals in the aforementioned McFarlane case, despite noting that 'the Tribunal had given insufficient consideration as to whether erasure would be an appropriate sanction given the serious and persistent nature of the dishonesty'. See chapter 3, source referred to in n.227, [5].
56 Adlington and others 2015: 1
57 British Medical Association 2017: 1.
58 Although see our reference below to the legal obligation that NHS organisations now have to hold registers stating conflicts of interests which their staff are required to declare (text accompanying nn.64 and 65).
59 BMA 2017: 2.
60 Adlington and others 2015: 2; McCartney 2018; Iacobucci 2018a.
61 Mahase 2019.
62 Independent Medicines and Medical Devices Safety Review 2020: 188, recommendation 8.
63 Charlie Cooper, 'Scandal of doctors who get cash from healthcare firms for patient referrals', *The Independent* (London, 29 January 2015). The GMC repeated the need for legislative power in order to make such a change in 2019.

in the Medical Register, there does not appear to be an appetite to include the compulsory declaration of competing interests.[64] And although, since 2017, individual NHS organisations such as CCGs have been required to hold a register of interests declared by staff, including doctors,[65] this system has been critiqued for being 'inconsistent and often impossible for patients to find and make sense of'.[66]

Counterarguments to the disclosure of conflicts of interest are identified by Sperling. First, to counteract any anticipated rejection of a certain treatment provider because doctors have disclosed a financial interest in this provider, for example, doctors could offer more biased advice to their patients. Secondly, the burden of the relevance of a conflict of interest is shifted on to the patient rather than being addressed. And, thirdly, heavy burdens would be placed on doctors to disclose self-interests during patient consultations, thereby taking time away from and distorting the therapeutic relationship. Finally, Sperling notes that there is 'hardly any substantial or strong evidence' that a conflict between the doctor's self-interest (by way of a relationship with 'industry') and the patient's interests will seriously threaten health care.[67]

We would challenge each of these claims. First, although there may be a hypothetical risk that doctors could provide more biased advice where they have a financial interest in one of the available treatment providers, should they do so, this would equally violate the duty stated in the GMC Guidance above, since they must not try to influence patients' choice of health care services to benefit themselves.[68] On the second point, if the regulatory bodies fail to address conflicts of interests adequately, as has been argued in respect of the GMC by Adlington et al, doctors would not feel *compelled* to disclose. Consequently, no party would shoulder the responsibility of conflict of interest. The outcome of shifting the burden to the patient should be avoided if the GMC takes seriously any breaches of professional duty regarding conflicts of interest. Thirdly, if the

---

64 GMC, 'Developing the Medical Register, 23 February 2017', at https://www.gmc-uk.org/-/media/documents/M06___Developing_the_UK_medical_register.pdf_69417294.pdf accessed 8 July 2020; McCartney 2018a: 1. Although see Mahase 2019, in which a GMC spokesperson is quoted as follows: 'it is possible attitudes are shifting over time – in which case having more flexible legislation would allow us to explore this option in the future. We have been pushing for legislative change for some years now, including having the flexibility to gather certain types of information.'

65 NHS England, 'Managing Conflicts of Interest: Revised Statutory Guidance for CCGs' 2017, available at https://www.england.nhs.uk/publication/managing-conflicts-of-interest-revised-statutory-guidance-for-ccgs-2017/ accessed 9 March 2020.

66 By Margaret McCartney, in Lacobucci 2018a. And the law in respect of CCGs declaring their conflicts of interests, such as direct financial benefits received from private companies and charities (se NHS England 2017), may not be being followed properly in practice. See Adlington and others 2015: 1; Moberly 2018. According to a report from the Centre for Health and the Public Interest, only 19 of the 265 NHS consultants who own shares or equipment in and work in private hospitals have had these interests declared publicly by their trust: Rowland 2019: 12.

67 Sperling 2017: 183–184.

68 General Medical Council 2013a: [14] and [15].

disclosure of conflicts of interests were to be made through a central register, then this should not lead to any heavy burden being placed upon doctors to disclose such interests to every patient during each consultation. To pre-empt arguments against a central register, such as 'a fear that the information disclosed will be misinterpreted' and the existence of research suggesting that patients don't 'look for such information in public websites',[69] the register would need to be accessible, easily searchable, and its existence and purpose would have to be well-publicised. It would serve the important purpose of reinforcing responsibilities regarding conflicts of interest, and knowing that an accessible, mandatory register of conflicts of interests exist could encourage public trust.

Finally, whilst there may be no conclusive empirical evidence that a conflict between the doctor's self-interest and the patient's interests seriously threatens health care, we are unaware of any conclusive evidence demonstrating that it does not. And although it could also be contended that disclosing conflicts of interest *might* have a negative effect by placing patients on guard and encouraging them to adopt a more wary attitude towards their doctors' medical advice and judgement,[70] again, we are unaware of any empirical study that has proven that this is likely to occur.[71] However, since the duty to act in the patient's interests and not out of self-interest is a core duty existing within the doctor-patient relationship, the onus should be upon those who claim that acting contrary to this duty would not be damaging to prove that this is indeed the case. Absent such proof, we argue that the mandatory disclosure of conflicts of interests by all doctors in a central, publicly accessible register, and rigorous enforcement of this duty by the GMC, are required.[72]

4) The appropriate legal response

i) *The piecemeal protection under the existing law*

Building on our exploration of the existing law in earlier chapters,[73] our focus here is on whether exploitation in the doctor-patient relationship is captured within an appropriate legal framework. We have already established that a range of laws could potentially be applicable. For instance, consider that although not specifically directed at the mischief of exploitative behaviour, examples of criminal laws exist that are designed to address medical and scientific behaviour under the Human Tissue Act 2004 (such as removing, storing or use human tissue

---

69 Sperling 2017: 184.
70 Hall 2005: 159. On adopting such a sceptical stance on trust, see Hall 2005: 158, 164–165.
71 Although it has been argued that 'ineffective disclosure may undermine patients' trust in their doctors': Oakes and others 2015: 38.
72 Whilst we have chosen to focus on the matter of regulating conflicts of interest here, we also note that the GMC has been criticised for its failure to act for some time on concerns regarding complaints about Ian Paterson's malpractice that were first raised in 2007 (with Paterson only being suspended in 2012): Paterson Inquiry 2020: 187–188 and 192.
73 Chapter 3, section 8; chapter 5, part 2, sections 1–3; chapter 6, sections 1 and 4.

without appropriate consent and trafficking in human tissue for transplantation purposes)[74] and the Human Fertilisation and Embryology Acts 1990 and 2008 (such as creating, using or keeping an embryo without a licence).[75] These laws could catch certain behaviour that constitutes exploitation, for example, a doctor taking advantage of *B's* serious financial hardship by offering her £1,000 for one of her kidneys. And, as we have discussed, there are also particular criminal offences that apply to certain categories of persons, including health care professionals (such as sexual offences where the parties are in a relationship of care and one party has a mental disorder impeding choice).[76] Other offences catch serious wrongs that can involve exploitation perpetrated by anyone.[77]

Private law also offers options for addressing some types of exploitative behaviour. In chapter 3,[78] we noted the existence of doctrine in contract law that can protect patients in the private sector from exploitative behaviour which the patient has consented to, such as undue influence. And, as we explored in chapter 5,[79] the law of torts may offer redress for wrongfully exploited patients who have had their legally protected interests invaded by their doctors.[80] What is notable about the availability of a remedy through tort law, however, is that it is dependent on an invasion of a protected interest – it is not enough just to establish that the doctor acted wrongfully, as we discuss in the subsection below. Thus, significantly, even a law that is not directed towards censure or prevention, like the criminal law,[81] requires more than wrongful behaviour.

Each of these possible legal avenues of protection and remedy for a doctor's exploitative behaviour is limited in scope, and the overall picture painted is of a law that targets certain behaviour that happens to be exploitative, rather than a law that *directly* responds to the wrong of exploitation. If, therefore, our argument that exploitation in the doctor-patient relationship is distinctive is accepted, does this mean that there should be a new criminal offence or tort of exploitation?

ii) *A tailored legal response: A new criminal offence, or tort, of exploitation?*

In crimes where the wrongdoer fails to respect another person as a human being, such as murder, sexual offences, kidnap, racially aggravated assault,

---

74 Ss.5 and 32 of the Human Tissue Act 2004.
75 S.41 of the Human Fertilisation and Embryology Act 1990.
76 Ss. 38–41 of the Sexual Offences Act 2003 (SOA).
77 Such as the offences of rape and sexual assault under ss.1 and 3 of the SOA.
78 Chapter 3, section 8.
79 Chapter 5, part 2, section 2.
80 Ashworth 2000: 233: 'Tort liability, as its very name suggests, marks out the defendant's conduct as wrongful … the central function of tort law is … to provide a remedy to the victim for the invasion of protected interests, usually damages but sometimes injunctive or other relief.'
81 Ibid: 233.

blackmail and crime related to identity theft, the concept of exploitation can shed light on the essence of the harm that has been caused and draws attention to the way in which 'the harm is partly constituted by the wrong'.[82] Indeed, there has been increased attention paid to exploitative behaviour by the common law in various contexts.[83] This has led Collins to remark that the scant attention paid to the task of 'elucidating the contours and limits of the wrong of exploitation' by criminal law theorists and commentators is 'astonishing'.[84]

Besides being a label attached to the wrong done in the type of crimes noted above, and 'a policy argument marshalled in opposition'[85] to certain practices, the case might be made that exploitation is a special type of wrongful behaviour that warrants a specific, tailored legal response: an offence that criminalises wrongful exploitation that occurs in the context of the doctor-patient relationship. Throughout this work, we have argued that, when wrongful exploitation occurs in the doctor-patient relationship, it is especially wrongful and harmful and should, therefore, be seen as a special case. But even though on the basis of such an approach, criminalisation would only extend to wrongful exploitation in this relationship (and perhaps other professional relationships that share the same characteristics of trust and unequal power), a broad spectrum of behaviour would still potentially be criminalised.

This brings us to the crux of the matter, and the reason why it is difficult to envisage either an offence or civil wrong of exploitation. The palpable reason why exploitation is not categorised as a category of legal wrong, in and of itself, is because it would be too vague and too complex for criminal or civil regulation. It would be too vague because the label of exploitation can be applied to such a wide variety of behaviours, as recognised by the Court of Appeal in *R v. SK*.[86] It would be too complex because of the ambiguity surrounding the essential elements of exploitation: some agreement would surely have to be reached as to when behaviour constitutes exploitation and whether this evaluation is process or outcome based, or a combination of the two. Lawmakers would face a challenging and perhaps impossible task to create a legal concept of exploitation that could be utilised in statute, that could regulate behaviour, and that the criminal and/or civil courts could apply. For the law requires a legally workable concept,

---

82 Duff 2007: 128.
83 Collins 2017: 169.
84 Collins 2015: 69.
85 Hill 1994: 650.
86 [2011] EWCA Crim 1691: 'In the modern world exploitation can and does take place, in many different forms. Perhaps the most obvious is that in which one human being is treated by another as an object under his or her control for a sexual purpose. But "slavery or servitude" and "forced labour" are not confined to exploitation of that sort. One person may exploit another in many different ways.' ([41] (Lindblom J)). Note also Chuang's warning about the 'overinclusiveness that increased attention to exploitation writ large [as a legal definition] might inspire.': Chuang 2014: 641.

the existence or non-existence of which can be evidenced.[87] This is a point made neatly by Ashcroft in his explanation of why it is consent, as opposed to autonomy, that is a legal concept:

> While the body of law relating to consent is enormous, and discussions of autonomy as the moral foundation for consent are similarly extensive, it is consent which is entrenched in legal discourse, in case law and in legislation, in large part because while 'consent' can be tested in various ways in litigation, 'autonomy' is more elusive ... So while the concept of 'autonomy' has an explanatory role in discussion *of* the law, it plays at most a small part *in* the law.[88]

Moreover, there is the difficult matter of harm. One of the roles of both the civil and criminal law is to hold the wrongdoer accountable for the harm caused. But there will be no accountability or redress for the wronged party unless the harm they suffer is recognised at law. We set out the way in which a doctor's exploitation will frequently wrong the patient *and* harm the patient's interests in chapter 2. Whilst the law does recognise and protect certain moral rights, thereby prohibiting some wrongs,[89] it is usually harms connected to setback to interests that the law recognises as actionable, as we have already noted.[90] The civil law generally requires proof of actual harm to the patient's interests caused by the doctor's actions.[91] For

---

87 This is no doubt the reason why s.3 of the Modern Slavery Act 2015, titled 'Meaning of exploitation', does not, in fact, provide a definition of exploitation, but simply refers to the commission of certain offences and 'securing services etc by force, threats or deception' or 'securing services etc from children and vulnerable persons'. But some statutory definitions do exist, and we discuss the statutory definition of exploitation specified to correspond with the offence under s.53(A) of the SOA in n.100 below.
88 Ashcroft 2018: 72 (emphasis in original). Foster and Herring have challenged the claim that autonomy's part in the law is small, noting that Article 8 of the European Convention on Human Rights 'gives autonomy, in its legal incarnation, its shape': Foster and Herring 2018: 73. However, Ashcroft is correct in his assertion that autonomy is not a legislative or common law concept because of the ambiguity surrounding it. This is not to say, however, that consent is an unproblematic legal concept, as we explored in chapter 5, part 2, section 1, text accompanying nn.24–39.
89 Such as the right to private life under Article 8 of the European Convention of Human Rights, protected under English domestic law by the tort of breach of confidence (or misuse of confidential information). See, e.g. *Campbell* v. *MGN* [2004] UKHL 22.
90 See the previous section, text accompanying nn.80–81.
91 We do not mean to include the tort of breach of confidence as an exception here (regarding which it was stated in *X* v. *Y* [1988] RPC 379, 391 (Rose J) and *R* v. *Department of Health, ex p Source Informatics* (1999) 49 BMLR 41 (Latham J), that the breach of confidence might in itself constitute harm), because we argued earlier that we have an interest in privacy that can be intruded on by others and set back if it is left in a worse condition than it was prior to the invasion. See chapter 2, text accompanying n.197. Likewise, the tort of battery, where the harm comprises of unconsented-to touching *per se* (a violation of the right to bodily integrity), also involves an interest that can be set back: the interest in liberty. See generally Scanlon 2009: 72.

instance, a violation of the right to autonomy could constitute medical negligence, and therefore an actionable wrong, if the doctor fails to inform the patient of a material risk of the proposed surgery that the reasonable person in the patient's position would wish to know about, and the patient consequently suffers harm due to that risk eventualising.[92]

Further, different types of exploitative behaviour can, of course, cause varying levels of harm. Some harms might warrant criminal liability, others may warrant civil law accountability, and some could warrant no legal regulation at all. This is not necessarily problematic. The law is capable of distinguishing between levels of a broad typology of the same behaviour and the degree of harm caused; for example, where there is a breach of duty, negligent behaviour that causes injury is caught by the tort of negligence and, when such negligence is gross and causes death, this constitutes a criminal wrong.[93] But what all of this demonstrates is that there can be no 'one-size-fits-all' approach to the legal regulation of exploitation.

Related to the above, there is a need to ensure that, in particular, the blunt weapon of the criminal law does not become relied on too readily.[94] Given the severe consequences for the individual who is prosecuted, and its stigmatising effects, the criminal law should never be utilised as a first resort. This is especially the case when appropriate civil law remedies are available, or the matter in question can be adjudicated by the doctors' professional regulatory body, the GMC. We concur with Collins's call for a cautious response to the push towards criminalisation of exploitation,[95] because exploitation is too opaque a concept to offer a sound basis for the creation of a generic criminal offence.[96] We have already highlighted the difficulty of producing a workable legal concept of exploitation because of the broadness and vagueness of the term. However, as Collins notes, 'conceptual clarity is improved if different types of interpersonal exploitation are identified, and if wrongfulness is explained in relation to a specific type of interpersonal exploitation'.[97] This explains the targeting of exploitative behaviour related to specific wrongs by

---

92   *Montgomery* v. *Lanarkshire Health Board*; *Chester* v. *Afshar* [18] (Lord Steyn): 'A rule requiring a doctor to abstain from performing an operation without the informed consent of a patient serves two purposes. It tends to avoid the occurrence of the particular physical injury the risk of which a patient is not prepared to accept. *It also ensures that due respect is given to the autonomy and dignity of each patient.*' (Emphasis added.)
93   *R* v. *Adomako* [1994] UKHL 6.
94   Also, we should be wary of adopting an overly punitive legal response in order to respond to the intense public reaction to breaches of trust and doctors' exploitation of patients. As Hall comments, 'due to the strength and emotional tenor of trust in physicians, patients … are subject to extreme feelings of betrayal once the limits of trust are breached': Hall 2005: 161.
95   Collins 2017.
96   Ibid: 172.
97   Ibid: 181.

the legislature.[98] When the Modern Slavery Act 2015 was at its Public Bill Committee stage in the House of Commons, for example, Karen Bradley MP stated that:

> Looked at as an offence on its own ... exploitation could cover some banal conduct ... We have a moral imperative here ... to help stamp out slavery from our society. I do not want to detract from what we are doing by creating offences that could undermine that desire ... If we are to achieve it, we need to ensure that we create clear offences that are focused on the severe abuse that amounts to modern slavery ... Seeking to cover any form of exploitation in our society risks diluting the effect of the Bill by potentially making a criminal of every one of us, confusing law enforcement and undermining the focus on the victims of serious abuse.[99]

It is for these are reasons that the offences which we have proposed in this book are specific and designed to target exploitative behaviour that we have argued is particularly wrongful and harmful. Our proposed offences are focused on certain variants of exploitative behaviour (sexual exploitation by doctors that is unlikely to be captured by existing offences, and persuading a person to request an assisted death through undue influence) in a similar way to the existing offence of paying for the sexual services of a prostitute subjected to force,[100] for example. Beyond this, neither a broader crime nor a tort of exploitation would be workable, or appropriate.

---

98 See also ibid.
99 Hansard, House of Commons Public Bill Committee on the Modern Slavery Bill 2014-15, col.102, at https://publications.parliament.uk/pa/cm201415/cmpublic/modernslavery/140902/pm/140902s01.htm accessed 9 March 2020.
100 SOA, s.53A. This offence occurs where C induces a prostitute to provide services for which A has made or promises payment. A narrow legislative definition of exploitative conduct then follows: 'C engages in exploitative conduct if—(a) C uses force, threats (whether or not relating to violence) or any other form of coercion, or (b) C practises any form of deception' (S.53A(3)). Furthermore, C must have 'engaged in that conduct for or in the expectation of gain for C or another person (apart from A or B)' (s.53A(1)(C)). Notably, when the provision was being debated during Committee stage in the House of Lords, Lord Brett noted that amendments had been made to address 'the fear that [the clause], as originally drafted, was too wide and that its definition could go beyond the exploitative and coercive circumstances which the offence was intended to cover': Hansard, vol.712, col.271, 1 July 2009, at https://publications.parliament.uk/pa/ld200809/ldhansrd/text/90701-0009.htm accessed 9 March 2020. Note also that the explanation of exploitation as it applies to the sexual exploitation offences under the SOA (ss.48–50) is also specific. According to s.51(2) SOA: 'For the purposes of sections 48 to 50, a person (B) is sexually exploited if—(a) on at least one occasion and whether or not compelled to do so, B offers or provides sexual services to another person in return for payment or a promise of payment to B or a third person, or (b) an indecent image of B is recorded [or streamed or otherwise transmitted]; and "sexual exploitation" is to be interpreted accordingly.'

iii) Modifying existing legal frameworks: a more feasible alternative?

a) Extending undue influence beyond the contractual context

> The doctrine of undue influence has a long pedigree as a means of aiding vulnerable persons whose will has been overborne by another ... there are powerful moral grounds for extending the law as it is developed in transaction contexts so that it offers protection proportionate to the vulnerability and interests of patients in the context of medical treatment.[101]

As noted above and discussed in chapter 3, the law already recognises that patients can be vulnerable to exploitation through presumed undue influence in a doctor-patient relationship which is based in contract law, and the courts of equity have applied a liberal approach, providing relief in a variety of cases involving relationships where one party exercises dominion over the other.[102] But of course, not all health care is provided under a contract, especially in countries which have a publicly funded health care system such as the UK. Whilst it may be true that, in considering (reputational) implications for a defendant, contract law can be more appropriately expansive in its regulation than criminal or tort law,[103] the nature of the wrongful behaviour in question remains the same whether it occurs in private contractual or publicly funded health care.[104] As Smith observes:

> Wrongful behaviour in a contractual situation is the same as wrongful behaviour generally in private law, that is, it is an infringement of another person's rights. Thus what counts as wrongdoing ... is established on general considerations determining what rights and duties people have and not on considerations unique to contract law. *The existence of a contract is peripheral to the application of the wrongdoing principle.*[105]

Given this, there are surely grounds to consider whether the protection that undue influence can offer should also be offered to patients who face exploitation perpetrated through pressure or the overbearing of their will outwith a contractual relationship with their doctor. Indeed, it is arguably inequitable that those who are in a position to pay (and thus, those who tend to be more

---

101 Pattinson 2002: 305–306.
102 Bell 2007: 561.
103 'A refusal to enforce a contract is typically less serious than a finding of criminal or tortious liability ... For this reason, there is in principle a gap between what is unlawful generally and what is wrongful behaviour in a contractual situation – as English courts recognise.': Smith 1997: 351–352.
104 As demonstrated by the accounts of the wrongs done to them by Ian Paterson's private and NHS patients. See Paterson Inquiry 2020: 12-97.
105 Smith 1997: 351 (emphasis added).

equal in social standing to the doctor upon whom they rely) are offered protection through undue influence and other established contractual doctrines, when patients who cannot afford to pay for their health care are not shielded in the same manner.

We are not the first to advocate for the extension of undue influence beyond the confines of contractual law to the wider medical context. Pattinson has proposed a new category of presumed undue influence where the patient can prove:

a   the relationship between the parties is one of patient and medical advisor;
b   the medical advisor has put pressure on the patient to reach a particular decision (i.e. the decision reached); and
c   the patient needs persuasion for reasons other than an initial failure to understand the full details of relevant medical science.[106]

Whilst Pattinson limits his proposal to decisions pertaining to medical treatment, we have considered undue influence as a tool that could address not only exploitation which relates to such decisions, but also to patients' decisions to engage in sexual behaviour with their doctors, and patients' decisions to request an assisted death. We have proposed a new criminal law offence of sexual exploitation that includes the element of undue influence where the doctor obtains the patient's acquiescence through making a coercive or irresistible inducement to catch sexually exploitative behaviour that could well fall outside current criminal law offences.[107] We have also cautiously supported the application of undue influence within the tort of battery as another means of catching such exploitative behaviour, albeit that our advocacy of this alternative was more muted because we do not perceive battery as being the best fit for the doctor's exploitation.[108] Finally, we suggested that undue influence could be the means through which to deal with the risk of exploitation by way of relatives or carers pressurising patients into requesting an assisted death.[109]

In seeking to extend undue influence beyond the law of contract there are, however, a number of challenges and limitations that need to be acknowledged. First, there is the ambiguity surrounding the concept of undue influence that we alluded to in chapter 6.[110] Whilst the existence of various legal accounts of undue influence offers flexibility, this flexibility also poses a notable challenge: the lack of clear meaning. As Bell explains, undue influence:

---

106 Pattinson 2002: 310–311.
107 See chapter 5, part 2, section 1.
108 To recap, the wrong of unconsented-to touching fails to convey the essence of the wrong perpetrated by the doctor – the violation of trust and wrongful exploitation within a dependent relationship, the breach of duty to act in the patient's best interests rather than self-interest. See chapter 5, part 2, section 2.i.
109 See chapter 6, section 4.
110 Ibid.

is ill-defined in scope, for the courts [of equity] have consistently refused to fetter their discretion by rigid rules ... The problem is compounded by the fact that undue influence is an unhelpfully diverse doctrine: although it is typically applied in cases of personal relationships, it is also capable of applying in other contexts ... [in] relationships of trust and confidence and relationships of authority ...[111]

At the crux of the matter is how to conceptualise the level of influence that brings into question the true nature of the patient's consent. In the words of Staughton LJ in *Re T*, 'in order for an apparent consent or refusal of consent to be less than a true consent or refusal, there must be such a degree of external influence as to persuade the patient to depart from her own wishes, to an extent that the law regards it as undue. I can suggest no more precise test than that.'[112] In large part, this is because the level of pressure needed in order to make influence undue is variable. 'The degree of pressure required will inevitably depend on the *nature* of the relationship, taking into account ... "the *forcefulness* of the personality of the other"'[113] and how *vulnerable* one is to the other's pressure. What is more, 'both at law and in equity it has long been recognised that an influence may be subtle [and] insidious ... The degree of pressure to turn persuasion or appeals to affection into undue influence may ... be very little.'[114]

In this work, we have followed Birks' definition that 'undue influence consists in unconscionable exploitation of influence'.[115] To answer the critical question as to 'whether or not the influence has invaded the free volition of the [person] to withstand the influence',[116] we have advocated a (modified) existing assessment of undue influence model which could offer a means of resolving the matter of when influence becomes undue.[117] However, we recognise that the variability of this, and the need for this to be assessed on a case-by-case basis, will continue.

The second challenge is the potential judicial unwillingness to extend the application of undue influence to the doctor-patient relationship outside the laws of contract and equity, as expressed by Staughton LJ:

> The cases on undue influence in the law of property and contract are not, in my opinion, applicable in the different context of consent to

---

111 Bell 2007: 556. See also Quinn and others 2010: 114.
112 *Re T (Adult: Refusal of Treatment)* [1993] Fam 95 (CA), [57].
113 Bell 2006: 558, quoting *Daniel v. Drew* [2005] EWCA Civ 507, [32] (Ward LJ) (emphasis added).
114 *Re T (Adult: Refusal of Treatment)* [1993] Fam 95 (CA), [50] (Butler-Sloss P).
115 Birks 2004: 34. See chapter 3, text accompanying n.241; chapter 6, section 4.
116 *Thompson v. Foy* [2009] EWHC 1076 (Ch), [101] (Lewison J).
117 See chapter 6, section 4. Aspects of this model are directed towards an assisted dying request, but these parts could be removed in an undue influence assessment model of wider applicability.

medical or surgical treatment. The wife who guarantees her husband's debts, or the widower who leaves all his property to his housekeeper, are not in the same situation as a patient faced with the need for medical treatment.[118]

We have noted, however, that more recent judicial analysis of undue influence has placed emphasis on one party's unfair exploitation of a relationship with another in which they have greater power.[119] Moreover, we concur with Pattison that, given that medical treatment decisions are of 'potentially greater importance' than decisions such as those alluded to by Staughton LJ above, this strengthens the case for extending the doctrine of undue influence to the doctor-patient relationship regardless of whether the relationship is of a contractual nature. And although we should not assume that all patients are automatically vulnerable, especially if seeking medical treatment for a minor ailment, for example, our argument that all patients are potentially vulnerable also supports this extension.[120]

The fact remains, however, that without the existence of a contract between patient and health care provider, an alternative doctrinal framework in which to situate exploitative behaviour – a means of legal categorisation – is required. As discussed above, we have considered the potential that both criminal and tort law have to house a legal wrong involving undue influence, and proposed that the criminal law should only be resorted to when the wrong is of sufficient magnitude. In other cases, where a doctor's exploitation is facilitated through undue influence, we suggest that the law of equity could offer a suitable venue: namely fiduciary law. We explore this further in the next subsection.

Finally, even if it proves possible to extrapolate basic principle of contractual doctrine to doctor-patient relationships in non-contractual situations, we wish to highlight the limitation that undue influence is not applicable to *all* exploitation in this relationship. The protection that the doctrine offers only applies where consent has been given because of undue influence. It would thus fail to catch exploitative behaviour in other contexts, such as where the patient exploited is unconscious, or is unaware of the doctor's (exploitative) behaviour, such as in our *Dr X* and *Mr Y* scenario.[121] But, as we will explore next, fiduciary law could offer the doctrinal framework that catches *all* exploitative behaviour which involves a doctor acting out of self-interest, and, notably, the connection

---

118 *Re T (Adult: Refusal of Treatment)* [1993] Fam 95 (CA), [57] (Staughton LJ) (see also [50] (Butler-Sloss P); *U* v. *Centre for Reproductive Medicine* [2002] EWCA Civ 565; *A Local Authority* v. *Mrs A and Mr A* [2010] EWHC 1549 (Fam); Pattison 2002.
119 See chapter 3, section 8.
120 Pattison 2002: 309; chapter 4, section 2.
121 See chapter 2, section 3.iii, text accompanying nn.160–174.

between (presumed) undue influence[122] and fiduciary law arguably already exists.[123]

b) Pushing the boundaries of recognised fiduciary obligations

In the earlier section on the professional response to exploitation in the doctor-patient relationship, we proposed that the doctor as fiduciary should be the explicit ethical premise that is at foundation of medical ethics education and CPD. What we propose here would yield a symmetrical approach between law and medical ethics, for we are taking forward the argument we made in chapter 5 in the specific context of sexual exploitation, and calling for recognition of fiduciary obligations to tackle exploitation in the doctor-patient relationship.[124]

Our immediate challenge is to manoeuvre around the afore-discussed apparent judicial reluctance to apply fiduciary law in this jurisdiction, which might be partly explained because English law has tended to view the concept of fiduciary relationship as only existing within the confines of property law and in respect

---

122 For our earlier discussion of presumed and actual undue influence, see chapter 3, section 8, text accompanying nn.243–244.

123 See Haughey 2012: 134. Whilst defending jurisprudence of the courts in England and Wales that supports this connection, such as *Hammond* v. *Osborn* [2002] EWCA Civ 885, Haughey critiques the House of Lords judgment in *Royal Bank of Scotland* v. *Etridge* [2001] (see chapter 3, nn.243–244) which, he argues, fails to recognise the correlation between presumed undue influence and fiduciary obligation: Haughey 2012: 144–147. He argues that, in the case of presumed undue influence, 'the trusting party reposes trust and confidence (deferential trust) in a trusted party, they are giving that trusted party access to their decision-making faculties (asset)... for the defined and limited purpose of acting in their interest. Thus, a limited access arrangement occurs. The result is that the trusted party *is* a fiduciary, at least to the extent of the scope of the limited access. Therefore, the trusted party is prohibited from deriving an unauthorized benefit from that arrangement.' (Emphasis in original.) Note that Haughey follows Flannigan's position that a limited access arrangement to the trusting party's assets is the test for the existence of a fiduciary arrangement: Haughey 2012: 131; Flannigan 2009: 379. This fiduciary, limited access arrangement exists between doctor and patient as the latter provides the doctor with access to his body, confidential information and decision-making faculties (assets), in order that the doctor can treat him (Haughey 2012: 131 and 134, n.33). Support for finding synergy between presumed undue influence and fiduciary law can also be found in Duggan 2003. For a contrasting view, see Conaglen 2010.

124 Readers may thus wish to revisit the discussion of fiduciary obligations in chapter 5, part 2, section 3 at this point. We note that the argument we present here in respect of fiduciary duties may not extend to the medical research context. We chose to look at medical research to illustrate our account of vulnerability in chapter 4 rather than embarking on a broader consideration of exploitation in medical research (see chapter 1, text accompanying n.25, for our rationale for so doing). However, it is worth noting that the fiduciary duty that we have argued exists in the doctor-patient relationship may be more arguable in respect of researchers who are not also the participants' doctors, since there could be a 'considerable tension between the interests of the researchers and subjects'. See further Wertheimer 2011: 114.

of equitable limitations on ownership.[125] Fiduciary law would need to be conceived as more than a mechanism for controlling the *abuse of property* improperly obtained from relationships of trust,[126] to also being a means to address the *abuse (or misuse) of the person* in such relationships. In short, the recognition of fiducial obligations under the law in England and Wales would need to extend to the protection of the patient's non-material interests in the doctor-patient relationship, a reflection of McLachlin J's approach in the Supreme Court of Canada in *Norberg* v. *Wynrib*:

> Society has an abiding interest in ensuring that the power entrusted to physicians by us, both collectively and individually, [should] not be used in corrupt ways ... the plaintiff ... has a striking personal interest in obtaining professional medical care *free of exploitation for the physician's private purposes* ...[127]

McLachlin J appears to have had in mind the interest all patients have in placing their trust in the medical profession to receive medical care and treatment without exploitation, with the doctor's primary concern being to protect their patients' (non-material) interests rather than serving their own. As we see it, this is what causes fiduciary law to be the most appropriate means for dealing with the wrong and harm of a doctor's exploitation of her patient. This wrong is committed by the doctor through allowing the conflict to arise between her duty of loyalty[128] to the patient and her own self-interest. The doctor's gain is facilitated through her breach of the patient's deferential trust[129] and an abuse of her more powerful position. Fiduciary obligations thereby incorporate a wider moral lens that is able to recognise the 'totality'[130] of the wrong of this behaviour.[131]

We are not advocating the extension of fiduciary law and the law of equity to other doctor-patient contexts, absent exploitation, such as failing to allow a patient access to her medical records. There has been a resistance to construe all a doctor's obligations as being fiducial, and case law recognises that '[a]

---

125 Shepherd 1981: 52.
126 Which would explain why Browne-Wilkinson LJ seemed prepared to accept the possible existence of a fiduciary duty relating to an abuse of trust for the doctor's personal profit in *Sidaway*; the fiduciary relationship would exist over the profit through the imposition of a constructive trust.
127 *Norberg* v. *Wynrib* [1992] 2 SCR 226, [74] (emphasis added). See also the broader construction of assets in n.123; Joyce 2002.
128 On loyalty as a fiduciary duty or a juridical constraint upon fiduciaries, see Samet 2014; Smith 2014. On the application of fiduciary obligations to the doctor-patient relationship, see Haughey 2012: 131.
129 On deferential trust, see n.123 and chapter 3, n.72.
130 *Norberg* v. *Wynrib*, [61] (McLachlin J).
131 It should thus be clear that we disagree with those authors who challenge such a moral conception of the fiduciary obligation and reject the argument that being a fiduciary involves a duty to avoid a conflict of interest. See Penner 2014; Conaglen 2010: chapter 5.

relationship may properly be described as "fiduciary" for some purposes, but not for others.'[132] To adopt an alternative, broad status-based approach[133] to finding fiduciary obligations, and thereby extend the remit of fiduciary law to all areas of a doctor's interaction with a patient, would result in both an unwieldy and overbroad legal response. Advocating such an approach would be unlikely to quell judicial reluctance to accept fiduciary obligations in the doctor-patient relationship in this jurisdiction.

An initial application of fiduciary law to sexual exploitation, as we proposed in chapter 5, may help appease such judicial concerns, however. If it proves possible to take the initial step of extending fiducial obligations in this particular context, connections between the breach of the professional duty not to act out of self-interest could then be drawn to advocate the limited further extension to other instances of exploitation in the doctor-patient relationship, such as those cases we discussed involving infertility doctors using their own sperm in their patients' artificial insemination treatment and doctors offering patients inappropriate and unjustified medical treatment.[134] Our contention that fiduciary obligations should only apply in circumstances involving exploitation chimes with Flannigan's identification of the fundamental prohibition that gives rise to a fiduciary obligation: not to act out of self-interest.[135] This supports our proposed exclusion of any behaviour absent such self-interest (for instance, failing to inform the patient of risks attached to medical treatment because the doctor considers the risks to be negligible, refusing to grant patients access to their medical records, or breaching confidentiality in order to protect others[136]) from the scope of fiduciary law. It is also notable that existing avenues for legal redress exist in relation to such behaviour. As Sopinka J has cautioned, 'fiduciary duties should not be superimposed on these common law duties simply to improve the nature or extent of the remedy.'[137]

Next, we need to address the question of *when* exploitation should be actionable under fiduciary law.[138] That is, would the patient need to establish that the exploitation caused harm, such as a recognised psychiatric condition, or would mental distress suffice? We have highlighted the way in which a doctor's exploitation and breach of trust can cause mental distress and feelings of shame and betrayal, for instance, and the cases that we have examined demonstrate how a doctor's exploitation of his patient is so often harmful to the patient's interests.

---

132 *McInerney* v. *MacDonald* [1992] 2 SCR 138, 149 (La Forest J).
133 Bartlett 1997: 195–196.
134 See chapter 3, section 4.
135 Flannigan 2004: 52.
136 Note that whilst Flannigan argues that the function of the law of breach of confidence is akin to that of the law of fiduciary obligations, he is considering the context in which confidence is breached for reasons relating to opportunism: ibid: 71. However, this essential element of acting in self-interest is not present where confidentiality in the doctor-patient relationship is breached to protect others in cases such as *W* v. *Egdell* [1990] Ch. 359 CA.
137 *Norberg* v. *Wynrib*, [147] (Sopinka J).
138 On the matter of remedies, see Ost 2016: 229–230.

As we see it, therefore, where a patient can establish that his doctor's exploitation caused him to suffer mental distress then this should constitute actionable damage *without* the need to prove that this has led to a psychiatric condition.[139] We agree with Allen's observation, albeit in a broader context, that 'the harm is real, even if it is not a psychiatric disorder'[140] and, in a professional relationship so dependent on trust, the need to deter the abuse of power is clear.[141]

Finally, here we should consider whether our call for recognition of fiduciary obligations could be expanded to include exploitative behaviour in other intimate and confidential professional relationships. Whilst other such relationships are not the focus of this work, and we do not have the necessary space to offer any detailed analysis, any extension of fiduciary law to exploitation in the doctor-patient relationship has the *potential* to be extrapolated further to similar intimate and confidential relationships. That is provided that they give rise to the same fundamental obligation to act in the party with inferior power's interests and not to serve the professional's own, such as in the case of lawyer and client.[142] Although we perceive the doctor-patient relationship to be the paradigm example of such relationships, for the same reasons that we provided when considering the application of our proposed sexual exploitation offence,[143] we would support the application of fiduciary obligations to all professionals who act in an exploitative way in intimate and confidential professional relationships of trust.

5) Final thoughts

Our aim throughout this work has been to shed light on a much-used but lesser-explored concept in health care ethics and law in the particular context and dynamics of the doctor-patient relationship. Through our conceptual, theoretical analysis and our case studies, we have endeavoured to reveal the complexities of exploitation as it occurs in this relationship, and to reveal the nature of wrong – the violation of the ethos of a distinctive intimate and confidential professional relationship – and the harms that it causes. We have drawn attention to the elements that facilitate exploitation's occurrence and suggested what further steps could, and should, be taken in professional medical ethics and regulation and at law to tackle and respond to exploitation. In drawing this work to a conclusion, we wish to make two final observations.

---

139 Note that, under the existing law (in relation to property of a trust), it is not necessary to establish that the beneficiary suffered harm provided that the fiduciary benefits from their breach of duty: see *Boardman v. Phipps* [1967] 2 AC 46, 116; Haughey 2012: 131.
140 Allen 1996: 76.
141 Ibid.
142 We also note that undue influence has specifically been recognised to occur in religious/spiritual advisor relationships in English law for centuries, in cases including *Norton v. Relly* (1764) 2 Eden 286 (actual undue influence) and *Allcard v. Skinner* (1887) 36 ChD 145 (presumed undue influence). See further Bell 2007: 592–594.
143 See chapter 5, part 2, section 1, text accompanying nn.51–55.

First, we do not advocate the overuse of exploitation as a shorthand concept.[144] Invoking exploitation without proper explanation of what is meant by the term cannot provide a means of analysing and finding resolution for relevant bioethical dilemmas involving the doctor-patient relationship. We must be clear on what does and does not amount to exploitation, and on different variants of exploitation, in order to cast light on what it is that underpins our ethical opposition to certain practices. Consider, for instance, that our analysis has revealed more than one variant of exploitation in the doctor-patient relationship, the most significant of which we have found to be:

1 where the doctor misuses the patient by taking advantage of a vulnerability and, in some cases, the patient is, and may remain, unaware of the exploitation; and
2 where the doctor (or another) takes advantage of and misuses the patient through exercising undue influence.

These are both variants of the same wrong, and there may sometimes be a degree of overlap between them,[145] but we risk clarity of understanding and finding an effective means (regulatory and legal) of redress if we fail to recognise that exploitation can be perpetrated in different ways through the targeting of particular vulnerabilities and circumstances which make a person more susceptible to pressure or coercion.

Secondly, we recognise that, just as in other contexts, it is not possible to *eliminate* exploitation in the doctor-patient relationship. As Wood notes, 'exploitation is ... a pervasive fact of the social life of human beings'.[146] We can attempt to combat it and take preventative measures but, even then, we cannot realistically eradicate it. In an earlier chapter, we provided the example of gynaecologist Dr Levy[147] who exploited patients by secretly taking explicit photographs of their genitals. When accused of being at fault for not discovering his actions earlier, a lawyer acting for the hospital concerned commented that 'it's one of those situations where no matter what rules and regulations you put in place ... there's not a thing you can do to prevent [it]'.[148] Of course, such a claim may have a ring of defensiveness about it, but a doctor who is determined to exploit her

---

144 See also Wertheimer 2007: 254.
145 Say, for instance, a doctor at a private sector clinic uses very selective success rates to persuade and pressurise women in their forties seeking assisted reproduction services to undergo fertility treatment at the clinic (see chapter 3, n.75). She would be taking advantage of patients' susceptibility to her offer because of their desperate desire to have a child (a vulnerability) *and* exercising undue influence.
146 Wood 1995: 156.
147 See chapter 3, section 2.
148 Matt Pearce, 'Johns Hopkins gynecologist with camera: Victims to get $190 million', *Los Angeles Times* (Los Angeles) 21 July 2014, available at http://www.latimes.com/nation/nationnow/la-na-nn-johns-hopkins-gynecologist-photos-settlement-20140721-story.html accessed 14 April 2020.

patients will almost inevitably be presented with opportunities to do so because of the intimate, confidential nature of the relationship. And we have noted that, outwith our specific focus, exploitation exists in health care beyond the doctor exploiting the patient, to the patient as the exploiter within this relationship, and to other health care professionals who have intimate professional relationship with patients such as nurses. We leave further analysis of exploitation in health care to other authors, but hope that this work has provided the groundwork for future research by identifying some of the critical issues that will need to be explored in such a broader-scoped study, and by offering a detailed, theoretically informed account of exploitation in the doctor-patient relationship that can be taken forward.

References

Accreditation Council for Graduate Medical Education, *ACGME Common Program Requirements (Post-Doctoral Educational Program)* (ACGME 2020a).

Accreditation Council for Graduate Medical Education, *ACGME Common Program Requirements (Residency)* (ACGME 2020b).

Adlington K and others, 'The General Medical Council and Doctors' Financial Interests' (2015) 350 *British Medical Journal* h474.

Allen T, 'Civil liability for Sexual Exploitation in Professional Relationships' (1996) 59 *Modern Law Review* 56.

Almeida L and others, 'Why Healthy Subjects Volunteer for Phase I Studies and How They Perceive Their Participation' (2007) 63 *European Journal of Clinical Pharmacology* 207.

American Medical Association, *AMA Code of Medical Ethics* (2016), at: https://www.ama-assn.org/sites/ama-assn.org/files/corp/media-browser/principles-of-medical-ethics.pdf accessed 22 July 2020.

Anderson J, 'Autonomy and Vulnerability Entwined' in Mackenzie C and others (eds) *Vulnerability: New Essays in Ethics and Feminist Philosophy* (Oxford University Press 2013).

Anderson Spickard W and others, 'A Continuing Medical Education Approach to Improve Sexual Boundaries of Physicians' (2008) 72 *Bulletin of the Menninger Clinic* 38.

Archard D, 'Exploited Consent' (1994) 25(3) *Journal of Social Philosophy* 92.

Archard D, *Sexual Consent* (Westview Press 1998).

Archard D, 'The Wrong of Rape' (2007) 57(228) *Philosophical Quarterly* 374.

Aristotle and others, *The Nicomachean Ethics* (Oxford University Press 2009).

Ashcroft RE and others, 'Teaching Medical Ethics and Law Within Medical Education: A Model for the UK Core Curriculum' (1998) 24 *Journal of Medical Ethics* 188.

Ashcroft RE, 'Law and the Perils of Philosophical Grafts' (2018) 44 *Journal of Medical Ethics* 72.

Ashworth A, 'Is the Criminal Law a Lost Cause?' (2000) 116 *Law Quarterly Review* 225.

Askola H, *Legal Responses to Trafficking in Women for Sexual Exploitation in the European Union.* (Hart 2007).

Australian Health Practitioner Regulation Agency and National Board, *Guidelines: Mandatory Notifications about Registered Health Practitioners* (AHPRA 2020).

Baier A, 'Trust and Antitrust' (1986) 96 *Ethics* 231.

Ballantyne A, 'Benefits to Research Subjects in International Trials: Do They Reduce Exploitation or Increase Undue Inducement?' (2008) 8 *Developing World Bioethics* 178.

Barnard D, 'Vulnerability and Trustworthiness: Polestars of Professionalism in Healthcare' (2016) 25 *Cambridge Quarterly of Healthcare Ethics* 288.

Bartlett P, 'Doctors as Fiduciaries: Equitable Regulation of the Doctor-Patient Relationship' (1997) 5 *Medical Law Review* 193.

Battin MP and others, 'Legal Physician-assisted Dying in Oregon and the Impact on Patients in "Vulnerable" Groups' (2007) 33 *Journal of Medical Ethics* 591.

Bauman AE and others, 'Getting it Right: Why Bother with Patient-centred Care?' (2003) 179 *Medical Journal of Australia* 253.

Beauchamp TL, *Standing on Principles: Collected Essays* (Oxford University Press 2010).

Beauchamp TL and Childress JF, *Principles of Biomedical Ethics* (7th edn, Oxford University Press 2013).

Beecher H, 'Ethics and Clinical Research' (1966) 274 *New England Journal of Medicine* 1354.

Bell A, 'Abuse of a Relationship: Undue Influence in English and French Law' (2007) 15 *European Review of Private Law* 555.

Benn SI, 'Privacy, Freedom, and Respect for Persons', in Schoeman FD (ed), *Philosophical Dimensions of Privacy: An Anthology* (Cambridge University Press 1984).

Bennett, B, 'Posthumous Reproduction and the Meanings of Autonomy' (1999) 23 *Melbourne University Law Review* 286.

Bickel J, 'Human Values in Teaching Program in the Clinical Education of Medical Students' (1987) 62 *Journal of Medical Education* 369.

Biggs H, 'Madonna Minus Child. Or – Wanted: Dead or Alive! The Right to Have a Dead Partner's Child' (1997) 5 *Feminist Legal Studies* 225.

Biggs H, 'I Don't Want to be a Burden! A Feminist Reflects on Women's Experiences of Death and Dying' in Sheldon S and Thomson M (eds), *Feminist Perspectives in Health Care Law* (Cavendish 1998).

Biggs H, *Death with Dignity and the Law* (Hart 2001).

Biggs, H 'Criminalising Carers: Death Desires and Assisted Dying Outlaws' in Brooks-Gordon, B and others (eds), *Death Rites and Rights* (Hart 2007).

Biggs H, 'Legitimate compassion or compassionate legitimation? Reflections on the policy for prosecutors in respect of cases of encouraging or assisting suicide' (2011) 19 *Feminist Legal Studies* 83.

Bigwood R, 'Undue Influence: "Impaired Consent" or "Wicked Exploitation"?' (1996) 16 *Oxford Journal of Legal Studies* 503.

Birks P, 'Undue Influence as Wrongful Exploitation' (2004) 120 *Law Quarterly Review* 34.

Bismark M and others, 'Sexual Misconduct by Health Professionals in Australia, 2011–2016: A Retrospective Analysis of Notifications to Health Regulators' (2020) *Medical Journal of Australia* doi:10.5694/mja2.50706.

Bogart JH, 'Reconsidering Rape: Rethinking the Conceptual Foundations of Rape Law' (1995) 8(1) *Canadian Journal of Law and Jurisprudence* 159.

Bogg A and Stanton-Ife J, 'Protecting the Vulnerable: Legality, Harm and Theft' (2003) 23 *Legal Studies* 402.

Bracken-Roche D and others, 'The Concept of "Vulnerability" in Research Ethics: An In-depth Analysis of Policies and Guidelines' (2017) 15 *Health Research Policy and Systems* 8.

Bratuskins PA and others, 'Sexual Harassment of Australian Female General Practitioners by Patients' (2013) 199 *Medical Journal of Australia* 454.

Brazier M, 'Do No Harm – Do Patients Have Responsibilities Too?' (2006) 65 *Cambridge Law Journal* 397.

Brazier M 'Exploitation and Enrichment: The Paradox of Medical Experimentation' (2008) 34 *Journal of Medical Ethics* 180.

Brazier M and Ost S, *Medicine and Bioethics in the 'Theatre' of the Criminal Process* (Cambridge University Press 2013).

British Medical Association, *Transparency and Doctors with Competing Interests: Guidance from the BMA* (British Medical Association 2017).

Brody H, *Ethical Decisions in Medicine* (2nd edn, Little, Brown and Company 1981).

Brody H, *The Healer's Power* (Yale University Press 1992).

Buchanan A, *Ethics, Efficiency, and the Market*. (Rowman and Allanheld 1985).

Buchhandler-Raphael M, 'Criminalizing Coerced Submission in the Workplace and in the Academy' (2010a) 19 *Columbia Journal of Gender and Law* 409.

Buchhandler-Raphael M, 'Sexual Abuse of Power' (2010b) 21 *University of Florida Journal of Law & Public Policy* 77.

Buchhandler-Raphael M, 'The Failure of Consent: Re-Conceptualizing Rape as Sexual Abuse of Power' (2011) 18 *Michigan Journal of Gender & Law* 147.

Butler J, 'The Modern Doctor's Dilemma: Rationing and Ethics in Healthcare' (1999) 92 *Journal of the Royal Society of Medicine* 416.

Butler J, *Precarious Life: The Powers of Mourning and Violence* (Verso Books 2004).

Care Quality Commission, *The State of Care in Independent Acute Hospitals* (Care Quality Commission 2018).

Carrese JA and others, 'The Essential Role of Medical Ethics Education in Achieving Professionalism: The Romanell Report' (2015) 90(6) *Academic Medicine* 744.

Case P, *Compensating Child Sexual Abuse in England and Wales* (Cambridge University Press 2007).

Chadwick R and others (eds), *The Right to Know and the Right Not to Know: Genetic Privacy and Responsibility* (2nd edn, Cambridge University Press 2014).

Chamberlain E, 'Revisiting Canada's Approach to Fiduciary Relationships', in Robertson A and Tilbury M (eds), *Divergences in Private Law* (Hart 2016).

Chamberlain JM, 'Malpractice, Criminality and Medical Regulation: Reforming the Role of the GMC in Fitness to Practise Panels' (2017) 25(1) *Medical Law Review* 1.

Charles C and others, 'Decision-Making in the Physician-Patient Encounter: Revisiting the Shared Treatment Decision-Making Model' (1999) 49 *Social Science & Medicine* 651.

Chen-Wishart M, 'Undue Influence: Beyond Impaired Consent and Wrongdoing towards a Relational Analysis' in A Burrows and A Roger (eds), *Mapping the Law: Essays in Honour of Peter Birks* (Oxford University Press 2006).

Chisholm A and others, *Setting Standards: The Views of Members of the Public and Doctors on the Standards of Care and Practice They Expect of Doctors* (Picker Institute 2006).

Christman J, *The Politics of Persons, Individual Autonomy and Socio-Historical Selves* (Cambridge University Press 2009).

Chuang J, 'Exploitation Creep and the Unmaking of Human Trafficking Law' (2014) 108 *The American Journal of International Law* 609.

Clark CC and Kimsma GK, '"Medical Friendships" in Assisted Dying' (2004) 13 *Cambridge Quarterly of Healthcare Ethics* 61.

Clarke HF and Driever MJ, (1983) 'Vulnerability: The Development of a Construct for Nursing', in Chinn PL (ed) *Advances in Nursing Theory Development* (Aspen 1983).

Clough B, 'Disability and Vulnerability: Challenging the Capacity/Incapacity Binary' (2017) 16 *Social Policy and Society* 469.

Coggon J, 'Varied and Principled Understandings of Autonomy in English Law: Justifiable Inconsistency or Blinkered Moralism?' (2007) 15 *Health Care Analysis* 235.

Coggon J, 'Would Responsible Medical Lawyers Lose Their Patients?' (2012) 20 *Medical Law Review* 130.

Coggon J, 'Mental Capacity Law, Autonomy and Best Interests: An Argument for Conceptual and Practical Clarity in the Court of Protection' (2016) 24 *Medical Law Review* 396.

Cohen M and others, 'Sanctions Against Sexual Abuse of Patients by Doctors: Sex Differences in Attitudes Among Young Family Physicians' (1995) 153 *Canadian Medical Association Journal* 169.

Colburn B, 'Autonomy, Voluntariness and Assisted Dying' (2020) 46 *Journal of Medical Ethics* 316.

Coleman P, 'Sex in Power Dependency Relationships: Taking Unfair Advantage of the "Fair" Sex' (1988) 53 *Albany Law Review* 95.

College of Physicians and Surgeons of Ontario, *Final Report of the Task Force on Sexual Abuse of Patients* (College of Physicians and Surgeons of Ontario 1991).

College of Physicians and Surgeons of Ontario, *Maintaining Appropriate Boundaries and Preventing Sexual Abuse* (College of Physicians and Surgeons of Ontario 2008).

Collins J, 'The Contours of "Vulnerability"' in Wallbank J and Herring J (eds), *Vulnerabilities, Care and Family Law* (Routledge 2013).

Collins J, *'A Study of Exploitation for the Criminal Law'* (DPhil thesis, University of Oxford, 2015).

Collins J, 'Exploitation of Persons and the Limits of the Criminal Law' (2017) 3 *Criminal Law Review* 169.

Colt H and others, *The Picture of Health: Medical Ethics and the Movies* (Oxford University Press 2011).

Competition and Markets Authority (CMA), *Private Healthcare Market Investigation: Private Report* CMA 25 (HMSO 2014).

Competition and Markets Authority (CMA), 'Private Healthcare Market Investigation: Explanatory Note to Accompany the Private Healthcare Market Investigation (Variation and Commencement) Order 2017' (2017), at https://assets.publishing.service.gov.uk/media/59034b6140f0b606e3000273/private-healthcare-variation-order-2017-explanatory-note.pdf accessed 22 July 2020.

Conaglen M, *Fiduciary Loyalty: Protecting the Due Performance of Non-Fiduciary Duties* (Hart 2010)

Coney S, *The Unfortunate Experiment* (Penguin Books 1988).

Conrad P, *The Medicalization of Society: On the Transformation of Human Conditions* (JHU Press 2007).

Cooper Z and others, *The Price Ain't Right? Hospital Prices and Health Spending on the Privately Insured* (Health Care Pricing Project 2015), at http://www.healthcarepricingproject.org/papers/paper-1 accessed 22 July 2020.

Corfield L and others, 'Prepared for practice? UK Foundation doctors' confidence in dealing with ethical issues in the workplace' (2020) *Journal of Medical Ethics* Published Online First: 10 April 2020. doi: 10.1136/medethics-2019-105961

Corlett A, 'The Nature and Value of the Moral Right to Privacy' (2002) 16 *Public Affairs Quarterly* 329.

Coulter A, *The Autonomous Patient* (Nuffield Trust 2002).

Council for Healthcare Regulatory Excellence, *Clear Sexual Boundaries between Healthcare Professionals and Patients: Responsibilities of Healthcare Professionals* (CHRE 2008a).

Council for Healthcare Regulatory Excellence, *Learning about Sexual Boundaries between Healthcare Professionals and Patients: a Report on Education and Training* (CHRE 2008b).

Council on Ethical and Judicial Affairs, American Medical Association, 'Sexual Misconduct in the Practice of Medicine (1991) 266 *Journal of the American Medical Association* 2741.

Coverdale JH and Turbott SH, 'Teaching Medical Students about the Appropriateness of Social and Sexual Contact Between Doctors and their Patients: Evaluation of a Programme' (1997) 31 *Medical Education* 335.

Coverdale JH and others, 'National Survey on Physicians' Attitudes Toward Social and Sexual Contact with Patients' (1994) 87 *Southern Medical Journal* 1067.

Coyle L and Atkinson S, 'Vulnerability as Practice in Diagnosing Multiple Conditions' (2019) 45 *BMJ Medical Humanities* 278.

Cristel RT and others, 'Evaluation of Selfies and Filtered Selfies and Effects on First Impressions' (2021) 41 *Aesthetic Surgery Journal* 122.

Crown Prosecution Service, *Code for Crown Prosecutors* (8th edn, CPS 2018).

Cullen RM, 'Arguments for Zero Tolerance of Sexual Contact between Doctors and Patients' (1999) 25 *Journal of Medical Ethics* 482.

Cummins Gauthier C, 'The Virtue of Moral Responsibility and the Obligations of Patients' (2005) 30 *The Journal of Medicine and Philosophy* 153.

Dan-Cohen M, *Harmful Thoughts: Essays on Law, Self and Morality* (Princeton University Press 2002).

Daniels KR and others, 'Relationships between Doctors and Patients in Obstetrics and Gynaecology' (1995) 35(3) *Australian and New Zealand Journal of Obstetrics and Gynaecology* 286.

Davies M, *Medical Self-Regulation: Crisis and Change* (Ashgate 2007).

Davies M, 'Crossing Boundaries: Dealing with Amorous Advances by Doctors and Patients' *BMJ Careers* 18 November 2015.

Dean J, 'Private practice is unethical—and doctors should give it up' (2015) 350 *British Medical Journal* h2299.

de Boer ME and others, 'Pressure in Dealing with Requests for Euthanasia or Assisted Suicide. Experiences of General Practitioners' (2019) 45 *Journal of Medical Ethics* 425.

DeCew JW, 'The Priority of Privacy for Medical Information' (2000) 17 *Social Philosophy and Policy* 213.

Department of Health, *Committee of Inquiry – Independent Investigation into How the NHS Handled Allegations About the Conduct of Clifford Ayling* (HMSO 2004a).

Department of Health, *NHS Waiting Times for Elective Care in England* HC 964 (HMSO 2004b).

Department of Health, *The Kerr/Haslam Inquiry: Full Report* Cm 6640 (HMSO 2005).

Department of Health, *Trust, Assurance and Safety – The Regulation of Health Professionals in the 21st Century* Cm 7013 (HMSO 2007).

Department of Health, *Transforming Care: A National Response to Winterbourne View Hospital: Final Report* (HMSO 2012).

Department of Health and Social Care, *Review of the Regulation of Cosmetic Interventions* (HMSO 2013).

Department of Health and Social Care, *The NHS Constitution for England* (HMSO 2015).

Dorr Goold S and Lipkin M, 'The Doctor–Patient Relationship: Challenges, Opportunities, and Strategies' (1999) 14 (Suppl 1) *Journal of General Internal Medicine* S26.

Draper H and Sorell T, 'Patients' Responsibilities in Medical Ethics' (2002) 16 *Bioethics* 335.

Duff RA, 'Harms and Wrongs' (2001) 5 *Buffalo Criminal Law Review* 13.

Duff RA, 'Restoration and Retribution' in von Hirsch A and others (eds), *Restorative Justice and Criminal Justice: Competing or Reconcilable Paradigms?* (Hart 2003).

Duff RA, *Answering for Crime* (Hart 2007).

Duffy M, 'Vulnerability' in Given LM (ed), *The Sage Encyclopaedia of Qualitative Research Methods* (Sage 2008).

Duggan AJ, 'Undue Influence' in Parkinson P (ed), *The Principles of Equity* (Lawbook Co 2003).

Dunn MC and others, 'To Empower or to Protect? Constructing the "vulnerable adult" in English Law and Public Policy' (2008) 28 *Legal Studies* 234.

Dworkin R, *Taking Rights Seriously* (Harvard University Press 1977).

Dworkin R, 'Rights as Trumps' in Waldron J (ed), *Theories of Rights* (Oxford University Press 1984).

Dyer AR and Bloch S, 'Informed Consent and the Psychiatric Patient' (1987) 13 *Journal of Medical Ethics* 12.

Dyer C, 'Stem cell therapy doctor exploited desperate patients, GMC finds' (2010) 341 *British Medical Journal*, c5001.

Dyer C, 'Rogue Surgeon Paterson is Sentenced to 15 Years After Performing Unnecessary Operations' (2017a) 357 *British Medical Journal* 2678.

Dyer, C, 'Oral Surgeon Whose Misconduct was "Serious, Persistent, and Shocking" is Struck Off' (2017b) 358 *British Medical Journal* j4225.

Ehrlich S, '"Inferring" Consent in the Context of Rape and Sexual Assault', in Solan L and others (eds.), *Speaking of Language and Law: Conversations on the Work of Peter Tiersma* (New York: Oxford University Press 2015).

El-Gingihy Y, *How to Dismantle the NHS in 10 Easy Steps* (Zero Books 2015).

Elliott C and de Than C, 'The Case for a Rational Reconstruction of Consent in Criminal Law' (2007) 70(2) *Modern Law Review* 225.

Elliott J (ed), *Oxford Compact Dictionary and Thesaurus* (Oxford University Press 1997).

Ellison L and Munro VE, 'Of "Normal Sex" and "Real Rape": Exploring the Use of Socio-Sexual Scripts in (Mock) Jury Deliberation' (2009) 18 *Social & Legal Studies* 291.

Ells C, 'Foucault, Feminism, and Informed Choice' (2003) 24 *Journal of Medical Humanities* 213.

Emanuel EJ, 'Undue Inducement: Nonsense on Stilts' (2005) 5 *American Journal of Bioethics* 9.

Emanuel EJ and Battin MP, 'What are the Potential Cost Savings from Legalizing Physician-Assisted Suicide?' (1998) 339 *New England Journal of Medicine* 167.

Engel GL, 'The Need for a New Medical Model: a Challenge for Biomedicine' (1977) 196 *Science* 129.

Englehardt T, 'The Many Faces of Autonomy' (2001) 9 *Health Care Analysis* 283.

Enman SR, 'Doctrines of Unconscionability in England, Canada and the Commonwealth' (1987) 16 *Anglo-American Law Review* 191.

Eskridge WM, 'The Many Faces of Sexual Consent' (1995) 37 *William and Mary Law Review* 47.

Eyres White G and others, 'Can One be a Good Doctor and have a Sexual Relationship with One's Patient?' (1994) 11(4) *Family Practice* 389.

Fahy T and Fisher N, 'Sexual Contact Between Doctors and Patients: Almost Always Harmful' (1992) 304(6841) *British Medical Journal* 1519.

Farber N and others, 'Physicians' Experiences with Patients who Transgress Boundaries' (2000) 15 *Journal of General Internal Medicine* 770.

Feinberg J, *The Moral Limits of the Criminal Law: Harm to Others*, vol.1 (Oxford University Press 1984).

Feinberg J, 'Victims' Excuses: The Case of Fraudulently Procured Consent' (1986) 96 *Ethics* 330.

Feinberg J, *The Moral Limits of the Criminal Law: Harmless Wrongdoing*, vol.4 (Oxford University Press 1988).

Finch E and Munro VE, 'Breaking Boundaries? Sexual Consent in the Jury Room' (2006) 26 *Legal Studies* 303.

Fineman MA, *The Autonomy Myth* (The New Press 2004).

Fineman MA, 'The Vulnerable Subject: Anchoring Equality in the Human Condition' (2008) 20(1) *Yale Journal of Law & Feminism* 1.

Fineman MA, 'The Vulnerable Subject and the Responsive State' (2010) 60(2) *Emory Law Journal* 251.

Fineman MA, '"Elderly" as Vulnerable: Rethinking the Nature of Individual and Societal Responsibility' (2012) 20 *Elder Law Journal* 71.

Fineman MA, 'Equality, Autonomy, and the Vulnerable Subject in Law and Politics', in Fineman MA and Grear A (eds), *Vulnerability: Reflections on the New Ethical Foundation for Law and Politics* (Ashgate 2013).

Fineman MA, 'Vulnerability, Resilience, and LGBT Youth' (2014) 23 *Temple Political & Civil Rights Law Review* 307.

Fineman MA, 'Vulnerability and Inevitable Inequality' (2017) 4 *Oslo Law Review* 133.

Fineman MA, 'Vulnerability and Social Justice' (2019) 53 *Valparaiso University Law Review* 341.

Fineman MA and Grear A (eds), *Vulnerability: Reflections on the New Ethical Foundation for Law and Politics* (Ashgate 2013).

Flannigan R, 'The Fiduciary Obligation' (1989) 9 *Oxford Journal of Legal Studies* 285.

Flannigan R, 'The Boundaries of Fiduciary Accountability' (2004) 83 *Canadian Bar Review* 35.

Flannigan R, 'The Core Nature of Fiduciary Accountability' (2009) 3 *New Zealand Law Review* 375.

Formby A and others, 'Cost Analysis of the Legal Declaratory Relief Requirement for Withdrawing Clinically Assisted Nutrition and Hydration (CANH) from Patients in the Permanent Vegetative State (PVS) in England and Wales' (2015) Research paper 108 Centre for Health Economics.

Formosa P, 'The Role of Vulnerability in Kantian Ethics' in Mackenzie C and others (eds), *Vulnerability: New Essays in Ethics and Feminist Philosophy* (Oxford University Press 2013).

Foster C, *Human Dignity in Bioethics and Law* (Hart 2011).

Foster C and Herring J, 'Identity, personhood and the law: a response to Ashcroft and McGee' (2018) 44(1) *Journal of Medical Ethics* 73.

Foster C and Miola J, 'Who's in Charge? The Relationship Between Medical Law, Medical Ethics and Medical Morality' (2015) 23(4) *Medical Law Review* 505.

Fovargue S, 'The (Ab)use of those with No Other Hope? Ethical and Legal Safeguards for Recipients of Experimental Procedures' (2013) 22 *Cambridge Quarterly of Healthcare Ethics* 181.

Fox M, 'Research Bodies: Feminist Perspectives on Clinical Research' in Sheldon S and Thomson M (eds), *Feminist Perspectives on Health Care Law* (Cavendish 1998).

Fox-Decent E and Criddle E, 'The Fiduciary Constitution of Human Rights' (2009) 15 *Legal Theory* 301.

Friere de Andrade Neves M, 'States of Uncertainty: Plural Laws and Affective Governance in the Context of Assisted Suicide in Germany' (2018) 50 *Journal of Legal Pluralism and Unofficial Law* 317.

Friesen P, 'Educational Pelvic Exams on Anesthetized Women: Why Consent Matters' (2018) 32 *Bioethics* 298.

Galletly, C 'Sexual Misconduct by Doctors: A Problem that has Not Gone Away' (2020) 23 *Medical Journal of Australia* 216.

Ganguli Mitra A and Biller-Andorno N, 'Vulnerability and Exploitation in a Globalized World' (2013) 6 *International Journal of Feminist Approaches to Bioethics* 91.

Garbutt G and Davies P, 'Should the Practice of Medicine be a Deontological or Utilitarian Enterprise?' (2011) 37(5) *Journal of Medical Ethics* 267.

Gardner J, 'The Opposite of Rape' (2018) 38(1) *Oxford Journal of Legal Studies* 48.

Gardner J and Shute S, 'The Wrongness of Rape' in Gardner J (ed), *Offences and Defences: Selected Essays in the Philosophy of Criminal Law* (Oxford University Press 2007).

Gartrell N and others, 'Physician-patient Sexual Contact: Prevalence and Problems' (1992) 157 *Western Journal of Medicine* 139.

Garzino FR, 'Undue Economic Influence on Physician-Assisted Suicide' (1997) 1 *DePaul Journal of Health Care Law* 537.

Gearty C, 'The Place of Private Nuisance in the Modern Law of Torts' (1989) 48 *Cambridge Law Journal* 214.

General Medical Council, *Tomorrow's Doctors* (GMC 1993).

General Medical Council, *Consent: Patients and Doctors Making Decisions Together* (GMC 2008).

General Medical Council, *Reform of the Fitness to Practise Procedures at the GMC* (GMC 2011).

General Medical Council, *Financial and Commercial Arrangements and Conflicts of Interest* (GMC 2013a).

General Medical Council, *Good Medical Practice* (GMC 2013b).

General Medical Council, *Good Practice in Research and Consent to Research* (GMC 2013c).

General Medical Council, *Maintaining a Professional Boundary Between You and Your Patient* (GMC 2013d).

General Medical Council, *Achieving Good Medical Practice: Guidance for Medical Students* (GMC 2016a).

General Medical Council, *Guidance for Doctors Who Offer Cosmetic Interventions* (GMC, 2016b).

General Medical Council, *Guidance on Supporting Information for Appraisal and Revalidation* (GMC 2018a)

General Medical Council, *Outcomes for Graduates* (GMC 2018b).

Gerteis M and others (eds), *Through the Patient's Eyes: Understanding and Promoting Patient-centered Care* (Jossey-Bass 1993).

Gill V and others, *The Standards Expected of Doctors: Patient & Public Attitudes* (National Centre for Social Research 2012).

Gillespie AA, *Sexual Exploitation of Children: Law and Punishment* (Round Hall 2008a).

Gillespie AA, '"Upskirts" and "Down-blouses": Voyeurism and the Law' (2008b) *Criminal Law Review* 370.

Gillespie AA and Ost S, 'The "Higher" Age of Consent and the Concept of Sexual Exploitation' in Reed A and Bohlander M (eds), *Consent: Domestic and Comparative Perspectives* (Ashgate 2016).

Gillon R, *Philosophical Medical Ethics* (Wiley 1986).

Glesne C and Peshkin A, *Becoming Qualitative Researchers: An Introduction* (Longman 1992).

Godlee F and others, 'Wakefield's Article Linking MMR Vaccine and Autism was Fraudulent' (2011) 342 *British Medical Journal* 7452.

Goldie J and others, 'Sex and the Surgery: Students' Attitudes and Potential Behaviour as They Pass Through a Modern Medical Curriculum' (2004) 30 *Journal of Medical Ethics* 480.

Goodin RE, *Protecting the Vulnerable: A Reanalysis of Our Social Responsibilities* (University of Chicago Press 1985).

Goodin RE, 'Exploiting a Situation and Exploiting a Person' in Reeve A (ed), *Modern Theories of Exploitation* (Sage 1987).

Goodyear-Smith F and Buetow S, 'Power Issues in the Doctor-Patient Relationship (2001) 9 *Health Care Analysis* 449.

Gordijn B and Janssens R, 'Euthanasia and Palliative Care in the Netherlands: An Analysis of the Latest Developments' (2004) 12 *Health Care Analysis* 195.

Gornall J, 'The Truth about Cash for Referrals' (2015) 350 *British Medical Journal* h396.

Gosport Independent Panel, *Gosport War Memorial Hospital: The Report of the Gosport Independent Panel* HC1084 (HMSO 2018).

Greenfield S and Osborn G, 'Unconscionability and Contract: The creeping shoots of Bundy' (1992) 7 *Denning Law Journal* 65.

Greenspan P, 'The Problem with Manipulation' (2003) 40 *American Philosophical Quarterly* 155.

Griffiths D and Mullock A, 'Cosmetic Surgery: Regulatory Challenges in a Global Beauty Market' (2018) 26 *Health Care Analysis* 220.

Grubb A, 'Sexual Assault by Doctor: Breach of Fiduciary Duty, *Taylor v McGillivray*' (1995) 3 *Medical Law Review* 108.

Guy, M, 'Between "Going Private" and "NHS Privatisation": Patient choice, competition reforms and the relationship between the NHS and private healthcare in England' (2019) 39 *Legal Studies* 479.

Hall MA, 'The Importance of Trust for Ethics, Law, and Public Policy' (2005) 14 *Cambridge Quarterly of Healthcare Ethics* 156.

Hall MI, 'Relational Autonomy, Vulnerability Theory, Older Adults and the Law: Making It Real' (2018) 12 *Elder Law Review* i.

Halter M and others, *Sexual Boundary Violations by Health Professionals – An Overview of the Published Empirical Literature* (CHRE 2007).

Hamilton K and others, 'A Sheep in Wolf's Clothing: Exploring Researcher Vulnerability' (2006) 33 *NA - Advances in Consumer Research* 672.

Harding M, 'Trust and Fiduciary Law' (2013) 33 *Oxford Journal of Legal Studies* 81.

Harper J and others, 'Adjuncts in the IVF Laboratory: Where is the Evidence for "Add-on" Interventions?' (2017) 32 *Human Reproduction* 485.

Harper RB, 'The Application of Contributory Negligence Principles to the Doctor/patient Relationship' (2001) 9 *Torts Law Journal* 180.

Harris R and Slater K, *Analysis of Cases Resulting in Doctors Being Erased or Suspended From the Medical Register* (DJS Research 2015).

Hart HLA, *The Concept of Law* (Oxford University Press 1961).

Haughey M, 'The Fiduciary Explanation for Presumed Undue Influence' (2012) 50 *Alberta Law Review* 129.

Held V, 'Coercion and Coercive Offers' in Pennock JR and Chapman JW (eds), *Coercion* (Aldine 1972).

Henderson GE and others, 'Vulnerability to Influence: A Two Way Street' (2004) 4 *American Journal of Bioethics* 50.

Her Majesty's Inspectorate of Constabulary and Fire & Rescue Services, *PEEL Spotlight Report Shining a Spotlight on Betrayal: Abuse of Position for a Sexual Purpose* (HMICFRS 2019).

Hesketh W, '*Conceptualising Medico-Crime in the UK*' (DPhil thesis, University of Ulster, 2011).

Hill JL, 'Exploitation' (1994) 79 *Cornell Law Review* 631.

Hoff T, 'Why a Deteriorating Doctor-patient Relationship Should Worry us', OUP Blog, 24 August 2017, at: https://blog.oup.com/2017/08/deteriorating-doctor-patient-relationship/ accessed 12 January 2021.

Holland S and Kydd A, 'Ethical Issues When Involving People Newly Diagnosed with Dementia in Research' (2015) 22 *Nurse Researcher* 25.

Holm S, *Ethical Problems in Clinical Practice* (Manchester University Press 1997).

Holtug N, 'The Harm Principle' (2002) 5 *Ethical Theory and Moral Practice* 357.

Hook J and Devereux D, 'Boundary Violations in Therapy: the Patient's Experience of Harm' (2018) 24 *BJPsych Advances* 366.

Horder J, *Ashworth's Principles of Criminal Law*, (9th edn, Oxford University Press 2019).

House of Lords Select Committee on Medical Ethics, *Report of the Select Committee on Medical Ethics* HL Paper 21 (HMSO 1994).

House of Lords Select Committee on the Long-Term Sustainability of the NHS, *The Long-Term Sustainability of the NHS and Adult Social Care* Report of Session 2016–2017 HL Paper 151 (HMSO 2017).

Howard LC and Hammond SP, (2019) 'Researcher Vulnerability: Implications for Educational Research and Practice' (2019) 32 *International Journal of Qualitative Studies in Education* 411.

Hunter DJ, 'From Tribalism to Corporatism: The Continuing Managerial Challenge to Medical Dominance' in Kelleher D and others (eds), *Challenging Medicine* (Routledge 2006).

Husak D, *Overcriminalization* (Oxford University Press 2008).

Hutter BM and Lloyd-Bostock S, *Regulatory Crisis* (Cambridge University Press 2017).

Independent Medicines and Medical Devices Safety Review, *First Do No Harm: the Report of the Independent Medicines and Medical Devices Safety Review* (HMSO 2020).

Ingelfinger FJ, 'Arrogance' (1980) 303(26) *New England Journal of Medicine* 1507.

Irvine D, 'Patients, Professionalism, and Revalidation' (2005) 330 *British Medical Journal* 1265.

Irvine D, 'A Short History of the General Medical Council' (2006) 40(3) *Medical Education* 202.

Ivanova E and others, 'Ethical Aspects of Vulnerable Groups of Patients in Clinical Trials' in Prostran M (ed), *Clinical Trials in Vulnerable Populations* (IntecOpen 2017).

Jackson S and Hafemeister T, *Financial Abuse of Elderly People vs. Other Forms of Elder Abuse: Assessing Their Dynamics, Risk Factors, and Society's Response* (Final report presented to the National Institute of Justice 2010), at https://www.ncjrs.gov/pdffiles1/nij/grants/233613.pdf accessed 22 July 2020.

Jansen LA and Wall S, 'Rethinking Exploitation: A Process-Centred Account' (2013) 23 *Kennedy Institute of Ethics Journal* 381.

References

Jansen-van der Weide MC and Onwuteaka-Philipsen BD, 'Granted, Undecided, Withdrawn, and Refused Requests for Euthanasia and Physician-Assisted Suicide' (2005) 165 *Archives Internal Medicine* 1698.

Jones JH, *Bad Blood: The Tuskegee Syphilis Experiment* (Free Press 1981).

Joyce R, 'Fiduciary Law and Non-Economic Interests' (2002) 28 *Monash University Law Review* 239.

Justice Department, 'Farid Fata Victim Impact Statements', 2:13-cr-20600-PDB-DRG Doc # 135-2 (2015), at https://fm.cnbc.com/applications/cnbc.com/resources/editorialfiles/2016/09/13/Farid%20Fata%20Victim%20Impact%20Statements_0.pdf accessed 22 July 2020.

Kant I, *Groundwork of the Metaphysics of Morals*, in Kant I and Gregor MJ (eds), *Practical Philosophy* (Cambridge University Press 1999).

Katz D and others, 'All Gifts Large and Small: Towards an Understanding of the Ethics of Pharmaceutical Industry Gift-giving' (2003) 3(3) *American Journal of Bioethics* 39.

Kay A, *This is Going to Hurt: Secret Diaries of a Junior Doctor* (Picador 2018).

Kelleher D, 'Self-help Groups and their Relationship to Medicine' in Kelleher D and others (eds), *Challenging Medicine* (Routledge 2006).

Kelleher D and others (eds), *Challenging Medicine* (Routledge 2006).

Kennedy I, 'The Fiduciary Relationship and its Application to Doctors' in Birks P (ed), *Wrongs and Remedies in the Twenty-First Century* (Clarendon Press 1986).

Kimsma GK and van Leeuwen E, 'The Role of Family in Euthanasia Decision Making' (2007) 19 *Healthcare Ethics Committee Forum* 365.

Kittay E, *Love's Labour: Essays on Women, Equality, and Dependency* (Routledge 1999).

Kitty E and others, 'Dependency, Difference and the Global Ethic of Long Term Care' (2005) 13 *Journal of Political Philosophy* 443.

Knight S, 'Libertarian Critiques of Consent in Sexual Offences' (2012) 1 *UCL Journal of Law and Jurisprudence* 137.

Kon A, 'The Shared Decision-Making Continuum' (2010) 304 *Journal of American Medical Association* 903.

Korsgaard C, 'The Reasons we can Share: an Attack on the Distinction Between Agent-Relative and Agent-Neutral Values' (1993) 10 *Social Philosophy and Policy* 24.

Laar A, 'Researcher Vulnerability: An Overlooked Issue in Vulnerability Discourses' (2014) 9 *Scientific Research and Essays* 737.

Lacey N, 'Unspeakable Subjects, Impossible Rights: Sexuality, Integrity and Criminal Law' (1998) 9 *Canadian Journal of Law and Jurisprudence* 47.

Lacobucci G, 'GMC Should Hold Conflicts of Interests Register for all Doctors, Says McCartney' (2018a) 363 *British Medical Journal* k4230.

Lacobucci G, 'Trust in GPs Remains High but Patients Report More Difficulties Getting an Appointment' (2018b) 362 *British Medical Journal* k3488.

Lacobucci G, 'Cash-strapped CCGs ask GPs not to refer some patients to hospital' (2019) 366 *British Medical Journal* 5484.

Lamond G, 'Coercion, Threats, and the Puzzle of Blackmail' in Simester AP and Smith ATH (eds), *Harm and Culpability* (Clarendon Press 1996).

Lamond G, 'Coercion', in LaFollette H (ed), *International Encyclopaedia of Ethics* (Blackwells 2013).

Lass A and Brinsden P, 'How Do Patients Choose Private In Vitro Fertilization Treatment? A Customer Survey in a Tertiary Fertility Center in the United Kingdom' (2001) 75 *Fertility and Sterility* 893.

Latham M, 'The Shape of Things to Come: Feminism, Regulation and Cosmetic Surgery' (2008) 16 *Medical Law Review* 437.

Launer J Sexual harassment of women in medicine: a problem for men to address' (2018) 94 *Postgraduate Medical Journal* 129.

Law Commission, *Mental Incapacity* Report No 231 (HMSO 1995).

Law Commission, *Hate Crime: the Case for Extending the Existing Offences* Consultation Paper No 231 (HMSO 2013).

Law Commission, *Reforming Misconduct in Public Office: a Consultation Paper* Consultation Paper No 229 (HMSO 2016).

Lazarus ES, 'Theoretical Considerations for the Study of the Doctor-patient Relationship: Implications of a Perinatal Study' (1988) 2(1) *Medical Anthropology Quarterly* 34.

Lederer S, *Subjected to Science: Human Experimentation in America Before the Second World War* (John Hopkins University Press 1995).

Lewis P, 'The Medical Exception' (2012) 65 *Current Legal Problems* 355.

Logar T, 'Exploitation as Wrongful Use: Beyond Taking Advantage of Vulnerabilities' (2010) 25 *Acta Analytica* 329.

Lowenberg JS and Davis F, 'Beyond Medicalisation: The Case of Holistic Health' (1994) 16(5) *Sociology of Health and Illness* 579.

Luna F, 'Elucidating the Concept of Vulnerability: Layers not Labels' (2009) 2 *International Journal of Feminist Approaches to Bioethics* 121.

McCartney, M, 'Margaret McCartney: Hiding and Seeking Doctors' Conflicts of Interests' (2018) 360 *British Medical Journal* k135.

McHale J, 'Children, Cosmetic Surgery and Perfectionism: A Case for Legal Regulation' in Ferguson P and Laurie G (eds), *Inspiring a Medico-Legal Revolution: Essays in Honour of Shelia McLean* (Ashgate 2015).

Mackenzie C, 'The Importance of Relational Autonomy and Capabilities for an Ethics of Vulnerability' in Mackenzie C and others (eds) *Vulnerability: New Essays in Ethics and Feminist Philosophy* (Oxford University Press 2013).

Mackenzie C and Soljar N, *Relational Autonomy: Feminist Perspectives on Autonomy, Agency, and the Social Self* (Oxford University Press 2000).

MacKinnon C, *Women's Lives, Men's Laws* (Harvard University Press 2005).

McLean S, *Assisted Dying: Reflections on the Need for Law Reform* (Routledge-Cavendish 2007).

Macklin R, '"Due" and "Undue" Inducements: Subjects on Paying Money to Research Subjects' (1981) 3 *IRB: A Review of Human Subjects Research* 1.

Macklin R, 'Bioethics, Vulnerability and Protection' (2003) 17 *Bioethics* 472.

Macklin R, 'A Global Ethics Approach to Vulnerability' (2012) 4 *International Journal of Feminist Approaches to Bioethics* 64.

McNeill PM, *The Ethics of Human Experimentation* (Cambridge University Press 1993).

McPherson CJ and others, 'Feeling Like a Burden to Others: A Systematic Review Focusing on the End of Life' (2007) 21 *Palliative Medicine* 115.

Madden Dempsey M and Herring J, 'Why Sexual Penetration Requires Justification' (2007) 27(3) *Oxford Journal of Legal Studies* 67.

Mahase E, RCGP Calls on GMC to Introduce Mandatory and Public Declaration of Interests Register' (2019) 367 *British Medical Journal* l6695.

Mandeville K, 'My Life as a Guinea Pig' (2006) 332 *British Medical Journal* 735.

Mappes TA, 'Sexual Morality and the Concept of Using Another Person', in Mappes TA and Zembaty JS (eds) *Social Ethics: Morality and Social Policy* (McGraw-Hill 1985).

Marshall SE and Duff RA, 'Criminalization and Shared Wrongs' (1998) XI(1) *Canadian Journal of Law and Jurisprudence* 7.

Mayer R, 'What's Wrong with Exploitation?' (2007) 24 *Journal of Applied Philosophy* 137.

Mayo DJ and Gunderson M, 'Physician Assisted Death and Hard Choices' (1993) 18 *Journal of Medicine and Philosophy* 329.

Medical Council of New Zealand, *'Trust in the Doctor-Patient Relationship'* (Medical Council of New Zealand 1994).

Medical Council of New Zealand, *Sexual Boundaries in the Doctor-Patient Relationship: A Resource for Doctors* (Medical Council of New Zealand 2004).

Miles JK, 'Taking Patient Virtue Seriously' (2019) 40 *Theoretical Medicine and Bioethics* 141.

Mill JS, *On Liberty* (originally published 1859) (Everyman 1996).

Millbank J, 'Female Health Practitioners Disciplined for Sexual Misconduct' (2020a) 43 *University of New South Wales Law Journal* 1244.

Millbank J, 'Sexual Relationships Between Health Practitioner and Former Patients: When is it Misconduct?' (2020b) 213 *Medical Journal of Australia* 212.

Millenson ML, 'When "Patient Centred" is no Longer Enough: The Challenge of Collaborative Health' (2017) 358 *British Medical Journal* j3048.

Miller P, 'A Theory of Fiduciary Liability' (2011) 56 *McGill Law Journal* 235.

Miller P and Weijer C, 'Fiduciary Obligation in Clinical Research' (2006) *Journal of Law, Medicine & Ethics* 424.

Ministry of Health, Welfare and Sport *Outcome Based Healthcare 2018–2022* (2018), at https://www.government.nl/documents/reports/2018/07/02/outcome-based-healthcare-2018-2022 accessed 22 July 2020.

Minkina N, 'Can #MeToo Abolish Sexual Harassment and Discrimination in Medicine?' (2019) 394(10196) *Lancet* 383.

Miola J, 'Autonomy Ruled Ok?' (2006) 14 *Medical Law Review* 108.

Mngadi KT and others, 'Undue Inducement: A case study in CAPRISA 008' (2017) 43 *Journal of Medical Ethics* 824.

Moberly T, 'The Pharma Deals that CCGs Fail to Declare' (2018) 360 *British Medical Journal* j5915.

Moline J, 'Professionals and Professions: A Philosophical Examination of an Ideal' (1986) 22(5) *Social Science & Medicine* 501.

Monzini P, *Sex Traffic: Prostitution, Crime and Exploitation* (Zed 2005).

Moore LW and Miller M, 'Initiating Research with Doubly Vulnerable Populations' (1999) 30 *Journal of Advanced Nursing* 1034.

Morgan D and Lee RG, 'In the Name of the Father? *Ex parte Blood*: Dealing with Novelty and Anomaly' (1997) 60 *Modern Law Review* 840.

Morgan JF and Porter S, 'Sexual Harassment of Psychiatric Trainees: Experiences and Attitudes' (1999) 75 *Postgraduate Medical Journal* 410.

Morse JM, 'Researching Illness and Injury: Methodological Considerations' (2000) 11 *Qualitative Health Research* 538.

Murdoch I, *The Sovereignty of Good* (Routledge 1971).

Murphy J, 'Misfeasance in a Public Office: A Tort Law Misfit?' (2012) 32 *Oxford Journal of Legal Studies* 51.

Murphy J and Witting C, *Street on Torts* (13th edn, Oxford University Press 2012).

National Audit Office, *Health and Social Care Integration* HC 1011 (HMSO 2017).

National Commission for the Protection of Human Subjects of Biomedical and Behavioral Research, *The Belmont Report: Ethical Principles and Guidelines for the Protection of Human Subjects of Research* (US Government Printing Office 1979) at https://www.hhs.gov/ohrp/sites/default/files/the-belmont-report-508c_FINAL.pdf accessed 12 January 2020.

NHS England, *Managing Conflicts of Interest in the NHS* (NHS England 2017).

Norwood F, 'Nothing More to Do: Euthanasia, General Practice, and End-of-Life Discourse in the Netherlands' (2007) 26 *Medical Anthropology* 139.

Nuffield Council on Bioethics, *Animal-to-Human Transplants: The Ethics of Xenotransplantation* (Nuffield Council on Bioethics 1996).

Nuffield Council on Bioethics, *The Ethics of Research Related to Healthcare in Developing Countries* (Nuffield Council on Bioethics 2002).

Nuremberg Code 1947 (1996) 313 *British Medical Journal* 1448.

Oakes JM and others, 'How Should Doctors Disclose Conflicts of Interest to Patients? A Focus Group Investigation' (January 2015) Minnesota Medicine, at https://www.mnmed.org/MMA/media/Minnesota-Medicine-Magazine/clinical_oakes_1501.pdf accessed 22 July 2020.

O'Neill O, *Autonomy and Trust in Bioethics* (Cambridge University Press 2002).

Oregon Health Authority, Oregon Public Health Division, *Oregon Death with Dignity Act Data Summary 2018* (Public Health Division 2019), at https://www.oregon.gov/oha/PH/PROVIDERPARTNERRESOURCES/EVALUATIONRESEARCH/DEATHWITHDIGNITYACT/Documents/year21.pdf accessed 22 July 2020.

Ost S, 'Euthanasia and the Defence of Necessity: Advocating a more appropriate legal response' in Erin CA and Ost S (eds), *The Criminal Justice System and Health Care* (Oxford University Press 2007).

Ost S, 'The De-medicalisation of Assisted Dying: Is a Less Medicalised Model the Way Forward?' (2010) 18(4) *Medical Law Review* 497.

Ost S, 'Breaching the Sexual Boundaries: Should English Law Recognise Fiduciary Duties in the Doctor-Patient Relationship?' (2016) 24(2) *Medical Law Review* 206.

Ost S, 'Drs Bramhall and Bawa-Garba and the Rightful Domain of the Criminal Law' (2019) 49(3) *Journal of Medical Ethics* 151.

Ost S, 'The Medical Professional as Special Before the Criminal Law', in Bogg A and others (eds), *Criminality at Work* (Oxford University Press 2020).

Ost S and Biggs H, '"Consensual" Sexual Activity between Doctors and Patients: A Matter for the Criminal Law?', in Alghrani A and others (eds), *The Criminal Law and Bioethical Conflict* (Cambridge University Press 2012).

Ost S and Biggs H, '(I love you!) I do, I do, I do, I do, I do: Breaches of Sexual Boundaries by Patients in their Relationships with Health Care Professionals' in Stanton C and others (eds), *Pioneering Healthcare Law: Essays in Honour of the Work of Margaret Brazier* (Routledge 2016).

Ost S and Erin CA, 'An Ill-Suited and Inappropriate Union? Exploring the Relationship between the Criminal Justice System and Health Care' in Erin CA and Ost S (eds), *The Criminal Justice System and Health Care* (Oxford University Press 2007).

Pachana NA and others, 'Can We Do Better? Researchers' Experiences with Ethical Review Boards on Projects with Later Life as a Focus' (2015) 43 *Journal of Alzheimer's Disease* 701.

Parker J, 'Junior Doctors and Moral Exploitation' (2019) 45 *Journal of Medical Ethics* 571.

Paterson Inquiry, *Report of the Independent Inquiry into the Issues raised by Paterson* (HMSO 2020).

Pattinson SD, 'Undue Influence in the Context of Medical Treatment' (2002) 5 *Medical Law International* 305.

Peerenboom R, 'Rights, Interests, and the Interest in Rights in China' (1995) 31 *Stanford Journal of International Law* 359.

Pellegrino ED and Thomasma DC, *The Virtues in Medical Practice* (Oxford University Press 1993).

Penfold S, *Sexual Abuse by Health Professionals* (University of Toronto Press 1998).

Penner J, 'Is Loyalty a Virtue, and Even if it is, Does it Really Help Explain Fiduciary Liability?', in Gold AS and Miller PB, (eds), *Philosophical Foundations of Fiduciary Law* (Oxford University Press 2014).

Pereira T and others, 'Aesthetic Journeys: a Review of Cosmetic Surgery Tourism' (2018) *Journal of Travel Medicine* 1.

Petkova H, and others, 'Incidence of Anorexia Nervosa in Young People in the UK and Ireland: a National Surveillance Study' (2019) 9 *BMJ Open* e027339.

Phang A, 'Doctrine and Fairness in the Law of Contract' (2009) 29 *Legal Studies* 534.

Phillips SP and Schneider MS, 'Sexual Harassment of Female Doctors by Patients' (1993) 329(26) *New England Journal of Medicine* 1936.

Pilnick A and Dingwall R, 'On the Remarkable Persistence of Asymmetry in Doctor/patient Interaction: A Critical Review' (2011) 72 *Social Science & Medicine* 1374.

Plotkin DA and others, 'Assessing Undue Influence' (2016) 44 *Journal of the American Academy of Psychiatry and the Law* 344.

Price D, (1997) Giving Blood: Posthumous Fertility Treatment and a Good Old British Compromise? (1997) 11 *International Review of Law, Computers & Technology* 299.

Price D, 'Exploitation, Akrasia, and Goldilocks: How Many Pounds for Flesh for Medical Uses?' (2013) 21 *Medical Law Review* 519.

Pritchard-Jones L, 'The Good, the Bad, and the "Vulnerable Older Adult"' (2016) 38(1) *Journal of Social Welfare and Family Law* 51.

Puglise, SM, '"Calling Dr. Love": The Physician-Patient Sexual Relationship as Grounds for Medical Malpractice – Society Pays While the Doctor and Patient Play' (2000) 14 *Journal of Law and Health* 321.

Quinn MJ and others, *Undue Influence: Definitions and Applications* (California Superior Court 2010).

Quinn MJ and others, 'Developing an Undue Influence Screening Tool for Adult Protective Services' (2017) 29 *Journal of Elder Abuse & Neglect* 157.

Ragg M, 'McBride Guilty of Scientific Fraud' (1993) 341 *The Lancet* 550.

Regan S and others, 'Physician Attitudes Toward Personal Relationships with Patients' (2010) 48 *Medical Care* 547.

Richman J, 'Sanctioned Assisting Suicide: Impact on Family Relations' (1987) 3 *Issues in Law and Medicine* 53.

Rhodes R, 'Understanding the Trusted Doctor and Constructing a Theory of Bioethics' (2001) 22 *Theoretical Medicine* 493.

Ries NM and Thomson M, 'Bioethics and Universal Vulnerability: Exploring the Ethics and Practices of Research Participation' (2020) 28 *Medical Law Review* 293.

Rimmer A, 'Eighteen Doctors were Struck Off for Sexual Assault or Rape in the Past Four Years' (2018) 369 *British Medical Journal* 913.

Rimmer A, 'My Patient Has Left Me Money in Their Will. Can I Accept?' (2019) 363 *British Medical Journal* l66.

Robertson R and others, *Understanding NHS Financial Pressures: How are they Affecting Patient Care?* (The King's Fund 2017).

Roest B and others, 'The Involvement of Family in the Dutch Practice of Euthanasia and Physician Assisted Suicide: A Systematic Mixed Studies Review' (2019) 20 *BMC Medical Ethics* 1.

Rogers W and Ballantyne A, 'Gender and Trust in Medicine: Vulnerabilities, Abuses and Remedies' (2008) 1(1) *International Journal of Feminist Approaches to Bioethics* 48.

Rogers W and others, *Special Issue on Vulnerability* (2012a) 5(2) *International Journal of Feminist Approaches to Bioethics*.

Rogers W and others, 'Why Bioethics Needs a Concept of Vulnerability' (2012b) 5 *International Journal of Feminist Approaches to Bioethics* 11.

Rotman L, 'Fiduciary Law's "Holy Grail": Reconciling Theory and Practice in Fiduciary Jurisprudence' (2011) 91 *Boston University Law Review* 921.

Rowland D, *Pounds for Patients: How Private Hospitals use Financial Incentives to Win the Business of Medical Consultants* (Centre for Health and the Public Interest 2019).

Royal College of Surgeons, *Professional Standards for Cosmetic Surgery* (Royal College of Surgeons of England, 2016).

Rudinow J, 'Manipulation' (1978) 88 *Ethics* 338.

Samanta J and Samanta A, 'Awake and (Only Just) Aware? A Typology, Taxonomy, and Holistic Framework for Withdrawing Clinically Assisted Nutrition and Hydration in the Minimally Conscious State' (2018) 26(4) *Medical Law Review* 633.

Samet I, 'Fiduciary Loyalty as Kantian Virtue' in Gold AS and Miller PB, (eds), *Philosophical Foundations of Fiduciary Law* (Oxford University Press 2014).

Sample RJ, *Exploitation: What It Is and Why It's Wrong* (Rowman & Littlefield 2003).

Scanlon TM, 'Rights and Interests' in Basu K and Kanbur R (eds), *Arguments for a Better World: Essays in Honor of Amartya Sen* (Oxford University Press 2009).

Schneebaum G, 'What is Wrong with Sex in Authority Relations? A Study in Law and Social Theory' (2015) 105 *Journal of Criminal Law & Criminology* 345.

Schneider MS and Phillips SP, 'A Qualitative Study of Sexual Harassment of Female Doctors by Patients' (1997) 45(5) *Social Science and Medicine* 669.

Schulhofer SJ, *Unwanted Sex: The Culture of Intimidation and the Failure of the Law* (Harvard University Press 1998).

Schwartz J, 'What's Wrong with Exploitation?' (1995) 29 *Noûs* 158.

Searle RH and others, *Bad Apples? Bad Barrels? Or Bad Cellars? Antecedents and Processes of Professional Misconduct in UK Health and Social Care: Insights into Sexual Misconduct and Dishonesty* (Coventry University 2017).

Shamoo AE and Resnik DB, *Responsible Conduct of Research* (Oxford University Press 2003).

Shaw D and Moreton A 'Counting the Cost of Denying Assisted Dying' (2020) 15 *Clinical Ethics* 65.

Shepherd JC, *The Law of Fiduciaries* (Carswell 1981).

Sherwin S, 'Whither Bioethics? How Feminism Can Help Reorient Bioethics' (2008) 1 *International Journal of Feminist Approaches to Bioethics* 7.

Shmueli A and Savage E, 'Private and Public Patients in Public Hospitals in Australia' (2014) 115 (2–3) *Health Policy* 189.

Sikic Micanovi L and others, 'Who Else Needs Protection? Reflecting on Researcher Vulnerability in Sensitive Research' (2020) 10 *Societies* 1.

Simester A and von Hirsch A, *Crimes, Harms and Wrongs* (Hart 2011).

Slote M, *Morals from Motives* (Oxford University Press 2001).

Smith DH and Newton L, 'Physician and Patient: Respect for Mutuality' (1984) 5 *Theoretical Medicine and Bioethics* 43.

Smith HE, 'Why Fiduciary Law Is Equitable', in Gold AS and Miller PB (eds), *Philosophical Foundations of Fiduciary Law* (Oxford University Press, 2014).

Smith J, *Disguising Death* (HMSO 2002).

Smith J, *Safeguarding Patients: Lessons from the Past-Proposals for the Future, the Shipman Inquiry* (HMSO 2004).

Smith RG, *Medical Discipline: The Professional Conduct Jurisdiction of the GMC 1858-1990* (Clarendon Press 1994).

Smith SA, Contracting Under Pressure: a Theory of Duress' (1997) 56 *Cambridge Law Journal* 343.

Snijdewind MC and others, '(Complexities in Euthanasia or Physician-Assisted Suicide as Perceived by Dutch Physicians and Patients' Relatives' (2014) 48 *Journal of Pain and Symptom Management* 1125.

Sperling D, '(Re)disclosing Physician Financial Interests: Rebuilding Trust or Making Unreasonable Burdens on Physicians?' (2017) 20 *Medicine, Health Care and Philosophy* 179.

Spiegel W and others, 'Sexual feelings in the Physician-patient Relationship: Recommendations for Teachers' (2003) 37 *Medical Education* 840.

Spiegel W and others, 'Private or Intimate Relations between Doctor and Patient: Is Zero Tolerance Warranted?' (2005) 31 *Journal of Medical Ethics* 27.

Spiers J, 'New Perspectives on Vulnerability using Emic and Etic Approaches' (2000) 31 *Journal of Advanced Nursing* 715.

Stewart H, 'Harms, Wrongs, and Set-backs in Feinberg's Moral Limits of the Criminal Law' 2001 5 *Buffalo Criminal Law Review* 47.

Stirrat GM and others, 'Medical ethics and law for doctors of tomorrow: The 1998 Consensus Statement updated' (2010) 36 *Journal of Medical Ethics* 55.

Stone J, (2002) 'Race and Healthcare Disparities: Overcoming Vulnerability' (2002) 23 *Theoretical Medicine* 499.

Subotsky F, 'Psychiatry: Responding to the Kerr/Haslam Inquiry' in Subotsky F and others (eds), *Abuse of the Doctor-patient Relationship* (Routledge 2010).

Subotsky F and others (eds), *Abuse of the Doctor-patient Relationship* (Routledge 2010).

Swift J, 'A Modest Proposal for Preventing the Children of Poor People in Ireland, from Being a Burden on their Parents or Country, and for Making them Beneficial to the Publick' (originally published 1729) in Birch D and Hooper K (eds), *The Concise Oxford Companion to English Literature* (4th edn, Oxford University Press 2012).

Tadros V, *Criminal Responsibility* (Oxford University Press 2005).

Tan D, 'Sexual Misconduct by Doctors and the Intervention of Equity' (1997) 4 *Journal of Law and Medicine* 243.

ten Cate K and others, 'Considerations on Requests for Euthanasia or Assisted Suicide; a Qualitative Study with Dutch General Practitioners' (2017) 34 *Family Practice* 723.

ten Have H, *Vulnerability: Challenging Bioethics* (Routledge 2016).

Tauber AI, *Patient Autonomy and the Ethics of Responsibility* (Mit Press 2005).

Thomson M, 'Bioethics and Vulnerability: Recasting the Objects of Ethical Concern' (2018) 67 *Emory Law Journal* 1208.

Tremain SL, 'Stemming the Tide of Normalisation: An Expanded Feminist Analysis of the Ethics and Social Impact of Embryonic Stem Cell Research' (2006) 3 *Journal of Bioethical Inquiry* 33.

Tschan W, 'Abuse in Doctor-Patient Relationships' (2013) 178 *Key Issues in Mental Health* 129.

Turoldo F and Barilan Y, 'The Concept of Responsibility: Three Stages in its Evolution within Bioethics' (2008) 17 *Cambridge Quarterly of Healthcare Ethics* 114.

Twemlow SW and Gabbard GO, 'The Lovesick Therapist' in Gabbard GO (ed), *Sexual Exploitation in Professional Relationships* (American Psychiatric Press, 1989).

Uniacke S, 'Harming and Wronging: The Importance of Normative Context', in Oderberg DS and Chappell T (eds), *Human Values: New Essays on Ethics and Natural Law* (Palgrave Macmillan 2004).

United Nations Office on Drugs and Crime, *The Concept of 'Exploitation' in the Trafficking in Persons Protocol* (UNDOC 2015).

Valdman M, 'A Theory of Wrongful Exploitation' (2009) 9(6) *Philosophers' Imprint* 1.

van Marwijk H and Haverkate I, 'Impact of Euthanasia on Primary Care Physicians in the Netherlands' (2007) 21 *Palliative Medicine* 609.

Veitch K, 'Obligation and the Changing Nature of Publicly Funded Healthcare' (2019) 27 *Medical Law Review* 267.

Viglianti EM and others, 'Sexual Harassment and Abuse: When the Patient is the Perpetrator (2018) 392 *Lancet* 368.

Von Fragstein M and others, 'UK consensus statement on the content of communication curricula in undergraduate medical education' (2008) 42(11) *Medical Education* 1100.

Waddams SM, 'Unconscionability in Contracts' (1976) 39 *Modern Law Review* 369.

Waldron J (ed), *Theories of Rights* (Oxford University Press 1984).

Wang Y, 'Smiling Through Clenched Teeth: Why Compassion Cannot be Written into the Rules' (2016) 42 *Journal of Medical Ethics* 7.

Ward PR and others, 'A Qualitative Study of Patient (Dis)Trust in Public and Private Hospitals: the Importance of Choice and Pragmatic Acceptance for Trust Considerations in South Australia' (2015) 15 *BMC Health Services Research* 297.

Wellman C, *Medical Law and Moral Rights* (Springer 2005).

Wendland C, 'Research, Therapy, and Bioethical Hegemony: The Controversy over Perinatal AZT Trials in Africa' (2008) 51 *African Studies Review* 1.

Wendler D and others, 'Why Patients Continue to Participate in Clinical Research' (2008) 168 *Archives of Internal Medicine* 1294.

Wertheimer A, *Coercion* (Princeton University Press 1987).

Wertheimer A, *Exploitation* (Princeton University Press 1996).

Wertheimer A, *Consent to Sexual Relations* (Cambridge University Press 2003).

Wertheimer A, 'Exploitation in Health Care', in RE Ashcroft, A Dawson, H Draper and JR McMillan, *Principles of Health Care Ethics* (2nd edn, Wiley, 2007), 247–254.

Wertheimer A, *Rethinking the Ethics of Clinical Research: Widening the Lens* (Oxford University Press 2011).

Westen P, *The Logic of Consent: The Diversity and Deceptiveness of Consent as a Defense to Criminal Conduct* (Ashgate 2004).

White G, 'Medical Students' Learning Needs About Setting and Maintaining Social and Sexual Boundaries: A Report' (2003) 37 *Medical Education* 1017.

Wiles R and Higgins J, 'Doctor-patient Relationships in the Private Sector: Patients' Perceptions' (1996) 18(3) *Sociology of Health & Illness* 341.

Wilkinson J and others, 'Don't Abandon RCTs in IVF. We Don't Even Understand Them' (2019) 34 *Human Reproduction* 2093

Wilkinson S, *Bodies for Sale: Ethics and Exploitation in the Human Body Trade* (Routledge 2003).

Wilkinson, S, 'Exploitation in International Paid Surrogacy Arrangements' (2016) 33 *Journal of Applied Philosophy* 125.

Witting C, 'NHS Rationing: Implications for the Standard of Care' (2001) 21 *Oxford Journal of Legal Studies* 443.

Wolf SM, 'Physician-Assisted Suicide in the Context of Managed Care' (1996) 35 *Duquesne Law Review* 455.
Wolff J, 'Marx and Exploitation' (1999) 3 *The Journal of Ethics* 105.
Wood AM, 'Exploitation' (1995) 12 *Social Philosophy and Policy* 136.
Young IM, 'Responsibility and Global Justice: A Social Connection Model' (2006) 23 *Social Philosophy and Policy* 102.
Zagzebski L, *Divine Motivation Theory* (Cambridge University Press 2004).
Zia Mansoor F, 'Exploitation of Child Domestic Labourers: The Limits of the Current Law' (2006) 8(3) *International Journal of Discrimination and the Law* 169.
Zuckerman D, 'Teenagers and Cosmetic Surgery' (2005) 7 *Virtual Mentor: Ethics Journal of the American Medical Association* 253.

Index

Accreditation Council for Graduate Medical Education, US 206
acquiescent exploitation 33–6
Allen T 130–1, 158, 225
ambiguous concept of exploitation 12, 13
American Medical Association (AMA) (Council on Ethical and Judicial Affairs) 115, 119, 121, 135
Anderson J 97
anonymised cases for research publication 57
Archard D 37–8, 43, 48, 50, 91, 145
Ashcroft RE 215
assisted dying 167–8, 203; burden perception, identifying undue influence (screening and assessing) 187–98; burden perception and relatives/carers 168–75; burden perception and society 176–86; doctor vulnerability 186–7; legal regulation 183–5
Assisted Dying Bill: (2014–2015) 178, 188; (2019–2021) 194, 196
Association for Palliative Medicine 169
autonomy: assisted dying and 172; assisted reproduction 'rights' (*Blood* case) and 1, 3, 33; consent vs 50–1, 215; diminished 96, 204; paternalism vs 50, 94, 98, 105; principle of 77–8; relational 108–9, 204; relationship with vulnerability 95–9, 204
Ayling C 129

Baez F 129
Baier A 52
Balmont Report, US 99–100
basic needs, taking advantage of 20–1, 23
battery, sexual assault under tort of 156–60, 161

Beauchamp TL and Childress JF 77–8, 81, 82
Bell A 219–20
Bingham Lord 169–70
Birks P 87, 189, 220
blackmail and sexual exploitation 126–7, 164–5
Blood case 1, 3, 33
Bogart JH 126
Bradley K 217
Bramhall S 2, 201
British Medical Association (BMA) 84
Buchhandler-Raphael M 118, 147, 150, 152
burden perception *see* assisted dying

Canada: Discipline Committee of the College of Physicians and Surgeons of Ontario 136–7; *Norberg* v. *Wynrib* 123, 125–6, 145, 157, 158–9, 162, 164, 201, 223; Protecting Patients Act (217) 119; Task Force on Sexual Abuse of Patients 119, 120–1
CAPRISA (HIV prevention) study, South Africa 102–3
Chen-Wishart M 88
civil law 155–61; sexual exploitation 157–8; vs criminal offence of exploitation 213–17
coercion: assisted dying and 169; exploitation vs 124–5
coercive and irresistible inducements (sexual exploitation) 122–30, 152, 201
collaborative health care 63
Colt H and others 2
Competition and Markets Authority (CMA) 69, 70, 210
confidential and intimate professional relationships 48–50, 89–90

conflicts of interest 70, 209–12
consent: acquiescent exploitation 33–6; autonomy vs 50–1, 215; rationality and 21–2; research participants 99–100, 101, 102; trust and 50–1, 52, 53, 57; undue influence and 220; vulnerability and 95–6, 103; *see also* sexual exploitation
consequentialism 79
continuing professional development (CPD) 208, 209
contract law 86–9, 158–9, 213
contractual model of health care 59
Conway case 169, 192
corporate manslaughter and assisted dying 183–4
cosmetic surgery: private health care 106–10, 111, 112; sexual exploitation and consent 129–30
cost saving: assisted dying 177–81, 182–4; withdrawal of treatment (PDofC) 180–1
COVID-19 109; private tests for 3, 75
criminal law: sexual exploitation 145–55; tort of exploitation vs 213–17
Cullen RM 119, 121, 122

Daniels KR and others 117, 122
de Boer ME and others 175
decision-making *see* consent; shared decision-making model
Declaration of Helsinki 112
degradation, exploitation as 19–20
deontological ethics 78, 83
Dignitas 184
Dignity in Dying 184
Director of Public Prosecutions (DPP): policy on assisted dying 170–1
disability and old age: assumption of vulnerability 181–2
doctor-patient relationship 47–8; contemporary model of 58, 61, 209; fiduciary duty *see* fiduciary duty of doctor; intimate and confidential professional relationships 48–50, 89–90; legal responses to exploitation 85–9, 212–25; philosophical medical ethics 77–82; power inequality *see* power inequality; professional ethics *see* professional/regulatory medical ethics; as special case 5, 89–90, 200–2; trust and reliance 50–7; variants of exploitation and impossibility of elimination 226–7; *see also* private

health care; publicly funded health care/NHS
Dorr Goold S and Lipkin M 68, 70, 79
Dyer AR and Bloch S 60

European Convention on Human Rights 169
exploitation (key themes) 3–6
exploitation (philosophical foundations): commonalities in definitions 22–4; concept and dictionary definitions of 10–12; essential elements 25–33; existing conceptions 12–24

Fata F 55, 201
Feinberg J 13–16, 20, 22–4, 36, 37, 41, 42, 43, 45, 73–4, 75
female doctors' sexual exploitation of male patients 118
female patient-initiated boundary breaches 164–5
feminist medical ethics 80–1
fertility treatment: *Blood* case 1, 3, 33; private health care 110, 111, 112; sexual exploitation 127–8
fiduciary duty of doctor 5–6, 58–60; legal recognition of 222–5; medical education and professional ethics 206–7, 208; sexual exploitation and 161–3, 224
financial incentives 68–70; medical research 31–2, 103; private health care 73–5; *see also* conflicts of interest
Fineman MA 93–5, 105, 111, 112, 182
Formosa P 98–9
framing conditions 21–2, 23
Freeman v. *Home Office* 156–8

Ganguli Mitra A and Biller-Andorno N 81, 204
Garbutt G and Davies P 78
Gardner J 51
Gartrell N and others 132, 133
gender and sexual exploitation 116–18, 164
General Medical Council (GMC) 82–3, 84, 85, 109; conflicts of interest 209–12; medical education and professional ethics 206–7, 208; sexual exploitation cases and reports 114–15, 117; sexual exploitation and ethics committee 137, 140; sexual exploitation regulation/guidance 118–19, 133, 135–6, 154–5

Ghabbour N 136–7
Goodin RE 11, 16–20, 22, 23, 24, 60–1, 92, 96
Goodyear-Smith F and Buetow S 204–5
Gosport War Memorial Hospital, England: Independent Panel report 184–5
GPs: assisted dying 175, 193; prescribing incentive scheme 68–9, 79; sexual exploitation 120, 132, 133, 134; trust 70
Griffiths D and Mullock A 106, 107, 108, 109–10
Grubb A 157–8

Halter M and others 131
harming and wronging 41–6
Hesketh W 62
Hill JL 12, 13, 18, 24, 124–5
Hoff T 71
Human Fertilisation and Embryology Acts 1990 and 2008 212–13
Human Fertilisation and Embryology Authority 110–11
Human Tissue Act 2004, UK 212–13

illness, vulnerability and diminished autonomy 95–9
integrated provision of health and social care and information sharing 71
intention to gain 23–4
intimate and confidential professional relationships 48–50, 89–90

James D 170–1
Jansen LA and Wall S 13, 21–2, 23, 26, 31, 52–4, 78

Kantian moral philosophy 19, 46; autonomy and vulnerability 98–9; exploitation and vulnerability 202–3; misuse 27–8, 30–1; and principles of biomedical ethics (Beauchamp and Childress) 78; violation of moral rights 37–8, 40
Karbatt J 65
Kerr/Haslam Inquiry 54, 114

Lacey N 152
Lamond G 126
Latham M 108–9
Law Commission 150, 153–4, 182
legal responses to exploitation 85–9, 212–25; *see also* sexual exploitation

Levy N 3, 54–5, 64, 201, 226
Logar T 20–1

McFarlane A 84–5
McHale J 106
Mackenzie C 97–8
McLachlin J 2, 162, 223
management reforms, NHS 71–2
Mappes TA 124
Mayo DJ and Gunderson M 176–7
means to an end, misuse as 30–1
medical education: and professional regulatory ethics 205–12; sexual boundary crossing 137–9
medical ethics, philosophical 77–82
medical insurance 76–7
Medical Practitioners Tribunal Service (MPTS) Panel, GMC 114–15, 117, 118–19, 154–5
medical research *see* research
Mental Capacity Act 2005 100
mental health professionals, vulnerability assessment by 195
Millenson ML 63
misconduct in medical research 104
misuse 27–32
Modern Slavery Act 2015 217
Moore LW and Miller M 96
Moore v. *Regents of the University of California* 83
moral rights, violation of 36–41
moralised concept of exploitation 3–4, 11–12, 25
morally neutral definition of exploitation 11–12
Murdoch I 80

National Clinical Assessment Service 115
National Institute for Health and Care Excellence (NICE) 67
negligence, sexual assault under 160–1
Netherlands: assisted dying 174–5, 185, 186–7, 188, 193–4
New Zealand: sexual exploitation 117, 119
NHS *see* publicly funded health care/ NHS
Nicklinson case 170, 181, 197
Nicolson Baroness 178
Norberg v. *Wynrib* 123, 125–6, 145, 157, 158–9, 162, 164, 201, 223
Norwood F 193
Nuffield Council on Bioethics 102

old age and disability: assumption of vulnerability 181–2
one's own ends, exploitation for 32–3
online research projects on health 63
opportunities to exploit: power inequality and 60–6; undue influence and 201
outcome-based conceptions of exploitation 13; Feinberg 13–15; Goodin 16–19; Wertheimer 15–16

palliative and social care: assisted dying 185–6
paternalism: autonomy vs 50, 94, 98, 105; beneficence principle and 78; fiduciary duty of doctor and 58; vulnerability and 98, 112, 137, 182
Paterson I 2–3, 64, 65–6, 72–3, 201
patient responsibility 82
Pattison SD 3, 219, 221
Phang A 88–9
philosophical medical ethics 77–82
Plotkin DA and others 195
potential vulnerability 94, 98, 100, 104, 105, 112–13, 204
power inequality 48; characteristics 91; and opportunity to exploit 60–6; sexual exploitation 117–18, 120, 130–1, 164; sexual exploitation and civil law 157–8; sexual exploitation and criminal law 145–55; and vulnerability 94, 97; *see also* undue influence
prescribing incentive scheme 68–9, 79
Pretty v. *DPP* 169–70
Price D 125, 127
principlism 77–8, 81, 82
private finance initiative (PFI) 178–9
private health care 69; contract law 86–9; doctor-patient relationship 72–7; vulnerability in 105–12, 113
Private Healthcare Information Network (PHIN) 70
process-based conceptions of exploitation 13; Feinberg 13–15; Goodin 16–19; Jansen and Wall 21–2; Sample 19–21
Professional Conduct Committee, GMC 114
professional/regulatory medical ethics 82–5, 205–12; sexual exploitation 118–22
Protecting Patients Act 2017, Canada 119
psychiatrists, sexual misconduct of 114, 118, 120, 136–7

public interest, abuse of trust and sexual contact 153–4
public knowledge and trust 208–9
publicly funded health care/NHS 66–72, 75–6, 79; cost saving and assisted dying 177–9, 182–3, 185–6; power inequality 63

Quinn JM and others 192–3, 194, 195

rationality and consent 21–2
Re Z (assisted dying case) 171
regulation *see* professional/regulatory medical ethics
relational autonomy 108–9, 204
relational vulnerability 92, 98, 104
relatives/carers, burden perception and assisted dying 168–75
religious belief and assisted dying 190–1
research: case studies in scientific papers 56–7; inducements 31–2, 102–3; vulnerability in 99–105, 112, 113
researchers, vulnerability of 104
Richman J 168–9
Rogers W and Ballantyne A 116–18, 208–9
Romanell Report, US 206
Royal College of Surgeons 109
Rudinow J 129, 193

Sample RJ 19–20, 21, 23
Scarman Lord 88, 162
Schneebaum G 146–7, 150
Schneider MS and Phillips SP 116
Searle RH and others 115, 155
setback to interests 41–6
sex in authority relations (SAR), concept of 146–7
sexual exploitation 54–5, 209; by patients of doctors 164–5; civil law approach (England and Wales) 155–61; consent, contentious issue of 122–34; consent, legal focus on 165–6; criminal law approach (England and Wales) 142–55; fiduciary approach 161–3, 224; gender and 116–18, 164; incidence 114–15; Kerr/Haslam Inquiry 54, 114; power inequality *see* power inequality; professional ethics and regulation 118–22; as public wrong 154; undue influence 201; vulnerability 117–18; zero-tolerance approach: requirements and possible dilution 134–41

Sexual Offences Act 2003 (SOA), England and Wales 143–4, 149
sexualised behaviour, definition of 116
shared decision-making model 59–60; and shared vulnerability 204–5
Shelton D 127–8, 145
Sherlock Baroness 178
Shipman Inquiry (Smith J) 64
Sidaway case 162–3
Smith RG 114
Smith SA 218
Snijdewind MC and others 171
Sopinka J 159–60, 161, 163, 224
South Africa: CAPRISA (HIV prevention) study 102–3
special case, doctor-patient relationship as 5, 89–90, 200–2
Sperling D 211
Spiegel W and others 121, 137–9, 140
Staughton LJ 220–1
structural injustices and pressures 81, 203–4
subjective states of mind 21–2
Sumption Lord 181, 197

taking advantage 26–7; of basic needs 20–1, 23; *see also* misuse; unfairness; vulnerability
Tauber AI 51–2
ten Have H 94, 97
tort law *see* civil law
Trossel R 64–5
trust 50–7; exploitation as breach of 5; in publicly funded health care system 70–2; sexual exploitation and abuse of 149–53; *see also* fiduciary duty of doctor
Twemlow SW and Gabbard GO 56

unconsciousness 29, 34
undue influence: assisted dying and burden perception 187–98; contract law doctrine of 86–7, 158–9; doctor as fiduciary 5–6; legal response 218–22; sexual exploitation 201 (*see also* coercive and irresistible inducements)
unfairness: misuse and 31–2; taking unfair advantage 15–18, 22–3
universal vulnerability theories 93–5
US: cost saving and assisted dying 179–80; medical education and ethics 206; Texas Penal Code: non-consent to sexual contact 148–9
utilitarianism 79

Veitch K 72, 178–9
virtue ethics 80
vulnerability: assisted dying and 170–2, 181–2, 186–7, 189–90, 191, 194–5; consent and 95–6, 103; cosmetic surgery and 109; dictionary definitions of 92; of doctor 186–7; fertility treatment and 111; illness and 95–9; inducements and 31–2, 102–3; misuse as taking advantage of 28–31; potential 94, 98, 100, 104, 105, 112–13, 204; in private health care 105–12, 113; relational 92, 98, 104; relationship with autonomy 95–9, 204; relationship with exploitation 4–5, 91–3, 200, 202–5; in research 99–105, 112, 113; of researchers 104; in sexual exploitation 117–18, 129–30, 135–7; shared 204–5; structural injustices and pressures 81, 203–4; unconsciousness 29, 34; undue influence and 218; universal vulnerability theories (Fineman) 93–5

Wagner B 179–80
Wang Y 59
Wertheimer A 11, 15–16, 22, 23, 24, 52, 57, 125, 127
Wiles R and Higgins J 73, 105–6
wrongfulness *see* moralised concept of exploitation; unfairness

Zuckerman D 106–7, 109

Printed in the United States
by Baker & Taylor Publisher Services